PHILOSOPHY AND THEURGY
IN LATE ANTIQUITY

Algis Uždavinys

Philosophy
&
Theurgy

IN LATE ANTIQUITY

Angelico Press
Sophia Perennis

First published in the USA
by Sophia Perennis
© Algis Uzdavinys 2010
Angelico Press / Sophia Perennis edition 2014
All rights reserved

Series editor: James R. Wetmore

For information, address:
Angelico Press, Ltd.
4709 Briar Knoll Dr. Kettering, OH 45429
www.angelicopress.com

Library of Congress Cataloging-in-Publication Data

Uzdavinys, Algis
Philosophy and theurgy in late antiquity
by Algis Uzdavinys.—1st ed.

p. cm.
Includes bibliographical references
ISBN 978 1 59731 086 4 (pbk.: alk. paper)
1. Plato. 2. Neoplatonism. 3. Philosophy, Ancient.
4. Theurgy—History I. Title.
B395.U93 2008
186'.4—dc22   2008022417

Cover image credit:
Detail of Libations from *Initiation into the Cult of Dionysus,*
Fresco Cycle at the Villa of Mysteries, Pompeii

Cover design: Cristy Deming

CONTENTS

4: METAPHYSICAL SYMBOLS AND THEIR FUNCTION IN THEURGY

5: DIVINE RITES AND PHILOSOPHY IN NEOPLATONISM

FOREWORD

Philosophy, Theurgy, and the Gods

NEAR THE BEGINNING of Ani's *Book of Going Forth by Day*, the soul of Ani (a scribe in ancient Egypt) states what he expects to have gained in the next life after leading a holy life on earth following the path laid down by the gods:

> May you grant power in the sky, might on earth, and vindication in the God's Domain, a journeying downstream to Busiris as a living soul and a journeying upstream to Abydos as a heron; to go in and out without hindrance at all the gates of the Duat.[1]

This ancient text, beautifully illustrated and written in the second millennium BCE, marks in a very early form the hopes and expectations of the religious elite: a special place in the next world with a right to come and go back to the land of the living at will. It also shows the importance of the gods in the process and—even more especially—the bond between the believer and those gods. In other passages it is clear that Ani has become a god himself, and is in fact Osiris when he joins the god in the underworld. The path to Osiris is not easy, and there is much knowledge that Ani must have attained on earth in order to navigate the underworld safely and eventually come successfully through the weighing of his heart (Plate 3) to the presence of the gods (Plates 4, 30, and 36). The entire process is therefore marked by Ani's wisdom granted him by the gods. The process involved mutually gods and human beings.

Although it is most probably true that the ancient Greeks from

---

1. O. Goelet, R. Faulkner, and C. Andrews, *The Egyptian Book of the Dead: The Book of Going Forth by Day*, 2nd revised edition (San Francisco, 1998), Plate 2.

the fifth century BCE onwards could not have had access to *The Book of Going Forth by Day*, the so-called Egyptian Books of the Dead, buried as it they were their creators, and that even if they had had such access they could not have deciphered the hieroglyphic writings in them, the fact remains that the ideas contained in this Egyptian text were still available to them. The strange tales related by Herodotus (c. 484–c. 425 BCE) in book II of his *Histories* show the power that Egypt had for capturing the Greek imagination, and even at that time several works on this ancient nation and its religious beliefs were available. After the death of Alexander the Great in 323 BCE, his general Ptolemy took control of Egypt, and his family retained control of the country until the Romans took it over after the death of Cleopatra in 30 BCE. During that time, it is clear that even more works about the country and its ways were written, many of which were about their religious beliefs. Thereafter Egypt remained the land known for wisdom and magic.

There is, then, a discernible literary and traditional path from Ani's book to Iamblichus' philosophy. In chapter two, below, Dr. Uzdavinys considers the role and meaning of theurgy in Iamblichean philosophy. He rightly shows that the word *theourgia* is one of many that Iamblichus and his fellow Platonists use for the relationship between gods and mortals. It is also clear that Iamblichus believed that his version of theurgy had ancient roots that extended back to the Egyptians. Indeed, he wrote his most famous work, *On the Mysteries*, under the persona of an Egyptian priest.

Iamblichus (c. 245–c. 325 CE) probably took the term 'theurgy' from the *Chaldaean Oracles*, sacred texts assembled by the father/son team Julian the Chaldaean and Julian the Theurgist in the second century CE.[2] As Dr. Uzdavinys has argued, the term has been misapplied by scholars for many years, but more recently (thanks especially to the excellent scholarship of J.M. Dillon, G. Shaw, E.C. Clarke, and others) a better understanding of the meaning of the term has emerged along with a new vision of how theurgy and

---

2. *On the Oracles*, see especially R. Majercik, *The Chaldaean Oracles: Text, Translation, and Commentary* (Leiden, 1989), pp. 1–46.

philosophy are interconnected in Iamblichean Neoplatonism. Interestingly, what has emerged is a view of theurgy that is very much akin to Ani's Egyptian beliefs.

Dr. Uzdavinys' learned work elucidates many of the connections between Iamblichus and the ancient Egyptians, and I will not belabor them here. I will instead briefly suggest how Iamblichus interpreted the (now lost) writings on ancient Egypt and the *Chaldaean Oracles* and created a brand of Neoplatonism that would stand for centuries after him. I should add too that the founders of the *Chaldaean Oracles*, the two Julii, were (like Numenius, a Neopythagorean contemporary with them who also had Platonic leanings) from Apamea. This adds a Syrian connection to theurgical rite, which should not be ignored. Indeed, as Dillon argues,[3] Iamblichus likely set up his own Syrian school in Apamea. Thus, Iamblichus is clearly setting himself, his school, and his philosophy in Eastern as well as Egyptian currents of learning.

This desire to attach Platonism to earlier traditions is an important aspect of Iamblichus' philosophical goal: the unity of Pagan teachings. In his *De Mysteriis*, he argues at length against the narrowly Greek and narrowly (skeptical) philosophical beliefs articulated by Porphyry. For Iamblichus, Platonic philosophy is more than Greek texts and what he would see as narrow philosophical eristics. Plato himself, he would argue, knew ancient wisdom and used it, and so it is imperative that Greek philosophers now do the same or risk misunderstanding Plato. Theurgy is the means of bringing ancients and Plato together.

What then is theurgy, and how does it make use of the Greek philosophical tradition along with the Egyptian/Chaldaean/Syrian mysticism? As Dr. Uzdavinys argues throughout this book, the cultures and philosophies are all linked in diverse ways. As he also points out, the meaning of 'theurgy' has been often misunderstood. 'Theurgy' is literally 'gods' work' (from *theoi* = 'gods' and *ergon* = 'work, activity, operation'). In the *De Mysteriis*, Iamblichus argues that this does not mean that we human beings force the gods to do

---

3. J. F. Finamore and J. M. Dillon, *Iamblichus, De Anima: Text, Translation, and Commentary* (Leiden 2002), pp. 5–6.

work for us. The gods, as Plato had laid out in the *Symposium* (202b–203a), do not interact directly with human beings. They are separate and superior, and interaction is accomplished via daemons, intermediary demigods that carry our prayers to the gods and the gods' gifts to us. So we mortals would have been cut-off from the gods except for the intermediaries, which Iamblichus identifies with angels, daemons, and heroes. These exist below the Moon and on earth and can range as high as the ethereal bodies of the visible gods above (planets and stars). Thus, one way that theurgic rituals work is via these intermediaries.

Iamblichus, however, did not remove this earthly realm from interactions with the gods. Also in the *De Mysteriis*, especially in book III, he lays out his theory of illumination (*ellampsis*). The gods shine a light from their ethereal bodies, and though they themselves stay separate from the material realm here on earth, they nonetheless can illuminate objects and persons and interact with them in that way.

This in turn brings up a third essential ingredient of theurgic rites: the person involved, the theurgist, initiate, or sacred object/ person, must be adapted to receive the divine rays. For us human beings, this means that we must be appropriately purified. To take the lowest exemplum, if the theurgist wishes to use a child as a medium in a rite, then the theurgist must prepare the child for reception by purifying the child-recipient's ethereal body. The ritual purifying renders the child fit for receiving the divine rays.

On a higher level, if theurgists wish to channel the divine through their own body, then they will have more preparation to do. Certainly they will have to purify themselves via ascetic living, etc., but there is more involved because, in the case of children, the child's intellect is not being engaged in the rite. Indeed, the child is unaware of what is happening when the god's light surrounds him. For theurgists, however, the intellect must be engaged, which in turn means that they must purify not only their bodies and lower souls but also their minds. This would involve a regimen of study that includes not only philosophy but also sacred ritual. As we saw in Ani's case, the two sorts of study, though separate, coalesce in meetings with the gods.

If these three ingredients are present—a god working through intermediaries and emitting a light down below to a person or object adapted for its receipt—then the presiding theurgist will establish contact with the divine. At the lowest level, this means that the child or object receives the divine illumination. When it is the theurgist that is involved or one of the theurgist's advanced initiates through the theurgist, when (that is) the mind of the recipient is engaged and the recipient has done the appropriate study and preparation, the divine rays lift the soul of the theurgist or initiate out of the body and up to the heavens, where it joins with the god.[4] In this way, Iamblichus has preserved Plato's requirement in the *Symposium* that the god does not descend and yet has assured that our ascent is possible.

Thus, Iamblichus can conclude that this is no base magical rite of the sort we encounter in the *Greek Magical Papyri*. This is a philosophical/theurgical ritual in which the soul ascends to the gods not by forcing the gods but by submitting to the divine will and dictates. In the *De Mysteriis*, Iamblichus is careful to distinguish base magic, which leaves everything to chance and may lead its practitioners to consort with falsity and evil daemons, and higher magic or theurgy. The latter is a guarantor of truth and happiness, combined as it is with the life of the gods.

And so in ritual as after death, theurgy—'god's work' performed willingly by the gods for those who prepare themselves appropriately—brings the philosopher/theurgist to the gods and perfects our divine, rational selves. We are reminded again of Ani facing Osiris. His prayer was for vindication and the ability to move freely between realms. The goal of Iamblichus is not entirely dissimilar. The knowledge we gain on earth guarantees us a place in heaven (and we are 'divine' in that sense, though not literally gods), and

---

4. Since we human beings have an ethereal 'vehicle', that is an ethereal substance that houses the rational and irrational souls, the ethereal light of the god mixes with the ethereal body and lifts it (together with the two souls) heavenward until our ethereal vehicle unites with the god's ethereal body. Further, our rational soul unites with that of the god, and this in turn would allow further ascent so that the rational soul could encounter Divine Intellect and even the One itself.

that place means that our rational souls are united to the universal powers and thus we, qua minds, can 'travel' between realms: ethereal, Intelligible, and that of the One. Theurgy brings peace, contentment, power, vindication, and a divine-like status.

JOHN F. FINAMORE
University of Iowa

INTRODUCTION

THE HISTORICALLY UNCONTEXTUALIZED use of philosophy, mysticism, or ritual practice is problematic in many respects, because it presupposes various self-evident and uncontested categories of thought and culture which, far from being 'universal' (at least in the popular positivistic sense), are in fact contextually conditioned, and may thus be constructed as idealized and fabulous castles based upon normative socio-religious fantasies.

This crucial insight, however, and the subsequent critical approach towards all sorts of cultural constructions, or towards certain discursive veils, textual tricks, and rhetorical devises which are now taken as 'tradition', can neither dismiss nor compromise the ineffable divine transcendence, nor that set of metaphysical principles which is truly archetypal. There is no question that human thought is inevitably inclined toward culturally determined and ideologically shaped generalizations (or simply toward certain sweet illusions), and it has a 'legal' right to do so, because manifested reality ('constructed' or manifested in the sense of Neoplatonic *ellampsis*, irradiation) is itself a sort of Myth, a Myth of the 'Divine Play'.

This ontological conviction, expressed in the terms of mythical and theological images, is neither an obligatory article of faith nor a solemn assertion of 'perennial wisdom'; far from it. The Socratic irony and Shaivic laughter, dancing on the deconstructed corpses of the past, is not a hindrance 'to behold the secret and ineffable figures in the inaccessible places', as Proclus used to say (*In Euclid.* 141.22).

We remain attentive to historical contexts (to the extent that they are actually 'historical'; nonetheless, we suspect that these contexts themselves are hermeneutically constructed so as to function as organizing teleological visions and selective sets of memories, or rather as text-like *mandalas* of interrelated social and metaphysical fields. In a sense, all texts, all signs and symbols, and all phenomena are spurious and may be likened to a drunken hallucination, a

mirage. This mirage, however, is rooted in the mystery of the immanent divine self-disclosure, which resembles an endless arabesque
reflecting the image of archetypal Ouroboros. Therefore our investigation, though being sensitive to all available historical testimonies and details, cannot exclude or avoid certain metaphysical
premises, more or less a-historical comparisons, 'unprovable' noetic
intuitions and even (sometimes pretended) 'creative misunder-
standings' (as Pierre Hadot perhaps would say).

This 'holy myth-making' in the widest cultural and ecological
sense (including the perennial presence of error and self-delusion)
is not simply a heavenly sanctioned 'human norm', but the only
means of survival for our teleologically 'constructed' civilization,
the only thin g that allows it to bear its heavy burden of *paideia*.
This is so because our whole life and its rhythmic pattern increas-
ingly consists of inherited, constructed, determined, and always creatively (hermeneutically) re-constructed myths and dialectically
performed rites of being.

Bearing in mind all these reservations, we try to avoid thoroughly
dogmatic assertions while presenting an integral but nonetheless
selective picture of ancient philosophy and related ritual practices
in the Hellenic, Egyptian, and Mesopotamian contexts. While
revealing striking parallels and analogies, we are not inclined to the
often too naïve theories of 'influences', 'borrowings', and 'diffusions'.
Such theories may be correct or not, but by themselves they are
unable to explain neither the meaning of current ideas and images
(not to say the meaning of life), nor their role in the metaphysical
and social economies of human existence.

The present monograph is devoted to the philosophy of late
antiquity (especially, to Neoplatonism) understood as a way of life
and as a path of inner transformation in one's search for spiritual
rebirth and unity with the divine principles. When regarded as a
science of purification and restoration of unity, philosophy is no
less than a rite of becoming like God, and in this respect it is inseparable from the traditional sacred rituals, now partly or entirely interiorized.

The religious ideas and practices of the Mediterranean, Egypt
and the Near East serve as a background for both philosophy (*philo-*

sophia) and theurgy (*theourgia*). They equally include contemplation and action (sometimes described as an ascent to Heaven), conceived of as a way of living perfectly—that is, in accordance with the divine patterns and archetypes—thereby fulfilling man's last end (*telos*) which is to subsist at the level of *Nous* (the divine Intellect), to return to the One.

This monograph consists of five chapters, all of them written in 2007, except the last one, *Divine Rites and Philosophy in Neoplatonism*, which was first delivered as a paper at the conference *Platonism, Neoplatonism, and Literature*, presented by the International Society for Neoplatonic Studies in Orono, Maine, USA, 28 June–1 July, 2002. The short version of the first chapter was presented as a key-note lecture at the conference *Philosophy: Its Essence, Power and Energy*, organized by The Prometheus Trust in Glastonbury, UK, 28 June–1 July, 2007. I am grateful to Tim Addey who invited me to present a key-note lecture at this conference and published my another monograph, namely, *Philosophy as a Rite of Rebirth, From Ancient Egypt to Neoplatonism* in 2008.

The three remaining chapters (2, 3, and 4) were written at the La Trobe University in Bendigo, Australia. *The Limits of Speculation in Neoplatonism*, an article which appears as an appendix, was initially a paper presented at the Third Annual Conference of the Prometheus Trust (2008, Glastonbury, Somerset, UK).

The present monograph is the result of prolonged studies which started long before my Ph.D. dissertation on Proclus (in Lithuanian) was defended in 2000; consequently I must express my gratitude to the late Professor A. Hillary Armstrong (though he was a bit skeptical regarding my growing interest in Egyptian matters), and the late Professor Henry J. Blumenthal, my supervisor at the University of Liverpool, which I visited as an Honorary Research Fellow of the British Academy. Due to the kind attention of Ilsetraut Hadot and Pierre Hadot, I was also able to spend six months at the Centre National de la Recherche Scientifique (CNRS) in Paris in 1997–1998.

Many colleagues and friends have contributed to my studies by their own academic research, their presence in various conferences and private meetings, and all sorts of assistance. They include Martin Lings, Kathleen Raine, John Dillon, John Finamore, Jay Bregman,

Gregory Shaw, Peter Kingsley, Anne Sheppard, Sara Rappe, Richard Sorabji and others.

During the winter and spring of 2005, the Andrew Mellon fellowship afforded me the occasion to spend three months at the American Center for Oriental Research in Amman and opportunity to visit numerous ancient sites in Jordan. I am particularly grateful to Pierre and Patricia Bikai and the staff of ACOR. Last but not least, I want to acknowledge the unwavering support of my wife Virginia and my two daughters, Dorothea and Ruta.

ALGIS UZDAVINYS
Kaunas (Lithuania)
November 2008

1

THE ORIGINS AND MEANING OF PHILOSOPHY

Really there can only be one kind of knowledge. And rationality is simply mysticism misunderstood.[1]

Truth itself is in danger of being extinguished. Men will experience its sunset since they are unable to endure its divine dawn (*ten theian anatolen*).[2]

EIDOTHEA AND PROTEUS:
THE VEILED IMAGES OF PHILOSOPHY

There are numerous definitions of philosophy and many different interpretations of what it really is: either the art of living (in response to the fundamental question: *pos bioteon*, 'how should we live?') or an epistemological project serving a certain demonic will to power and the increasing madness of positivism—a contradictory and fruitless occupation which has nothing in common with genuine wisdom, 'since its basic principle of exhaustive verbal adequacy is opposed to any liberating finality, to any transcending of the sphere of words.'[3]

But if the sphere of words must be transcended (because philosophy's concern with language and logic is only preliminary to more important tasks), the term *philosophia* itself must not be improperly idolized. Just as the same term may designate different things in

---

1. Peter Kingsley, *Reality*, Inverness, CA: The Golden Sufi Center, 2003, p. 148.
2. Damascius *Phil. Hist.* 36 BC.
3. Frithjof Schuon, *Logic and Transcendence*, tr. Peter N. Townsend, London: Perennial Books, 1984, p. 27.

different historical and ideological contexts, so the same reality may be alluded by different terms as well, and the term 'philosophy' is no exception, especially when it denotes an introduction to the 'unified silence' which is ineffable and superior to all knowledge.

Ancient Hellenic and modern European 'philosophy' have nothing in common but the name. Ch. C. Evangeliou therefore contests the uncritical assumption that ancient Hellenic philosophy is the origin of Western or European 'philosophy', arguing instead that the Socratic tradition, to which Plato and Aristotle belong, has more affinity with the Egyptian wisdom and the 'remote philosophies of India and China'.[4]

However, though the Orphico-Pythagorean and Platonic spiritual traditions practice philosophy as a means for escaping from reincarnation by detachment from that 'barbaric dirt' (*pelon*) where the soul's eye is buried (as if lying in the 'karmic dirt', *karma varana*, of the Jains) and then returning to one's native star, the place beyond the heavens, it would be incorrect to suppose that all Eastern philosophical schools are concerned with liberation, *moksha*. To take at face value their claim that they possess an exceptional spirituality would be naïve; likewise, to imagine (in accordance with a common fiction) that Western philosophy from Aristotle onwards is deficient in its orientation and, being mere a shallow mental plaything, does not lead to a spiritual disciple and liberation, in whatever sense this 'liberation' may be understood, would be equally naïve.

Orphism and Pythagoreanism, which may be safely regarded as the font of the whole Greek philosophical tradition, were perhaps partly related to contemporary Indian speculations, medical theories and spiritual practices (especially, those of Ajivikism and Jainism), but they depended more directly on a re-shaping of the Egyptian and Mesopotamian cultural heritage. As regards 'philosophy's' allegedly Egyptian origins, Ch. E. Evangeliou says:

---

4. Christos C. Evangeliou, *The Hellenic Philosophy: Between Europe, Asia and Africa*, Binghamton: Institute of Global Cultural Studies, Binghamton University, 1997, pp. II–III.

Evidently, by the channel of the Pythagorean tradition, some seeds and certain roots of Egyptian wisdom reached Hellas where they grew into the magnificent tree of Platonism.[5]

In order not to be entirely deceived by the names and rhetorical devices which sometimes function as veiled images and spectacular masks in the cosmic theatre, we should turn our attention to the hidden kernel of what is called philosophy, be it a chariot for traveling into another world; a mighty method, 'stolen from the gods' and subsequently corrupted, turned upside down; a crafty stratagem; or a means of achieving and experiencing indivisible objects—that is, of living 'another life' where the self is assimilated to Dionysus, the god both of tragedy and of comedy. Accordingly, we intend to describe the chief goals (*skopoi*) of this method—a method that constitutes only one particular form of mediation between the transcendent divine wisdom and our human existence, one of the various ways based on certain archetypal patterns, and our intellectual powers as shaped according to these patterns, as well as on our historically determined visions and metaphysical hopes, of dealing with reality.

In this respect, philosophy resembles the dynamic interchange between Proteus, Eidothea and Menelaus, as it is depicted by Proclus. Proteus, being an angelic intellect (*nous*) in the 'chain' (*seira*) of Poseidon, 'contains in himself the forms of all things in the world' (*ta eide panta ton genneton: In Remp.* 1.112.28–29). His name seems a variant of *protistos* (*primus*, first) but more probably Proteus is another form of Hapy, the shape-shifting Nile god, an 'old man of the sea', who symbolizes the permanent transformation and continuity of theophanies, immersed in the immanent stream of becoming; his name is related to Egyptian *prouti*, a biform of *per-aa*, 'great house' (in the sense of cosmic temple, household of truth, *maat*)—that is, 'pharaoh'.[6]

---

5. Ibid., p.119.
6. R. Drew Griffith, *Sailing to Elysium: Menelaus' Afterlife (Odyssey 4.561–569) and Egyptian Religion.—Phoenix*, vol. 55, 2001, 3–4, p.213.

We should remember that Proteus (who is *Ra sa,* son of Ra, or *anthropos teleios,* the royal *axis mundi* in this respect) tells Menelaus that he will not die: the gods will put him in Elysium instead. The name Elysium (*Elusion*), which represents the ultimate reward of the human hero and, undoubtedly, of the philosopher, derives from the Egyptian *sekhet iaru,* the Osirian 'Field of Reeds'. Likewise the word *makares* (blessed), an epithet of the Elysian plain (*Elusion pedion*), comes from the Egyptian *maa-kheru,* the righteous dead, one who has successfully passed the Netherworld judgement and now possesses the magical ability to create his own psychic reality by using the words of power, *hekau,* thereby participating in the demiurgic activities of the Osirian (or Hathorian) *mundus imaginalis.*

According to Proclus, Eidothea, who contemplates the Forms through Proteus, functions as mediator between the fragmented, embodied soul of Menelaus and the angelic *nous.*[7] As a daimonic soul she participates in Menelaus' imperfect mode of perception, but as a soul of the highest order, equal to the angelic *nous,* she is able to grasp the whole of Proteus' identity, the integral pleroma of the Forms represented by the *Logos*-like pharaoh, the royal paradigm and prototype of the perfect philosopher.

When Proteus is perceived by a fragmentary soul immersed in time and therefore unable to see these Forms simultaneously, he appears to pass from one shape to another, though simultaneously containing all possible shapes. Therefore Eidothea's instruction consists of a method as to how to shift one's consciousness from the screen of ever-changing fragmentary images to the true Protean identity at the noetic level of being—that is, to reduce the phenomenal plurality into the intelligible unity or divine oneness, as if leading Odysseus through the great wanderings of life towards 'the mystical harbor of the soul' (*ho mustikos hormos tes psuches*: Proclus *In Parm.* 1025A, 32ff).

7. Robert Lamberton, *Homer the Theologian. Neoplatonist Allegorical Reading and the Growth of the Epic Tradition,* Berkeley: University of California Press, 1986, p. 227.

Only the life according to intellect (*he kata noun zoë*) has stability, and this is precisely the philosophical life which represents a path to one's true noetic essence, accomplished through the intervention of divine grace—for instance, in the form of Hermes' gift (*dosis*), liberating Odysseus' understanding from the chains of the Poseidonian imagination. Following the paradigm of Homeric Odysseus, philosophy generally denotes a work of transition involving the transformation of one's very existence. Regarded as 'much-wandering' or 'very cunning' (*polutropos*), Odysseus, in this respect, is figuratively sailing to the 'beautiful west' (*Amentet*), as if returning from darkness to the intelligible light. No wonder that the Greek word *noös*, mind, is related to the verb *neomai*, 'to return home', indicating a return from death, a release from the sweet prison of Calypso's arms—the verb *kalupto*, to hide, to veil, suggesting both darkness and death.

THE DISTINCTION BETWEEN PHILOSOPHICAL LIFE AND PHILOSOPHICAL DISCOURSE

The philosophical transformation leads to the 'better lot', be it considered as supreme wisdom, virtue, spiritual understanding, one's noetic identity, or mystical union, and this transition (identifiable with the constant exercise of *metis*, skillfulness and practical intelligence, renewed at every instant) may be accomplished by different means and at different levels of consciousness. These means of integral training and psychagogy, aimed at one's spiritual equilibrium and purity, may include not only the inner struggle with oneself for truth, goodness and beauty, but also the exercise of logic, physics and ethics.

In addition to the sacrificial rites and acts of devotion directed to the gods and goddesses of wisdom, at certain historical point various scientific activities and related hermeneutical attitudes developed, which consisted of speculative commentaries on the divine names, attributes, myths, texts, liturgies and life strategies. Consequently the Egyptians, renowned both for their piety and their practical wisdom (*eusebeia kai phronesis*), introduced, according to Isocrates, the practice of philosophy for the cultivation of the soul, 'a pursuit which has the power, not only to establish laws but also to investigate the nature of the universe'. Pythagoras, on a visit to Egypt, 'became a student of the religion of the people, and was first to bring to the Greeks all philosophy' (*Busiris* 21–23).

It appears that liturgy gradually became transformed into philosophical discourse, which began, essentially, as a description of divine names and qualities, thus making philosophy (in a sense of a striving for wisdom, a conformity to the archetypal models and the sacred iconography) a kind of pious life that includes, as its integral part, a particular mode of discourse. This discourse may consist of magic spells or gnostic formulas, theurgic hymns, aretologies, and/ or hieratic assertions, all related to the realm of *sumbolike theoria* (symbolic understanding, or contemplation).The contemplation of symbols and interpretation of the paradigmatic mythologems sooner or later developed into the more general form of theoretical discourse.

But the life aimed at proximity to the gods and the realization of truth (the Egyptian *maat*), must not be *reduced* to such discourse, be it simply liturgical—that is, limited to certain sacred formulas— or physical, as when speculative cosmology is more or less 'emancipated' or 'naturalized', and transformed into a rational exegesis of the traditional world order. Therefore a distinction between philosophy and philosophical discourse, explicitly formulated in Hellenistic philosophy and recently reformulated by P. Hadot, is crucial for understanding that philosophical discourse is analogous to *ta legomena*, 'things recited' or sacred accounts (*hieroi logoi*), in the Eleusinian mysteries.

However, such recitations or interpretations of hieratic stories (which may sometimes include the questions of the mystagogue and the responses of the initiate, a form that can be regarded as one prototype of the philosophical dialogue, or the philosophical contest, the *agon*) are not the same as *ta dromena*, 'things performed'. Eventually, neither *legomena* nor *dromena* can replace or be equivalent to *epopteia*, the mystical vision, which is both the highest stage of initiation and the goal of Platonic contemplative philosophy. As P. Hadot insists, while emphasizing the central role that discourse plays in the philosophical life:

In Antiquity the philosopher regards himself a philosopher not because he develops a philosophical discourse, but because he lives philosophically.[8]

Those, according to Damascius, who are truly in love with philosophy have to be tested like gold in the fire (*Phil.Hist.* 66F).[9] The true lover of wisdom must be 'full of truth in his behavior and speech', and thus a living example 'in piety and overall philosophy of life' (*epi eusebeia te kai hole biou philosophia: Phil.Hist.* 111). Damascius clearly distinguishes between being a philosopher in one's way of life and being one in the realm of knowledge (*episteme, dialektike*: ibid., 71b).

However, the simple distinction between philosophical discourse and philosophical way of life is not enough. It is necessary to emphasize that this way is in fact the way of purification and actualization of the divine in the human, leading the soul to a living, concrete union with the divine Intellect and the Good, or the Neoplatonic One, which is *epekeina tes ousias*, beyond Being and Intellect. Understood as an ascent (*anabasis*) which follows a descent (*katabasis*), philosophical life is tantamount to an esoteric rite of transformation.

Philosophical discourse may in fact be linked to personal *askesis*, to a concrete *praxis*, and in this sense it is the true spiritual *ergon*: both incorporeal and corporeal work. Likewise, hermeneutical interpretation should be regarded as an integral part of contemplative practice—analogous to the contemplation of hieratic statues (*agalmata*) and geometric diagrams (*schemata*), which possesses an anagogic function. The discourse considered abstractly, as a written and formally structured text, is one of philosophy's semi-political tools, sometimes used in contests of rhetoric as a magical instrument. In modern times, however, what was originally a tool serving the kind of philosophical education that requires, in the context of the rivalry between schools (*haireseis*), that dogma be fixed in the

8. Pierre Hadot, *Philosophy as a Way of Life. Spiritual Exercises from Socrates to Foucault,* ed.Arnold I. Davidson, tr. Michael Chase, Oxford: Blackwell, 1995, p. 27.

9. Damascius, *The Philosophical History,* text with translation and notes, ed. and tr. Polymnia Athanassiadi, Athens: Apameia, 1999.

mind, becomes the only object of professional study, thereby reducing philosophy to philosophical discourse, and discourse itself to one particular type of demythologized and desacralized prose. To quote Damascius once again:

> I have indeed chanced upon some who are outwardly splendid philosophers in their rich memory of a multitude of theories; in the shrewd flexibility of their countless syllogisms; in the constant power of their extraordinary perceptiveness. Yet within they are poor in matters of the soul and destitute of true knowledge. (*Phil.Hist.* 14).

One who dedicates his labor to things mortal and human may have a sharp intelligence and an incredible amount of contradictory or systematic discursive knowledge, but 'would never go far towards the acquisition of the great divine wisdom' (*ten theoprepe kai megalen sophian*: ibid., 34d) or far in approaching 'the truly hieratic truth which lies hidden in the depths' (*ten en butho kekrummenes hos alethos hieras aletheias*: ibid., 35b). This truth is almost imperceptible within the impious and hypnotic context of the technical language reserved for specialists in the modern university, a set which reinforces the tendency to take refuge in the comfortable universe of concepts. According to the aptly remark of Simplicius:

> Chrysippus did not write on this subject (the nature of man) with the goal of being interpreted and understood, but so that one makes of his writings in life. If therefore I make use of his writings in life, at that very moment I participate in the good they contain. But if I admire the exegete because he provides good explanations, and if I can understand and myself interpret the text, and if, quite frankly, everything falls to my lot except the fact of making use of these writings in life, would I have become anything other than a grammarian instead of a philosopher?[10]

---

10. From Simplicius' *Commentary on Epictetus' Manual* cited by Arnold I. Davidson "Introduction: Pierre Hadot and the Spiritual Phenomenon of Ancient Philosophy".—Pierre Hadot, *Philosophy as a Way of Life*, p. 27.

It is fairly evident that whatever Damascius and his remote *kathe-gemon*, Plato, mean by 'philosophy', it radically differs from what contemporary textbooks mean by this now rather devalued term, though ancient Platonists and especially Peripatetics sometimes did pursue their secondary activity of explaining the world too vigorously, and that indeed led to a too theoretical and abstract view of things. The modern scholarly pursuit also too often resembles a sort of self-confident obsession enacted by a host of hypercritical and angry 'grammarians'. The emancipated philosophical discourse— their object of torture—is treated in accordance with certain language games and an imagined history which, paradoxically, ends by rejecting as 'irrational' the love of wisdom itself.

The postmodern battle against philosophy (understood, first of all, as a kind of 'writing', as a heap of idolized and scrutinized texts) is a sheer parody of the true deconstruction of error by means of the *elenchus*. Being thoroughly parasitic, it involves an element of ruse and dissimulation in an attempt to shake the philosopher's confidence in reason—but instead of leading to the reason-transcending noetic unity, it invokes a Typhonian fragmentation, partiality, dissolution, alienation, simulation, 'otherness' (*heterotes*, as the opposite of the Platonic 'sameness', *tautotes*), and nonbeing. As Ch. Griswold says, 'it is Socraticism without the Good,'[11] i.e., without the One or any other metaphysical principle.

Though Plato's Socrates asserts in *Symposium* that the mediative daimonic *eros* is a 'philosopher through all of life (*philosophon dia pantos tou biou*), a clever sorcerer and enchanter and sophist' (*goes kai pharmakeus kai sophistes*: Symp. 203d 7–8), the postmodern pseudo-philosophical writings are devoid of that elevating erotic power which leads to the realm of the divine. As N. Garver concludes:

> In the end ... we find no metaphysics, no logic, no linguistics, no semantics, and no grammatology left to carry on, but only the brilliant scholarly mischievousness.[12]

11. Ch. Griswold, *Plato's Metaphilosophy.—Platonic Investigations*, ed. Dominic J. O'Meara, Washington, DC: The Catholic University of America Press, 1985, p.18.

12. N. Garver, *Derrida on Rousseau on Writing.—Journal of Philosophy* 74, 1977, p.673, cited by Ch. Griswold, ibid., p.17.

STANDING FACE TO FACE WITH IMMORTALITY

If philosophy for the ancients is a comprehensive and extremely demanding art of living which cures human illness and purifies souls (thus presupposing that the present human condition is corrupted and deviated from the archetypal standards), why modern representation of ancient philosophy depicts it as an exclusively conceptual edifice, that is, as a system-building and system-demolishing activity? I. Hadot rightly observes that philosophy in Graeco-Roman antiquity is not in the first instance a systematic thought-structure *a la* Hegel intended to serve as the theoretical explanation of the world and the events of the world, [but is] above all an education towards a happy life.[13]

However, I. Hadot is not entirely correct when she considers that this happy life essentially means 'life here and not only in some hypothetical life after death', because the initial task of *philosophia* in its Orphico-Pythagorean and Platonic sense (which is not, primarily, a theoretical explanation of the world, but a rite of rebirth) consists in transcending the realm of so-called Calypsian happiness in the 'cave', the corporeal prison. Therefore A.H. Armstrong reflects the modern sensibilities when he argues that 'the primary purpose of the intense meditation on the last things practiced and commended by the philosophers is not to prepare us for any sort of life after death.'[14]

The aim of philosophical life includes an ability to live well here and now, because the noetic background of one's very being is everywhere and the ineffable One is always immediately present. Nevertheless, it culminates in transition—in Egyptian terms— to the Osirian realm (*Duat*), the alchemical body of the goddess Nut (Heaven), sometimes represented as the macrocosmic temple in the form of a cow. Damascius emphasizes this solemn point of departure when he describes the physical death of Hermeias, the Alexandrian philosopher and disciple of Syrianus:

13. Ilsetraut Hadot, "The Spiritual Guide".—*Classical Mediterranean Spirituality. Egyptian, Greek, Roman*, ed. A.H. Armstrong, London: Routledge and Kegan Paul, 1986, p. 444.

14. A. Hilary Armstrong, *Expectations of Immortality in Late Antiquity*, Milwaukee: Marquette University Press, 1987, pp. 23–24.

It is said that as he was dying he swore to Aegyptus that the soul is immortal and imperishable (*athanaton einai kai ano-lethron ten psuchen*). What gave him this courage was his virtu-ous life disowning the bodily nature, turning to the inner self and experiencing the detachment [from the mortal body] as it already stood face to face with immortality (*Phil. Hist.* 54).

Hence, 'learning to live' presupposes 'learning to die', and this philosophical *paideia* is analogous to the building of one's own 'royal tomb', that is, the symbolic and text-like *mandala* of theurgic words (*hekau*) and animated hieroglyphs (*medu neter*)—the visual embodiment of the Platonic Forms. Such 'philosophical tomb' serves for one's own initiation and post-mortem alchemical trans-formation in the Osirian temple-like Duat. In this respect, we are not concerned with those agnostic philosophical traditions in Greece which, while dogmatically denying any life after death, nev-ertheless, regarded learning to die and detachment from the greedy pursuit of worldly goods as important for one's happy existence. We are dealing instead with that philosophical perspective from which the term itself initially stems. The Greek word *philosophos* is an equivalent or even an exact translation of the Egyptian *mer rekh*, 'lover of knowledge', that is, one who is in pious pursuit of *gnosis*, liberating wisdom, provided by Thoth and other gods for the accomplishment of transformation and spiritual resurrection in the realm of Osiris-Ra.

This perspective is based on the Egyptian doctrine of the intelligi-ble solar life at the level of *Atum-Ra* and the immortality of the winged soul (itself a sort of solar manifestation, *ba*), subsequently modernized and adapted for the Hellenic culture during the so-called Pythagorean-Platonic intellectual revolution. As a substitute for the Horus-like pharaoh, the real *theios aner*, the Platonic philos-opher is, in this respect, a remote inheritor of the interiorized Egyp-tian temple mysteries. Accordingly, he hopes after death for disembodied immortality, for vision of the noetic pantheon and union with the divine principles (*neteru*), as if entering the solar barque of *Ra*. The solar *Atum-Ra* is tantamount to the divine Intel-lect, or to the entire noetic cosmos (*kosmos noetos*) of spiritual lights.

Since early Christianity presented itself as a *philosophia*, a sacramental way of life in conformity with the divine *Logos*, it vehemently rejected all those rival aspects of ancient Hellenic philosophy which pursued the same goals but by different dialectical and theurgic means. Porphyry divided the Christians into two groups: the *polloi kai alloi* (the unlearned many, the 'many other', other than the learned minority) and the *hairetikoi* (the learned few, namely, Gnostics) who had a *hairesis* derived from the ancient philosophy.[15]

The so-called Gnostics were exterminated by the Christians themselves, and the later *ekklesia* predominately turned away from Plato's *verissima philosophia* towards the less demanding 'lesser mysteries' (to say it in Neoplatonic terms) of Peripatetic sensualism. The mainly logical and physico-cosmological aspects of philosophy were consequently accepted, while at the same time all 'pagan' spirituality was furiously rejected, especially in those cases where it resisted being tacitly Christianized and integrated into the fabric of Christian mythology and mysticism. The Iamblichean-Procline metaphysics and theurgy, for example, were transformed into the mystical theology of Dionysius the Areopagite, but the sacramental and theurgic dimension of the Neoplatonism proper[16] was utterly demonized and demolished.

Since Christianity had annexed the privileged path to immortality, philosophy was able to survive only in the form of auxiliary rational discourse which is separated from any independent soteriological claims and spiritual practices. As A.I. Davidson aptly remarks, ancient spiritual exercises were no longer considered a part of philosophy, but were integrated into Christian spirituality, and every Christian thinker, even if still called a 'philosopher', was in fact an initiate of the anti-Hellenic ecclesiastic mysteries:

---

15. J. Igal, "The Gnostics and 'the Ancient Philosophy' in Porphyry and Plotinus".—*Neoplatonism and Early Christian Thought, Essays in Honour of A.H. Armstrong*, ed. H.J. Blumenthal and R.A. Markus, London: Variorum Publications, 1981, p.139.

16. Algis Uzdavinys, "Putting on the Form of the Gods: Sacramental Theurgy in Neoplatonism".—*Sacred Web. A Journal of Tradition and Modernity*, vol. 5, 2000, pp. 107–120.

Philosophical speculation thus became a purely abstract and theoretical activity, which was set strictly apart from theological thought and religious practice and spirituality.[17]

The Islamic civilization has its own Quranic paradigms, spiritual practices and methods to approach God as well. Therefore the assiduous acceptance and assimilation of the considerably Christianized Hellenic heritage during the Abbasid period was highly selective, and 'philosophy' (*falsafah*) came to be identified with the particular Neoaristotelian trend of thought whose logic and cosmology to some extent served Islamic theology. Thereby philosophy as such became synonymous with the discursive Peripatetic philosophy, and when Shihab al-Din al-Suhrawardi, the Persian mystic from the Syrian city of Aleppo, introduced his philosophy of illumination (*hikmat al-ishraq*),[18] partly based on Sufi esoterism, this philosophy was largely a new version of the Athenian Neoplatonism and the Egyptian Hermetic wisdom.

Since the word *ishraq* means either 'the rising of the Sun' or 'illumination', ultimately we are referred back to the remote roots of Platonism—as far back as the Egyptian *Book of the Dead* (*pert em hru*), the original title of which means 'coming forth by the [noetic] day', with the rising Sun, *Ra*. In the Egyptian metaphysical thought, *Ra* (*Re, Phre, Pre*) is called by many different names. Along with his attendants in the solar barque, he generally functions as the noetic Creator and stands for the divine Intellect.[19]

17. Arnold I. Davidson, "Introduction": *Pierre Hadot and the Spiritual Phenomenon of Ancient Philosophy*, p. 32.

18. Suhrawardi, *The Philosophy of Illumination: A New Critical Edition of the Text of Hikmat al-Ishraq*, tr. John Walbridge and Hossein Ziai, Provo, Utah: Brigham Young University Press, 1999; Algis Uzdavinys, "Divine Light in Plotinus and al-Suhrawardi".—*Sacred Web. A Journal of Tradition and Modernity*, vol. 10, 2003, pp. 73–89.

19. Algis Uzdavinys, "The Egyptian Book of the Dead and Neoplatonic Philosophy".—*History of Platonism: Plato Redivivus*, ed. Robert Berchman and John Finamore, New Orleans: University Press of the South, 2005, pp. 163–180.

PHILOSOPHY AND THE HIERATIC RITES OF ASCENT

For Proclus, the Athenian Neoplatonist, full access to the noetic cosmos can be achieved only by a revelation and theophany which transcends our discursive knowledge of the Forms. Only an illumination from the intellective gods renders us capable of being connected to the intelligible Forms; therefore Proclus, following Plato's Socrates (*Phaedr.* 249d) compares their contemplation to mystery-rites (*teletais*), initiations (*muesesi*) and noetic visions (*epopteias: In Parm.* IV.949). It means that discursive philosophical accounts and symbolic descriptions of the higher divine orders (*taxeis*), as well as meditations and interpretations of the privileged sacred texts, prepare the soul for spiritual vision. As J. Bussanich remarks,

> the soul ascends to the noetic or henadic realm by relying both on philosophy and theology, on reason and revelation.[20]

However, the assistance of gods in one's attempt to ascend to the divine *gnosis* through the 'knowledge in us', which is different from the divine sort, is of crucial importance. Since, as A.C. Lloyd argues, Neoplatonic hypostases are experiences and types of consciousness, the content of personal experience (or mystical vision) cannot be derived from the philosophical system itself: it is an unpredictable gift from the gods.[21]

Proclus insists that Plato's divinely inspired (*entheastikos*) and at the same time strictly scientific theology is in accord with the mystic traditions of Orpheus, Musaeus, Homer, and Hesiod, as well as the Assyrian and ancient Egyptian sages, though Plato mainly delivers his teachings about the gods and first principles in a scientific manner, rejecting the dramatic element (*tragikon*) of mythic discourse. Proclus subordinates philosophical reasoning to theology, understood as a metaphysics confirmed by the revelations of the gods themselves, since theology ('talk about the gods') is concerned with

---

20. John Bussanich, "Mystical Theology and Spiritual Experience in Proclus' Platonic Theology".- *Proclus et la Theologie Platonicienne*, ed. A.Ph. Segonds and C.Steel, Leuven: University Press, 2000, p.298

21. A.C. Lloyd, *The Anatomy of Neoplatonism*, Oxford: Clarendon Press, 1991, p.126.

the One and the whole henadic realm with which the primary gods are to be identified, and which transcends both discursive reason and intellection.[22] Hence, philosophy in its deepest essence is analogous to the hieratic rite of ascent. As Proclus says:

> We must demonstrate that each of these doctrines is in accord (*sumphonos*) with the first principles of Plato and with the mystic traditions of the theologians; for the whole of Hellenic theology is the offspring of Orpheus mystagogy, Pythagoras being the first to have learned the initiation rites (*orgia*) of the gods from Aglaophamus, while Plato in turn received from the Pythagorean and Orphic writings the complete science of these matters (*Plat. Theol.* 1.5, pp. 25–26 Saffrey-Westerink).

Similarly, the revelatory and soteriological nature of philosophy (if it remains faithful to the perennial theurgic standards) is asserted by Iamblichus. He sees a unity between the theologies of the Egyptians, the Chaldeans (sometimes called Assyrians), and of Pythagoras and Plato, at the same time stressing the dependence of Hellenic philosophers on the Egyptian priests. All the sciences are conveyed by the gods. The divine philosophy of Pythagoras, being inseparable from cultic practices, is rather composite in its historical development:

> . . . some things being learnt from the Orphics, some from the Egyptian priests, some from the Chaldean mages, some from the Eleusinian rites. . . .' (*Vita Pyth.* 84.14–18)

For Iamblichus, the highest purpose of the cultic practices and hieratic rites is to ascend to the One (*De myster.* 230.12–13), 'a useful statement of the purpose of theurgy . . . even as it is that of theoretical philosophy', according to his modern commentators.[23] This

---

22. John Dillon, "Philosophy and Theology in Proclus. Some Remarks on the 'Philosophical' and 'Theological' Modes of Exegesis in Proclus' Platonic Commentaries".—*From Augustine to Eriugena: Essays on Neoplatonism and Christianity in Honor of John O'Meara*, ed. F. X. Martin et alii, Washington, DC: The Catholic University of America Press, 1991, p. 76.

23. Iamblichus, *On the Mysteries/De mysteriis,* tr. with an Introduction and Notes by Emma C. Clarke, John M. Dillon and Jackson P. Hersbell, Atlanta: Society of Biblical Literature, 2003, p. 265.

ascension is pursued by 'those who love to contemplate theurgic truth' (*tes theourgikes aletheias*: ibid., 228.12). The theurgic operation (*he telesiourgia tes hieratikes*: ibid., 230.2) purifies and liberates from the bonds of generation, making us like to the gods and rendering us worthy to enjoy their friendship (*philia*). This sacrificial *hierourgia* is able to

> assimilate what is in us to the gods, even as the fire assimilates all that is solid and resistant to luminous and subtle bodies, and leads us up by means of sacrifices and sacrificial fire towards the fire of the gods' (*pros to ton theon pur:* ibid., 215.1–4).

Hence, it is not thought (*ennoia*) or philosophy (in the sense of philosophical discourse or discursive thinking, rational human speculation), but the ritual accomplishment (*telesiourgia*) of ineffable acts (*erga*), the hieratic mystagogy (*hieratike mustagogia*) or hierurgy (*hierourgia*, holy work) that is a method of salvation for the soul. Otherwise, Iamblichus asks, 'what would hinder those who engage in contemplative philosophy (*tous theoretikos philosophounta*) from having theurgic union with the gods?' (ibid., 96.11–12). For Iamblichus—the Syrian aristocrat with the indigenous Arabic racial background—as J. F. Finamore remarks: 'The world of philosophy has moved from the armchair to the altar.'[24] Or rather, philosophy has been translated back to hierurgy, as if regaining its initial Egyptian (that is, theurgic) form and function. 'By means of this divine philosophy, the soul in the contemplation of the blessed visions' (*ta makaria theamata*, cf. Plat. *Phaedr.* 247a4) exchanges one life for another and, having abandoned its own life, it gains the most blessed activity (*energeia*) of the gods (ibid., 41.12–13). Therefore Iamblichus, while maintaining an ambiguity of the term *philosophia*, categorically asserts as follows:

> Yet if you put forward a philosophical question, we will settle this also for you by recourse to the ancient stelae of Hermes (*kata tas Hermou palaias stelas*), to which Plato before us, and

24. John F. Finamore, "Plotinus and Iamblichus on Magic and Theurgy."— *Dionysius*, vol. XVII, December 1999, p. 85.

Pythagoras too, gave careful study in the establishment of their philosophy (ibid., 5.12–6.4).

However, according to the popular Western myth which is partly of Peripatetic origin, philosophy begins with the appearance of books written in Greek prose at a time when political power in Miletus passed from Lydians to Persians and the local wise men (*sophoi* or *sophistai*) started to speak about *phusis* of 'everything' and especially of the genesis and structure of the world. This incredible tale stands as a foundational dogma of the deliberately constructed self-image of contemporary rationalism.

THE TASK OF 'EGYPTIAN PHILOSOPHY':
TO CONNECT THE END TO THE BEGINNING

Sometimes it is supposed that since the term *philosophia* in its 'true' sense was coined by Pythagoras or even later by Plato, philosophy itself is the original achievement of the Greeks who suddenly decided to replace witnessing the festivals of the gods with witnessing the well ordered cosmos of 'things that are' (*ta onta*), still calling this latter enterprise by the same word, *theoria*.[25] Thus thinking posits itself as autonomous: its proofs and arguments are to be strictly correlated with rational comprehension, speaking, and being, even though tradition ('ancient custom' aided with *logos*: Plat. *Leg*.890d) and philosophy, in this context, still form two aspects of a single cult. In reality, however, there is a continuity of *eusebeia* (integral religious devotion, now allied with mathematical formulae), and Plato's Academy itself is a sanctuary of the Muses, the angelic beings who provide revelations. As W. Burkert pointed out:

> What mystery priests had sought to make credible in ritual thus becomes the certainty of the highest rationality... The word which in the epic tradition distinguished the gods from men becomes the ineradicable seal of the essential personality,

25. Walter Burkert, *Greek Religion*, tr. John Raffan, Cambridge, MA: Harvard University Press, 2000, p.311.

athanatos . . . the soul can no longer be abandoned by the gods: on the contrary, it is called on to ascend.[26]

Damascius, being well versed in questions of 'Egyptian philosophy' (*en tois Aiguptiois philosophemasi*), maintains, nevertheless, that hieratic art (*hieratike*) and philosophy stem from different principles. He argues that to certain Platonists philosophy is primary (as to Plotinus and Porphyry), while to others (as to Iamblichus, Syrianus, and Proclus), hieratic practice is Philosophy, according to Damascius, descends from the one cause of all things to the lowest level of being. Hieratic art, instead, has its roots in the pericosmic causes: its subject is, as he says, 'the immortality of the soul (*psuchon peri athanasias*), on which the philosophy of the Egyptians is the same' (*hoti kata auta kai Aiguptiois philosopheitai: Phil.Hist.* 4a).

Hence Egyptian philosophy is regarded as partly, at least, identical with theurgy, namely, the worship (*therapeia*) of the gods which 'ties the ropes of heavenbound salvation (*tes anagogou soterias*) on the third, pericosmic level, that of generation' (ibid., 4A). Damascius argues that Plato has united these two sides of meta-philosophy by calling the philosopher a 'Bacchus':

> . . . for by using the notion of a man who has detached himself from genesis as an intermediate term, we can identify the one with the other. Still, it remains evident that he intends to honor the philosopher by the title of Bacchus, as we honor the Intelligence by calling it God, or profane light by giving it the same name as mystic light (*In Phaed.* 1.172.5-7).

Just before conditionally dividing all Platonists into the categories of *philosophoi* and *hieratikoi*, Damascius (himself being a ferocious researcher—*aner zetetikotatos*, a superb logician, as P. Athanassiadi remarks)[27] describes philosophy as the initiatory rites (*hai teletai*) and explains what it means to call the philosopher a Bacchus, as

---

26. Ibid., p.323.
27. Polymnia Athanassiadi, "Introduction".—Damascius, *The Philosophical History*, p.55.

the Egyptian philosopher and theurgist Heraiscus, is called, for example:

> The first Bacchus is Dionysus, whose ecstasy manifests itself in dancing (*basis*) and shouting (*iache*), that is, in every form of movement of which he is the cause according to the *Laws* (II. 672a5–d4); but one who has dedicated himself to Dionysus, having become his image, shares his name also. And when a man leads a Dionysian life (*ho de zon Dionusiakos*), his troubles are already ended and he is free from his bonds and released from custody, or rather from the confined form of life; such a man is the philosopher in the stage of purification (*In Phaed.* 1.171.1–6).

L.G. Westerink supposes that Damascius, in spite of his attempt at impartiality, evidently prefers the 'hieratic school' (*hoi hieratikoi*)[28] and, consequently, 'the theosophy which comes from the gods' (*ten apo ton theon . . . theosophian: Phil.Hist.* 46d). Damascius indeed maintains that the higher wisdom, namely, the Orphic and Chaldean lore (*ten Orphiken te kai Chaldaiken ten hupseloteran sophian*) transcends philosophical common sense (*ton koinon philosophias:* ibid., 85a). However, sometimes he seems to straightforwardly equate philosophy with the hieratic rites and with their esoteric interpretation. Consequently, to divulge *tes philosophias aporrheta*, the esoteric mysteries of philosophy, means to expose the hieratic statues and symbols from the secret temple of Isis at Menuthis (destroyed by the Christians in AD 488/9) and to describe the iconographic characteristics of those images in the presence of the Alexandrian ecclesiastical authorities (ibid., 58a).

Be that as it may, Damascius emphasizes that nothing is exclusive in the Greek philosophy itself, since philosophy, contrary to B. Russell's dogmatic claims, is not to be regarded as a miraculous Greek invention for the sake of B. Russell's future glory:

---

28. *The Greek Commentaries on Plato's Phaedo, vol. II: Damascius,* ed.and tr. L.G. Westerink, Amsterdam: North-Holland Publishing Company, 1977, p.104.

So that it is easy, if one wishes, to adapt Hellenic notions to conform with Egyptian ones. The Egyptians were the first men to philosophize on these things (*Aiguptioi de tauta eisin hoi protoi philosophountes*). Indeed it is from the Egyptians that the Pythagoreans introduced all these matters to the Greeks (*Phil. Hist.* 4a).

'All these things' include the Egyptian soteriology, centered on the immortality of the soul, on one's reassembling after multiple division or after being rent asunder and having taken an earthly body, as well as the idea of the fusion with the divine (*theokrasia*), of the perfect union (*henosis*) and 'the return of our souls to God' (*epanodos ton hemeteron psuchon pros to theion*: ibid., 4a). The soul (*psuche*) is no longer regarded as the phantom (*phasma*), or the ghostly double (*eidolon*), as it is depicted in Homer, but rather viewed as the immortal soul (like the Egyptian *ba*, destined to be transformed into the pure noetic light, *akh*) which constitutes one's real being, one's immaterial and divine essence to be delivered from the illusory prison-like body and reintegrated into the divine realm of eternal archetypes.

This initially esoteric Orphico-Pythagorean perspective, accepted and rationalized by Plato, places its emphasis—contrary to the earlier Homeric practices—on purification, concentration, unification, remembrance, separation of the soul and spiritual ascent, aimed at the mystic (*aporrhetos*) union with Dionysus (*Osiris*) and Apollo (*Horus-Ra*). Therefore to be a philosopher in the Egyptian-Pythagorean-Platonic manner would mean, as J.-P.Vernant has pointed out, to turn oneself away from the perishable body-simulacrum of the soul in order to return to that of which the soul itself is the simulacrum, namely, the divine Intellect and the One:

> In the *Phaedo*, before explaining his theory of *anamnesis*, Plato defines philosophy in a way that conforms to what he calls an ancient tradition, naming it a *melete thanatou*. By this he means a discipline or a rehearsal for death which consists in purifying the soul through a process of concentration that, starting from all the points of the body where it has been dispersed, gathers the soul back to itself so that, reassembled and

unified, it can unbind itself from the body and escape from it (*Phaed.* 67c3ff, 80e2ff).[29]

The philosopher tries to make his soul as pure, justified, illuminated, emancipated and separated in his life as it will be after death, thus following the paradigm of the Egyptian temple initiations and attempting 'to connect the end to the beginning', since the gnostic Osirian initiations in the Egyptian temples anticipated, prepared for and prefigured the ultimate initiation into the mysteries of the Duat, the Osirian realm of the dead. No wonder that philosophy, as an enterprise of raising (*anagein*) the soul to the level of the divine *eidos* and uniting (*sunagein*) it to the divine, is, according to Isidore, the master of Damascius, tantamount to prayer:

> He used to say that when the soul is in holy prayer (*en tais hierais euchais*) facing the mighty ocean of the divine, at first, disengaged from the body, it concentrates on itself; then it abandons its own habits, withdrawing from logical into intuitive thinking (*apo ton logikon ennoion epi tas to no sungeneis*); finally, at a third stage, it is possessed by the divine and drifts into an extraordinary serenity befitting gods rather than men' (*Phil. Hist.* 22).

THE KRONIAN LIFE OF SPECTATOR:
'TO FOLLOW ONE'S HEART IN THE TOMB'

The Greek verb *theorein* means 'to look at, behold, observe, perceive, speculate', therefore *theorema* refers both to a sight or spectacle and to an object of speculation. As G. A. Press pointed out:

> While *theasthai* before Plato seems always to refer to a looking or viewing with the eyes, *theoria* can also mean a viewing with the mind or contemplation, being a spectator at the games or the theater, or being a *theoros*, a state ambassador.[30]

29. Jean-Pierre Vernant, *Mortals and Immortals. Collected Essays,* ed., Froma I. Zeitlin, Princeton: Princeton University Press, 1991, p. 191.

30. Gerald A. Press, "Knowledge as Vision in Plato's Dialogues".—*The Journal of Neoplatonic Studies,* vol. III, no. 2, Spring 1995, p. 75.

Theoros is not only the official title of state ambassador to sacred festivals (where divine epiphanies or cultic icons are contemplated): it also signifies the envoy sent to consult an oracle and thereby is related with the concept of revelation. Since knowledge is regarded as spectacle, a philosopher as *theoros* is spectator at the cosmic games, the play of the gods (*paidia ton theon*), one who simply comes to look on (*theorein*) while attuning his ears to the undying divine laughter (*asbestos gelos*). From his love of knowledge (*philosopheon*), he may travel to Egypt, like Solon, for the purpose of seeing *ta thaumata*, wonders what are to be contemplated, for example, the animated statues (*agalmata*) and hieroglyphs, themselves tantamount to the miraculous embodiment of the gods.

In this respect, the spectator and traveler is *philotheoros*, 'lover of contemplation', since contemplation of the hieratic symbols and icons reveals that 'every image is a kind of knowledge and wisdom' (*episteme kai sophia hekaston estin agalma: Enn.* V.8.6.8–9), as Plotinus maintains. To him the true wisdom is ontological substance, or noetic being, and the true substance is wisdom (*he ara alethine sophia ousia, kai he alethine ousia sophia: Enn.* v.8.5.15–16).

Therefore J. Assmann rightly observes that for those Egyptians who regarded their land as a holy of holies, as the *templum mundi*, the temple of the world, and a sort of sacred 'otherworldly realm' in the world of the living,

> the festival was the medium of an advantage in the next life that was already acquired on earth, as was also the case later with the Orphic and Eleusinian mysteries. Here, for the first time, we are able to grasp a central point in the connection between Egyptian festivals and Greek mysteries that the Greek writers constantly stressed. During life, the festival already opened up a next-worldly space where the deceased could hope to return after death.[31]

What the Egyptian initiate seeks is the proximity to the gods: both in the temple cult and in the Osirian Netherworld (Duat) the

---

31. Jan Assmann, *Death and Salvation in Ancient Egypt*, tr. David Lorton, Ithaca and London: Cornell University Press, 2005, pp. 232–233.

goal is to 'gaze upon the face of the gods'. This is exactly the goal of Plato's philosophy: to gaze upon and contemplate the noetic Forms, or Ideas. This 'embalming glance' with which the Egyptians beheld the world (seeing it as a set of heliophanies, of living images that reflect their intelligible archetypes and function as cultic vehicles for the *bau* of the gods, the *neteru*) was not dissecting and separating, but integrative and anagogic.

Therefore theoretical knowledge, concerned with what exists, is an essential constituent of true wisdom, and all those substances (*ousiai*) which do not possess wisdom in themselves, are not true substances, according to Plotinus. But the Ideas in Intellect are concrete living realities and true substances, not mental abstractions, and these noetic realities (*akhu* in the Egyptian theology) are the objects of Platonic *theoria*. This *theoria* or vision (analogous to the Eleusinian *epopteia*) refers to something inner, immediate, comprehensive, experiential and supra-rational: it will not take the form of an argument or proposition in their usual technical sense. Platonic *theoria* is more related to the realm of sacred liturgies and mysticism, because its gaze is synthetic rather than analytic, inclusive and integrative rather than exclusive and scattering. As Plotinus observes:

> One must not then suppose that the gods or the 'exceedingly blessed spectators' (*hupereudaimonas*) in the higher world contemplate propositions, but all the Forms we speak about are beautiful images (*kala agalmata*) in that world, of the kind which someone imagined to exist in the soul of the wise man, images not painted but real (*agalmata de ou gegrammena, alla onta*). This is why the ancients said that the Ideas were realities and substances (*Enn.* v.8.5.20–24, Armstrong).

Likewise, a general theory of knowledge for Plato is a vision which one has to experience in a manner of the Sufi 'unveiling' (*kashf*) rather than a doctrine of what knowledge is at the level of discursive propositions. Even Aristotle's theoretical knowledge retains the sense of *theoria* as the observation of festival, statue, or spectacle, since this knowledge is not merely belief about the first principles of movement, and manipulation of the related mental puzzles, but also a self-moved way of life which involves a sort of

'Osirification'—not for the sake of profane advantage but of certain holy *eudaimonia*, the godlike status which (as Aristotle supposes) depends on the leisure necessary for the concentration that allows one to philosophize.

The true aim of philosophy is not to produce discursive accounts but rather to re-kindle the ever-present inner spark of the divine within us and to raise the soul to the noetic cosmos either by the theurgic 'ropes' of worship (analogous to the rays of the Sun), or by means of contemplation and dialectical ascent. Thus Serapion, the Alexandrian philosopher and Damascius' spiritual grandfather, is regarded by the contemporary Platonists as a model (*paradeigma*) of sainthood characteristic of the golden age of Kronos. Since Kronos is identified with the divine Intellect, the Kronian life is the true philosophical life in obedience to the immortal element within us, the life ruled by *nous*.[32] And this Kronian *bios* is equivalent to the way leading to the golden tower of Kronos: 'There winds sweep from the Ocean across the Island of the Blessed' (Pindar *Olymp.* II.70–73). As Damascius relates about Serapion:

> But most of the time he spent at home, leading a life which was not that of a man, but quite simply a god-like existence, constantly addressing prayers and hymns to himself or to the divine (*pros heauton e pros to theion*), or rather meditating in silence. A seeker of the Truth and a man with a theoretical cast of mind (*theoretikos*), he could not bear to occupy himself with the technicalities of philosophy (*ta technikotera tes philosophias*), but immersed himself in those vigorous concepts (or inspired intellections) which feel one with God. For this reason he possessed and read almost nothing except the writings of Orpheus. . . . (*Phil. Hist.* III Athanassiadi).

Serapion is here depicted as being *theoretikos*, the theoretical philosopher, in spite of his complete lack of interest in dialectical inquiry (*zetesis*) or in discursive theological games, and his rather monastic Orphic *askesis*, close to that of the later Sufi saints (*awliya'*).

---

32. John Dillon, "Plato and the Golden Age".—*Hermathena. A Trinity College Dublin Review*, no. CLIII, winter 1992, p. 32.

Therefore let us see what it means to be a theoretical philosopher, according to Opympiodorus, another Alexandrian Neo-platonist:

The contemplative philosopher (*ho theoretikos*) knows sensible things insofar as he reduces them from their own plurality to the unity of the intelligible; but since in the intelligible there is not only unity but also plurality, he reduces the unity in the intelligible to the unity that is in God (*anagei to hen to en to noeto epi to hen to en to theo*), which is unity proper without multiplicity, for God is nothing but a monad without multiplicity' (*In Phaed.* 4.3.7–10 Westerink).

Wisdom, being the most finished of the forms of knowledge, is loved and aimed at by those who regard contemplation and contemplative dialectic as the art of purification (*katharsis*), and who have already had started the journey of the great return whose end is the full grasp of the noetic unity of all reality. This theoretical wisdom is concealed in the shrine of that truth which initially is expressed in myth and only slowly revealed to the man who can lift up to God the sacred light of his soul, according to Damascius (*Phil. Hist.*2a). For such a man, involved in contemplation (*theoria*) of the overwhelming noetic beauty (which gods themselves continuously contemplate), partly reflected in earthly images, in ways of life and the soul's restored inward purity, being is not a dead thing, devoid of life and intelligence, but 'Intellect and Being are one and the same thing' (*nous de kai on tauton*: Plotinus *Enn.* v.4.2.44).

The *bios theoretikos* of Hellenic philosophers is directly related to what is called 'following one's heart' (*shemes-ib*) by the Egyptians. In the Late Period Egypt, religious and contemplative persons (regarded as 'philosophers' by Chaeremon), while still alive, used to seek meditative seclusion in the temples or in the gardened rock-tombs, thereby following their heart-intellect—that is, retiring into the alchemical tomb-temple. W. Federn argues that *shemes-ib* (*sms-ib*) might be rendered in Greek as *scholazein*, 'to have leisure'.[33] Now to be at leisure means 'to follow one's heart in the tomb' or 'in the

33. Walter Federn, The "'Transformations' in the Coffin Texts: A New Approach".—*Journal of Near Eastern Studies*, vol. xix, no. 4, Oct. 1960, p. 248.

garden', to experience certain blissful Protean transformations and become a 'silent man'. Consequently, it means to concentrate one's spiritual eye on divine objects, eternal archetypes and intelligible lights, as if embalming oneself at the 'holy ground' (*kheret-neter*) of divine Presence.

THAUMA IDESTHAI: 'A WONDER TO BEHOLD'

Proclus reminds us that wonder is the beginning of philosophy, and for this reason Iris is called the daughter of Wonder (*In Alcib.* 42). This passage is based on Plato's discussion of the problem of incommensurability in geometry and 'our power to render successively rational what at each lower dimension is still irrational, thus bringing about ever more comprehensive rational order.'[34] Plato's text runs as follows:

> *Theaetetus:* By the gods, Socrates, I am lost in wonder (*thaumazo*) when I think of all these things, and sometimes when I regard them it really makes my head swim. *Socrates:* . . . this sense of wonder (*to thaumazein*) is the mark of the philosopher, since wonder is the only beginning of philosophy, and he was a good genealogist who made Iris the daughter of Thaumas (*Thaetet.* 155d).

This amazement and philosophical wonder may be understood in different senses, because epistemological, mathematical or metaphysical puzzles are not the only genuine causes for wonder. It may also be caused by the cultic masks of God, while facing the external play of multiple theophanies and inwardly contemplating the undivided noetic lights. The greatest wonder, for the ancient Egyptian initiate 'like unto the dead', is to 'find the gods dancing before your gaze, the Ennead bidding you welcome,' when 'your hand will be taken by Ra himself' among the crew of his barque, and 'when they see you, making your appearance as a god' at the side of Ra, so 'that you may see the god, and the god see you.'[35]

34. Rosemary Desjardins, *The Rational Enterprise: Logos in Plato's Theaetetus*, Albany: SUNY Press, 1990, p. 189.
35. Jan Assmann, *Death and Salvation in Ancient Egypt*, p. 62.

Iris is the messenger of the gods, and the seven-fold rainbow. In Akkadian myth, the rainbow is likened to a *gamlu* weapon, the divine curved scythe which is the weapon of the gods: the rainbow surrounds the Sun like a *gamlu*, being Ishtar's cosmic jewelry, symbolically depicted as a chain of flies.[36] It appears after the *abubu*, the Great Flood, signifying the restored covenant of peace and *philia* between the gods and human beings, that is, the reconstructed bridge of 'philosophy' which connects two different ontological realms, like the smoke-pillar of the sacrifice. This necklace of Ishtar, the celestial omen that causes an awful and joyous amazement, confirms that the irrational powers, plotting against the life of intellect, are now pacified.

In this respect, Ishtar is similar to Athena Soteria, the mistress of philosophy, whose function is to preserve the heart of Dionysus undivided. This heart stands for the unparticipated Intellect (*Nous*). The Orphic Dionysus is torn asunder into seven pieces (like a rainbow) by the Titans, an action that indicates a seven-fold division of the Soul. Ishtar (who may in another aspect be equated to Persephone) is analogous to God's Presence, *Shekhinah*, 'virgin of light', with whom the Jewish mystic seeks to be united, following considerably older Assyrian paradigms. As S. Parpola rightly observes:

> This notion of the *Shekhinah* agrees perfectly with the role played by Ishtar in Assyrian ecstatic prophecy, where she represents the Word of God manifested through prophetic spirit (*to pneuma*, 'spiritus sanctus').[37]

When the solar disk of Ashur (*Assur*) is turned into the eight-pointed star, it becomes the symbol of Ashur's daughter, Ishtar, the Beauty of God. Her birth-process, conceived almost as a constructive flow of Pythagorean numbers, is to be likened to the divine

---

36. Anne Draffkorn Kilmer, "The Symbolism of the Flies in the Mesopotamian Flood Myth and Some Future Implications".—*Language, Literature, and History: Philological and Historical Studies Presented to Erica Reiner*, ed. Francesca Rocherberg-Halton, New Haven: American Oriental Society, 1987, p.179.

37. Simo Parpola, "The Assyrian Tree of Life: Tracing the Origins of Jewish Monotheism and Greek Philosophy".—*Journal of Near Easten Studies*, vol. 52, no. 3, 1993, p.181.

stream emanating from the winged disk above the sacred Assyrian Tree of Life, the prototype of the later Sephirotic Tree in Jewish esoterism. The star of Ishtar represents the divine *pleroma* in the form of a four-spoked wheel.[38] It refers to the rotation of the macrocosmic wheel, moved by her erotic power and imitated by the theurgic instruments, such as the top of Hekate (*Hekatikos strophalos*), namely, the golden *sphaira*, in Chaldean Platonism.

The manifested wheel of Ishtar's noetic fire—or the beautiful cosmic *agalma*, to say it in Plato's own terms—is a wonder to behold (*thauma idesthai*). This Greek expression is used mostly in the demiurgic contexts, and one should remember that the function of the philosophers in the cosmic state of the gods, in which wisdom (*sophia*, namely, order, measure, right proportion, like the Egyptian *maat*) is maintained, is to be the crafters, or *demiourgoi*. Their 'royal' task is to determine the functions of the rest of the body-like state, fixing their gaze upon the things of the eternal and unchanging order.

All cosmic (or rather *cosmetic*) arrangements, divine orders (*taxeis*), theophanies and creations are *thauma idesthai*, 'a wonder to behold'. They are like *daidaleia*, the works of Daidalos, that is, the Near Eastern and Egyptian artifacts, the animated cultic statues, things endowed with life. They display autokinetic powers like the tripods of Hephaistos, or imaginary golden maidens endowed with mind, voice, and strength.[39]

For Plato, human beings are precisely such animated puppets, made by the gods, 'possibly as a plaything, or possibly with some more serious purpose' (*Leg.* 644d), whose existential show is *thauma idesthai*: it causes perplexity and marks the beginning of philosophy, the path of remembrance. This attempt to recover the original memory and comprehend the truth through remembering the origins and meaning of the puppet-play is focused not merely upon how things are, but upon why they are the way they are.

For Platonists, the word *aletheia* (truth) itself indicates that this

38. Ibid., p.189.

39. Sarah P. Morris, *Daidalos and the Origins of Greek Art*, Princeton: Princeton University Press, 1992, p. 226.

knowledge is a dispelling of oblivion (*lethe*). This philosophical recollection of the 'great light of Apsu', the wisdom-gushing fountain
of *kosmos noetos*, is like Etana's ascent to heaven in order 'to disclose
concealed things'. (Etana is the legendary Sumerian king of Kish, 'a
shepherd who ascended to heaven'.) Every lover of wisdom (*nemequ*
in Akkadian) follows the paradigm of Etana and the other mythical
apkallus, that is, the archetypal avataras and sages whose spiritual
legacy, albeit tacitly, is 'still very much alive in Jewish, Christian, and
Oriental mysticism and philosophies.'[40]

Aristotle says that it is owing to their wonder that men

> both now begin and at first began to philosophize.... And a
> man who is puzzled and wonders thinks himself ignorant:
> whence even the lover of myths is in a sense a lover of wisdom,
> for myth is composed of wonders (*Metaph*.982b).

Aristotle equates the lovers of myths and the philosophers, arguing that philosophy should be distinguished from the science of
production (*poietike*), because theoretical or philosophical knowledge transcends the specificities of time and place. Being the study
of first principles, it is pursued for no earthly purpose. The philosopher tries to reach a kind of *apotheosis* which takes place at the end
of the Peripatetic road. Accordingly, *logos* must yield to non-discursive *nous*, to seeing the entire cosmos noetically. This noetic accomplishment is regarded as a change into 'a better state', since God is in
'a better state', and life belongs to God. For Aristotle, God is identical to the divine Intellect. As Ch. C. Evangeliou remarks:

> Following along the path suggested by Aristotelian dialectic,
> we can see that the eternally energized Divine Intellect and the
> dialectically perfected, and thus noetically transformed, mind
> of the true philosopher are identified as being essentially the
> same... In this new noetic light, Aristotle's philosophy, and the
> Platonic tradition to which he belongs, would appear to be
> closer to the Eastern ways of thinking... than to the narrowly
> defined 'Western rationality', if by this expression is meant the

40. Simo Parpola, ibid., p.199.

kind of calculative and manipulative *ratio*, in the service of utilitarian, technological and ideological goals.[41]

THE INVINCIBLE WARRIORS
AS MODELS OF PHILOSOPHICAL LIFE

In a sense, philosophy is the *via dialectica*, dialectic way, following the paradigmatic Orphic formula: *bios-thanatos-bios* (life-death-life). In a *makarismos* of the golden lamellae (from a tomb in Pelinna), themselves shaped as two stylized heart-form ivy leaves, this formula is explained as follows:

> Now you have died and now you have come into being, O thrice happy one, on the same day. Tell Persephone that Bakchios himself has set you free.[42]

This sacred way of liberation, opened to the Orphic initiates (*mustai kai bakchoi*) is the 'mystic road to Rhadamanthus' (*mustikon oimon epi Rhadamanthum*),[43] Rhadamanthus meaning 'man of *Amenta*' (*r(w)d-Imntt*), of the Osirian Netherworld.[44] The Orphic eschatology, which regards death as the way to real life, promises the vindicated gnostic (analogous to the Egyptian *maakheru*, from which derives the Greek word *makarios*, 'blessed') that he may be a god instead of a mortal. This immortalization is achieved after one's transformation and acceptance into the Elysian Fields. The word *Elysium* (gr. *Elusion pedion*) itself derives from the Egyptian word *ealu* (or *iaru*), 'reeds', referring to the Osirian Field of Reeds.[45]

---

41. Christos C. Evangeliou, *The Hellenic Philosophy: Between Europe, Asia and Africa*, pp. 50–51.

42. Fritz Graf, "Dionysian and Orphic Eschatology: New Texts and Old Questions".—*Masks of Dionysus*, ed. Thomas H.Carpenter and Christopher A. Faraone, Ithaca and London: Cornell University Press, 1993, p. 241.

43. Susan Guettel Cole, "Voices from Beyond the Grave: Dionysus and the Dead.—*Masks of Dionysus*, p.278.

44. R. Drew Griffith, *Sailing to Elysium: Menelaus' Afterlife (Odyssey 4.561–569) and Egyptian Religion*, p.220.

45. Jan Assmann, *Death and Salvation in Ancient Egypt*, p.392.

At the level of individual human choice (or *metanastasis*, a change of address), the image of a journey with stages and stations along the road became a schema for the moral life, especially in the Hellenistic period. Heracles, the paradigmatic embodiment of the true philosopher, is depicted as sitting and looking down two roads, that of Vice and Virtue, laid out before him.[46] The road which marks advances in moral, intellectual, and spiritual development (for example, those leading from the realm of images to the realm of archetypes, and from knowledge of the self to knowledge of God) requires a mystagogue, the guide upon the road.

Philo of Alexandria, at once the Jewish *hermeneus* and Middle Platonist (labeled *ho Puthagoreios* by Clement of Alexandria) speaks of the 'royal' road which the Hebrews traveled on their way to the 'promised land' as the way leading to God. This road itself is curiously called *philosophia* (philosophy being understood as a means by which a mortal human being is immortalized) and Moses regarded as *pansophos* and *philosophos*, the greatest of philosophers,[47] who 'had both reached the apex of philosophy (*philosophias ep' auten phthasas akroteta*) and had been taught by oracles the most significant and essential aspects of nature' (*De opificio mundi* 8). Philo outlines the progress leading to the contemplative life as follows:

> after relinquishing mortal things, the soul is to receive a vision of things immortal and the ability to contemplate them (*epideixin kai theorian ton athanaton*)'[48]

For the Homeric Greeks, this road of 'migration' is the road of 'homecoming'. It is traveled by means of toil and suffering, a performance of the Twelve Labors, a passing through the Twelve Night Hours of the Egyptian Duat. Therefore Heracles (sometimes

46. Herold Weiss, "A Schema of 'the Road' in Philo and Lucan".—*The Studia Philonica Annual: Studies in Hellenistic Judaism*, vol. I, ed. David T. Runia, Atlanta: Scholars Press, 1989, p. 43.

47. Gregory E. Sterling, "Platonizing Moses: Philo and Middle Platonism".— *The Studia Philonica Annual: Studies in Hellenistic Judaism*, vol. v, ed. David T. Runia, Atlanta: Scholars Press, 1993, p. 99.

48. Herold Weiss, ibid., p. 51.

identified as the Egyptian god Khonsu, the Phoenician Melqart) is considered as the greatest example (*paradeigma*) of the philosophical life, demonstrating how a human being can become a god. Those who have been educated after the pattern of Heracles are called 'sons of Zeus' (*Dios paidas*), transferred (*methastasthai*) into the company of the gods, since Heracles, pictured as the ideal warrior, king, and philosopher, is viewed by Dio Chrisostom as 'the savior of the world and humanity' (*tes ges kai ton anthropon sotera*).[49]

Heracles is designated as a *heros theos*, a hero-god, to be imitated by philosophers and ascetics. He is regarded as skilled in prophecy, dialectic, and logic, like Philo's Moses, who was not a Hebrew Moses, but rather a Middle Platonist,[50] a 'divine man' (*theios aner*), or even a god (*theos*), whose divinity is understood as a reflection of the divine ruling power (*basilike dunamis*). According to W.E. Helleman:

> Philo indicates that in receiving the vision Moses, being divinely inspired, becomes divine, for the prophetic mind becomes like the monad, leaving behind its mortal and dual nature to become pure *nous*, a unity.[51]

The Heraclean paradigm makes it clear that for one's immortalization both philosophical *paideia* and hieratic initiation are required. Initiation is the starting-point of stepping into another world for those lovers of wisdom who are 'men of knowledge', who travel the sacred road and descend while alive into the Underworld (like mythical Heracles and Orpheus), following the example of Persephone and her Akkadian prototype, the goddess Ishtar, or Inanna.

Ishtar represents the descending and ascending soul, both *anima mundi* and the individual *psuche*, by whatever term we may call it. The personal salvation of the initiate may be symbolized by Ishtar's

---

49. David E. Aune, "Heracles and Christ: Heracles Imagery in the Christology of Early Christianity".—*Greeks, Romans, and Christians. Essays in Honor of Abraham J. Malherbe*, ed. David L. Balch et alii, Minneapolis: Fortress Press, 1990, p.9.

50. Gregory E.Sterling, ibid., p.111.

51. Wendy E. Helleman, *Philo of Alexandria on Deification and Assimilation to God.—The Studia Philonica Annual. Studies in Hellenistic Judaism*, vol. 11, ed. David T. Runia, Atlanta: Scholars Press, 1990, p.69.

release from the Netherworld, accomplished (as an inward alchemical work) by the devotees of Nabu (the Babylonian equivalent of
Thoth, the Egyptian divine scribe, regarded as Hermes by the
Greeks) through intensive philosophical study, philosophical meditation, exegesis of *hieroi logoi*, and esoteric cult practices related to
the Heraclean figure of Ninurta, a son of Enlil, whose spiritual perfection (like that of Philonian *Logos*) is symbolized by the sacred
Tree of Life.

Both Nabu and Ninurta are viewed as God's weapons, as powers
of Marduk. The Tree itself (the prototype of the Pythagorean *tetractys* and Sephirotic *pleroma*, or the Garden of Knowledge, *kosmos
noetos*) represents a royal mystical path of spiritual growth and
ascent, starting from its roots (the realm of Nergal) and leading
towards the winged disk, the crown of divine Light ('the apex of
philosophy'), the symbol of both Anu and Enlil, or Marduk, but in
Assyria a symbol of Ashur by virtue of his equation with Anu and
Enlil. As S. Parpola relates:

> In a Neo-Assyrian hymn glorifying Ninurta, his body is
> described as encompassing the whole universe, with different
> gods equated with his limbs, his face being the sun.... It
> should be stressed that just as Christ and the Father are one, so
> is triumphant Ninurta/Nabu one with his Father: both Mar-
> duk and Enlil are included among Ninurta's limbs....
> Ninurta's triumphal chariot is identified with what is called
> Marduk's chariot.... Against this background, it is not acci-
> dental that the throne of God in Ezek. 1 and Dan. 77 is known
> as the Chariot in Jewish tradition; the aspect of God seated
> upon it is that of God triumphing over evil and sin....
> According to the doctrine of the Tree, the power to combat evil
> also resided in man: the man who succeeded in conquering sin
> would become the Son of God himself and eventually triumph
> in Heaven.[52]

Being a son of the king of the gods, Ninurta in some respect is
analogous to the Egyptian Horus acting through the ruling human

---

52. Simo Parpola, ibid., pp. 204–205.

king. Horus-like pharaoh maintains truth and cosmic order in the heliophanic state, keeping equilibrium between opposing forces through the mediation of Thoth (an aspect of universal intelligence, namely articulating creative Sound—that is, the light-like *Logos*). Likewise, the heart of a human being who is the lover of *Maat* (*Maat* being Thoth's feminine counterpart, his *dunamis*, or *shakti*) is the heart in which Horus dwells. This truth-loving heart is attuned to *maat* and lives on *maat*, because to 'do *maat*' and to 'speak *maat*' is the same as 'to philosophize', 'to make bright *maat*' which Ra loves'. Since truth (*maat*) is bread by which Ra, the solar divine Intellect, lives, the true philosopher (the imitator of deity) is fed on its brightness too in order to move in an orderly and harmonious way, being theurgically united with the goddess *Maat*. As J. Naydler says:

> She is literally the bread by which Ra lives, and so by implication she is the food of all the gods, who are but the limbs of Ra. What better substance than truth could there be for the gods to feed on?[53]

Ninurta, the invincible divine warrior, also fights for truth against disorder and error. His triumphal return to the celestial home, Ekur, after his victory against a terrible monster, Asakku, the symbol of the fallen material existence, death, and sickness, is a model for the spiritual combat and *askesis*, directed against irrational and evil forces. In addition, Ninurta is the perfect king (*sharru gitmalu*) or perfect man/hero (*etlu/qarradu gitmalu*, that is, *anthropos teleios*, like *al-insan al-kamil* in Sufism). The perfect man is the paradigmatic sage, or philosopher (in the initial archetypal sense), the provider of light and wisdom, dispensing the medicine of life (*shammu sha balati*). Ninurta holds the book of life, the tablet of destinies. In Mesopotamian gnosis, by imitation of Ninurta's deeds and qualities the initiate is resurrected from the dead and glorified in Heaven. According to S. Parpola:

> This idea certainly was central to the myth of Ishtar's Descent to the Netherworld, which provided the Mesopotamian para-

---

53. Jeremy Naydler, *Temple of the Cosmos. The Ancient Egyptian Experience of the Sacred*, Rochester: Inner Traditions, 1996, p.94.

digm par excellence for the salvation of man. Since the motif of the 'jewel-studded garment' in the *Hymn of the Pearl* clearly derives from Ishtar's Descent, its integration with motifs from Ninurta mythology suggests that the idea of personal salvation was inherent in the Ninurta myths as well. Thus interpreted, these myths had relevance to any individual who, having 'vanquished' the material world, had attained divine perfection, symbolized by the 'jewel-studded garment'. Personal salvation indeed appears to have been the essential goal of the cult of Nabu, the son of Marduk who since the late second millennium BCE was syncretized with Ninurta. The devotees of Nabu appear to have striven for salvation through intensive study and exegesis of canonical scripture; the cult itself was esoteric and, like the cult of Ishtar, has affinities with Gnosticism, Hermeticism and Mithraism.[54]

THE INWARD JOURNEY TO THE PLACE OF TRUTH

Parmenides, a priest and a 'son' of Apollo, in his journey to meet the goddess (presumably Persephone, that is, Ishtar), travels to the *peirata* of universe, the ultimate boundaries of existence. After receiving paradoxical revelations, he becomes a messenger of the goddess, the founder of logic which itself initially had a rather soteriological function. As P. Kingsley relates:

> That was the job of the hero who manages to touch the borderline between the human and divine; to reach the realm of Persephone. Most typically of all, though, it described the daily route followed by the sun as it makes its way to the other side of the ocean surrounding the known world and arrives in the Mansions of Night.[55]

---

54. Simo Parpola, "Mesopotamian Precursors of the Hymn of the Pearl".— *Melammu Symposia II: Mythology and Mythologies. Methodological Approaches to Intercultural Influences*, ed. R. M. Whiting, Helsinki: The Neo-Assyrian Text Corpus Project, 2001, p.192.
55. Peter Kingsley, *Reality*, p. 279.

This route is followed by all spiritual heroes, those who imitate the Sun's voyage around a circular cosmos of heliophanies, the perfect cultic paradigm and icon of the ouroboros-like *Nous* in his external cyclic epiphany. In Egypt, the *Book of Amduat*, in which the centrality of knowledge (*rekh*) is emphasized, seems to be 'the first religious treatise to insert the king consistently into the daily course of the sun.'[56]

During this paradigmatic journey, at the very depths of the Duat, the Sun (the *ba* of Ra) reaches the water hole filled with *Nun*, the ineffable primeval substance, where Ra (as *ba*, the self-revealing noetic *eidos*) and Osiris (as the ideal *sah*-form of Ra, his corpse depicted as *Sokar*) are united. Thereby the Eye of Horus is healed by Thoth and the rebirth of Ra occurs, moving through the body of the cosmic Serpent (the World-encircler) backward, from tail to mouth. Likewise, the resurrection of the 'dead' philosopher, the follower of Ra, restored like the solar Eye, conforms to the same pattern.

The Egyptian journey of Ra's *ba*, known as 'the path of the two ways', is followed both by the soul of the dead and that of the hero, the initiate-philosopher who 'dies' before his actual physical death. N. Marinatos shows that both Gilgamesh and Odysseus perform this cosmic journey at the edges of the earth (*perata ges*).[57]

In Egypt, the *ba*'s journey (performed by the deceased or the initiate) is to 'yonder shore, upon which the gods stand' (*Book of the Dead* 98). The lover of truth and wisdom wishes to reach the place 'where Maat is' (*Coffin Texts* III.143)—to settle there, beneath the holy sycamore, which is like the Assyrian Tree of Life. Though his journey has the character of an official trip, imitation into the solar course is granted only to the righteous (to the *siddiq*, in Aramaic and Arabic Sufi terms) who is to be rejuvenated in the goddess' womb and united with Ra in that 'primeval place' where he first 'came into being (*kheper*) out of Ra'.[58]

---

56. Erik Hornung, *The Egyptian Books of the Afterlife*, tr. David Lorton, Ithaca and London: Cornell University Press, 1999, p. 34.

57. Nanno Marinatos, "The Cosmic Journey of Odysseus".—*Numen*, vol. 48, Leiden: Koninklijke Brill NV, 2001, p.381.

58. Jan Assmann, *Death and Salvation in Ancient Egypt*, p.180.

The Sun God is not only the life-giving demiurgic Intellect (whose *ba* unites with the cultic body of Osiris in the Duat), but also the supreme *hermeneus*, that is, translator or interpreter. Whoever wishes to enter the Osirian Duat needs to be helped by the knowledge of Ra himself. This is why, according to the *Book of Amduat*, it is necessary for the initiate on earth to follow Ra (the solar *Nous*) on his journey to noetic rebirth.[59] Hence, he must practice theurgic rites and philosophy in a sense of 'living on Maat' and 'sitting in the hand of Amun-Ra' or 'putting the god in one's heart'. This attitude stands in strict accord with Plato's definition of philosophy as training for death and preparation for the spiritual journey through the Netherworld, ultimately aimed at the return to the all-encompassing One.

The inward journey requires the traveler to withstand a series of examinations which include knowledge of the secret divine names, and of one's true identity and destination. The philosopher, as a traveler striking out towards the throne of Osiris, beyond the 'horizon' (*akhet*), is identified to Horus. The path of *bau* (souls, manifestations, psychic entities) is opened to his *ba* by *Upawet* (or *Wepwawet*, a manifestation of the 'victorious Horus'), the Opener of the Ways and the chief Mystagogue, sometimes identified with Anubis.

The jackal-headed god Anubis is the master of mummification, 'He who is over the mystery'; he is able to re-unite *membra disiecta* of the dead body and turn it into an image of Osiris, his eternal *eidos* and visible theurgic hieroglyph. The embalmer produces the 'head of mystery' (*tep sheta*) which is the 'head of a god' that enables the deceased or the initiate to see and act as a god.

Maat is the permanent driving force, the assistant, and the directed *telos* of this ritualized esoteric journey, each stage of which is equivalent to an iconographic constellation of particular keywords, symbols, and the related divine powers, experienced as an externalized psychic environment. The voyage itself is only possible

---

59. Theodor Abt and Erik Hornung, *Knowledge for the Afterlife. The Egyptian Amduat—A Quest for Immortality,* Zurich: Living Human Heritage Publication, 2003, p. 28.

when a 'mystical ship' is built by the sole means of theurgic language. Thereby the dismembered ship (like the *ochema*, the shining vehicle of the soul in Neoplatonism) is reconstructed and animated. Simultaneously one's bodily limbs are 'sacramentally interpreted' (to use J. Assmann's term) by equating each part of the initiate's body with a particular deity.

This initiatory journey through a deliberately-constructed, text-like reality, by means of a particular transformative knowledge (*gnosis*) and a powerful theurgic language, consists of relating all roles and events back to their archetypes in the divine realm of *akh*. The initiate wards off any threat by recognizing it and by calling it by name, thereby confirming its place within the textual *mandala*.

By knowing the metaphysical structure and iconography of the *mundus imaginalis* related to the particular noetic principles (*neteru*), the initiate is certain that he knows everything (*panta ta onta*, to say it in Greek philosophical language). Philosophy itself is sometimes defined as *gnosis ton onton he onta esti*, that is, as the knowledge of those noetic realities that really exist, though such realities (tantamount to the Egyptian divine Ennead, the noetic *pleroma* of principles and their subsequent articulation) are not easily grasped by the impoverished modern mind.

TO BE LIKE OSIRIS

The philosopher is willing to die, according to Olympiodorus, and he is striving for death, namely the separation of the soul from the body. However, as the Alexandrian Neoplatonist says:

> Preparation for death is not an end in itself . . . for the real end is being dead. For the same reason 'dying' is distinct from 'being dead'; one in search of purification, who is training himself for death, is 'dying', that is to say, purifying himself of affects, while the contemplative is already 'dead', because he is free from affects, and therefore he will not make dying his object (*In Phaed.* 3.3.2–6).

To be dead is to be like Osiris who waits to be united with the *ba* of Ra, and this union in the Duat belongs to one's integral philosophical life. To philosophize in the Osirian Netherworld entails using the knowledge necessary to effect the alchemical transformation required in order to be vindicated and become *maa-kheru*. J. Assmann says:

> The accumulation of such an enormous body of knowledge based on pure speculation and meant to insure individual salvation (i.e. in the sense of overcoming death) reminds one of the Gnosis and must surely represent one of its roots. Purity, in the sense of deliverance from the burdens of earthly existence, may only be attained through knowledge. Purity and knowledge, these two concept are closely interwoven; does not the deceased assert: 'I know the names. . . . I am pure'?[60]

Through his purity and knowledge the deceased (the initiate 'philosopher') steps face to face with the gods, or the noetic Forms. In the inscription from the tomb of Djehutiemheb (the reign of Ramesses II), the owner of the tomb prays to Hathor:

> Give me your countenance, let me praise it, grant your beauty, that I may gaze upon your form. . . .[61]

The deceased declares himself to be truly a servant of Hathor, the Serpent goddess from the eastern horizon, Lady of the Sycamore Tree, who initiates ascent to Heaven for those who love her as the paradigm of integrity and the source of joyous inspiration, or 'sober drunkenness'. Being regarded as the Eye of Ra (or *Wedjat*-eye, the whole and re-assembled eye which like an active mirror irradiates and expresses Ra's intelligible beauty), she acts as the theurgic power of divine Intellect. In this respect, Hathor is the *Iret*-eye, *iret* meaning 'doer'.[62] The Eye's work may be understood both as creative contemplation (as in later Plotinian sense of that word) and as theurgic accomplishment, *ergon*, by means of which the initiate is integrated

60. Jan Assmann, "Death and Initiation in the Funerary Religion of Ancient Egypt".—*Religion and Philosophy in Ancient Egypt*, ed. J. P. Allen et alii, New Haven: Yale University Press, 1989, p.144.

61. Jan Assmann, *Death and Salvation in Ancient Egypt*, p.199.

62. Alison Roberts, *Hathor Rising. The Serpent Power of Ancient Egypt*, Rottingdean: Northgate Publishers, 2001, p.9.

into the Golden Cow (Hathor), and placed in the womb-like tomb for the noetic rebirth.

The above mentioned servant of Hathor (the name Hathor meaning 'the house of Horus') receives certain revelations or philosophical instructions from the goddess. As he says, she spoke to him with her own mouth and came to instruct; so the servant declares:

> I do not reject the speech of your mouth,
> I do not disregard your teaching.
> I am on the way that you yourself have ordained,
> On the path that you yourself have prepared.
> Blessed be he who knows you!
> He who beholds you is blessed.
> How happy is he who rests at your side,
> Who enters into your shadow.
> It is you who prophesied my tomb at the beginning,
> When it was first planned.[63]

This revealed path of gnosis and vision, understood as an initiation into the mysteries of the realm of the dead, constitutes the essential core of the historically much later Platonic philosophy. The Hellenic *philosophoi*, regarded as solar heroes, formally replaced the Egyptian solar initiates whose chief spiritual master (*telesiourgos*) was the Horus-like king, son of Ra, able to receive revelations and ascend to his father Atum-Ra in order to be united in His embrace. The solar hierophanies, viewed as faces of the noetic fire, were rationalized and turned into the Ideas.

In any case, the solar heroes traveling the sacred Apollonian road of Orpheus, Pythagoras, and Parmenides (the road which 'carries the wise man through all cities' and which is the same as that of Odysseus) have an exclusive knowledge of how to pass through darkness to light, through death to life. This great intelligence enabled Sisyphus (sometimes regarded as the father of Odysseus) to persuade Persephone with wily words and 'return from death'.[64]

---

63. Jan Assmann, *Death and Salvation in Ancient Egypt*, p.199.

64. Douglas Frame, *The Myth of Return in Early Greek Epic*, New Haven and London: Yale University Press, 1978, p.36.

This transition may be imagined as a ceremonial movement through the temple gates and halls which the initiate must cross in order to reach the place of justification, in the innermost part of the temple, where Osiris sits enthroned. According to J. Assmann:

> The path of the deceased to Osiris corresponds to the path of the priest on his way to the innermost sanctuary of the god. The path of the priest is furthermore sacramentally explained as an ascent to the heavens.[65]

THE DEATH WHICH DETACHES FROM THE INFERIOR

In the context of Egyptian journey to the Field of Reeds (or the Field of Offerings, *sekhet hetep*) and the noetic Isle of Flame, purification and initiation are inseparable, like the purification (*katharsis*) and separation (*chorismos*) in Plotinus' philosophy. Since *ta noeta*, the noetic realities, are completely free (*katharotaton*) from body, the soul must separate (*choriai*) itself from body also, thereby becoming form (*eidos*) and formative power (*Enn.* IV.7.8.14–24; I.6.6.14–16). Being completely purified is a stripping (*aphairesis*) of anything alien (*Enn.* I.2.4.6) and restoring one's true identity: in this way, Plotinus says, 'it becomes clear what we are made to be like and with what god we are identified' (*Enn.* I.2.5.1–3).

Plato himself argues that death is a release (*lusis*) and separation from the body (in the sense of the Egyptian *khat*, or *shat*: the disanimated corpse, the *soma*), thus linking purification with the life of the philosopher who seeks wisdom and knowledge.[66] However, death from above and death from below are not the same, according to Damascius: death as such is not identical with purification, only that death which detaches from the inferior (*In Phaed.* I.127.1–2)— that is, the death which corresponds to initiation and ascent (*anagoge*).

---

65. Jan Assmann, *Death and Initiation in the Funerary Religion of Ancient Egypt*, p. 149.

66. Robert Musser, "Notes on Plotinian Purification".—*The Journal of Neoplatonic Studies*, vol. v, no. 1, fall 1996, p. 79.

In the *Pyramid Texts*, the ultimate primeval hieratic model of all subsequent 'anagogic philosophy' (or rather, an esoteric paradigm of the 'theurgic Platonism', established at least two thousand years before Plato), it is proclaimed:

> *Akh* (light-like intellect, spirit) belongs to the Heaven, *khat* (corpse, physical body) to the Earth (*PT* 305).

Plato's *Phaedo, Phaedrus*, and *Symposium* are, in fact, only the distant and marginal post-scriptum commentaries to this Heliopolitan metaphysics, adapted to the noisy Athenian market-place.

When the pharaoh sheds all his impurities and all accretions of physical plurality, the Heaven opens to him and he joins Ra in his solar barque where the daughters of Ra, namely Maat and Hathor, stand erect at the prow. The pharaoh, son of Ra whose noetic identity is to be re-actualized, in his prayer states the epistemological *telos* of his 'cosmic dialectic' aimed at reintegration and return to the divine *Nous*:

> See me, Ra, recognize me, Ra. I belong to those that know you, so know me (*PT* 311).

W. Burkert is perhaps unaware of this *Pyramid Texts* tradition when he describes as a 'bold assertion' an epigram to those Hellenes who fell in war in 432 BC, running as follows:

> The aither has received the souls, earth the bodies.[67]

At death, the body returns to the earth, as earth to earth, but the immortal *psuche* returns to the *aither*. Even if Homeric religion 'had not an inkling' that there is in man an immortal divine element, his *nous*, which is part of the universal *Nous*, this claim cannot be taken as a proof that the doctrine itself is a 'revolutionary' discovery or some 'fascinating' invention of early Pre-Socratic thinkers. W. Burkert perhaps understands this himself when he says:

67. Walter Burkert, *Greek Religion*, tr. John Raffan, Cambridge, MA: Harvard University Press, 2000, p. 320.

The Mysteries had taught comparable ideas in secret: the divine origin of man and his goal of unity with the divine. This now becomes explicit through natural philosophy, with a claim to objective truth.[68]

For Plotinus, it is dialectic which constitutes the contemplative path upward to Intellect, the path by which the Forms (*eide*) descend from, and ascend to, the throne of the King.[69] Since wisdom (*sophia*) is an intellectual, purificatory, and anagogic activity which turns away from the things below, the dialectical wisdom (or the science of dialectic) enables the soul, when it is purified, to become an *eidos* belonging to the plenitude of God. In order to turn away from shadowy multiplicity and attain union with the Intellect, and finally with the One, the Soul must strip off what she put on in her descent:

> just as for those who go up to the celebrations of sacred rites (*ta hagia ton hieron*) there are purifications, and strippings off of the clothes they wore before. . . . (*Enn.* 1.6.7.3–4).

ENTERING THE SOLAR BARQUE OF ATUM-RA

The target (*skopos*) of the initiatory rites, according to Damascius, is to elevate (*anagagein*) souls back to their final destination which is the same starting-point from which they first set out on their downward journey and where the undivided Dionysus gave them being, seated on his father's throne (*In Phaed.*I.168.1–5). Hence the philosopher wishes to identify his fate with that of Dionysus, who is the cause of soul's deliverance (and is therefore named *Luseos*), like the Egyptian initiate identified his with that of Osiris. The Neoplatonists belonging to Iamblichus' school maintain that the soul is a single and uncomposite essence which, nonetheless, undergoes various changes when it enters the body. However, the rational and

---

68. Walter Burkert, ibid., p.320.
69. Peter A. Kay, "Dialectic as the Science of Wisdom in Plotinus".—*The Journal of Neoplatonic Studies*, vol. IV, no. 1, fall 1995, p.32.

irrational powers, which include imagination (*phantasia*), perception, opinion, discursive thought, desire, and intellection, survive death. These powers are present to both the disembodied and embodied soul, though in different ways. As Proclus explains, discussing why the *agalma*-like cosmos as a whole does not require sense-organs:

> In this passage he (i.e., Plato in *Timaeus* 33c) is obviously doing nothing else than freeing the universe from the mode of life proper to individuals and the organs appropriate to this [life], which are attached to us when we descend into generation; for when we remain above we have no need of such multifarious life-modes and the particular organs that go with them, but there the luminous vehicle (*ochema augoeides*) suffices for us, which contains in a unified mode all the senses. So seeing that we ourselves, when we have dispensed with generation, are free from all life of that sort, what are we to assume in the case of the universe? (*In Tim.* 2.81.21ff).

Both Numenius and Iamblichus argue that there are two souls, rational and irrational, presenting this distinction as the doctrine of the Egyptians. The soul which is rational (able to practice intellection, *noesis*, and noetic union with its source) belongs to the intelligible cosmos (the realm of *akhu*), being created by the Demiurge (the Ra or Ptah of the Egyptians). The irrational soul, instead, is received from the circuit of the heavens and is created by the younger gods of Plato's *Timaeus*.

Iamblichus possibly thought that the rational soul, when embodied, itself develops irrational powers that it activates through the irrational soul (also regarded as being immortal, but only at the level of lower cosmic existence, like the Egyptian *ka* which returns to the vital realm of the 'ancestors'). Therefore there is an innate weakness even in the pure rational soul (like the Osirian 'weakness', since Osiris is called the 'weary of heart' when dissolved into a disparate multiplicity and unable to realize his centralizing function as the monadic heart-intellect) which cannot prevent the irrational Sethian powers to be actualized in human life. According to J.F. Finamore and J.M. Dillon:

This, it would seem, is in keeping with the *Phaedrus* myth, where the disembodied soul slips and falls.[70]

Hence the perpetual contest and battle between Horus and Seth, the opposite psychic forces which are to be reconciled at the higher level of Osirian re-integration: just as Osiris triumphed over death, so every deceased person or initiate would triumph over death, irrationality, impurity, and disorder, though in the Field of Reeds he is given both 'the Horian places and the Sethian places'. The inscription from the Theban tomb of Neferhotep states as follows:

There is none who does not arrive there.
The time one spends on earth is but a dream.
But 'Welcome, safe and sound!' is said to the one who has reached the West.[71]

The arrival of the deceased in the West (*Amentet*), being the first stage of the transformative path to the barque of Ra which transcends the psychic Osirian domain, assumes the character of a homecoming: 'he becomes a divine *ba* like the Ennead',[72] that is, like the archetypal totality of the noetic gods. But before 'going forth by day from the earth as a living *ba* to behold the Sun disk', one must first descend into the realm of psycho-physical genesis, and this descent (down from the Isle of Fire) is compared to the fall into the realm of death. As an oft-used hieratic formula declares:

May your *ba* ascend, may your *khat* descend.

The *khat* (corpse), which stands in this context for the irrational soul (her bodily vehicle), is equivalent in a certain respect to the psychosomatic realm of the 'underworld' which constitutes the basis for (or the inner side of) the external visible set of phenomena.

The downward journey (*katabasis*) is repeated as a ritual descent into the underworld, or rather *Amentet*, the realm of *anima mundi*, equivalent to the inner cosmic body of the goddess Nut (Heaven),

70. John F. Finamore and John M. Dillon, "Commentary to the De Anima".— *Iamblichus, De Anima*, text, translation, and commentary by John F. Finamore and John M. Dillon, Leiden: J. E. Brill, 2002, p. 117.

71. Jan Assmann, *Death and Salvation in Ancient Egypt*, p. 119.

72. Jan Assmann, ibid., p. 177.

of Hathor, or of Osiris-Sokar himself. The Egyptian royal tombs are designed to represent this otherworldly temple (which may be likened to the third hypostasis in Plotinus' philosophy), thereby equating the entombment of the pharaoh to a *descensus ad inferos* on the path of the Sun god Ra, sailing in his barque.

The *descensus* (like the spiritual death through initiation and gnosis) is necessary for the subsequent *ascensio*, the ascent to the noetic realm—that is, the act of entering the solar barque and being united with Atum-Ra. Atum, being the god of preexistence, floating in *Nun* (like the One-Being, *hen on*, in the ineffable One, *to hen*, of the Neoplatonists), symbolizes both nonbeing and all-being, that is, the whole noetic meta-structure in its archetypal fullness. As the Lord of All (*neb tem*), he says:

> I am Atum when alone in the primeval waters, I am Ra when he appears in glory and begins ruling what he has created.[73]

Atum, being the henadic source of the Ennead (in the sense of the nine-fold divine *Paradeigma*), and father of the gods (first of all—father of Shu and Tefnut, that is, of Life, *ankh*, and Order, *maat*, analogous to the Pythagorean pair of *Apeiria* and *Peras* respectively), is 'lord of noetic totality'. According to J. P. Allen:

> The name Atum (*j.tmw*) is a form of the verb *tm*—probably a 'noun of action' of the same type as *j.qdw* 'builder' from the verb *qd*. *Tm* means both 'complete, finish' and 'not be'. Both connotations are associated with Atum.[74]

Since Atum is the 'complete one', the initiate strives to be 'complete as Atum' (*PT* 1298b), to be integrated into the realm of Ra, and describes his spiritual homecoming in following terms:

> Ra has extended his arms to me, and his crew will not drive me back.[75]

73. Erik Iversen, *Egyptian and Hermetic Doctrine*, Copenhagen: Museum Tusculanum Press, 1984, p.14.

74. James P. Allen, *Genesis in Egypt. The Philosophy of Ancient Egyptian Creation Accounts*, New Haven: Yale University, 1988, p.9.

75. Jan Assmann, *Death and Salvation in Ancient Egypt*, p.397.

According to Damascius, who cites the Chaldean oracle in this respect, those realized philosophers who live with the gods and belong to their community, at the same time sharing in their theurgic government, 'rest in God, breathing the midday rays' (*In Phaed.* 1.169.3; fr.130.2).

The initiate Platonist lives with the gods in accordance with the design of the gods of initiation (*ton teleounton theon:* ibid., 1.168.5). To say it in another terms, the soul dies to the body (corpse, *soma,* or *khat,* symbolized by a fish, the Sethian creature which swims in the lower Nile of genesis) and is reborn to intelligent life in communion with the gods and, finally, with the Good (the hyper-noetic ineffable Nile) itself. To the extent of her purity, self-knowledge, and recollection (*anamnesis,* which 'is the practice of death')[76] the soul restores her own unchanging nature—that is, her immortality—at the level of the luminous solar *ochema* of Ra.

PHILOSOPHICAL INITIATIONS
IN THE NETHERWORLD

Damascius regards initiatory rites (*hai teletai*) as being twofold: those here below, which are a kind of preparation for the Netherworld mysteries, and those in the hereafter. This important distinction implies that the soul continues to philosophize in the hereafter and that the main philosophical *ergon* begins only after one enters into the realm of Persephone. These two levels of philosophical activity are analogous to the Egyptian model of initiatory practice.

According to the *Book of Amduat,* the knowledge of the mysterious *bau* (*rekh ba shetau*) and of the secret names (*renu-sen-shetau*) is acquired by a living person upon earth, the 'philosopher' who voluntarily becomes 'dead' still in his earthly tomb-like body. Therefore the gnostic inwardly approaches the places where Osiris is enthroned (initiation itself being an altered rite of coronation) by the means of spiritual exercises— namely, sacramental interpretations, meditations, and creative iconographic visualizations.

---

76. J. C. Marler, "Proclus on Causal Reasoning: I Alcibiades and the Doctrine of Anamnesis".—*The Journal of Neoplatonic Studies,* vol. I, no. II, Spring 1993, p. 33.

Only he who already knows Ra in his innermost heart is prevented from entering the place of annihilation: instead he hears Ra's voice in the Netherworld, sees the animating divine light, ties the golden rope in the noetic barque, and is transformed into an excellent *akhu*. However, the main alchemical transformation of the soul, albeit based on her purity and already acquired knowledge, in most of cases occurs within the macrocosmic cycle of solar journey (into which the microcosmic cycle of earthly life is integrated) after one's physical death.

Both initiations involve 'two ways', that of gnosis and that of praxis, as it is revealed in the *Book of Amduat* and the *Book of Gates*, analogous to *philosophia* and *hierourgia* respectively.

The two need not be mutually exclusive. The ultimate end would be to become 'the likeness of the great god himself.[77]

In the *Book of Two Ways* of the Middle Kingdom, two zigzag paths are depicted that form a kind of map for the deceased (or the initiate of Thoth). Thoth, equated to the 'Great Name who made his light', 'the Eye of Horus, excellent in the night, which makes flame with its beauty' (*CT* 1053), leads the initiate to the house of Maat. Among the destinations of the deceased gnostic in the *Book of Two Ways*, as L.H. Lesko observes, are not only the Field of Reeds (or Offerings, *hetep*), but also the palace of Osiris and the solar barque of Ra.[78] The transformed initiate as Ra (by virtue of being united with the divine *Nous*) rides in the solar barque in the companionship of Thoth, standing before Hu (the creative divine Word) and Sia (Perception, Wisdom).

Damascius maintains that the initiatory rites performed in the hereafter also are twofold: 1) those which purify the pneumatic vehicle (*peri ton pneumatikon chitona*), as rites here below purify the shell-like (*peri ton ostreinon*) body; 2) those which purify the luminous, solar vehicle (*peri ton augoeide*):

---

77. Edward F. Wente, "Mysticism in Pharaonic Egypt?"—*Journal of Near Eastern Studies*, vol. 41, no. 3, 1982, p.178.

78. Leonard H. Lesko, *The Ancient Egyptian Book of Two Ways*, Berkeley: University of California Press, 1977, p.6.

In other words, the way upward through initiation has three
degrees, as the way through philosophy also has: the philosopher's way to perfection takes three thousand years, as it is said
in the *Phaedrus* (249a3–5), the number one-thousand representing a full life and a complete period. Therefore the "uninitiated" (*atelestos*), because farthest remote from his destination,
"lies in slime", both here and even more hereafter, where his
place is in the "dregs of creation" (*en gar te trugi tes geneseos*),
Tartarus itself. Of course the text (*ho logos*) mentions only the
extremes, but there is also a wide range of intermediate states.
The way by which philosophy leads us upwards can be thought
of in analogous terms, though the communion achieved
through them is not perfect nor equal to the mystic union (*kata
ten aporrheton henosin poiountai ten sunaphen*). If it is true that
a man who pursues philosophy without eagerness will not have
the benefit of its results, it is no less true that a man who follows
the way of initiation (*telestike*) without total commitment will
not reap its fruits (*In Phaed.* 1.168.7–16)

Damascius complains that those who are lifted to the upper Earth
(depicted in Plato's *Phaedo* as a *sphaira* made of an ether-like substance and containing, like the Osirian Field of Reeds, long-lived
pneumatic bodies) are not always seekers for wisdom, that is, they
are not eager to 'philosophize' (*ou pantes philosophousin*). This
means that they do not seek for the final release and union with Ra,
the divine Intellect, being content instead with the paradisal existence within the upper regions of *anima mundi* and its imaginal
abodes, analogous to the *'alam al-khayal* in the Ishraqi and Sufi mysticism. These inhabitants of the Osirian paradise are carried up by
Justice, because they led a life of habitual virtue without philosophy
(*In Phaed.* 1.529.1–5).

Hence, the true philosopher, like the Upanishadic sage, is not
content with an ancestral way (*pitryana*), but rather pursues a divine
way (*devayana*), and seeks to become aware of his imperishable solar
self-identity, his noetic Atum-Ra-nature in union with the supreme
Seer who emerges from the ineffable depths of Nun, the boundless
Good of Platonic theology.

SELF-KNOWLEDGE AND RETURN
TO ONE'S INNERMOST SELF

For Proclus and other Neoplatonists, the knowledge of ourselves (*he heauton gnosis*) is the beginning (*arche*) of all philosophy, based on *anamnesis*, or recollection, understood as an ordering of knowledge toward the causes of human nature—that is, a reversion (*epistrophe*) and withdrawal from unlikeness to likeness, from image to its archetype, from diversity to unity. The concept of *epistrophe pros heauton* as return to one's innermost self-identity may be regarded as concentration at the level of intellect.

Nous is identical with the Forms and knows itself by knowing them, though this divine self-knowledge is the knowledge of noetic being, 'not the knowledge of a mysterious private self.'[79]

For Neoplatonists, whatever is self-reflective has an existence separable (*choristen ousian*) from the body. Through self-reflectivity the soul 'philosophizes'—that is, she realizes her immortal essence, following the exhortation of the Delphic Apollo. Though the Delphic *gnothi seauton* may be interpreted and understood as meaning 'know yourself as a man and not a god' by those uninitiated who, like A.D. Nock, are content to indulge in their own concepts of life,[80] the realization of one's mortality (in the sense of the Sufi *fana*, namely, 'annihilation', the Plotinian 'putting off' of everything) paradoxically reveals one's subsistence in the reaffirmed divine *eidos* (the Sufi *baqa*).

As Hermeias of Alexandria, the disciple of Syrianus says, commenting Plato's passage (*Phaedrus* 229c–230a), it is clear that he who knows himself knows everything (*delon gar hoti ho heauton gnous ta panta oiden: In Phaedr* 31.15c). Philoponus even maintains that when the philosopher turns to himself and studies the nature

---

79. Lloyd P. Gerson, Επιστροφη προς εαυτον: "History and Meaning".—*Documenti e studi sulla tradizione filosofica Medievale: An International Journal on the Philosophical Tradition from Antiquity to the Late Middle Ages*, vol. VIII, 1997, p.16.

80. Arthur Darby Nock, "Notes on Ruler-Cult I–IV".—*Essays on Religion and the Ancient World*, vol. I, Selected and edited, with an Introduction, Bibliography of Nock's writings and indexes, by Zeph Stewart, Oxford: Clarendon Press, 1986, p.145.

of the soul he is being active in a purificatory mode, *kathartikos energei*.[81] According to L. P. Gerson:

> Self-knowledge is knowledge of what is above because in general the effect is contained within the cause and in knowing the latter one must know the former.[82]

This 'return to one's innermost self' means traveling on the path of purification and discerning the truth in oneself through recollection awakened either by prayers, rites, and initiations (*teletai*) or by philosophical exercises understood as the science of dialectic. In the context of discursive dialectic, *anamnesis* means unification of cause and effect, a self-knowledge according to the reversion of man upon himself.[83] In the realm of metaphysics and theological myth, the sequence of dialectical reasoning depicts the release of the 'imprisoned' divinity, or rather its projective manifestation (*ba*) which was once a god (*neter*) among the other gods (divine archetypes, noeric intellects, spiritual lights, *akhu*), now descended into a body. However, being purified and reborn as a pharaoh (*anthropos teleios*, the paradigm of perfect *philosophos*, lover of Maat), means being ready to return to the company of the gods in Heaven, as depicted in Plato's *Phaedrus* and in countless Egyptian texts.

This reversion towards our intelligible causes, first through discursive *episteme* and then through non-discursive self-knowledge, is accomplished by the elevating power of Athena, a 'lover of war and wisdom', who establishes us in the 'harbor of the Father' (*to hormo tou patros:* Proclus *In Crat.* CLXXXV, p.113.2)—that is, in the divine *Nous*, the noetic plenitude of Atum-Ra. These purificatory and 'intellect-awakening rites' (*egersinooisi teletesi*) lead up to wisdom (*sophia*), the final goal of philosophy. The ascent itself is an impossible task without the providential care and help provided by Atum's own intelligible rays, his *bau*-like powers, 'the leaders to bright-shining wisdom' (*sophies erilampeos hegemones*) who 'bring to light

---

81. Henry J. Blumenthal, *Aristotle and Neoplatonism in Late Antiquity. Interpretations of the De anima*, London: Duckworth, 1996, p.4.

82. Lloyd P. Gerson, ibid., pp. 24–25.

83. J. C. Marler, ibid., p.44.

the rites and initiations of the holy myths' (*orgia kai teletas hieron anaphainete muthon*), as Proclus sings in his fourth hymn.[84]

This position of the particular soul (*ba*), viewed as an image (*tut*) of the luminous divine *Ba*, means that 'all processions and all conversions are accomplished through likeness' (*dia ten tes homoiotetos aitian*: Proclus *Plat.Theol.* VI.3.17.1–22). Since only the divine *Nous*, the miraculous Eye of Heka ('one whom the Sole Lord made before two things had developed… when He sent his Sole Eye': *Coffin Texts* 261), is capable of contemplating its own noetic Forms, it is necessary to attain pure unification with the divine *Nous* and its intelligible-intellective totality.

Nous in us (the microcosmic *ba* of Ra-intelligence, as an *imago dei*, reflected in the mirror of one's scarab-like heart) 'ascends' to his father Atum 'on the road of the followers of Ra' in order to be taken into His embrace, to 'moor' the soul in the Father of the universe, the Lord of All (*neb tem*, that is, Atum), who is therefore regarded by Proclus as 'the paternal harbor' (*ho patrikos hormos*). As P.M. Van der Berg remarks:

> This is what Proclus means when he says that our light is linked with a light that is more beautiful, more noeric and simpler than the light of *episteme*.[85]

Through *anamnesis*, the soul (transformed into *akh*, luminous intellect) realizes one single bond of friendship (*philia*) which embraces the totality of manifestations (the *kheperu* of Atum-Ra, himself likened to the golden noetic Scarab, Khepera or Khepri), 'effecting this bond', as Iamblichus says, 'through an ineffable process of communion', (*ton sundesmon touton dia tinos arrhetou koinonias*: *De myster.* 211.12–13).

Being 'dead' and detached from her myth-like life story, like Heracles is detached from his *eidolon*, the lower image, himself (*autos*)

---

84. Robert M. Van den Berg, "Towards the Paternal Harbour: Proclean Theurgy and the Contemplation of the Forms".—*Proclus et la Theologie Platonicienne*, ed. A. Ph. Segonds and C. Steel, Leuven: University Press, Paris: Les Belles Lettres, 2000, p.434.

85. Robert M. Van der Berg, ibid., p.428.

rejoicing in abundance with the immortal gods (*Odyssey* XI. 601–604), the soul is able to recollect her identity as a god. In a sense, however, this is not her identity at all, if she is not separated from the lower soul, from the impure psychic residues, and translated to the solar barque of Ra, to the Plotinian *Nous*, where every divine intelligence is rapt in eternal contemplation of the Father's Face and has no earthly memories.

The soul-intellect is integrated into the glory of *pantheos* which contains all gods. It thereby contains the entire universe in its archetypal unity, like the Lord of All (*neb tem*), the One Existent (*hen on*), to put it in Neoplatonic terms. Atum, regarded as Heka (miraculous power of creation, the supreme Magic), from His own mouth irradiates all that exists (*netet un*), producing 'repeated millions'. According to this point of view, the entire multi-leveled creation is a theophany, Atum's self-disclosure, through the miraculous force of Heka which finally brings all manifestations (*kheperu*) back to their ultimate source. As Th. McEvilley says:

> The Orphics held that release is obtained through recollection of one's own god-nature, and Plato's doctrine of recollection implies that for him this means that one must, in effect, become omniscient. In Platonic passages which preserve the Orphic strain it is said (as it is so often said in the Upanishads) that the knowledge in question is non-discursive and cannot be communicated by words. As in India, ethical emphasis is on loss of the ordinary desire habits. In the *Cratylus* (493), speaking in Orphic terms, Plato says that it is desire which turns the soul 'upside down' for its downward plunge into matter; it is the soul's forgetful desire which keeps it embodied, and this desire must be corrected by recollection of its true nature. . . .[86]

---

86. Thomas McEvilley, *The Shape of Ancient Thought: Comparative Studies in Greek and Indian Philosophies*, New York: Allworth Press, 2002, p.101.

THE RECOVERED UNITY OF DIONYSUS IN OURSELVES

According to Damascius, the one who practice philosophy in the right way (*philosophountes orthos*), perfects the God that is within him (*ton en heauto theon teleioi: In Phaed.* 1.30.3). L.G. Westerink, however, argues that *ton en heauto theon* is not to be understood that the human soul could be called God in the strict sense, that is, a divine henad, since the 'one of the soul' is only a 'one-like' faculty which enables us to know the divine:

> The human soul shares in the divine only through the God to whose 'retinue' it belongs, and only in this restricted sense can Damascius speak of the 'Dionysus' in ourselves.[87]

However, following the Orphic myth which is the central metaphysical axis of all Platonic theology and dialectic, Damascius equates the Titanic mode of life (*he titanike zoë*) with the irrational mode, by which rational life, that is, the Dionysus (or Osiris) in ourselves is torn asunder:

> While in this condition, we are Titans, but when we recover that lost unity, we become Dionysus and we attain what can be truly called completeness (*In Phaed.* 1.9.6–8).

This Osirian paradigm stands as the chief model for all Platonic logic and dialectic, following the central Orphic doctrine of an esoteric monism, namely, that 'all things are born from the One and all things are resolved back into it.'[88] The One's light is 'as it were' (*hosper*) broken into fragments by *Nous*, according to Plotinus, thus producing the multiple noetic unities which are the Forms and contemplative noeric intellects, constituting the radiant and luminous totality of *kosmos noetos*, likened to a living *sphaira*, 'to a globe radiant with faces all living' (*Enn.* VI.7.15.24ff). This radiant and living globe is equivalent to the noetic Heliopolis, the place of dazzling illumination where the primordial Lotus emerges.

The articulated *archetypus mundus* may be depicted as the pure

---

87. *The Greek Commentaries on Plato's Phaedo, vol. II: Damascius*, p. 41.
88. Thomas McEvilley, ibid., p. 27.

primordial Lotus, as the Isle (*iu*) of the Egg, or the Isle of Fire which contains Heka, namely, the hidden magical forces of all subsequent demiurgy. It is the solar *ben-ben*, the tomb-like stone of Heliopolis, and 'stone' or 'tomb' in this respect is the same as 'egg' in the Orphic cosmogony. *Ben-ben* emerges from the abyss of the ineffable One. This supreme pyramid-like Stone, on the top of which rests the Egyptian Phoenix, the *bennu* bird (the original *Logos*—and in Middle Kingdom terms, the *ba* of Osiris),[89] is both a symbol of eternal life and a prototype of the 'philosophical stone' in alchemy.

This Stone, or the High Sand, represents the supreme threshold (*akhet*) of intelligible light, symbolized by the pyramid (*akhet*) here below and serving as the theurgic instrument for the king's immortalization. For this reason, the 'road of philosophy' and the 'avenue to salvation' in Egypt are cast in stone. Stone stands for the noetic fire, stability, and immortality. Inside the stony *akhet*, the images of contained noetic Forms are made visible. They are hieroglyphs (*medu neter*), eternalized as the ritually 'animated' inscriptions, namely, the *Pyramid Texts*. J. Assmann explains:

> The central topic of these texts is the idea of ascent to heaven. Their recitation and the accompanying rites aided the king in his ascent to heaven and incorporation in the circuit of the sun. The Egyptian word for this ritual function, like the word *akhet*, derives from the root meaning 'blaze, be radiant'; it is the causative form that signifies 'to make into a spirit of light'. This function of the Pyramid Texts replicate[s] the architectural form of the pyramids, which are themselves the symbolic realization of the king's ascent to heaven and inclusion within the circuit of the sun.[90]

The soul's return to this shining noetic 'barque' is not a temporal event in one's personal history of life: when consciousness returns to the stage of pure intellection (*noesis*), simplification (*haplosis*),

---

89. R.T. Rundle-Clark, *Myth and Symbol in Ancient Egypt*, London: Thames and Hudson, 1991, p. 246.

90. Jan Assmann, *The Mind of Egypt. History and Meaning in the Time of the Pharaohs*, tr. Andrew Jenkins, New York: Metropolitan Books, 2002, pp. 58–59.

presence (*parousia*), and union (*henosis*), where 'the two become one' (*ta duo hen ginetai*), it is no longer 'soul', no longer 'man', but rather the divine *Nous* itself. P. Mamo rightly argues that since 'soul', for Plotinus, is a label for a variety of psychic and intellectual activities, not for a stable and permanent nature, neither the human soul, much less 'this ordinary man, this pitiful fragment of the cosmos' can ever be called 'God'. This means that

> the individuality of the soul comes close to being an illusion, an addition of non-being, clearly something to be overcome before a higher stage in the expansion towards totality (*pas*) can be reached.[91]

Within the multi-dimensional hierarchy of theophanies, inside the differentiated body of Ptah (to say it in accordance with the Egyptian Ramesside concept of divine transcendence and immanence, the declaration that 'All is One'), Dionysus is both the cause of individual life and the cause of deliverance. He appoints the term of the imprisonment for

> as long as it is better for embodied souls to be under restraint, in view of the final goal, which is deliverance by Dionysus (Damascius *In Phaed*. 1.12.1–3).

The final goal for the contemplative philosopher is to remember and rediscover Dionysus in himself, the Monad united with the superior principles. Through this monadic purity one hopes to touch the purity of the transcendent One, of the unspeakable and hidden Amun, *deus ineffabilis*. The supreme Amun of the late Theban theology surpasses all human and divine knowledge, veiling himself even before the gods, so that his essence is not known. This ineffable One, however, 'makes himself into millions', thus playing the dialectical game of unity and diversity. According to J. Assmann:

> This god transcended the world not only with respect to the mysterious hiddenness of his '*ba*-ness', in which no name could

---

91. Plato Mamo, "Is Plotinian Mysticism Monistic?".—*The Significance of Neoplatonism*, ed. R. Baine Harris, Norfolk: ISNS, Old Dominion University, 1976, p. 210.

name him and no representation could depict him, but also with respect to the human heart, which was filled with him. He was the hidden god who 'came from afar' yet was always present to the individual in the omniscience and omnipotence of his all-encompassing essence. He was not only the cosmos—in Egyptian, the totality of the 'millions', and also *neheh* and *djet*, 'plenitude of time' and 'unalterable duration' into which he unfolded himself—but also history.[92]

Ultimately, the searcher for God and lover of Wisdom is God himself, secretly involved both into 1) a self-disclosure (which actually appears as a magical self-veiling), creative irradiation, manifestation, descent of the soul, and 2) reintegration, redemption, deconstructive unveiling, liberation. As Damascius relates:

> When Dionysus had projected his reflection into the mirror, he followed it and was thus scattered over the universe. Apollo gathers him and brings him back to heaven, for he is the purifying God and truly the savior of Dionysus (*kathartikos on theos kai tou Dionusou soter hos alethos: In Phaed.* 1.129.1–4).

However, the soul is never united with the gods as an individual: through awareness and recollection it moves from particularity to universality, from plurality to unity, and, strictly speaking, this is not the individual's journey but the journey of Dionysus, the cosmic drama of Osiris, imitated at all levels of being.

PHILOSOPHICAL MUMMIFICATION
INSIDE THE COSMIC TOMB

The Egyptian tomb is a temple of Osiris, inside of which the mummy (*sah*) functions as a symbol of Osiris, as his restored and visible *eidos*, the re-collected and healed Eye of Horus. In this sense, mummification is a sort of initiation and 'Osirification', making one's *imago* cultically accessible and mythically valid. As R. Bjerre

---

92. Jan Assmann, *The Search for God in Ancient Egypt*, tr. David Lorton, Ithaca and London: Cornell University Press, 2001, pp. 241–242.

Finnestad pointed out:

> The mummification is a divinization, a transmutation of the human body to a god's body. From a religious point of view the mummification is no conservation of the human body but rather the opposite: the mummification is a ritual transformation of the human and mortal to the divine and eternal.[93]

The gathering of the Osirian *membra disiecta* is equivalent to transformation, as if collecting the scattered elements of one's being into the single text which establishes a community with the gods. Through the binding power of symbols (themselves regarded like *bau* of the gods, like the Neoplatonic *sunthemata*) the parts of the *sah*-body are identified with different deities, limb by limb, thereby asserting that no limb of the deceased is without its god (*neter*): he is entirely a god. With the help of symbolic forms, related to *eros* and *logos*, love and theurgic speech, what was torn apart is gathered together again, as in the process of philosophical dialectic.

The eidetic completion and perfection (*neferu*) necessarily imply life (*ankh*), beauty, imperishability, virtue, moral righteousness and ability to conform to the norms of truth and to the noetic standard, *maat*. Through the transfiguring power of *medu neter*— 'divine language', that is, written and animated hieroglyphs which are not to be 'read' but rather 'recited' (like the *Qur'an*)—the initiate is transformed into an *akh*, since he cannot approach the gods as a man. The deceased in the Duat (which is the hidden dimension of bodies, 'located' here and now) recollects those *logoi* which construct his unitary divine identity ('I recollect what I have forgotten'), as in the Orphic mysteries where the initiate (or *philosophos*) is to recollect what he has learned about the afterlife through the mysteries or during his philosophical training.

The Egyptian word *sakhu* ('making an *akh*') indicates the spiritual transformations produced by theurgic recitations, liturgies, and a sort of anagogic hermeneutics (interpretation itself being an esoteric rite), which are 'demonstrations of the power of Ra', of the

---

93. R. Bjerre Finnestad, "The Meaning and Purpose of Opening the Mouth in Mortuary Contexts".—*Numen*, vol. xxv, 2, p.128.

solar intelligence. The sacred texts themselves possess a transfiguring and awakening *dunamis*, but the basic principle of these rites of
separation, purification, recollection, interpretation, and unification (so as to restore the miraculous Eye) is the theurgic principle.
Accordingly, the cultic actions, recitations, and initiations

> are not carried out in the sense of a communication between
> man and god, but as the enacting of a drama in the divine
> world, between god and gods. . . . When the priest spoke, one
> god spoke to another, and the words manifested their trans-
> forming, performative, theurgic power, that is, their power to
> create divine presence.[94]

Knowledge of this mystery was the royal path to immortality, the
royal tombs being repositories of the 'philosophical knowledge' that
brought deliverance. As J. Assmann remarks, 'philosophy and practice were mutually dependent',[95] since one's tomb is built through
remembrance, virtue, and righteousness, the building process itself
being equivalent to the realization of truth (*maat*). This means that,
in a strict sense, neither descent, nor ascent of the soul (*ba*) are her
own activities but rather the ritual-like activities (*energeiai*) of the
One, accomplished through the plurality of the gods, 'who reveal
themselves in the bodily appearance of souls', as G. Shaw says,[96] and
in the orderly arrangements of the cosmic state which includes
landscapes and all meaningful sacred phenomena.

Therefore the sharp distinction between 'soul' (the whole
complicated psychic spectrum of *ka, ba*, and *akh*) and 'body' (both
khat and *sah*) seems to be a grave simplification. In addition, both
the heart (*ib*, or *ab*, the center of one's intelligence and feelings) and
the name (*ren*, which reveals a person's true nature or essence) may
be related to the overwhelming realm of 'soul' and its individualized
('named') articulations. How this ambiguous 'soul' corresponds

---

94. Jan Assmann, *Death and Salvation in Ancient Egypt*, pp. 245–246.
95. Jan Assmann, ibid., p. 38.
96. Gregory Shaw, "The Mortality and Anonymity of the Iamblichean Soul".—
Syllecta Classica, vol. 8: Iamblichus: the Philosopher, The University of Iowa, 1997,
p. 180.

with one's 'shadow' (*shuyt*) is unclear. As L. Bell mysteriously pointed out:

> The shade was both an emanation from a deity and a reflection of divine power (light); it was drawn as a silhouette of the body, and it symbolized divinity's indwelling of an object or being (roughly speaking, incarnation).[97]

In Egypt, the cosmic life itself was understood as the constant interaction of Osiris and Ra, of corpse-like *hupodoche* and active light-like *eidos*, thus joining, uniting, and knotting together the different divine limbs, or rather the countless *bau* of the One. As Olympiodorus says:

> Because the soul is a 'sacred image (*agalma*) that takes all forms', since it possesses the principles of all that is (*panton ton onton*), it can be aroused by sensible things to recollection of the principles that it has within itself and produce them: having observed a thing in this world, the soul realizes its absolute essence (*In Phaed.* 11.7.1–6).

Even for Plotinus, *psuche* and *soma* tend to have a relative meaning with respect to each other, because the physical universe is immersed within the great domain of *anima mundi* (or the hypostasis of divine *Psuche*, which is an image of *Nous*, active in the sense-perceived universe and animating its parts),[98] so that all bodies, as final external crystallizations of psychic activities, are already placed in the Duat, inside the cosmic body of Nut, or Osiris. As H. Oosthout argues:

> When one tries to determine what 'body' means in its strictest sense—what properties a body can have that should not be ascribed to the activity of the soul—then one is left with almost

97. Lanny Bell, "The New Kingdom 'Divine' Temple: The Example of Luxor".— *Temples of Ancient Egypt*, ed. Byron A. Shafer, London and New York: I.B. Tauris, 2005, p.130.

98. Hilary Armstrong, "Aristotle in Plotinus: The Continuity and Discontinuity of Psyche and Nous".—*Aristotle and the Later Tradition*, ed. Henry Blumenthal and Howard Robinson, Oxford: Clarendon Press, 1991, p.119.

nothing. 'Bodies' that are completely without a 'soul', and that do not partake in any *energeia* whatsoever, are reduced to sheer indeterminacy.[99]

PLATONIC DIALECTIC: THE SCIENCE OF PURIFICATION AND RESTORATION OF UNITY

Both Plato and Plotinus identify *dialektike*, which imitates the Osirian dismemberment and reintegration, as the proper method of philosophy for attainment of wisdom and truth through death (called supernatural, *huperhues*, death by Damascius, since the lower human 'soul' must die anyway) in order to recognize the greater life that this 'death' sustains.

The necessary separation from the mortal body does not mean that philosophy despises body as such which, in fact, constitutes an image of the higher realities, though the puppet-like body is turned into a living *agalma* only by the binding and animating power of 'soul' and 'intellect', of *ba* and *akh* respectively. Therefore the Egyptian mummy, as a symbolic form or hieroglyph, makes visible one's *eidos*, the image of regained integrity and identity in the 'golden' realm of archetypes.

Hence, justification through the alchemical transformation in the Duat (spiritually accessible here and now) is like a 'noetic mummification', since the word for the eidetic Osirian body, that is, for mummy, *sah*, also means 'noble', 'worthy', 'belonging to the realm of light'. The process of mummification is analogous to dialectic which cannot create realities but makes them evident for the human *nous* to contemplate. The dialectician rediscovers his true self which means a return to Intellect, the restoration of the damaged Eye of Horus through the healing wisdom of Thoth.

Therefore the purpose of dialectic is not *techne* (art) but *sophia* (wisdom): its aim is not production but the realization of noetic wholeness, and this recreative return may be described as a solar

---

99. Henri Oosthout, *Modes of Knowledge and the Transcendental. An Introduction to Plotinus Ennead* 5.3 (49) *with a Commentary and Translation*, Amsterdam: B.R. Gruner, 1991, p.48.

rebirth. This attainment of intellectual and spiritual perfection through *noesis* is modeled on the divine contemplation of *Nous* itself, for itself. Hence, as J. P. Anton remarks, the dialectician gains access to the invisible realm of *Nous* and *ta noeta*, the intelligible realities, since dialectic's domain is Intellect, not the One.[100]

Olympiodorus explains the difference between the contemplative (theoric, rational) philosophy and theurgy by saying that our soul is at first illuminated by *Nous* and its actions are directed by the contemplative virtues (and dialectic), but afterwards it becomes identical with the source of illumination (*ellampsis*) and acts in union with the One by the paradigmatic virtues. Therefore:

> The object of philosophy is to make us *nous* (*philosophias men ergon noun hemas poietai*), that of theurgy to unite us with the noetic principles (*theourgias de henosai hemas tois noetois*) and conform our activity to the paradigms (*In Phaed.* 8.2.19–20).

Thus dialectic ensures the completion of the preparatory work, reintegration, and ascent needed to make transition from the wholeness of *Nous* to the ineffable transcendence of the One, that is, from the solar Atum-Ra to the primordial Flood, Nun (or the hidden Amun, *deus absconditus et ineffabilis*). But dialectic, like the 'magic mourning', awakens and accomplishes reintegration of the 'justified' and 'vindicated' Osirian limbs after their division (*diairesis*), lifting up the synthesizing intellectual *djed*-pillar. Eventually it provides transition from the realm of Osiris to that of Ra. In this sense, dialectic is 'the method of attaining assimilation to God (*homoiosis theo*) through consciousness of the ultimate One-in-the-many, prior to the return to the One itself.'[101]

Understood in this sense, dialectic is not the art of refutation in the Aristotelian manner, but the science (*episteme*) of purification (*katharsis*), which transcends the domain of *dianoia* and *logismos*, the discursive reasoning, being aimed at the full grasp of the unity of *mundus intelligibilis*. Since it is the most valuable part of philosophy,

100. John P. Anton, "Plotinus and the Neoplatonic Conception of Dialectic".— *Journal of Neoplatonic Studies*, vol. 1, no. 1, fall 1992, pp. 15–16.
101. John P. Anton, ibid., p. 13.

dialectic is sometimes equated with the purest part of *nous* which stands for that wisdom which is concerned with real being. Philosophy as a whole covers the skills of logic and the investigation of the entire cosmic order, but through the science of Platonic dialectic it also prepares the 'lover of wisdom' to contemplate *nous* as unity and causes the soul to turn to itself. Consequently, the potentiality of human heart-intellect, as an *imago dei*, is translated into the actuality of divine *Nous*.

Dialectic, itself regarded as a gift of the gods (*dedosthai para theon*: Damascius *In Phileb.* 56), consists of division (*diairetike*), analysis (*analutike*), definition (*horistike*), and deduction (*apodeiktike, sullogistike*). The Platonic dialectic is based on the model of sacrifice (albeit interiorized and abstracted) which imitates the traditional cosmogony. Therefore the method of division (tantamount to dismemberment of Osiris, Dionysus, or the Vedic Purusha) is related to demiurgy, manifestation, ontological pluralization, and that of analysis to reversion, return, restoration of unity. Definition and deduction are intermediate, falling under the species of both division and analysis (or collection, *sunagoge*). Deduction produces effects from causes (thus representing the path of manifestation) and definition reduces a plurality of elements to a complex unity (thus standing for reversion, spiritual ascent).

Damascius, in this respect following the Pythagoreans rather than Plato's *Protagoras*, associates Prometheus with procession (*proodos*) and Epimetheus with reversion (*epistrophe*). The latter name, Epimetheus, is explained by Iamblichus as *epistrophe eis to noeton*, return to the noetic reality:

> Prometheus reveals the ways in which the gods proceed down into nature, Epimetheus the modes of their reversion to the intelligible realm. Iamblichus is stated to have said so on the authority of Pythagoras (Damascius *In Phileb.* 57).

PHILOSOPHY AS A RITE OF BECOMING LIKE GOD

This dialectical science of measurement and elevation, leading to the tower of Kronos, the disembodied realm of pure *Nous*, is the sacred way (*hodos*) traveled by *philosophos* (lover of wisdom) who stands in sharp contrast to *philodoxos* (lover of opinion).[102] Understood in this way, philosophy is not a case of mental gymnastics or a training in oratory and social management (as Isocrates supposes), but the process of becoming like God, in accord to Plato's axiomatic advice to 'flee this world and become like God as much as one can' (*phuge de homoiosis theo kata to dunaton: Theaet.* 176.6). Therefore W. E. Helleman says:

> As Socrates contrasts the evils which adhere to our mortal nature with the goodness characteristic of that other world where the gods dwell, *en theois . . . ekeise,* flight from this world is as it were equated with the process of becoming as much as possible like the divine.[103]

To realize this goal (*telos*) is to achieve the perfect wisdom (*sophia*) by cultivating that which is highest in the soul and already akin to the divine. It means to partake of or participate in (*metechein*) the immortal divine nature, exercising one's intellectual capacities by focusing on that which is eternal and unchanging. For Olympiodorus, the life beyond, in the realm of eternal noetic light, is to be called a temple (*hieron gar ho ekeise bios: In Phaed.* 1.3.9). Therefore the philosopher as imitator of God is on the way to this temple, on the way to the Father, being elevated to the temple by the gracious and death-bringing lightning of the Father, by his dialectico-erotic and telestic 'thunderbolt'. This is the fire of reversion, by which God reverts to Himself.

The process of becoming like God, linked to an ontological and epistemological reversion (*epistrophe*), covers the entire hierarchy of beings and their activities, culminating in the noetic unification (through the hieratic virtues, which belong to the godlike, *theoeides,* part of the soul) and mystical union (*henosis*). Arguing that for rational beings (*logikois*) the goal is the Good and for irrational beings (*alogoi*), pleasure (*In Phileb.* 258), Damascius equates philo-

---

102. Janet M. Atwill, *Rhetoric Reclaimed. Aristotle and the Liberal Arts Tradition,* Ithaca and London: Cornell University Press, 1999, p.136.

103. Wendy E. Helleman, *Philo of Alexandria on Deification and Assimilation to God,* p.53.

sophy with the 'de-Titanizing' dialectical enterprise, moving from the irrational differentiation to the noetic completeness—to Osiris *Unun-nefer*, 'who exists in completion' or 'in perfect beauty':

> Union (*he sunaphe*) is brought about by similarity (*homoiotetos*); therefore the wise (*ho sophos*) and good man, that is the philosopher, ennobled by virtue and knowledge, is united to the goodness and wisdom of the Gods. Goodness in the Gods is the activity (*energeia*) by which they provide for all things, wisdom that by which they know all things (*In Phaed.* 1. 40.1–4).

For Damascius, there are three kinds of hope: that of the crowd (*pandemos*), that of the philosopher (*philosophos*), and that of the theurgist (*hieratike: In Phaed.* 1.48.1–2). In this arrangement philosophy is given an intermediate place, like that of *eros* in Plato's *Symposium*. Socrates is purified and united to the divine through the daimonic realm of philosophy, which is concerned with separation of soul from body, refutation (*ho elenchos*), and leaving behind the *regio dissimilitudinis* where the soul, fallen into forgetfulness, suffers exile and defilement. Proclus says:

> Socrates looks toward the daimon and the daimon's forethought, and the daimon toward the god whose follower he is; Socrates is united to the divine (*sunaptetai to theio*) through the daimonic order, and he too exercises all his activity in accordance with God, since the daimon reveals to him the divine will (*In Alcib.* 159.6ff).

This daimonic and erotic philosophy is the rite of learning to die before one dies, accomplished through *anamnesis*, by which the soul is opened to union with its causes. This is like the 'loosening of the bond' (*luein ton desmon*) through which the dialectician can break the impasse, deal with pathlessness (*aporia*) and be united with the divine Beauty. The philosopher's soul alone recovers her wings, being ever initiated into the perfect mystery (*teleous aei teletas teleomenos*: Plato *Phaedr.* 249c).

THE ANCIENT LOGOS
AND ITS SACRAMENTAL FUNCTION

Since the standard definition of philosophy is *homoiosis gar theo he philosophia* (philosophy is assimilation to God), it seems that the Hellenic philosophy (or at least its dominating Pythagoreo-Platonic *hairesis*) is a late and 'modernized' version of that immemorial wisdom tradition which can be traced back not simply to the mythical theologies of ancient Egypt, Assyria and Babylonia, but ultimately to the forgotten dreams and visions of the Stone (if not the Golden) Age, whose 'holy silence' is impenetrable to our modern consciousness.

Therefore Celsus, the Middle Platonist, speaks about the 'ancient *logos*' which is 'true wisdom' (*alethes logos*), according to J.C.M. Van Widen's translation.[104] This ancient wisdom 'has existed from the beginning and has always been maintained by the wisest nations and cities and wise men' (Origen *Contra Celsum.* 1.14), namely, Egyptians, Assyrians, Indians, Persians, Odrysians, Samothracians, and Eleusinians. Evidently, both philosophy and the mysteries constitute this 'true *logos*' which modern commentators would rather describe as *muthos.*

However, if philosophy is defined as knowledge of the being (*episteme tou ontos*) or knowledge of the truth, sent down to men in order to bring them to God, then 'myth' may be regarded simply as a sort of symbolic *logos* whose sacramental function is to deal with transcendence. So understood, philosophy itself is a myth of liberation, of the ascending solar path for those who hope to become rational 'rulers', inward 'kings', to be assimilated to the demiurgic *Nous*, or God. As W.E. Helleman remarks:

> Just as the one universal mind rules the entire world, so also the human mind functions like a ruler (*hegemon*), and god (*theos*) within man. It is in using this divine faculty, the *nous*, that man is able to pursue his love of wisdom and contemplate

---

104. J.C.M. Van Winden, "True Philosophy—Ancient Philosophy".— ΣΟΦΙΗΣ ΜΑΙΗΤΟΡΕΣ *'Chercheurs de sagesse'. Hommage a Jean Pepin*, ed. Marie-Odile Goulet-Caze et alii, Paris: Institut d'Etudes Augustiniennes, 1992, p.198.

the heavens and the regions beyond, namely the intelligible cosmos and its patterns (*paradeigmata*) of all that is found in this world.[105]

Philosophy's 'post-scriptum' accretions, additions, and prolongations, that is, the agnostic philosophical discourse of Western modernity, instead of pursuing *demiourgike sophia* and *alethes logos*, adhere to the charms of material objects and mental passions.

J.M. Rist's ironic and factual denial of the possibility of success in the life of the philosopher-king is symptomatic:

> Plato's model for the action of the Guardians is that of the inspired lover. But the more cynical, or wise, may ask: how long will the strength of love endure?[106]

As regards modern philosophical discourse, it has entirely forgotten, derided, misunderstood, and neglected philosophy's initial purpose, viewing its *telos* as a religious fancy that belongs to the realm of irrational and despotic.

The ultimately Egyptian and Phoenician-Assyrian lineage of the Greek philosophical discourse which partly emerged under the Persian rule, perhaps inspired by the intellectual culture of the Lydian court at Sardis and the so-called Egyptian 'Saite Renaissance',[107] hardly can be disputed, in spite of the possible objection that different traditions may express the same reality, even without any direct influence upon one another. In an attempt to reveal the very core of Mesopotamian culture (in the Neo-Assyrian, Neo-Babylonian and Achaemenid empires), S. Parpola argues:

> As we have seen, Plato's teachings of the metaphysical world of ideas, of matter as the prison of the soul, and of the soul's divine origin, immortality and gradual ascent towards perfec-

---

105. W. E. Hellman, *Philo of Alexandria on Deification and Assimilation to God*, p. 57.

106. John M. Rist, *Plato Says That We Have Tripartite Souls. If He Is Right, What Can We Do About It?*—ΣΟΦΙΗΣ ΜΑΙΗΤΟΡΕΣ '*Chercheurs de sagesse*', p.123.

107. Jan Assmann, *The Mind of Egypt*, pp. 335–338.

tion, were also fundamental to the path of salvation encoded in the Assyrian sacred tree.[108]

Orpheus, the mythical founder of philosophical initiations in the form of mysteries, 'brings together a host of older Eastern traditions, Akkadian, Hurrite-Hittite, and Egyptian most of all,' as W. Burkert observes.[109] Parmenides is partly dependent on the Egyptian and Orphic theological paradigms, and Plato paraphrases Orpheus everywhere, as Olympiodorus asserts:

> Is it not evident, further, that Plato is adapting elements from the well-known Orphic myth (fr. 211)? The myth tells how Dionysus is torn to pieces by the Titans and is made whole by Apollo; so 'assembling and gathering itself together' means passing from the Titanic life to the unitary (*henoeide*) life. And there is Kore, too, who has to descend into Hades, but is brought up again by Demeter to dwell in her ancient home, which accounts for the 'dwelling'. Plato, indeed, borrows from Orpheus everywhere (*parodei gar pantachou ta Orpheos*). In the sequel (*Phaed.* 69c8–d1), he even quotes a line by him (fr. 235): 'Many carry the thyrsus, few become Bacchus' (*polloi men narthekophoroi, pauroi de te Bakchoi*). Those who carry the thyrsus without becoming Bacchus are philosophers still involved in civic life, while the thyrsus-bearers and Bacchants are those on the way to purification. This is why Dionysus, as we said already, is the cause both of life and of death: of death as the patron of prophecy, which excludes imagination.... (*In Phaed.* 7.10.3–15).

The late Hellenic Neoplatonists are aware that both the philosopher (who trains himself for death by means of dialectic, purification, and contemplation) and the theurgist are imitators of God, though sometimes they employ different methods in order to achieve the same or similar goals, even if theurgy may be regarded as

---

108. Simo Parpola, "The Mesopotamian Soul of Western Culture".—*Bulletin of Canadian Society for Mesopotamian Studies* 35, 2000, p. 34.

109. Walter Burkert, *Babylon. Memphis. Persepolis. Eastern Contexts of Greek Culture*, Cambridge, MA: Harvard University Press, 2004, p. 98.

transcending philosophy when the latter is understood as being merely *anthropine episteme*, a human science. For Proclus maintains that everything is to be saved and joined to the original causes, either through erotic madness (*dia tes erotikes manias*), through divine philosophy (*dia tes theias philosophias*), or again through theurgic power (*dia tes theourgikes dunameos*), which transcends human *episteme* (*Plat. Theol.* 1.25.112.25–113.10 Saffrey-Westerink). However, as A. Sheppard concludes, '*erotike mania, theia philosophia* and *theourgike dunamis* here really mean the same thing. They all refer to mystical union.'[110]

RIDDLES OF THE COSMIC MYTH

The arguments of Socrates in Plato's *Phaedo* may be divided into two categories: one mythical and Orphic (*muthikou kai Orphikou*), the other dialectical and philosophical (*dialektikou kai philoso-phou*), according to Olympiodorus (*In Phaed.* 1.1.5–6). The Orphic and mythical approach is viewed as being esoteric (*aporrhetos*), and the philosophical and dialectical as being demonstrative (*apodeikti-kos*). However, this distinction is not that as between *logos* and *muthos*, when *logos* is viewed in the sense of 'true account' and *muthos* regarded as a 'childish fiction'. All mythical assertions belong to the category of *logos*, because they are expressed in human language and may be understood by reason and intellect, even if presented in riddles (*ainigmata*). Certain privileged myths are treated as *theioi logoi*, 'divine accounts'. According to the Derveni papyrus:

> Orpheus did not mean to say in it (his poem) riddles that are contestable, but rather great things in riddles.[111]

Philosophical dialectic, in most of cases, is a sort of hermeneutical enterprise which enjoys in wrestling with riddles and logical puzzles within an accepted *a priori* framework of the constructed and therefore 'mythical' world picture. In this sense, philosophy's

---

110. Anne Sheppard, "Proclus' Attitude to Theurgy".—*Classical Quarterly* 32, 1, 1982, p. 220.

111. Peter T. Struck, *Birth of the Symbol. Ancient Readers at the Limits of their Texts*, Princeton: Princeton University Press, 2004, p. 31.

goal, as Aristotle supposes, is the extraction of truth from common opinions.[112] As regards literary myths proper, Plutarch, in his address to Clea, a priestess of both Dionysus and Osiris, declares that one must not use the myths as if they were entirely factual, but using the reason that comes from philosophy, take what is fitting (*prosphoron*) and in accord with truth (*kata ten homoioteta: De Iside et Osiride* 374c).

The entire manifested reality, or the *agalma*-like cosmos, may be regarded as a Myth, because its outer shell veils the inner realities and because myths themselves are divine (*theioi*), as Sallustius asserts, following Iamblichus in this respect:

> Myths represent the active operations (*energeias*) of the gods. The universe itself can be called a myth (*exesti gar kai ton kosmon muthon eipein*), since bodies and material objects are apparent in it, while souls and intellects are concealed. Furthermore, to wish to teach all men the truth about the gods causes the foolish to despise, because they cannot learn, and the good to be slothful, whereas to conceal the truth by myths prevents the former from despising philosophy and compels the later to study it (*De diis,* III. 8–15).

The myth-like universe may be likened to the *kheperu*, the ontological emanations and developments of the primeval Golden Scarab, Khepera, equivalent to Atum's miraculous self-disclosure through Heka, divine creative Magic, called Heikton by Iamblichus (*proton mageuma*, the first act or product of magic: *De myster.* 263.4). This conception is analogous to the Hindu doctrine of Maya, which far from being simply deception may be equated with the divine wisdom or the supreme measure (*maat*), working both by 'magic' and by 'logic', that disclose the demiurgic energies.

The demiurgic *Logos* creates the universe of theophanies which is a wonder to behold, *thauma idesthai*, and which may be designated as a Myth in the deepest metaphysical and ontological sense. A similar eidetic understanding of *muthos* is maintained by A. Losev, to

112. John J. Cleary, "Working Through Puzzles with Aristotle".—*The Journal of Neoplatonic Studies*, vol. I, no. 11, Spring 1993, p. 123.

whom the universal Myth is an ontological category on the noetic level, and to whom the Symbol is the outwardly-manifested face of the Myth.[113]

Why may the manifested universe be called both *muthos* and *logos*? Because the totality of creation, 'all things and all hiero-glyphs', to use the terms of so-called Memphite theology, uttered by Thoth, by the Tongue of Ptah, is able to transform the thoughts of the Heart into spoken and written language, namely, the universe. J. Assmann, in this respect, observes:

> If the distinction between a sphere of original Forms (Ideas) and a world of infinitely reproduced Images is a principle of Plato's philosophy, then the Egyptian division of creation expresses a primal, pretheoretical Platonism.[114]

Since myth is essentially an image of reality, of the noetic para-digms in the sequence of eidetic manifestation, any section of the Line in Plato's *Republic* (VI.509d1–511e5) may be called a 'myth' in relation to the preceding one, according to L.G. Westerink.[115] As Olympiodorus rather enigmatically explains:

> The word *muthos* is applied to ratiocinative knowledge (*ten dia sullogismou gnosin*) inasmuch as it is attained by means of the middle term and is not a direct vision of reality, just as intellec-tion (or thinking, *he noera*) could be called knowledge from images (*ex eikonon estin gnosis*) and is only a myth as com-pared to archetypal knowledge; and thus we see that the syllo-gistic method, of which the Peripatos is so proud, is called *muthos* by Plato (*In Phaed.* 10.3.2–6).

---

113. Oleg Bychkov, "Alexej Losev: A Neoplatonic View of the Dialectic of Absence and Presence in the Nature of Artistic Form".—*Neoplatonism and Contem-porary Thought*, part II, ed. R. Baine Harris, Albany: SUNY Press, 2002, p. 169. See A. Losev's writings in Russian, for example: *Bytije, imia, kosmos*, Moscow: Myslj, 1993.

114. Jan Assmann, *The Mind of Egypt*, p. 354.

115. *The Greek Commentaries on Plato's Phaedo, vol. 1: Olympiodorus*, p. 140.

PHILOSOPHY, MAGIC, AND LAUGHTER

Gazing at this myth-like manifested reality (*kheperu* in the Egyptian sense) marks the start of philosophy, that is, a striving for knowledge and a dialectical climbing from images to their noetic archetypes, to the divine Intellect, which is a limit and a standard of all things (*ta pragmata*). Philosophy (in whatever form it might be conceived) stands on the side of Horus, of the solar Ra, working to maintain cosmic order and restore the initial 'golden' purity. As Damascius has pointed out:

> Philosophy invisibly weaves the soul together and unifies it, while ignorance undoes it and tears it apart openly, that is, in this world of becoming (*In Phaed.* 1.358.1–3).

Therefore the Apollonian philosophy dispels ignorance both by gnosis and by magic. Philosophical discourse (written text), in this respect, is analogous to the magic *pharmakon*, the *Ephesia grammata* incised on the cult statue or tablet and containing 'evil-averting spells' (*alexipharmaka*). It is remarkable that the healing charms and incantations (*epodai*), as well as *voces magicae* (mantric sequences of vowels), are regarded as magical *logoi*. These *logoi* serve both for earthly protection and for eternal salvation.[116]

This talismanic function is tacitly inherited by the philosophical text, also containing *logoi*, sometimes appearing 'meaningless' to the uninitiated, as for example the famous *Ephesia grammata*, the mystic letters allegedly incised on the statue of Artemis of Ephesus. *Logos* is the usual term for the spoken part of magical action, as F. Graf observes.[117] The philosopher, in certain sense, resembles a crafty magician, who like the primal hunter roams after the realm of ideas and eats the still living flesh of his prey in the dialectical contest. Eventually, transcendence requires self-sacrifice and death.

P. Kingsley argues that 'those who know logic love to laugh,'

---

116. Roy Kotansky, "Incantations and Prayers for Salvation on Inscribed Greek Amulets".—*Magika Hiera: Ancient Greek Magic and Religion*, ed. Christopher A. Faraone, Dirk Obbink, Oxford: Oxford University Press, 1997, p.122.

117. Fritz Graf, "Prayer in Magic and Religious Ritual".—*Magika Hiera*, p. 189.

because being an impossibility to our minds, logic has laws but no fixed rules: 'Rules exist to trap us, but logic exists to set us free.'[118]

Now we could add that those who know philosophy also love to laugh. Why? Because real knowledge means that we know nothing, and this nothingness (*oudeneia*) is both the initial silence and silence as *telos*, as the final goal of philosophy. This holy silence may be interrupted only by the holy laughter of the gods. But for those of us who are neither perfect, nor wise, the love of endlessly talking and arguing about what is philosophy is not simply a waste of time, in spite of the paradoxical truth that 'the more learned we are, the worse things become.'[119]

The pious folk, according to Platonists, live on the heights of the upper pneumatic Earth, provided by the fruits of that region, fruits intermediate in character between those here below and the heavenly ones which the Hesperides proffer to those who have come to the end of their journey' (Damascius, *In Phaed.* 1.530.2–4).

The journey to the solar noetic realm is accomplished by philosophy which follows, in this respect, the hieratic models of Orphico-Dionysian initiation and those of the ancient Egyptian cultic practices. Therefore philosophy is aimed at the noetic *apotheosis* and *apokatastasis*: those who are purified by philosophy live in the spiritual realm of *akhu*, the Plotinian *kosmos noetos*, without bodies and without either earthly memories or their previous Titanic identities. Those who are ready to die 'in religious silence' (*en euphemia teleutan*), as Pythagoras used to say, are completely purified and return to the hypercosmic realm (*eis tou huperkosmion topon*) without bodies (Damascius *In Phaed.* 1.551.4–5). For those who perceive the real measure of the human tragedy, this return constitutes the sole meaning of philosophy.

118. Peter Kingsley, *Reality*, p. 192.
119. Ibid., p. 87.

2

VOICES OF THE FIRE:
ANCIENT THEURGY
AND ITS TOOLS

It is a sacrilege not to preserve the immortality of the soul, raising it to the level of the holy and uniting it to the divine with bonds which cannot be broken or loosened, but by contrast to pull and drag downwards the divine which is within us, confining it to the earthly, sinful and Giant- or Titan-like prison. [1]

Let us become fire, let us travel through fire. We have a free way to the ascent. The Father will guide us, unfolding the ways of fire; let us not flow with the lowly stream from forgetfulness.[2]

DEFINITIONS OF THEURGY IN ANTIQUITY

Contemporary Western scholars habitually repeat the standard assumption that the term *theourgia* was coined in the exotic circles of those misguided semi-Oriental (and, therefore, 'marginal') miracle-workers who imagined that the road to salvation lies not in the bright palace of 'reason' *a la* Sextus Empiricus, but in the pious hieratic rites. Consequently, on analogy with the term *theologia*, speaking of the divine things, they invented *theourgia*, namely, doing divine things, performing sacramental works.

The modern scholars affirm this rather artificial dichotomy too straightforwardly. They are, perhaps, unaware that rites also 'speak' and that they may include all kinds of *logoi*. For example, in ancient

1. Damascius *Phil.Hist*.19 Athanassiadi.
2. Proclus *De philosophia Chaldaica*, fr. 2.

Egyptian ritual, speech not only makes the archetypal realm of noetic realities manifest in the liturgical realm of visible symbolic tokens and actions, but also performatively accomplishes the theurgical transition and transposition of the cultic events into the divine realm, thereby establishing a relationship between the domain of noetic (*akhu*) Forms and the sequences of manifestation (*kheperu, bau*). In this hieratic context, the term *akhu* means 'radiant power', 'noetic light', 'solar intelligence', and is closely related to the conception of the eidetic and demiurgic name (*ran*, or *ren*). Only the gods (*neteru*) at the level of intelligible and intellective principles, iconographically depicted by the great Ennead (*pesedjet*), are able to use the 'radiant power of words' (*akhu typyw-ra*) in their truly creative ontological sense. Therefore,

> Sacred, radiantly powerful words report an otherworldly, divine sphere of meaning that is imposed on the reality of this world in a manner that explains and thus makes sense of it. Instead of supplying definitions, Egyptians would pronounce names, that is, the sacred and secret names of the things and actions that the priests had to know to exercise the radiant power of the words.[3]

We should wonder if the Greek term *theourgia* is not simply a rendering of some now forgotten Egyptian, Akkadian, or Aramaic term related to the complicated vocabulary of temple rites, festivals, and hermeneutical performances that follow the paradigms of cosmogony and serve as a vehicle of ascent conducted by the divine powers (*sekhemu, bau*) themselves. Accordingly, it would be incorrect to think that the Chaldean Platonists of Roman Syria, those who allegedly created and promoted this term *theourgia*, also invented the thing itself, that is, the tradition of hieratic arts and of their secret, theurgical understanding. Assuming the latter case, it would follow that this tradition, somewhat related to the solar metaphysics, royal cult, and reascension of the soul through the seven Babylonian planetary spheres (or through the branches and

---

3. Jan Assmann, *The Search for God in Ancient Egypt*, tr. David Lorton, Ithaca and London: Cornell University Press, 2001, p.92.

fruits of the Assyrian Sacred Tree) to the noetic Fire, is a dubious creation of those Chaldean philosophers who 'forged' (as modern positivists regard it) the so-called *Chaldean Oracles*, thereby forcing us to believe that the gods themselves, along with the luminous ghost of Plato, suddenly decided to reveal the final version of the Stoicized Middle Platonist metaphysics in the form of seductive 'manifestos of irrationalism'.

This is the ideological dogma established by E.R. Dodds and his countless predecessors. All of them feel an incredible pleasure in ridiculing the Ephesian theurgist Maximus and in mocking those who, instead of talking about the distant transcendent gods, allegedly 'create' them, following 'the superstitions of the time'.[4] This almost scandalous 'creation of gods' through the methods provided by certain telestic science (*he telestike episteme*) is often deliberately misunderstood. For E.R. Dodds, it is an 'animation of magic statues in order to obtain oracles from them'.[5] That sounds like a reinterpretation (employing 'magic' in a derogatory sense) of Proclus, who says that the telestic art, by the use of certain symbols (*dia tinon sumbolon*), establishes on earth places fitted for oracles and statues of the gods (*kai chresteria kai agalmata theon hidrusthai epi ges: In Tim.* III.155.18).

Telestike (the term derived from the verb *telein*, to consecrate, to initiate, to make perfect) is not a kind of rustic sorcery (*goeteia*). Rather it is a means to share or participate in the creative energies of the gods by constructing and consecrating their material receptacles, their cultic vehicles, which then function as anagogic tokens, as *sumbola* and *sunthemata*.

However, one should be careful not to fall into the trap of an improper one-sidedness when approaching the realm of ancient metaphysical concepts and related terms. The word 'theurgy' is not the term most frequently used by the ancient Neoplatonists when they discuss cosmological, soteriological or liturgical issues. As A. Louth openly states:

---

4. E.R. Dodds, *The Greeks and the Irrational*, Berkeley: University of California Press, 1984, p.286.
5. Ibid., p.292.

In Iamblichus, *theourgia* refers to the religious rituals—prayers, sacrifices, divinations—performed by the theurgist: it is one of a number of words—*theourgia, mustagogia, hiera hagisteia, threskeia, hieratike techne, theosophia, he theia episteme*—which have all more or less the same meaning and which are frequently simply translated *theurgie* by E. des Places....[6]

Damascius often prefers the terms *hiera hagisteia, hierourgia* (hierurgy, holy work, cultic operation) instead, or speaks of 'theosophy which comes from the gods' (*Phil. Hist.* 46d) and of the ancient traditions (*ta archaia nomina*) which contain the rules of divine worship (ibid., 42f). The Greek terms *hieratike* and *hieratike techne* (hieratic art, sacred method) are also rendered simply as 'theurgy' by the modern scholars.

For Damascius, *hieratike* is 'the worship of the gods' (*theon therapeia*) which 'ties the ropes of heavenbound salvation' (*Phil. Hist.* 4a), that is, raises the soul to the noetic cosmos by means of the ropes of worship, as in the Vedic and ancient Egyptian hieratic rites or the anagogic recitations of the Qur'an. This *hieratike techne* is designated as the 'Egyptian philosophy' which deals with certain spiritual alchemy consisting in gnostic *paideia* as well as in transformation, elevation, and immortalization of the soul (the winged *ba* of the true philosopher or the initiate).

The return of our souls to God presupposes either a fusion with the divine (*theokrasia*), or a perfect union (*henosis panteles*: ibid., 4a–c). This hieratic method of spiritual 'homecoming' is praised as the higher wisdom, namely, the Orphic and Chaldean lore which transcends philosophical common sense (*ten orphiken te kai chaldaiken ten hupseloteran sophian*: ibid., 85a).

For the late Neoplatonists, theurgy (including all traditional liturgies, rites, and sacrifices which are ordained, revealed, and, in fact, performed by the gods themselves) is essential if the initiate priest is to attain the divine through the ineffable acts which transcend all

6. Andrew Louth, "Pagan Theurgy and Christian Sacramentalism in Denys the Areopagite".—*The Journal of Theological Studies*, vol. 37, Oxford: Clarendon Press, 1986, p. 434.

intellection (*he ton ergon ton arrheton kai huper pasan noesin:* Iamblichus *De mysteriis* 96.43–14). Thus, a theurgic union with the gods is the accomplishment (*telesiourgia*) of the gods themselves acting through their sacramental tokens, *ta sunthemata*. The awakened divine symbols by themselves perform their holy work, thereby elevating the initiate to the gods whose ineffable power (*dunamis*) recognizes by itself its own images (*eikones*).

Dionysius the Areopagite borrows the term *theourgia* from Iamblichus and Proclus, but uses it not in the sense of religious rituals which have the purificatory, elevating, and unifying divine force. Now this term designates certain divine works or actions, such as the divine activity of Jesus Christ (*andrikes tou Iesou theourgias: CH* 181B). Dionysius the Areopagite also speaks of one's deification and *koinonia* (communion, participation) with God or an assimilation to God (*CH* 161 D 1–5) effected through participation in the sacraments. That means *henosis* (union) accomplished by partaking the most sacred symbols of the thearchic communion and of 'divine birth' achieved through the hermeneutical *anagoge* (ascent) and *epistrophe* (return to the Cause of All). However, as P. E. Rorem remarks,

> the uplifting does not occur by virtue of rites and symbols by themselves but rather by their interpretation, in the upward movement through the perceptible to the intelligible.[7]

Arguing that theurgical action directed by the gods and aimed at *theourgike henosis*, theurgical union, has nothing to do with wonder-working (*thaumatourgia*), Iamblichus regards theurgy as the cultic working of the gods (*theon erga*) or as divine acts (*theia erga*) in the metaphysical and ontological sense, which reveal the hidden henadic foundation of all manifested sequences of being, thereby re-affirming or re-collecting the ultimate divine presence in everything. As G. Shaw observes:

> That presence was ineffable, but what lay beyond man's intellectual grasp could nevertheless be entered and achieved

---

7. P.E. Rorem, *Biblical and Liturgical Symbolism within the Ps-Dionysian Synthesis,* Toronto: Pontifical Institute of Mediaeval Studies, 1984, p.116.

through ritual action, which is why Iamblichus argued that theurgy transcended all intellectual endeavors.[8]

If regarded as a term designating divine actions performed at different levels of manifested reality (which itself is nothing but the multi-dimensional fabric of *theon erga*, disclosed following the noetic paradigms of procession and reversion, *proödos* and *epistrophe*), then theurgy cannot be viewed simply as a ritualistic appendix to Platonism, but must rather be seen as its innermost core and its hidden essence. Consequently, not only may the Neoplatonic-Chaldean hieratic mystagogy be designated as 'theurgy', but also all hierurgical procedures (liturgies, invocations, visualizations, contemplations, prayers, sacramental actions, textual investigations, interpretations of symbols) which involve the direct assistance of the superior classes of beings (angels and semi-mythic teachers) and which activate the self-revelatory illumination in one's reascent from the inferior to the prior. All of them may be regarded as 'theurgical'.

Hence the *theurgical*, as universal and divine, is the opposite of anything particular and individualistic, anything based on one's subjective whims and egocentric drives. Without the fundamental realization of our own nothingness (*sunaisthesis ten peri heauton oudeneias: De myster.* 47.13–14), no one can be saved, because in theurgical union gods are united only with gods, or rather 'the divine is literally united with itself' (*auto to theion pros heauto sunesti*: ibid., 47.7–8). This should in no way be conceived as communication between the mortal man and the immortal divinity (as one person addressing another), but rather communication of the divine in us with the divine in the universe. According to Iamblichus:

It is plain, indeed, from the rites (*ergon*) themselves, that what we are speaking of just now is a method of salvation for the soul; for in the contemplation of the 'blessed visions' (*ta makaria theamata*) the soul exchanges one life for another and

---

8. Gregory Shaw, "Theurgy: Rituals of Unification in the Neoplatonism of Iamblichus".—*Traditio: Studies in Ancient and Medieval History, Thought, and Religion*, vol. XLI, New York: Fordham University Press, 1985, p.1.

exerts a different activity, and considers itself then to be no longer human—and quite rightly so: for often, having abandoned its own life, it has gained in exchange the most blessed activity of the gods. If, then, it is purification from passions and freedom from the toils of generation and unification with the divine first principle that the ascent through invocations procures for the priests (*henosin te pros ten theian archen he dia ton kleseon anodos parechei tois hiereusi*), how on earth one can attach the notion of passions to this process?' (*De myster.* 41.9–42.1).

DESCENDING LIGHTS
AND ANIMATED CULT IMAGES

The Egyptian temple rites, from which the Neoplatonic *hieratike* at least partly stems, may be called theurgical in the etymological sense of this word, because the Egyptian cult activity (itself staged as an interplay of divine masks) is based on a genuine encounter with the divine presence, with the immanent 'indwelling' of God's transcendent energies. The gods (*neteru*) do not literally dwell on earth in their cultic receptacles (statues, temples, human bodies, animals, plants), but rather install themselves there, thereby 'animating' images and symbols. A deity's *ba* (manifestation, noetic and life-giving power, descending 'soul') is to a degree united with the cult statues, processional barques, shrines, reliefs on the walls, sacred texts and the entire temple or the temple-like tomb.

The statue as a proper receptacle (*hupodoche*) for the divine irradiation is analogous to the purified human body of the royal person or of the 'dead' initiate, and the descent of a deity's *ba* resembles the approach of an active Platonic Form which informs the passive womb of matter and, consequently, establishes the manifested theatre of articulated and animated shapes. So the divine *ba* descends from the sky (or rather appears from the a-temporal inwardness, since theophanies *a priori* constitute all manifested reality) into his cult images (*sekhemu*) and the god's heart is united with these images.

Sekhem usually means 'power', but in this context it designates sign or symbol of power, as well as image or sacred icon. As Iamblichus remarks, 'the light of the gods illuminates its subject transcendently' (*kai ton theon to phos ellampei choristos: De myster.* 31.4), since even visible light (or the heliophany of Ra at the level of his shining Disk, *Aten*) proceeds throughout the visible cosmos:

> On the same principle, then, the world as a whole, spatially divided as it is, brings about division throughout itself of the single, indivisible light of the gods (*to hen kai ameriston ton theon phos*). This light is one and the same in its entirety everywhere, is present indivisibly to all things that are capable of participating in it, and has filled everything with its perfect power; by virtue of its unlimited causal superiority it brings to completion all things within itself, and, while remaining everywhere united to itself, brings together extremities with starting points. It is, indeed, in imitation of it that the whole heaven and cosmos performs its circular revolution, is united with itself, and leads the elements round in their cyclic dance. . . . (*De myster.* 31.9–32.2).

When the animating *ba* comes from the sky and descends (*hai*) on his image (*sekhem*), this metaphysical action (or divine work, *ergon*) simply indicates the special ritualistic re-actualization, re-affirmation, and re-petition of the cosmogonic scenario at the level of both cult images and purified human bodies who need to be re-assembled by the unifying divine spirit. This accomplishment (*telesiourgia*) is tantamount to the restoration of the Eye of Horus which is equated with 'offering' (*hetep*, or *hotep*), simultaneously defined as the harmonious reintegration of parts (parts of the scattered Osirian *eidos*, restored in accordance to the whole truth, *maat*), and as noetic satisfaction.

The cult statues presumably have two natures, one divine (when permeated by the *bau* of the gods, like the house of Ra is irradiated by his miraculous unifying rays) and one inanimate and material which must be consecrated in order to reveal the inner divine presence both in its perennial theophanic and its specialized cultic sense. Therefore J. Assmann says:

As creators of these statues, humans are reminded of their own divine origin, and by piously tending and worshiping them, they make the divine at home on earth.[9]

However, the daily rituals which consist in awakening, greeting, purifying, anointing, dressing, feeding, and worshiping the cult statue, as well as the process of sacrificial offerings (which are symbolically designated as the restored Eye of Horus and around which the ritual revolves), are not to be conceived 'as a communication between the human and the divine, but rather as an interaction between deities',[10] that is, as a real divine *ergon*, the holy work performed by the gods and all superior classes of beings.

According to the late Neoplatonists, the gods (like the Egyptian *neteru*) are present immaterially in the material things, therefore *ta sunthemata* (the theurgic seats of elevating power) are regarded as receptacles for the invisible divine irradiations (*ellampseis*) involved in the cosmic liturgy of descent and ascent. Since the body is an integral part of demiurgic work, in its perfect primordial form serving as an image (*eikon*) of divine self-disclosure, the condition and quality of embodied matter indicate the soul's internal condition.

The human body as a fixed eidetic statue or as an iconographically established sequence of dynamic hieroglyphic script (analogous to a series of Tantric *mudras*) is an instrument of divine presence, because this presence may be either concealed, or revealed. Therefore *telestike* is not to be thought as inducing the presence of a god (or of his representative daimon) in the artificially constructed receptacle (*hupodoche*) only. The divine *ba* can permeate the human body as well, thereby confirming the latter's ability to participate in the superior principles. When such 'incarnation' becomes permanent, the human body itself is transformed and turned into the spiritual 'golden statue'.

The incantations (*epodai*) are also to be viewed as the anagogic *sunthemata* which function as a means of maintaining the providential link between the ineffable henadic essences and their symbolic

9. Jan Assmann, ibid., p.41.
10. Ibid., p.49.

expressions, or between the noetic archetypes and their existential images, in order to complete the soul's divine measures and reveal its re-assembled immortal body (*sah*, which is symbolized by the Egyptian royal mummy). Since the body is an index (*deigma*) of the soul's capacity to receive a divine presence, separation from the lower somatic identifications and false identities requires us, as G. Shaw constantly argues,

> to determine the appropriate measures for that soul to engage the powers bestowed upon it by the Demiurge, and then to accelerate its growth into those measures by means of theurgic rites.[11]

It seems that the above mentioned measures are the ratios of the soul described in Plato's *Timaeus* (35b–36b; 43d–e). Therefore, through the correct performance of measured theurgic rites, the initiate imitates the activity of the Demiurge, conjoining parts to wholes and integrating the psychosomatic multiplicity into the presiding noetic unity.

FIGURES, NAMES, AND TOKENS OF THE DIVINE SPEECH

Arguing that as the soul's descent took place through many intermediary levels, so its ascent happens in an analogous manner, which includes dispensing with thinking through images, and dissolving 'the structure of life which it has compounded for itself'. Proclus compares *phantasia* (imagination) with

> those Stymphalian birds which fly about within us, inasmuch as they present to us evils of form and shape, not being able at all to grasp the non-figurative and partless Form (*In Parm.* 1025).

The Platonic philosopher, like the bird-shaped *ba* of the Egyptian initiate, indeed must re-grow his wings in order to fly up to the stars (visible symbols of the eternal noetic archetypes) and, standing on the back of the ouroboric universe, as on the back of the Egyptian

---

11. Gregory Shaw, *Theurgy as Demiurgy: Iamblichus' Solution to the Problem of Embodiment.*—Dionysius, vol. xii, Halifax: Dalhousie University Press, 1988, p.51.

goddess Nut, to contemplate what lies beyond and what is, therefore, formless and colorless.

However, in spite of this deconstructive rhetoric which makes a
sharp division between the things divine, directly perceived through
intellection (*noesis*), and those presented through verbally
expressed imagination (*lektike phantasia*), Proclus recognizes that
the one living on the level of intellect (*nous*) has a task appointed
for him to act by means of discursive reason and imagination. This
is so partly because all manifested realities, being merely playthings
of the gods (as Plato explicitly states: *Leg.*vii.803) appear as the
demiurgic dream of the Creator. The entire animated cosmos is like
the miraculous ship constructed by the Egyptian initiate in the
Duat, using the secret names and words of demiurgic (and, therefore, 'magic') power (*hekau*).

In this way both the Egyptian initiate, one who enters Duat
before his physical death, and the Platonic philosopher, follow the
divine Intellect (the solar Atum-Ra) who produces all things and 'in
his bottomless thoughts' contains causally and in single simplicity
the unified knowledge of all things and all divine works (*theia erga*),
which are accomplished by the very fact of his conceiving and noetically beholding them. It is, as Proclus says,

> as if by the very fact of imagining all these things in this way, he
> were to produce the external existence of all the things which
> he possessed within himself in his imagination. It is obvious
> that he himself, then, would be the cause of all those things
> which would befall the ship by reason of the winds on the sea,
> and thus, by contemplating his own thoughts, he would both
> create and know what is external, not requiring any effort of
> attention towards them (*In Parm.* 959).

Though the gods are without any visible shape or figure, they
may be viewed as a possessing figures in the psychic realm of the
imagination (in the microcosmic Duat, let us say, the Hathorian or
Osirian Netherworld of the soul), since each soul is the *pleroma* of
reality (*panton pleroma esti ton eidon: In Parm.* 896). So within the
soul, as on a magic screen, all things are contained inwardly in a
psychic mode. As S. Rappe reminds us:

At the borderland between the material world and the purely immaterial world of intellect, this space of imagination offers a transitional domain that the mind can come to inhabit. This visionary space does not contain external objects nor illusions nor hallucinations. Rather, it is above all a realm of self-illumination. . . .[12]

Therefore the soul is capable of seeing and knowing all things, including figures of the gods who essentially are without any shape and figure, in this 'Osirian' mode by entering into itself and awakening the inner powers which reveal the images (*eikones*) and symbols of the universal reality. Neither the outward nor the inward psychic seer is capable of seeing without images. Thus the nature of the things seen corresponds in each case to the nature and preparedness of the seer himself, that is, to the particular archetypal measures or configurations (those initially written on by *Nous*, the demiurgic Intellect) and to the actual contents of his existential and culturally shaped consciousness.

The Demiurge is the first and the only real seer and real speaker, whose 'speech' is tantamount to creative contemplation in the transcendent mirrors of imagination. Hence, his seeing and his speaking constitute manifestation itself. Therefore the creation of all things and the naming of them are one and the same.

The theurgic ascent (the reversion of creation, now assuming the form of sacramental deconstruction) is also regarded as a rite of divine invocation. In a certain sense, invocation, incantation, and psalmody show the sacred road (*hodos*) to the divine world, leading the initiated singer into the Netherworld. This knowledge of incantation constitutes the theurgic core of the Orphic way and provides the cosmological setting for the Egyptian temple liturgies, based on the luminous interplay of *heka* powers.

Likewise, in the context of ancient Greek epic poetry, the poet's song itself (the poet being simultaneously regarded as an inspired

---

12. Sara Rappe, *Reading Neoplatonism: Non-discursive Thinking in the Texts of Plotinus, Proclus, and Damascius*, Cambridge: Cambridge University Press, 2000, p. 173.

prophet-like *theologos*) is 'quite simply a journey into another world: a world where the past and future are as accessible and real as the present'.[13] The journey of these divinely inspired poets is their song. As P. Kingsley says:

> The poems they sing don't only describe their journeys; they're what makes the journey happen.[14]

For the late Hellenic Neoplatonists, even to read the philosophical or hieratic text (somewhat analogous to the cosmic text of stars and celestial omens, regarded as a display of divine hieroglyphs) is to take part in a theurgic ritual. S. Rape explains this as follows:

> The soul, as the channel of cosmic manifestation, reads the world under one of two signs: the world is 'other' than or outside the soul when it is engaged in the process of descent, whereas it is 'the same' as and within the ascending or returning soul. Both of these great names are thus pronounced and understood by the soul, while in the moment of its pronouncement, the world itself is expressed. In fact, the world as a whole is just such a system of signs, due again to the activity of the Demiurge.[15]

Hence, in the Neoplatonic view, all manifested reality consists of different modes of divine speech, or different levels of a revelation which operates with a system of signs and symbols that simultaneously manifest and conceal the One:

> Heaven and Earth are therefore signifiers, the one signifies the procession from there and other the return (Proclus *In Tim.* 1.273).

The name is an image (*eikon*) of a *paradeigma*, a copy of a model which is established at the noetic level. The Greek *onomata* means both 'names' and 'words', and these *onomata* are viewed as *agalmata* by Proclus. The cosmos as an *agalma*, an image, shrine, or statue of

---

13. Peter Kingsley, *In the Dark Places of Wisdom*, Inverness, CA: The Golden Sufi Center, 1999, p. 122.

14. Ibid., p. 123.

15. Sara Rappe, ibid., p. 181.

the everlasting gods (*ton aidion theon gigonos agalma*: Plato *Tim.* 37c), consists in the mysterious circularity of the great divine Name. Consequently, procession (*proodos*) and return (*epistrophe*) are the great names of the unspeakable Principle.

The ouroboric cosmos (ouroboric, because it resembles the circle-like body of the noetic Snake whose beginning and end are tied together) is to be viewed as the ontologically displayed divine text, the luminous golden globe filled with animated hieroglyphs. To say it in the Egyptian terms, the hieroglyphs are *medu neter*, 'divine words' (or modes of divine speech). This living *agalma*, or rather the entire constellation of *onomata*, *agalmata*, and *sunthemata*, is like a macrocosmic cult statue, a living embodiment of the divine Ideas, of the archetypal contents which constitute the plenitude of Atum.

While maintaining that *agalma* contains no implication of likeness and, therefore, is not a synonym of *eikon*, F.M. Cornford describes Proclus' attitude towards the cosmos as the holiest of shrines in following way. Plato, according to Proclus,

> speaks of the cosmos as an *agalma* of the everlasting gods because it is filled with the divinity of the intelligible gods, although it does not receive those gods themselves into itself any more than cult images (*agalmata*) receive the transcendent essences of the gods. The gods in the cosmos (the heavenly bodies) are, as it were, channels conveying a radiance emanating from the intelligible gods. Proclus calls the Demiurge the *agalmatopoios tou kosmou*, who makes the cosmos as an *agalma* and sets up within it the *agalmata* of the individual gods.[16]

The names of the gods are an objective eidetic expression of their henadic essence; therefore the deity is actually present in its name. The supreme Principle is likewise in his great names which constitute the manifested cosmos, since the One is the name of the procession of the universe, and the Good is the name of its reversion. This means that the universe, *to pan*, is a set of demiurgic and theurgic

---

16. Francis MacDonald Cornford, *Plato's Cosmology. The Timaeus of Plato*, Indianapolis: Hackett Publishing Company, 1997, p. 101.

tokens, like a hieratic statue with its body animated by soul. The stars, for example, are *agalmata* made by gods for their own habitation, and

> the cosmos with its eight moving circles is thought of as an *agalma* which awaits the presence of the divine beings who are to possess the motion symbolized.[17]

In Neoplatonism, names are likened to 'divine images' that are essentially symbolic and theurgic. They function within the metaphysical triad of remaining, procession, and reversion (*mone, proodos, epistrophe*), leading to the first principles and causes through their effects and traces. In addition, according to the otherwise unknown Democritus the Platonist (Damascius *In Phileb.* 24.3), the divine names are regarded as 'vocal images' or 'spoken statues' (*agalmata phoneenta*) of the gods.

Within the frame of the eternal demiurgic and theurgic work (*ergon*), there is no difference whether names are treated as being natural or conventional, *phusei* or *thesei*, because this opposition is too human, discursive, and partly illusory. For Proclus, at the level of human perception, things are 'natural' in four senses: like animals and their parts, like the faculties and activities of natural things, like shadows and reflections in mirrors, and like images fashioned by art (*technetai eikones*), those which resemble their archetypes. Names are regarded as being 'natural' in the fourth sense. Therefore A. Sheppard says:

> The view that names are naturally appropriate, like images fashioned by the painter's art which reflect the form of the object, accords with the Neoplatonist view that artistic images reflect the Platonic Forms rather than objects of the sensible world. It is also quite consistent with the view that names are *agalmata* espoused by Proclus in the *In Crat.* and also in the Alexandrian Neoplatonist Hierocles.[18]

17. Ibid., p. 102.
18. Anne Sheppard, "Proclus' Philosophical Method of Exegesis: The Use of Aristotle and the Stoics in the Commentary on the Cratylus".—*Proclus lecteur et interprete des anciens*, ed. Jean Pepin and H. D. Saffrey, Paris: CNRS, 1987, p. 149.

THE PROPHET BITYS AND THE
OVERWHELMING NAME OF GOD

The notion of theurgy as a divine work performed through the creative demiurgic Word and then through the ritual imitation of cosmogony is somewhat related to Bitys, the mysterious Egyptian prophet, sometimes described as the king. He is not attested, at least by this curious name, in the traditional Egyptian sources which constantly praise other divine sages instead, for example, Imhotep the Great. This divinized sage (Imhotep, sometimes forming a triad with Ptah and Hathor) is described as 'the lector priest, the servant of Thoth ... who fixes the plans of the god's temples,' 'by whom everyone lives' and 'who revivifies people in the state of death, who brings up the egg in the belly.'[19]

Iamblichus in *De mysteriis* describes certain aspects of the late Egyptian metaphysics and theurgy, arguing that

> Hermes also has set out this path (*ten hodon*); and the prophet Bitys (*Bitus prophetes*) has given an interpretation of it to King Ammon, having discovered it inscribed in hieroglyphic characters in a sanctuary in Sais in Egypt. He has handed down the Name of God, which extends throughout the whole cosmos (*to te tou theou onoma paredoke to diekon di' holou tou kosmou*); and there are many other treatises on the same subject.... (*De myster.* 267.11–268.4).

What sort of doctrine is attributed to Bitys by Iamblichus? It is a teaching about the supracosmic powers (*huperkosmioi te dunameis*), those which are worshiped by means of hieratic ritual (*tes hieratikes hagisteias*), thereby implying a clear distinction between the life of the soul and the intellective realm on the one side, and that of nature on the other. Hence the Egyptians (the followers of Thoth and Bitys) postulate intellect and reason (*noun te kai logon*) as the highest principles, subsisting on their own, and maintain that all

---

19. Dietrich Wildung, *Egyptian Saints. Deification in Pharaonic Egypt*, New York: New York University Press, 1977, p. 63 and p. 72.

things generated (in the sense of *kheperu*, manifested by Atum, 'lord of *kheperu*') are created by their means.

Iamblichus affirms that the ancient Egyptians recognized the highest Demiurge as forefather of all manifestations, attributing *he zotike dunamis*, the animating power, not only in the heavens but also prior to the heavens, since above the generated cosmos they postulate a pure Intellect (*katharon te noun huper ton kosmon pro-titheasi: De myster.* 267.4–5). This Intellect is indivisible in the universe as a whole, but divided at the level of the heavenly spheres.

The theory of the noetic cosmos involves conversion to the ungenerated principles and ascent to the noetic gods in order to unite ourselves to them, and thus, transcending the cosmic order, to 'partake in eternal life and in the activity of the supercelestial gods' (*aidiou te zoes kai ton huperouranion theon ten energeias metechein:* ibid., 271.8–9). Therefore, for the Egyptian followers of Thoth and Bitys, this is not merely a matter of doctrinal exposition of metaphysics, since

> they recommended that we ascend (*anabainein*) through the practice of hieratic theurgy (*dia tes hieratikes theourgias*) to the regions that are higher, more universal and superior to fate, towards the God who is the Demiurge (*pros ton theon kai demiourgon*), without calling in the aid of matter.... (ibid., 267.6–9).

The teaching of the legendary Bitys is ingeniously related to that of Plato by those Graeco-Egyptian alchemists who regarded philosophy as a way of inner transformation, speaking of the alchemical process as 'Osirification', as bringing Osiris back to life. Zosimus of Panopolis mentions the mysterious tablet (*pinax*), which presumably refers not so much to the concrete text, but rather represents the late Egyptian metaphysical tradition related to that proto-Hermetic cosmology, theology, and soteriology from which the Orphico-Platonic redemptive path of the immortal soul partly derives its initial patterns, namely, the paradigm of soul's ascent to the *huperouranios topos* in order to be united with Atum-Ra.

The tablet 'that Bitos (i.e., Bitys) wrote, and Plato the trice-great (*trismegas*) and Hermes the infinitely great (*muriomegas*)' allegedly contains the teaching about the inner man of light who is formed by the divine Intellect in its own image, like the Egyptian pharaoh who is the central image (*tut*) of God and, therefore, represents the theurgic axis of ascent. In this sense, the pharaoh, as a living Horus, is a son of Ra, of the solar demiurgic Intellect whose heliophanies constitute the *agalma*-like (or hieroglyph-resembling) cosmos. Consequently, J. Naydler regards Platonism as a re-expression (in accordance with Greek cultural norms) of Egyptian spiritual perspective, and says:

It may be that Plato's contribution to Western philosophy, like that of other early Greek philosophers, was that he put into terms understandable to his contemporaries, and thereby made accessible, teachings that were essentially esoteric and hitherto had been wrapped in secrecy, under the protection of the Egyptian priesthood.[20]

The Byzantine scholars still maintained that Plato followed the teachings of Hermes and Bitys. In this context, Hermes is to be viewed as the Hellenistic mask of Thoth, or Djehuti, the 'measurer' of all things, the god of wisdom, sacred rites, and hieroglyphic script (*medu neter*). The script itself, ontologically displayed, represents the Platonic Forms made visible by transferring the thoughts of Ra's (or Ptah's) heart into spoken and written language, that is, the articulated and visible universe, understood as a beautiful (*nefer*) symbolic text to be read, interpreted, and contemplated. As the universal Demiurge, Djehuti in the form of the sacred ibis hatched the world Egg at Hermopolis on the 'first occasion', *tep sepi*, that is, *in illo tempore*. This Egg is analogous to the noetic Egg of the Orphic myth.

According to the Hermopolitan theology, Djehuti (now tantamount to the Heliopolitan Atum) sends forth the primordial creative Sound still within the abyss of Nun (the ineffable One), thereby articulating the archetypal Ogdoad. This Ogdoad is not manifested and, therefore, it is pre-noetic. In other versions of theological account, Shu or Heka assumes the role of the creative Word, instead of Thoth,

---

20. Jeremy Naydler, "Plato, Shamanism and Ancient Egypt".—*Temenos Academy Review*, vol. 9, London, 2006, p. 91.

who is depicted as being either the heart or the tongue of Atum-Ra, that is, either the active demiurgic intelligence, or its power of expression, irradiation, manifestation, regulation, and ordering.

Since Thoth's feminine counterpart (his *shakti*) is Maat (truth, order, justice, proper limit, right proportion, canon), Thoth himself is to be viewed as a mediator of the noetic lights, of the divine Ideas, directing their ordered manifestation and revelation. In this respect, as a principle of gnostic revelations, magic incantations, symbolic representations, and initiatory mystagogies, he may be thought of, according to J. Naydler, as 'the universal principle that the Greeks were to call the *Logos*.'[21]

Consequently Bitys, who revealed the overwhelming Name of God, may be regarded as either Ra's, or Thoth's messenger or *avatara*. In Sanskrit, *avatarana* means a 'descent' (*katabasis*) of the immortal soul or of the All-Worker, Vishvakarman. The Doer of All Things, Vishvakarman, as the supreme monadic principle of all theurgies, gives names to the gods, thereby establishing their 'individual' being, since all gods function merely as the names of the nameless Father who in his ineffable unity is 'all things'. The countless names (which constitute the supreme Name revealed by Bitys) are given to God's 'presences' and 'powers' which thereby order the chains (*seirai* in post-Iamblichean Neoplatonism), streams, breaths, or rivers of manifestation. The original and inexhaustible Name (like the Vedic *Omkara*) is the noetic Sun which 'proceeds' as ever sounding light.

According to one of the Amun-Ra hymns, a late version of which survives in the Hibis temple:

> Hail, the One who makes himself into millions,
> Whose length and breadth are limitless!
> Power in readiness, who gave birth to himself,
> Uraeus with great flame;
> Great of magic (*heka*) with secret form,
> Secret *ba*, to whom respect is shown.[22]

---

21. Jeremy Naydler, *Temple of the Cosmos. The Ancient Egyptian Experience of the Sacred*, Rochester: Inner Traditions, 1996, p. 46.

The *bau* of God (Amun) are understood not as the visible cosmos in itself but as an archetypal decad of animating powers (among them the royal *ka* as the divine institution of kingship, which is a sort of metaphysical power embodied by the Horus-like pharaoh) that animate, sustain, keep, and govern the world. God is both one and many, both transcendent and immanent:

> There can scarcely be a clearer expression of the fact that the name too is only an aspect of the god which he uses when he exercises his rule over the world. As a nameless and secret *ba* the god is unlimited and omnipresent. The forms in which his power manifests itself are the millionfold totality.[23]

The Thothian tradition of Bitys (be this royal *hermeneus* a real or imagined person) is surely one of those maintained by scribes of the House of Life (*per ankh*). These Houses (depicted in the form of *mandala* with the figure of Osiris standing within a mummy case and gazing at the *ankh* hieroglyph, meaning both 'life' and 'mirror') were the initiatory centers in which the rite of death and rebirth was conducted for those attuned to *maat* and endowed with *heka*. This tradition (partly described by Zosimus of Panopolis at the turn of the fourth century) speaks about the inner man, the man of light (presumably, analogous to the ancient Egyptian *akh*), whose Greek name Phos means both 'light' and 'man'. When this *anthropos teleios* is imprisoned in the body, like Prometheus, his name is changed into Epimetheus, or Adam. The imprisoned Epimetheus should be rescued by the Son of God, that is, the royal Falcon, the son of Ra, whose pure 'rational' (or rather 'solar' and 'noetic', *akhu*) state is achieved when one's immortal *eidos* is germinated within the alchemical tomb. When the statue-like body is 'mortified', purified, and transformed by the descending divine rays, the spiritual illumination takes place.

Arguing that Bitys and Iamblichus provide a vital link between the Egyptian Hermetic lore and late Platonism, G. Fowden says:

22. Jan Assmann, *Moses the Egyptian. The Memory of Egypt in Western Monotheism,* MA: Harvard University Press, 1988, p. 204.

23. Ibid., p. 205.

To sum up, the *pinax* of Bitys, purportedly a translation of texts composed by Thoth-Hermes, and associated in some way with Plato too, discussed the theurgical ascent of the soul, and in doing so invoked two doctrines highly germane to theurgy, namely that of the *Anthropos*, which explains why Man can aspire to become—indeed already is—divine, and the theory of the two souls, which explains how the theurgist is purified from the taint of matter.[24]

THE DESCENDING AND ASCENDING PATHS OF HEKA

The so-called Greek Magical Papyri from Egypt give us a few scanty indications of the priest Bitys' realm of expertise—i.e., providing the spell of attraction over skull cups, attributed to the mythical king Pitys, and his prayer to Helios (Ra or Horus) to be delivered at sunset. The prayer contains the following cosmological and theological assertions:

> Borne on the breezes of the wand'ring winds,
> Golden-haired Helios, who wields the flame's
> Unresting fire, who turns in lofty paths
> Around the great pole, who creates all things
> Yourself, which you again reduce to nothing.
> From you, indeed, come elements which are
> Arranged to suit your laws which nourish all
> The world with its four yearly turning points
> (*PGM* IV.1955–1963)

> ... Because I call upon your four-part name:
> CHTHETHO NI LAILAM IAO ZOUCHE PIPTOE.
> I call upon your name, Horus, which is
> In number equal to the Moirai's names
> ACHAI PHOTHOTHO AIE IAE AI IAE AIE
> IAO THOTHO PHIACHA (36 letters).
> Be gracious unto me, O primal God,

---

24. Garth Fowden, *The Egyptian Hermes. A Historical Approach to the Late Pagan Mind,* Princeton: Princeton University Press, 1993, p.153.

O father of the world, self-gendered one
(*PGM* iv.1981–1989).[25]

The spurious letter of Pitys to King Ostanes mentions 'the holy god Osiris Kmephi Sro ('Osiris, Good Daimon, great prince', according to R.K. Ritner)[26] and contains the instructions on how the figure of Hekate is to be written, on a leaf of flax:

> Hekate with three heads and six hands, holding torches in her hands, on the right sides of her face having the head of a cow; and on the left sides the head of a dog; and in the middle the head of a maiden with sandals bound on her feet.[27]

The name Bitys, Bitos, Bithus itself may be related (at least, as one of possible puns and associative word-plays) with the Greek *buthos*, 'abyss', meaning the ineffable Silence (*sige*) of Nun and Naunet, the supreme syzygy, from which Atum-Kheprer-Ra emerges. For the Indian sages, this emergence of the intelligible light is an act of primordial sacrifice in the sense of contemplative *hieropoia* or 'making sacred'—that is, revealed, articulated, and divided in order to be re-integrated, re-united and 'put together' (*samdha* in Sanskrit). This act implies moving from darkness to light in both self-disclosure and self-sacrifice, a bringing to birth (or to death and rebirth) by means of the Word.

Thereby the lower Maya is born from the intelligible Maya, since *kha* and *purna*, void and plenum, to say it in Sanskrit, are identical, like nonbeing and plenitude of being in Atum's self-disclosure within the blind darkness of Nun. In Sanskrit, the words *maya* (magical means, creative power, matrix), *matr* (mother) and *matra* (measure) are closely related, because the first constituent part of all these words, namely, *ma*, to 'measure' (like the Egyptian *maat*) is constantly used in the contexts of creation, manifestation, giving birth to something, conferring form and definition.

---

25. *The Greek Magical Papyri in Translation Including the Demotic Spells*, ed. Hans Pieter Betz, Chicago and London: The University of Chicago Press, 1996, pp. 72–73.

26. Ibid., p. 72.

27. Ibid., p. 75.

In a sense, the 'measured' birth is a sort of sacrifice (*yajna* in Sanskrit), like Indra's slaying of the dragon Vritra who lies in the long darkness beneath the Waters. The solar Indra here means 'the most excellent incantation' (*mantra*) by which Prajapati, like the primordial Serpent, creeps forth from the darkness and becomes the Sun, the manifested and noetically articulated *Logos*. The Sun's shining is as much an utterance as a radiance, and this 'shining sound' (the great and hidden Name, *nama guhyam*) sets in motion the rounded Wheel of the Year. As A. K. Coomaraswamy relates:

> The Sacrifice is a spreading out, a making a tissue or web of the Truth (*satyam tanavamaha: SB* IX.5.1.18), a metaphor commonly employed elsewhere in connection with the raying of the fontal light, which forms the texture of the worlds. Just as the kindling of Agni is the making perceptible and evident of a hidden light, so the utterance of the chants is the making perceptible of a silent principle of sound. The spoken Word is a revelation of the Silence, that measures the trace of what is in itself immeasurable.[28]

If we return to the Egyptian Heliopolitan cosmogony, displayed in terms of *kheper* ('coming into being', 'making developments'), we should realize that Atum's singularity is articulated before his emergence from the ineffable Waters and, simultaneously, established as a unity-in-diversity at the level of manifested *kosmos noetos*. In the form of the golden Scarab (Kheprer, Khepera), Atum appears as the 'completed one', 'lord of totality' (*neb tem*).

There is a distinction made between the primordial Monad and the noetic Creator who bore all through his own mouth. Atum's self-disclosure begins as an Idea which is noetically expressed by means of Heka. The word Heka is usually translated as 'Magic', but, in fact, it is the all-sustaining noetic power that underlies all measured creation, that is, Atum's proceeding in a plurality of aspects, as many rays proceed from the one Sun. Therefore Heka is intimately connected with Maat, truth, justice, and right order.

28. A. K. Coomaraswamy, "The Vedic Doctrine of 'Silence'".—2. *Selected Papers. Metaphysics*, ed. Roger Lipsey, Princeton: Princeton University Press, 1987, p. 207.

Since Heka constitutes the primeval creative utterance of Atum-Kheprer through which all gods (*neteru*), as luminous names, came into being (*kheper*), Heka is frequently viewed as Father of all the gods and of all subsequent manifestations (*kheperu*), both spiritual and material. As the demiurgic Word and Power, Heka serves as the connecting link between Atum (the *pleroma* of noetic archetypes) and all that proceeds from Atum. In the *Coffin Texts*, Heka describes himself as a principle by which Atum gives life to the intelligible Ennead and produces everything from the primordial Monad:

> I am he whom the Sole Lord made
> Before two things had developed in this world,
> When he sent his Sole Eye,
> When he was alone.
> When something came from his mouth,
> When his million-fold *ka* was in the protection of
>   his associates,
> When he spoke with the One who developed with him,
> Than whom he is mightier,
> When he took Hu (Annunciation, Word) in his mouth.
> Truly, I am that son of the One who bore all,
> Being in protection of that which the Sole Lord commanded.
> I am he who gave life to the Ennead.
> I am Acts-As-He-Likes, Father of the gods
> (*CT* 261.5–17).

Heka is subordinated to Atum, though Atum himself, when he 'uses his own mouth' in Heliopolis, is Heka, both created and creator simultaneously. In short, Atum (or Ptah in other theological accounts) is the intelligible paradigm, the mediating power, and manifestation itself. When identified as Heka, 'Ptah is the joint principle of creative thought and utterance through which the Creator first operated. This is the same principle that continues to operate in the created world, in the Lord to the Limit's rule of nature and the pharaoh's rule of humanity.'[29]

---

29. James P. Allen, *Genesis in Egypt: The Philosophy of Ancient Egyptian Creation Accounts*, New Haven: Yale University, 1988, p.41.

The king and the initiate themselves must be united with Heka or 'become' Heka in order to conduct the theurgic ascent, because the mortal human personality cannot command the gods or be united with them. Only Heka, as Father or the gods and all-pervasive power of manifested being (Maya as the principle of both demiurgy and theurgy, of procession and reversion) can command the gods as his own hypercosmic and cosmic limbs, or his own 'words' (*hekau*).

Sometimes Heka is conflated with Shu, the primordial and infinite breath of life (*ankh*), analogous to the Pythagorean *apeiron*, whose counterpart Tefnut stands for *peras*, the 'fiery' limit and order (*maat*). Shu and Tefnut are the primeval diad which emerges from the ithyphallic Atum in the eternal Heliopolis:

> O Atum-Kheprer, when you became high, as the high ground, when you rose up as the *ben-ben* Stone in the Enclosure of the *Bennu*-bird (Phoenix) in On (Heliopolis), you sneezed Shu, you spat out Tefnut, and you set your arms about them as the arms of *ka*, that your *ka* might be in them. O Atum, set your arms about the Pharaoh, about his construction, and about this pyramid as the arms of *ka*, that the Pharaoh's *ka* may be in it, enduring for ever (*Pyramid Texts*, 600).

In a sense, *heka* is a life-giving essence from the Isle of Fire, the archetypal *topos*—'the place of everlasting light beyond the limits of the world, where the gods were born or revived'[30]—whose chief messenger is the solar *Bennu*-bird (Phoenix), embodiment of the Word, or the son of Ra 'in whom Atum appeared in the primeval nought, infinity, darkness and nowhere'.[31]

Accordingly, Heka may be viewed from many different sides and regarded as that 'magic force' of Being itself which starts to operate when Atum 'takes' Hu (the divine principle of creative speech, *Logos*, Annunciation, Utterance) in his mouth. Hu is conceived in a pair with Sia, the principle of noetic Perception, or Wisdom. Therefore Heka, as the creative power of Atum, may be equated with Wis-

---

30. R. T. Rundle Clark, *Myth and Symbol in Ancient Egypt*, London: Thames and Hudson, 1991, p. 247.
31. Ibid., p. 246.

dom, assuming the role of Thoth or Shu, and depicted as the mediating figure standing between Nut and Geb, between Heaven and Earth.

This mediating power, Heka, also represents the divine knowledge transmitted from the monadic plenitude 'down' through the archetypal Ennead. Geb (Earth), the son of Shu and the father of Osiris, contains all 'gnostic' *heka* power, legitimately received from the hands of Thoth. Geb's royal regalia (and, consequently, all esoteric teachings and paths of liberation) are inherited by the human pharaoh, the perfect *imago dei* (*tut neter*). His theurgic ascent, meaning the re-integration of an image (*tut*) into its living noetic archetype, is accomplished by assuming the form of all-embracing Heka.

Therefore the king on his ascending path eats the *heka* of the gods and of all things (putting their *heka* in his belly), and thereby becomes, or rather is able to re-collect, his initial noetic plenitude as *pantheos*, or *neb tem* (the Lord of All). Following this way of sacrificial or rather sacramental consumption (of collecting and eating the *heka* of all beings), the metaphysical *epistrophe* is accomplished and the entire manifested universe is symbolically reduced to the noetic *pleroma* of the initial Monad. Hence, the initiate (one who is 'dead' to all external multiplicity) may pronounce: 'I am Heka'.

THE SILENCE BEFORE THE GODS
AND ITS CREATIVE MAGIC

For most modern commentators on dark ancient texts, to say that 'I am Heka' means to be involved in hallucinations produced by the irrational and silly imagination of a sorcerer. A.H. Gardiner goes so far as to declare that there was no such thing as 'religion' in Egypt, but only *heka*, understood by him as a 'magic power'.[32] However, it may be labelled as 'magic' only when viewed from the presumably 'demythologized' modern perspective (itself rooted in the Judaeo-Christian mythologies), *a priori* assuming an entirely different onto-cosmology and accepting the 'sound and sterile' puritanism of

---

32. Jeremy Naydler, *Temple of the Cosmos. The Ancient Egyptian Experience of the Sacred*, p.124.

the positivistic sciences, whose tacit premises (if revisited) are even more 'fantastic' than those of sorcery.

If 'magic' is to be understood as denoting the driving force of anything 'coming into being', thereby producing a harmonious and logically arranged (both suprarational and rational) web of inter-relations, then we should accept this term, because any intentional mental act which produces certain subsequent effects is 'magical', in a sense. But moderns, as C.R. Phillips pointed out,

> have abstracted magic to cover all ancient religious phenom-ena that do not conform to their notions of 'true' religion and science.[33]

Therefore this view of 'magic', based on the tradition of Christian campaigns against the Pagans, as well as the anticlerical heritage of the Enlightenment, is 'the labelling theorist's dream',[34] tacitly shaped according to Judaeo-Christian and modern scientific stan-dards. If we still render the word *heka* by 'magic', we should remem-ber that, ultimately, this Magic (like the Hindu Maya) is a Magic of a highest order, because it appears as a power (*sekhem, dunamis, shakti*) of Atum-Kheprer-Ra in the act of creating the cosmos and arranging its hierarchies, as well as establishing the path of descent and the path of ascent.

Since Heka appears even before the first Utterance, the Egyptian Hu, he is equally related with the primordial Silence. Accordingly, Heka stands as the transcendent principle of any theurgy which operates through the creative divine speech, the irradiation of light-like names of power, themselves called *hekau* (in plural) and equiv-alent to the Hindu *mantras*. Brahman is both silent and audible (*mantram*). It fills up everything, but as the supreme Source remains transcendent and unaffected by whatever is irradiated from it or returned to it. As *Brhad Devata* of Shaunaka relates:

---

33. C.R. Phillips III, "Nullum Crimen sine Lege: Socioreligious Sanctions on Magic".—*Magika Hiera: Ancient Greek Magic and Religion*, New York and Oxford: Oxford University Press, 1991, p. 262.

34. Christina Larner's dictum quoted by C.R. Phillips III, p. 260.

Because of the magnitude of the Spirit (*mahatmyat*) a diversity of names is given (*vidhiyate*) . . . according to the distribution of their spheres (*sthanavibhagena*). It is inasmuch as they are 'differentiations', 'presences' (*vibhuti*), that the names are innumerable. But the shapers (*kavayah*) in their incantations (*mantresu*) say that the godhoods (*devatas*) have a common source; they are called by different names according to the spheres in which they established (*BD* I. 70–74).[35]

Iamblichus discusses some aspects of the Egyptian Hermetic (Thothian) theology, arguing that prior to the true beings (*ton ontos onton*) and to the universal principles (*ton holon archon*), The Egyptians posit one God (*theos heis*). Iamblichus also describes five Egyptian gods in descending order: 1) Heikton (reading Heikton instead of Eikton), 2) Kmeph (tantamount to the noetic Serpent, manifestation of Atum as the Creator of multiplicity), 3) Amon, 4) Ptah, and 5) Osiris. Heikton is described as 'the indivisible One' (*to hen ameres*) and as the 'first operation of magic' (*proton mageuma*):

> It is in him that there resides the primal intelligising element and the primal object of intellection (*to proton noeton*), which, it must be specified, is worshiped by means of silence alone (*De myster.* 263.4–5).

Now it is clear that the Iamblichean Heikton is the same as Heka. And the Egyptian Heka is viewed, we should remember, both as a god, *neter* (iconographically depicted with a frog on the top of his head, holding crossed serpents in his hands) and as an intrinsic cosmogonic force, equated with the divine 'magic'. Heka appeared within the totality of Atum before the initial duality, that is, before the emergence of Shu and Tefnut by means of Atum's masturbation or by means of his dynamic self-contemplation—by sending forth his Eye, the supreme *dunamis*, or the primeval *heka* power which establishes a certain proto-ontological 'horizon' for further creation. Within the ouroboric frame of this initial procession (*proödos*) and

---

35. A. K. Coomaraswamy, "Vedic 'Monotheism'".—2. *Selected Papers. Metaphysics*, ed. Roger Lipsey, Princeton: Princeton University Press, 1987, pp. 166–167.

return (*epistrophe*), which the miraculous gaze of Atum's Eye provides, all subsequent acts of creative 'magic' take place. Heka power, here revealed as the initial *ka* power of Atum, establishes the first metaphysical triad of Atum-Shu-Tefnut. Consequently, Atum's putting arms about Shu and Tefnut is regarded as a paradigm for the hieratic rite of 'animating' a cult statue through the intimate embrace.

Atum, in his mythic role of 'masturbator' (*iusau*) is sometimes regarded as androgynous Creator whose hand is personified as the goddess Nebet Hetepet. The Hand of Atum—also treated as Lady of the Vagina (*Hetepet*) or Lady of Offerings (*Hetepet*)—and another goddess, Iusaas (the force of growing and coming), are associated with Hathor. To certain extent, Hathor may be regarded as a counterpart of Heka at the level of Horus. But her 'true' name, in this case, should be something like 'Hekat'. Therefore we wonder if the goddess Hekate (viewed both as the supreme noetic Rhea and as the universal World Soul, Hathor proper) of the Neoplatonic-Chaldean metaphysics is not somewhat related to Heka. In spite of imagined or true Greek etymologies of the name Hekate, her role as the patroness of theurgy and magic conforms well to the theological horizon of Heka's competencies. It is worthy of mention that the frog goddess Heqet presides over birth and helps Khnum, her ram-headed divine husband, to shape the body of the human being along with its *ka*.

In the theological system presented by Iamblichus, Heka is tantamount to the One-Existent (*hen on*) of late Neoplatonic metaphysics. Being regarded as Silence previous to the gods, he is like a *huparxis* before the manifested noetic duality. J. Assmann maintains that the Heliopolitan theology which describes how Atum came into being (*kheper*) by himself and how everything else came into being (or assumed form) from him, is 'less a mythology than a germ of a philosophy.'[36]

Thus, the first truly manifested noetic triad (Atum-Shu-Tefnut) may be interpreted in many different ways. Mythologically, Atum himself emerges from the transcendent darkness of Nun. He appears

---

36. Jan Assmann, *The Search for God in Ancient Egypt*, p. 120.

(*kheper*) as the primeval mound (the metaphysical city of the Sun, Heliopolis) or as the lotus-like pillar of light. This vertical pillar, like the archetypal *axis mundi*, may be imagined as Atum's *lingam*, symbolically combined with a *naos* sistrum, the theurgic musical instrument of the golden Hathor, curiously regarded as the Hand of Atum.

Therefore creation starts both as a sexual act and as divine music. At the level of noetic *pleroma*, the ejaculated semen of creation appears as a miraculous Stone of light, as a pyramid-like Temple of *lux intelligibilis*, the womb-like tomb of all things. This is the shining *ben-ben* Stone of Heliopolis—the ultimate prototype of all subsequent sacred stones (symbols of noetic immortality) and all animated hieratic statues. Like a golden Egg, the Stone of Atum contains all subsequent demiurgic seeds, all the Platonic Ideas.

Since both Maat and Hathor are regarded as daughters of Ra and stand at the prow of the solar barque, they may be viewed together as a single figure of Hathor-Maat and equated to the noetic Eye of Ra. Now, as we remember, Heka is intimately related to Maat. Therefore Hathor, as the whole Uedjat-Eye, the Eye of Ra, initiates not only descent from, but also ascent to, Heaven, to the realm of divine Intellect. In this respect, A. Roberts aptly remarks:

> But as the *Iret*-eye, she also acts as the agent of the god's activity, since *iret* in Egyptian means 'doer'. The solar gaze becomes an activity as the eye—the instrument of divine energy and power—is projected out into the world.[37]

HEKATE'S GOLDEN BALL AS A ROTATING 'VOCAL IMAGE' OF THE FATHER

The holy teaching attributed to Bitys concerning 'the Name of God, which extends throughout the whole cosmos' seems to be basic to the Iamblichean understanding of theurgic practice. The whole cosmos is permeated and constituted by this Name whose creative expansion and contraction is maintained through the supreme Heka

---

37. Alison Roberts, *Hathor Rising: The Serpent Power of Ancient Egypt,* Rottingdean: Northgate Publishers, 1995, p.9.

power, thereby establishing the revolving noetic sphere and, consequently, the celestial and terrestrial spheres. These cosmic manifestations include the Sun's course viewed in ritual terms, the visible Sun being an image of the 'Lord of *maat*', Atum-Ra, or Amun-Ra.

In the hymn that discloses the Egyptian theological doctrines maintained during the reign of Hatshepsut and Tuthmosis III, Amun-Ra is described as one 'who grants a clear road to every eye that was created in Nun.'[38] Amun is simultaneously Lord of *maat* (truth) and Lord of the gods. He is identified as Atum, creator of both the gods and humankind, and as Ra-Kheprer, standing in his solar barque. He pours out his *bau* (manifestations, souls) in millions of forms: the light of the Sun is the *ba* of Ra, and the entire visible world may be called his *ba* as well.

Since Amun's cosmic body is the universe itself, this heliophanic body is permeated by the life-giving forces or eidetic essences which are his *bau*. These *bau* are experienced in the ordered world as the manifold ways in which God works. However, though being rich in marvelous manifestations, Amun keeps himself concealed as the One whose true nature is not revealed:

> None of the gods knows his true form;
> His image is not unfolded in books;
> Nothing certain is testified about him
> (*Leiden Amun Hymn* 200).[39]

In ancient civilizations, the One is symbolically imagined as the Centre or the invisible Pole of the sphere whose two points remain fixed. While discussing the meaning of *swastika* within the context of traditional Indo-european cosmologies, R. Guénon argues as follows:

> The Center communicates movement to all things, and, since movement represents life, the *swastika* becomes thereby a symbol of life, or, more exactly, the vivifying role of the Principle in relation to the cosmic order.[40]

---

38. Jan Assmann, *The Search for God in Ancient Egypt*, p. 196.
39. Jan Assmann, *Moses the Egyptian*, p. 196.
40. René Guénon, *Symbols of Sacred Science*, Hillsdale, NY: Sophia Perennis, 2004, p. 64.

As a symbol of life, *swastika* is analogous to the *ankh* hieroglyph, or rather it depicts the descending and ascending streams of life, related to the southern celestial gates of Seth, leading to genesis, ontological differentiation, reincarnation, dispersion, and to the northern gates of Horus, leading to the Circumpolars. These stars never disappear below the horizon and therefore stand for the eternal *archetypus mundus*, immortality, and liberation. Ultimately, this is the descent and ascent of the all-embracing Name of God whose spiral paths (which constitute the universe as a sort of *mahamantra*, as a dynamic display of *hekau*) are imitated by various theurgic instruments or *yantras*, to say it in Sanskrit terms. One of such instruments is the Chaldean top of Hekate (*Hekatikos strophalos*), described by Psellus, the Byzantine writer, as follows:

> Hekate's top is a golden ball (*Hekatikos strophalos sphaira esti chruse*), formed around a sapphire (or with lapis lazuli enclosed at the sphere's centre, according to S.Ronan),[41] whirled around by means of a rawhide thong, with characters [engraved] all over it. Whirling it, [the theurgist] used to make invocations (*epikleseis*). And they were accustomed to call these [tops] 'iynges', whether they were spherical or triangular or of some other shape. Whirling them, [the whirlers] gave forth indiscriminate sounds, or sounds like a beast, laughing and whipping the air. [The Oracle] teaches that the movement of the top, having an ineffable power (*dunamin aporrheton*), works the rite (*ten teleten energein*). It is called 'Hekate's top' because it is consecrated to Hekate.[42]

This Chaldean and Neoplatonic *yantra*, regarded as a vehicle for descending and ascending divine powers, is called Iynx (this is an English spelling, but in standard Greek transliteration: sg. *iunx*, pl. *iunges*), that literally means the wryneck bird. The Egyptian term *ba* (pl. *bau*) fits well this cosmological schema, because *ba*, depicted as

---

41. Stephen Ronan, "Hekate's Iynx: An Ancient Theurgical Tool".—*Alexandria*, vol. 1, Grand Rapids: Phanes Press, 1991, p. 322.

42. Sarah Iles Johnston, *Hekate Soteira: A Study of Hekate's Role in the Chaldean Oracles and Related Literature*, Atlanta: Scholars Press, 1990, p. 90.

a human-headed bird, both descends and ascends. In the Ramesside theology, the ten *bau* of Amun constitute something like the proto-Pythagorean decad of noetic archetypes. Five of these archetypal *bau* are related to the five life-giving cosmic elements and the five classes of life-endowed creatures. According to J. Assmann:

> This theology understands the *bau* of God not as the visible world itself, but as a decad of mediating powers that animate and sustain the world.[43]

The pharaoh belongs to the decad of *bau* and is equivalent to the central axis of the Chaldean *strophalos* (turbine), thereby mediating a divine energy of kingship endowed with soteriological and theurgical functions. As regards the symbolic meaning of the Chaldean Iynges (equated with the Thoughts of God, the Platonic Forms, themselves likened to a swarm of bees), Proclus describes them together with *teletarchai* (Masters of Initiation) and *sunocheis* (Connectors) as the gods that (at one particular level of manifestation) guard the poles, assembling the separate and unifying the manifold members of the whole. Proclus says:

> Other doctrines of a more secret kind assert that the Demiurge who presides over the cosmos rides upon the poles and through his divine love turns the whole towards himself. The Pythagoreans claimed that the pole should be called 'the seal of Rhea', as the place through which the life-giving goddess dispenses her mysterious and effective power to the All. . . . And if I may add my own conceit, the centers and the poles of all the spheres symbolize the wry-necked gods (*ton iungikon theon*) by limiting the mysterious union and synthesis which they effect; the axes represent the mainstays of all the cosmic orders, since they hold together the unities and revolutions in the visible cosmos, as the intelligible centers hold together the cosmos of the intelligibles; and the very spheres are likenesses of the perfect divinities (*autai de kai sphairai ton telesiourgon theon eikones eisin*), joining end to beginning (*archen telei sunaptousai*) and surpassing

---

43. Jan Assmann, *Moses the Egyptian*, p. 201.

all other figures in simplicity, uniformity, and perfection (*In Euclid*. II.90–91).[44]

Hence, the theurgic *strophalos* imitates the universe as a rotating vocal *agalma* of the Creator, by means of which the divine names, or powers, are both invoked and released, revealed and concealed. Strictly speaking, the work of this turbine represents the way in which the Platonic Forms proceed downward and the way all manifested realities return to their ultimate Source. Thereby end is joined to beginning 'under the tent-poles of the divine realm', to say it in the Egyptian terms. S. Ronan provides the following commentary on these Neoplatonic doctrines, indicating the equivalence between the Chaldean Iynges, the Platonic Forms, and the unspeakable divine names or symbols (*asema onomata, sumbola, sunthemata*):

> Essentially, this teaching holds that each god or goddess has an expression at every level of creation so that there are, for instance, solar human souls, solar animals, plants and minerals, etc. Expressing this in terms of Iynx equivalences, the sacred names are verbal Iynges, the symbols and sigils are visual Iynges, and the turbine (*strophalos*) is the Iynx as a ritual instrument. In each case, the Iynx serves to 'work the ritual' as Psellus puts it. We can see from our survey that the Iynx works at the hub of theurgy; it is a turbine which both generates and bears the divine power which alone, as Iamblichus tells us, makes ritual effective. As a force which vivifies and empowers ritual, the Iynx is dedicated to Hekate who is preeminently the vivifying power of the Chaldean universe.[45]

The Iynx was spun by means of cords passed through it, alternately pulling and relaxing the tension and thereby causing the Hekate's turbine to spin alternately one way (setting into motion the demiurgic thoughts of the Father, the noetic realities which think by themselves) and then the other (speeding back to the Father). The

44. Proclus, *A Commentary on the First Book of Euclid's Elements,* tr. Glenn R. Morrow, Princeton: Princeton University Press, 1992, pp. 74–75.

45. Stephen Ronan, ibid., p. 329.

ascending movement back to the One is tantamount to 'prayer', understood as reversion (*epistrophe*) to God at any ontological level of manifested reality. Hence, the movement of this turbine itself may be viewed as a sum of all prayers. 'All things pray except the First', according to Theodorus of Asine (Proclus *In Tim.* I.213.2–3).

For R. T. Wallis, this means that everything reverts upon its cause, and thereby upon the One, the cause of all. Therefore 'even inanimate objects aspire to imitate the Good . . . and it is the likeness to gods that they acquire by this reversion that for the later Neoplatonists justifies their use in theurgy.'[46]

THE SOUNDING BREATHS OF THE ALL-WORKING FIRE

The noise of the spinning (when the Chaldean Iynx is moved) imitates the noise of the divine Utterance, the Light-like Name of God. This noise is described by using the Greek verb *rhoizeo* ('whirl or spin with a whistling noise'). It is attested to in the Graeco-Egyptian Magical papyri as well. For example, the ritualist invites the Mistress of the entire world to heed her sacred symbols and give a whirring sound (*rhoizon*). In this case, whirring refers to the sistrum (*sesheshet*) of Hathor (PGM VII.883–884). The Mistress Selene the Egyptian, whose image is to be made in the form of the universe, is Hekate, lady of night, here described as Aphrodite Urania (Celestial Hathor). The spell itself belongs to certain rites of Heaven and the North Star.[47]

The Greek verb *rhoizeo* is frequently used to describe the cosmogonic noise of creation, imitated in the Oriental temple liturgies and festivals. In the Egyptian Sed-festival, aimed at the mystical rebirth of a pharaoh, the sacred music of Hathor (the Cow of Gold) was regarded as a means of cosmic deconstruction and subsequent re-creation of all *kheperu*.

As a fiery serpent goddess, Hathor is called Ueret-Hekau (the Great of Heka), sometimes depicted as a leonine-headed figure

---

46. R. T. Wallis, *Neoplatonism*, second ed. with a Foreword and Bibliography by Lloyd P. Gerson, London: Gerald Duckworth, 1995, p. 155.
47. *The Greek Magical Papyri*, ed. H. D. Betz, p. 141.

with a Sun disk and uraeus. Ueret-Hekau serves as an elevating force in the process of pharaoh's deification, that is, his ascent and union with Amun-Ra. Her elevating whistling music may be regarded as analogous to the whirring sound (*rhoizon*) of the Hekate's theurgic instrument which imitates both the harmony of the spheres and the rotation of the Platonic Ideas (the Chaldean Iynges, moving like the descending and ascending *bau* in the Egyptian Ramesside theology).

The word *iunx* (pl. *iunges*) is presumably derived from the verb *iuzo*, 'shout, cry out'. The *iunx*-wheel (like the macrocosmic wheel of creation) is moved by the erotic *heka* power. The sound made by the whirling wheel should be accompanied by invocations. In the Hellenic milieu, these invocations are based on the correct pronunciation of the seven Greek vowels, related with the seven planetary spheres of Babylonian-Hellenic cosmology, themselves belonging to one or another chain (*seira*) of manifestation. As S. I. Johnston remarks:

> The invocations of deities by pronunciation of the seven vowels is akin to the use of 'secret words' (*sumbola, sunthemata*), with which ... the iynges were connected or even identified.[48]

Here we see an analogy (or even identity) between the fundamental noetic principles and the sounding elements (*phoneenta stoicheia*) of the theophanic universe: 'The heavens sing, and the sound is that of the vowels.'[49]

This 'singing' stems from the silent One and shows the way back to Him. The roaring 'sounds' of divine irradiation (*ellampsis*) may be described as rays of light, as winds of spirit, or as the life-bringing breaths, rotating like the spokes of a wheel. According to the Vedic tradition, Vayu 'puts the inhalation and exhalation' (*pranapanau dadhati*) into man, like into the Egyptian statue-like body which receives the vital essence, *ka*.

The Sanskrit *pranah* (breath, vital spirit) is roughly equivalent to

---

48. Sarah Iles Johnston, *Hekate Soteira*, p. 98.
49. Patricia Cox Miller, "In Praise of Nonsense".—*Classical Mediterranean Spirituality. Egyptian, Greek, Roman*, ed. A.H. Armstrong, London: Routledge and Kegan Paul, 1986, p. 498.

the Greek *pneuma*. A.K. Coomaraswamy argues that these vital breaths of Brahma, Agni, or Vishvakarman (All-Worker) are imagined of as streams or torrents of light, sound, and life: they are the very waters (comparable to the Osirian Nile) that are released when Vritra is slain by Indra (*in illo tempore*, where the beginning and the end meet). These streams

> are called *nadyah* 'because they sounded (*anadata*)' as they went their way . . . and in the same way 'the Breath is a noise (*prano vai nadah*)', and when it sounds, all else resounds. . . .[50]

Agni, like the Chaldean noetic and paternal Fire, himself is the Breath, the ever-living Fire from which creative Speech is flowing down through the fiery channels, sometimes compared to the Seven Rays of the Sun. These Seven Rays may be identified to the Seven Rishis (*rsis*, divine seers, sages), or streams of wisdom, since the word *rsi* itself contains the root meaning 'rush, flow, shine'. Hence, the solar Vishvakarman, the supreme Agni, is the principle which transcends the seven lights (or rays) of manifestation. He is comparable to Atum-Ra, or Amun-Ra, that is, the divine Intellect. Essentially, Agni is beyond the seven *pneumata*, the pneumatic threads or wind-cords (*vata-rajjuh*) tied to the hypercosmic Sun, namely, Agni himself, or to the supercelestial Pole Star.

The fiery breaths or channels of Agni (the All-Working Fire) are analogous to the ethereal rays (*ochetai*) in the Neoplatonic cosmology and related soteriological rites. The luminous solar vehicle (*augoeides ochema*) of the immortal soul was thought to be able to inhale the Sun's rays and thereby return to the Sun, the visible *agalma* or *sunthema* of the Paternal Fire. The later Neoplatonists 'were firm believers in the theurgic rites of elevation', as J.F. Finamore pointed out.[51] They maintained that the soul (riding upon its purified solar vehicle) can be raised up by the rays of

---

50. A.K. Coomaraswamy, "On the Indian and Traditional Psychology, or Rather Pneumatology".—2: *Selected Papers. Metaphysics*, ed. Roger Lipsey, Princeton: Princeton University Press, 1987, p. 353.

51. John F. Finamore, "Julian and the Descent of Asclepius".—*The Journal of Neoplatonic Studies*, vol. 7, no. 2.

Helios, the noetic Sun shining through the visible Sun. The ascent of Heracles symbolized for them the soul's homecoming to the noetic realm; therefore Julian the Emperor said that Zeus elevated Heracles to himself

> through the thunderbolt (*dia tou kerauniou*), having ordered his son to come to his side by the divine *sunthema* of the ethe-real ray (*hupo to theio sunthemati tes aitherias auges: Or.* VII.220a).

THE ELEVATING RAYS OF THE RESOUNDING LIGHT

The Chaldean-Neoplatonic theurgist, 'guiding the works of fire' (*puros erga kubernon: Oracl.Chald.* fr.133), raises his soul upwards to the fiery noetic realm and even to the First Transcendent Fire (*pur epekeina to proton*) itself. He ascends by means of the mediating solar rays (the *bau* of Amun-Ra), or through the channels of fire equated to the ropes of worship.

All things are generated from One Fire (*henos puros*), or the Paternal Monad (*patrike monas*). From this monadic Fire, the Implacable Thunders (that is, the Platonic Ideas) leap forth along with the lightning-receiving womb of the shining ray of Hekate, and 'from there, all things begin to extend wonderful rays down below' (fr.35). According to the *Chaldean Oracles*, 'from the gods them-selves', as Proclus emphasizes, 'the Holy Name (*onoma semnon*) leaps with eternal circular motion into the *kosmoi* at the mighty order of the Father' (*In Crat.* 20.26–30; fr.87).

The Holy Name which extends throughout the entire manifested universe and, in fact, creates or develops it, may be likened to the whole solar Eye constituted by many parts—many 'names', 'signs', and 'symbols'. All of them are the shining and whirring thunder-bolts of the Father, that is, the intelligible archetypes irradiated and projected into the womb of the life-dispensing goddess, one who is an 'image' of the All. Thus, the *Chaldean Oracles* argue as follows:

> For the Paternal Intellect has sown the symbols throughout the cosmos, [the Paternal Intellect] which perceives the noetic relities. And [these noetic realities or their symbols] are called

ineffable beauties (*sumbola gar patrikos noos espeiren kata kosmon, hos ta noeta noei; kai kalle aphrasta kaleitai*: Proclus *In Crat.* 20.31–21.2; fr. 108).

The Chaldean Iynges, identified with the Platonic Ideas and the mystic solar rays, function as wheels binding together the noetic realm (the Seven-Rayed God, *ho heptaktis theos*: fr. 194) and the sensible world. R. Majercik maintains that they are not only the mediators of messages, but the message itself (or the revelation itself):

> For example, as the 'thoughts' or Ideas of the Father, the Iynges are actually magical names (*voces mysticae*) sent forth by the Father as 'couriers' in order to communicate with the theurgist. At this end, the magic wheel spun by the theurgist attracts these celestial Iynges and enables the theurgist (who alone is privy to the divine language of the gods) to communicate with the Father. But the message communicated by the Iynges is none other than their own magical names which, when uttered, enabled the theurgist to acquire certain divine powers.[52]

The cosmological extension of Iynges may be regarded as the sum of the wheel-like limbs which constitute the Gnostic *anthropos teleios* (Perfect Man and Son of God) coming out of the heart of the primeval Sea, that is, Ninurta, whose weapon is his 'Word'. This warlike Sumerian god, whose principal cult center was the temple E-shu-mesha at Nippur, was especially worshipped by the Neo-Assyrian kings, and their particular devotion to Ninurta had an esoteric dimension, related to the long-standing tradition of Mesopotamian gnosis.

When the monstrous lion-like bird, Anzu (or Imdugud), steals the archetypal tablets of destiny from Enki or from Enlil, this bird is killed by Ninurta and eventually reintegrated into Ninurta's own field of spiritual *energeia*. The Ninurta's chariot is drawn by the spirit of the Thunderbird Anzu, Donkey of Heaven (*imeru shami,*

---

52. Ruth Majercik, *The Chaldean Oracles: Text, Translation, and Commentary,* Leiden: E. J. Brill, 1989, p. 9.

like the Prophet's Buraq in Islamic mythology). In the Akkadian Anzu Epic, the feathers of Anzu, carried by the wind, 'convey the good news (like the *evangelium*) to the father Enlil.'[53]

The four whirling winds of Heaven are four winds created by Anu, those which disturbed Tiamat (the inert primordial Sea) in the dramatic Babylonian cosmogony of *Enuma elish*. In certain respect, these winds are to be equated with Anzu, envisioned as a thunder cloud or as an enormous bird, sometimes depicted as a lion-headed bird, sometimes as a winged lion with bird's tail. Ninurta (the divine archetype of the perfect warrior-king, the Messiah) is equated with the conquered Anzu. This rotating and whirring lion-headed bird becomes both his symbol and his loudly rumbling war chariot (the fiery, winged vehicle of the descending Ideas conceived of as Thunderbolts). As A. Annus remarks, himself following S. Parpola's suggestion, in Assyrian iconography

> the thunderbird Anzu is represented as a winged horse, based on the 'philological equation ANSU.KUR.RA = ANZU.KUR., donkey of the mountain/of the Netherworld = Anzu of the mountain/of the Netherworld.[54]

The Chaldean Connectors (*sunocheis*), another class of entities that issue from the Father (like the expanding rays of the Holy Name, transformed into the thunder, the lightning and the fiery channels), both establish true measure and harmony throughout the cosmos and function as the connective solar rays which conduct the initiate's soul upward to the fiery noetic realm. The theurgist acts like the Ninurta's or Ishtar's warrior of light. As the *Chaldean Oracles* say:

> Being dressed in the full-armored force of the resounding light (*photos keladontos*), And equipping the soul and the intellect with the weaponry of three-barbed strength, You must cast into your mind the complete *sunthema* of the Triad and wander

53. Amar Annus, "Ninurta and the Son of Man".—*Melammu Symposia II. Myth-ology and Mythologies. Methodological Approaches to Intercultural Influences*, ed. R. M. Whiting, Helsinki: The Neo-Assyrian Text Corpus Project, 2001, p. 10.

54. Ibid., p. 15.

Amongst the fiery rays not in a scattered manner but with concentration (Damascius *De princip.* 1.155.11–14; fr. 2, Johnston).

The elevating rays through which the soul (the holy warrior of Ninurta and of Ishtar-Hekate, guided by the Chaldean Teletarchs, 'Masters of Initiation') flies upward, carried by the re-collected paternal *sunthema* and the restored 'wing of fire', may be likened to chains of mantric names, the anagogic sounds of the sacred chants accompanied by inner visualizations and resulting in divine epiphanies. By their power the soul returns from images to their noetic archetypes. Therefore, as the Oracles say, the ascending souls 'sing a hymn to Paean' (fr. 131) and admonish us:

> You must hasten toward the light (*pros to phaos*) and toward the rays of the Father (*pros patros augas*), from where the soul, clothed in the mighty intellect, has been sent to you (fr. 115).

The ascent may be conducted only by those who 'listen to the voice of the Fire' (that is, those who accept the ineffable and intellective revelations from above) and travel the theurgic path of the noetic fire, represented by the upward movement of the Hekate's (or Ishtar's) *strophalos*.

The Iynges of the Chaldean-Neoplatonic cosmology are the Paternal Ideas dispensed throughout the cosmos and thereby constituting many different levels of *sumbola* and *sunthemata*: from the *sunthema* of the Sun (whose rays are to be inhaled with one's *augoeides soma*, the luminous vehicle of the immortal soul) to various divine numbers and geometric shapes, secret names (*arrheta onomata*) and material objects, all of them serving as theurgic tokens and means of elevation.

THE RITES OF HIERATIC INVOCATION AND ASCENT

According to Demetrius, the Egyptian priests employed the seven vowels (*phonetai*), uttering them in due succession when singing hymns (*On Style* 71). These 'words of power' (*hekau*) are uttered by the priest (playing the actual role of a god, *neter*) or by the *maa-kheru*, the 'dead' and vindicated initiate, one who already reached 'the nome of truth' or 'the land of silence', carried by a ferryman, and thereby equated to 'a divine *ba* like the Ennead' (*Pap. Leiden* I.350b 9–10).

The Egyptian hieroglyphs (*medu neter*, 'divine speech') perfectly correspond with music and are not to be 'read' but rather recited, sung, and contemplated. The sacred texts themselves have an anagogic function and are called *bau Rau*, 'demonstrations of the power of Ra', since by reciting them the elevating power of solar (that is, noetic) rays is re-actualized and brought into play.

To use an apt remark made by G. Shaw, in theurgy the sacred names are 'bodies' of the gods, because the names of the gods are 'individual theophanies in the same way that the cosmos was the universal theophany'.[55] The cosmos is a sounding *agalma* of Amun-Ra, echoed and imitated by all 'vocal constellations' that constitute the world and keep it in motion, through both the macrocosmic divine rites and the microcosmic liturgies of the Egyptian temples. Within the cosmos, conceived as a sacred drama of the miraculous creative Utterance (Hu), as a play of Heka's invisible rays,

> Cult was thus not carried out in the sense of a communication between man and god but as the enacting of a drama in the divine world, between gods and gods. If we do not shy away from an anachronistic usage first coined in late classical antiquity, we can call this principle of enacting events in the divine realm through the medium of cultic action and recitation 'theurgic'. What the most important advocate of theurgy, the Neoplatonic philosopher Iamblichus, wrote about these matters in his *On the Egyptian Mysteries* rests on deep insights into the meaning and function of cultic language, insights that are, *mutatis mutandis*, entirely appropriate to ancient Egypt.[56]

The Chaldean Iynges may be regarded as ferrymen (*diaporthmioi*) in many different ways, including that which concerns the transformative and salvatory rites. The Mesopotamian incantation-

---

55. Gregory Shaw, *Theurgy and the Soul: The Neoplatonism of Iamblichus*, University Park: The Pennsylvania University Press, 1995, p. 182.

56. Jan Assmann, *Death and Salvation in Ancient Egypt*, tr. David Lorton, Ithaca and London: Cornell University Press, 2005, p. 245.

priest (*ashipu*), for example, imagined himself able to journey to both the noetic realm and the netherworld in the guise of a star. While standing on a rooftop of the temple, he invoked the gods of the night sky in order himself to be incorporated into the court of these gods, the heavenly retinue of Anu and Antu (like the divine retinue depicted in Plato's *Phaedrus*), and afterwards serve as their messenger. T. Abush says:

> The speaker invoked the stars and other heavenly bodies in order to identify himself with these inhabitants of the night sky. . . . On a topographical level, this transformation is possible because he is in a locale that is not only terrestrial but also heavenly and that draws together the human and heavenly communities . . . the identification allows him to become a messenger of the gods. He imagined himself to be one of the stars and ascends into the sky and journeys through it to the netherworld. The identification has other purposes as well. Most of all, it serves to allow the ritual actor to take on the quality of wakefulness or sleeplessness associated with the stars.[57]

Damascius describes the Chaldean Iynges as 'magical fathers' (*mageion pateres: De princip.* II.201.3–4). They have an ability to transport all things from the noetic, demiurgical Monad to the material realm and back again (Proclus, *In Parm.* 1199.31–35). They are thought by the Father and also think themselves, like the intelligible lightnings turned into mysterious images, ineffable names, and world-ordering mantras. Thereby these Iynges lead 'the invisible into visibility and the visible into invisibility, causing one to mimic the other.'[58]

In both Vedic rituals and Tantric practices, *mantra* is regarded as a 'tool for thought' by which the initiate is identified with various divine powers that reveal themselves through the primeval, cosmogonic vibration and lead to the conscious realization of one's

---

57. Tzvi Abusch, "Ascent to the Stars in a Mesopotamian Ritual: Social Metaphor and Religious Experience".—*Death, Ecstasy, and Other Worldly Journeys*, ed. J.J. Collins and M. Fishbane, Albany: SUNY Press, 1995, p.25.
58. Sarah Iles Johnston, *Hekate Soteira*, p. 92.

transcendent Self, to identification and union, similar to the Egyptian immortalization and union with Atum-Ra, or with Amun-Ra. In Egypt, all temple rituals are based on the performative *heka* power, able to create divine presence and re-open the sound Eye of Horus through liturgies and recitations.

According to the Trika-Kaula traditions of Kashmiri Shaivism, the primordial Sound (*nada*) is arising eternally within the body of the initiate as a result of the movement of *pranah* in conjunction with the permanent vibration of the divine Shakti (the Serpent Power of Hathor-Sekhmet, the Solar Eye of Ra, the Mesopotamian goddess Ishtar, analogous to the Neoplatonic-Chaldean Hekate). The uncreated Sound (*anahatadhvani*) arises from within and reveals the unmanifest Absolute Reality (*avyakta*, the hidden Amun of the Ramesside theology) in the form of Sound. Therefore the ultimate Reality reveals itself in the form of the ever-vibrating Maya-Shakti that is continually creating the universe (*vishva*, the All) appearing as a mode of Parama Shiva's self-revelation via radiant demiurgic sounds and sacred mantras.

When the Parama Shiva reveals himself as the universe, he does not cease to have his integral self-experience as *Aham* (the supreme noetic self-identity). Therefore the initiate, in order to accomplish the rite of ascent and thereby to realize his integral nature (*svarupa*, like the re-collected and healed Eye of Horus),

should repeatedly utter and meditate on the significance of *Aham*, which is to be constituted by a combination of the seed *varna* (*bija-varna*) 'A', penultimate vowel AM, and the last vowel, HA (which is also a seed *varna*) in the order of A-HA-M. This *Aham* is not only a symbolic representation of the Supreme Self, it also represents the Essence of Paravak (Supreme Speech or Sound). The repeated *japa* (utterance) of *Aham*, followed by meditation on its significance, reveals to the *sadhaka* his integral *svarupa*, and also opens the path to its perfect realization.[59]

---

59. Deba Brata SenSharma, *The Philosophy of Sadhana, With Special Reference to the Trika Philosophy of Kashmir*, Albany: SUNY Press, 1990, p. 149.

In Egypt, the ascent conducted by the recitation of the divine names (themselves equivalent to the pneumatic solar rays) implies a sort of an *unio liturgica*. Ra extends his luminous, noetic arms towards the initiate, one who already is 'dead' before his physical death and who knows the liturgies of *archetypus mundus*, having the redemptive solar knowledge (*rekh*). Thus, it is said in the *Book of the Dead* (*Papyrus Nu* 133):

> Ra has led (the initiate speaker, the purified and vindicated reciter) into his barque: he (the initiate) has seen the sacredness of He-in-his-ouroboros. He has beheld Ra, namely, the free forms he assumes in the extension of his blaze of light... How good [it] is to gaze with the eyes, how good [it] is to hear truth with the ears! ... Osiris N. (the 'dead' initiate turned into Osiris) has not told what he has heard in the House of the Mysteries: the jubilation of Ra and the divine body of Ra crossing Nun among those who satisfy the divine *ka* with what it desires.

For Proclus, the theurgic ascent is also comparable to the rite of hieratic invocation, since, at the level of divine Intellect (to which the Neoplatonic philosopher aspires), creation and the act of naming are identical. Therefore the ascent to the noetic realm (and to the all-transcending Silence) is conducted by certain dialectical, contemplative, and theurgic use of names (*onomata*), appropriate for each level of theophany and equated to the divine images. There are many different levels and modes of theurgy. As L. Siorvanes observes:

> Manipulating the 'symbols' gives way to working with the Real Thing. Likewise, incantation gives way to pure invocation and ultimately to theurgic prayer. At the pinnacle of the operation, the priest-theurgist entrusts the soul's 'one' to the One itself. Through this leap of Faith, the 'one' unites cognitively with the One.[60]

---

60. Lucas Siorvanes, *Proclus. Neo-Platonic Philosophy and Science,* Edinburgh: Edinburgh University Press, 1996, p. 197.

THE TANTRIC ALCHEMY
AND THE OSIRIAN MUMMIFICATION

All Tantric worship assumes an identification of self (*ba*, in the case of Egyptian cult) with the divine, therefore the imposition of *mantras* upon the initiate's body effects its transformation, or 'Osirification', to say it in the Egyptian terms. Each *mantra* is identified with one or another deity and with the different parts of one's body. The 'acoustic images' (*mantramurtim*) of the Tantric gods are analogous to the Platonic *agalmata phoneenta*, the divine names regarded as 'vocal images' or 'vocal statues'.

Likewise, the different limbs of the Egyptian initiate's body are identified with different deities, and the 'cultic body' of the embalmed deceased is arranged not as a 'corpse', but as an *agalma* of a body or, to be more precise, an *agalma* of the separated soul (*ba*). The term *djet*, in fact, erased the distinction between symbolic representation and actual body. This *agalma* is constructed as an eidetic display of hieroglyphs (visible figures of divine speech), tantamount to the hieratic arrangement of Chaldean *sunthemata*.

Therefore the mummy (*sah*) symbolically represents one's real *djet*-body, the body of light (*sah*). It is the Osirian cult image located inside the book-and-sanctuary-like tomb. Being comparable to the alchemical egg 'that brought you forth', the mummy is an eidetic mirror for the separate *ba* to gaze upon. Thereby the winged *ba* comes to realize it as a divine statue whose golden mask is viewed as a 'head of a god'. Functioning as a sort of *yantra*, this head enables one to see and act as a god.

The initiate, transformed into the *sah*-body—that is, the Osirian mummy (gathered together out of its dismemberment and then awakened)—is divinized like a hieratic statue by means of sacramental rites, contemplative visualizations, and theological interpretations that imply knowledge (*rekh, gnosis*). The mummy is regarded as an animated statue and the statue is regarded as a mummy; both of them are transfigured 'forms' and instruments of divine *heka* powers.

In a recitation for the 'head of mystery' (*Book of the Dead*, 151), dedicated to the golden mummy mask, this 'head' is described as beautiful 'lord of vision' whom Ptah-Sokar has gathered and whom Shu has supported. The right eye of this head through which the dead initiate sees is identified with the solar night barque, the left eye with the solar day barque, the eyebrows with the divine Ennead, the crown with Anubis, the lock of hair with Ptah-Sokar and so on. Therefore J. Assmann rightly assumes that the mummy is not one's real body of the noetic light, but only the cultic instrument. He says:

> Cultic act and divine explanation are related to one another after the fashion of the *sensus literalis* and the *sensus mysticus* of medieval and early modern hermeneutics. Thus, an act such as purification (*sensus literalis*) is explained as rebirth (*sensus mysticus*), or provisioning (*sensus literalis*) as ascent to the sky (*sensus mysticus*).... It is not only a matter of explanation, however, but of a genuine transformation... Transformation is achieved through the establishment of a relationship between the cultic realm and the realm of the gods: something that happens in the cult is transformed into an event in the divine realm. This transformative function of spells is expressed by the word *sakh*. The recitation of spells with their sacramental explanation has a transformative power that rests on the interlocking of the two spheres of meaning. What belongs to this realm is transparent to the realm of the gods, and what is in the realm of the gods is visible to what is in this realm.[61]

In the Indian Tantric alchemy (*rasayana*), each part of the alchemist's body (like each part of the sanctuary) is consecrated with a particular *mantra*. By rites of consecration, all cultic instruments (including certain minerals, herbs, symbolic tokens, analogous to the Neoplatonic *sunthemata*) are transformed into so many *yantras* with which the universal energy that permeats both the cosmos and the initiate's body is awakened and re-activated. This re-activation is a part of the alchemical rites (understood as theurgy in etymological

---

61. Jan Assmann, *Death and Salvation in Ancient Egypt*, pp. 351–352.

sense, that is, as the real work of the gods) that will ultimately render the initiate a second Shiva.

To attain the state of Shiva (partly analogous to the state of Osiris-Ra) is to attain the state of gold reached through initiation (*diksha*) and alchemical transmutation (*vedha*). This path of one's immortalization consists in the generation of an immortal body, symbolized by the Osirian cultic body inside the *mandala*-like alchemical tomb which (being an icon of truth and righteousness, *maat*) served life, not death, and the construction of which (both in the architectural and the inner spiritual sense) was the goal of one's whole life, regarded as the royal path of gold-making.

The rites and techniques of this spiritual *rasayana* are ultimately based on the traditional metaphysical and cosmological doctrines. The Tantric universe, for example, is described as a rhythmical cosmic play between withdrawal (*nivritti*) and return (*pravritti*). This is like procession (*proödos*) and return (*epistrophe*) in Neoplatonism.

Therefore the yogic body (*yoga* indicating a binding connection or union) of the initiate is thought of as a microcosmic stage for God's (in the sense of *Ishvara*, like the personified Neoplatonic *Nous*) self-reversion and the re-interiorization of all his external cosmic projections. This path of return leads the initiate from images to their noetic archetypes. To say it another way, this is the descending and ascending path of *kundalini*, the miraculous power of both imprisoning and liberating Maya. The Serpent Kundalini in the Tantric mythology is analogous to the Hathorian 'serpent power', the fiery *dunamis* of the Paternal Intellect.

GOLDEN SEEDS OF THE NOETIC FIRE

In the pharaonic Egypt, gold symbolizes the bodies of the gods (*neteru*) and the immortal noetic substance. Gold (*nebu*) is regarded as a divine and imperishable metal related to the solar realm of Atum-Ra which includes the Golden Horus, that is, the official title of the pharaoh whose burial chamber is also described as the House of Gold. The sign for gold, *nebu*, is used in the same contexts as the festival sign *heb*, therefore these 'two images seem to be quite interchangeable, with deities and deceased persons being depicted on either sign.'[62]

Likewise, in the context of the Indian brahmanic sacrifice, the living substance of gold represents immortality and Vishvarupa's *eidos*. Vishvarupa ('omniform') is the name of Agni, the noetic Purusha: from his seed (like from Atum's seed) all distributive 'breaths' are emanating and one particular form (*rupa*) becomes gold.

The terrestrial gold germinates within the womb of the Earth: the gold mines are thought to be wombs of the Egyptian goddess Hathor. But the pure noetic gold constitutes the primeval Egg of Atum, or the Golden Egg (*hiranyagarbha*) of archetypes, viewed as a treasury of Agni's seed. Like the winged Orphic Phanes, the Vedic Prajapati (Brahma) himself is born *in illo tempore* from a primeval union of ineffable waters and the seed of Agni, that is, the supreme noetic Fire or *lux intelligibilis*, which emerges from the unspeakable Darkness.

One sort of gold (*prakrita-svarna*), the one belonging to the realm of phenomena, arose from that divine power which set the universe in motion. But another form of gold (*svahaja-svarna*) constitutes the noetic Egg at the top of Mount Meru (*huperouranios topos*), that is, the archetypal embryo from which the god Brahma emerges, like the Egyptian Atum-Kheprer-Ra is born in 'the first occasion' (*tep sepi*), understood as an 'interior time' of the spiritual archetypes, or as the 'ageless age' of the gods. As D. Gordon White remarks:

Here, it is the emanatory dynamic of the proto-Vedanta metaphysics of the Upanishads—a system that is very similar to the emanation and participation of Neoplatonist thought—that facilitates such analogies between the animal, vegetable, and mineral kingdoms. The universe in all its parts is a single organic entity, with all that exists on the great chain of being, the internal flux of a divinely constituted whole, to which all emanated form necessarily returns in the fullness of time. As such, all in the universe is shot through, 'like the scent in a

62. Richard H. Wilkinson, *Reading Egyptian Art: A Hieroglyphic Guide to Ancient Egyptian Painting and Sculpture*, London: Thames and Hudson, 1994, p. 171.

flower', with the divine essence. Moreover, since all exists on the same continuum of this divine outpouring, all is comparable, even identifiable.[63]

THEURGIC SPEECH OF THE BIRDS
AND SOLAR KNOWLEDGE

From Philostratus' passage about the golden Iynges in his *Life of Apollonius of Tyana* it is clear that these theurgic instruments (a sort of *yantras*, to say it in Indian Tantric terms) are compared to birds, and birds stand for angels, or divine messengers, in many of ancient traditions. The 'language of the birds' (sometimes equated with the oracular utterances), which Apollonius, the Neopythagorean sage, allegedly learned traveling among the Arabs (*Vita* 1.20), is called *mantiq at-tayr* or *lughah suryaniyyah* ('Syrian language') by the Arabs themselves. According to R. Guénon, it is related to the 'solar and angelic illumination', achieved through rhythmic sacred speech, the theurgic language of the gods:

> The same idea is contained in the word *dhikr*, which in Islamic esoterism is applied to rhythmic formulas corresponding exactly to Hindu *mantras*, formulas the repetition of which aims at producing a harmonization of the various elements of the being, and at determining vibrations which, by their repercussions through the series of states in their indefinite hierarchy, are capable of opening communication with the higher states; in a general way this is after all the essential and primordial purpose of all rites.[64]

This rhythmic speech, in a sense, imitates the whirring and whistling noise (*rhoizon*) of the demiurgic Word. To imitate the bird's motions and sounds implies that one assumes inwardly the bird-like (or angelic-like) status. Philosophically speaking, the initiate regrows the soul's wings lost in the process of descent,

---

63. David Gordon White, *The Alchemical Body. Siddha Traditions in Medieval India*, Chicago: The University of Chicago Press, 1996, pp. 189–190.

64. René Guénon, *Symbols of Sacred Science*, p. 52.

thereby separating his soul from body before body has separated itself from soul.

This separation means 'living the life of the inner man . . . vested in the higher or intellective part of soul and eventually in *Nous*',[65] like the Horus Falcon in the paternal light of Ra. Proclus, for example, explains the myth of Plato's *Phaedrus* as a journey upon which the soul encounters the divine *sunthemata* of the intelligible realm and accomplishes both the noetic union with the intelligible plenitude (or the Demiurge himself) and mystical union that occurs by unspeakable and unthinkable theurgic means.

Hence, the ascent (*anabasis, anagoge*) is conducted by initiation (*muesis*), contemplation (*theoria*), and esoteric knowledge (*gnosis*), or by the erotically energized *iunx*-wheel accompanied by invocation of the Holy Name. By restoring one's spiritual wings, the initiate is able to come back to the marvelous noetic womb of Rhea-Hekate, the font of all blessed substances that emanate from her with a whirling noise. For the Great Hekate, according to Damascius, 'sends forth a lifegiving whir' (*zoogonon rhoizema proiesi: De princip.* II.154.18). She sends forth the life-giving and divine (or angelic) speech (constituted by the noetic Iynges, equated with mysterious divine names, *onomata aporrheta*), afterwards to be imitated by the theurgists. Damascius, to whom the Orphic and Chaldean lore transcends 'philosophical common sense' (*Phil. Hist.* 85), says:

> Proclus was bemused by Isidore's imitation of the cries and noises produced by birds. Sometimes during the Chaldean rituals (*en tois Chaldaikois epitedeumasin*) he gave a display of his imitation of sparrows and hens and other birds fluttering their wings as they rouse themselves for flight (*Phil. Hist.* 59f).

These cries are analogous to the cries of the Egyptian Eastern *Bau*, a class of angelic beings who greet and worship the rising solar orb (*aten*). The Eastern *Bau* are depicted as apes (manifestations and symbols of Thoth, the god of hieroglyphs, scribal wisdom, rituals, and magic), frequently shown as holding the restored Uedjat

---

65. Andrew Smith, *Porphyry's Place in the Neoplatonic Tradition. A Study in Post-Plotinian Neoplatonism*, The Hague: Martinus Nijhoff, 1974, p. 23.

Eye or seated with Ra in his solar barque. Ra himself is sometimes represented as the Thothian ape within the Sun disk or as a migratory bird that enters the Netherworld (Duat) every night. Therefore the initiate's invocation to the nocturnal Sun is aimed at the direct equation of the 'deceased' (his winged soul, *ba*) with the *ba* of Ra or with Amun-Ra himself.

In the so-called *Litany of Ra*, the 'dead' initiate declares 'that he has a thorough knowledge of Ra's nocturnal forms of manifestation and their names; he adds his hope that they will open the netherworld for him and his *ba*, since he is indeed the image of the sun god and his *ba*. . . . 'I am one of you', he emphasizes, after which he again identifies himself with the sun god, with whom he shares the triumph 'over all his enemies in the sky and on earth', and thus in the afterlife as a whole.[66]

The vindicated dead or the initiate becomes one with the Eastern *Bau* through the divine knowledge, *gnosis*: he knows those words that the Eastern *Bau* speak and therefore enters into the crew of Ra. As the Sun priest, he joins the solar apes and becomes one of them by means of the theurgic *heka* power of Isis, that is, by singing hymns to the Sun. To know the language of the gods means to be transfigured already during one's lifetime, to join the Ennead and be united with Ra, the solar *Nous*. When this miraculous rebirth is accomplished,

> The god of Light-land extends his hands to you,
> You receive offerings on the altar of Ra.
> Your hands are grasped by the primeval ones.
> The god conducts you to the barque.
> You take your place in it, wherever you desire.
> You sit down, your legs unhindered.
>
> You fly up as Horus falcon,
> You roam (i.e., glide down) as a goose,
> A star that cannot set.
> Yours is *neheh*-eternity, your sustenance is *djet*-eternity.

---

66. Erik Hornung, *The Ancient Egyptian Books of the Afterlife*, tr. David Lorton, Ithaca and London: Cornell University Press, 1999, pp. 143–144.

A place has been granted you at the side of the Sole Lord,
You are his companion in the fields of Light-land[67]

TONGUES OF THE GODS AND THEIR SONGS

According to Philostratus (*Vita* 1.25), in a great judgement hall within the palace of the Babylonian king, the four golden Iynges are hung suspended from the ceiling, thus reminding the king of Adrasteia, goddess of Justice (analogous to the Egyptian Maat, the feminine counterpart of Thoth). The palace itself, whose roof tiles are gemstones of celestial blue, imitates the entire manifested cosmos, thus serving as a sacred *mandala* and as a theurgic *yantra*.

The suspended figures of Iynges, called 'the tongues of the gods' by Babylonian (Parthian) priests, are attuned in such way as to transmit the noetic energies up and down, carrying them between the divine realm and the king on his throne. The palace itself may be viewed as the royal theurgic instrument which unites political and spiritual power, both received from the gods like the shining *melammu*, the real noetic substance of the sacred kingship.

Likewise, in Indian Tantric Buddhism, a king is thought of as being magically emanated from the different limbs of the divinity and is re-divinized (or consecrated like a statue) by the coronation rites, rites that become a paradigm to be imitated by all subsequent esoteric rites and initiations. The *mandala*-like palace (*kutagara*) is an articulation of a political horizon with the *mantras* appropriate to the eight cosmic directions. Therefore the construction details, symbols, and technical vocabulary of *mandalas* are related to the architectural arrangement of palaces and temples, directed by Vajrapani, the Lord of the Mysteries and the commander of mysterious (*guhyaka*) yakshas (*yaksasenadhipati*). These yakshas, in some respect, function like the Chaldean Iynges and Teletarchs. As R.M. Davidson observes:

Vajrapani is also the guardian of the vehicle of secret spells, so he protects those possessing secret spells (*mantrin*). In this

---

67. Jan Assmann, *Death and Salvation in Ancient Egypt*, pp. 62–63.

role, the yaksha general uses his secret spells as a king employs secret counsel (*mantra*), and it is noteworthy that the king's counselors are identified as mantrins in Indian political nomenclature. Thus the secretaries associated with peace and war, the counselors of state, and many of the royal inner circle were designated mantrins.[68]

S.I. Johnston supposes that the Babylonian Iynges, described by Philostratus as 'tongues of the gods', are transmitters of divine knowledge and oracles to men, at the same time harmonizing the immortal and mortal elements of the universe.[69] The golden Iynges were hung up in one of the temples of Apollo at Delphi as well, being related to the hypercosmic and cosmic Sound of creation and revelation. They are described as 'having some of the persuasiveness (*peitho*) of the Sirens' (*Vita* 6.11), because the power of mantric sound is able to establish a theurgic bond between the invoker (or caller, *kletor*) and the attracted noetic fire.

However, the solar Apollo himself attracts the worshiper through 'persuasion' and through his sounding rays of *lux intelligibilis*. Since the Apollonian Iynges have the Sirenic power to attract and bind various realities by their miraculous sound, S.I. Johnston assumes that these golden wheels were intended to control 'individual celestial spheres by imitating not only the sphere's motion but also the specific tones that they contributed to the music of the spheres.'[70]

In this particular context, it is useful to remember the Pythagorean dictum which includes the question 'What is the Oracle of Delphi?' and the following answer: 'The Tetractys; that is, the harmony under which the Sirens sing' (Iamblichus, *Vita Pyth.* 85).

This is so because for the Pythagoreans the song of the Homeric Sirens is not destructive as for the later Platonists to whom to be attracted by the Sirens means to be bewitched (*katakeloumenoi*) and

---

68. Ronald M. Davidson, *Indian Esoteric Buddhism: Social History of the Tantric Movement,* Delhi: Motilal Banarsidas Publishers, 2004, p.143.

69. Sarah Iles Johnston, *Hekate Soteira*, p.97.

70. Ibid., p.101.

forget one's fatherland and one's ascent to the noetic realm (*tes eis to noeton anagoges*). Only after sailing past the Sirens, Odysseus is able to escape all the obstacles in the way of ascent of the soul, leaving them for his fatherland (Hermeias, *In Phaedr.* 259a).

But the Pythagoreans, as J. Pepin shows, regarded the song of the Homeric Sirens as representing the planetary music that not only enthralls souls after death but also in this life agitates to ascent, on the condition that their ears are not sealed by irrational passions as those of Odysseus' companions, blocked by wax.[71]

BACK TO THE LIFE-GIVING WOMBS
AND THE INEFFABLE SILENCE

If the Sirens are regarded as the evil daemons, those who hold back souls in the proximity of genesis, then Odysseus symbolizes one who passes through all stages of genesis and thereby 'returns to those beyond every wave who have no knowledge of the sea' (Porphyry, *De antro nympharum* 34). Here the Sirens represent the lures of pleasure and 'sweet irrationality' related with the world of becoming.

Therefore Odysseus, tied to the mast of his ship, may be viewed as one who has for pilot the Word (*Logos*) of God. To follow Odysseus in this respect means to be aided by a heavenly wind, or spiritual breath (*pneuma ouranion*, the animating and elevating power of Shu). According to Clement of Alexandria, the Christian writer, thereby one is initiated into the sacred mysteries and enjoys the hidden realities. For Clement, however, the wood to which Odysseus chains himself prefigures that of the Cross.[72]

But to stand upright tied up to the ship's mast, like the Osirian *djed* pillar or the cosmic *axis mundi* (depicted as the paradigmatic Sacred Tree by the Assyrian priests), is to be immobilized, to be turned into a mummy-like divine statue. This immobilization of body (like the Tantric *asana*) simultaneously presupposes the ascent of one's breath and one's mind by the ropes of the 'magic sound'

---

71. Jean Pepin, "The Platonic and Christian Ulysses".—*Neoplatonism and Christian Thought*, ed. Dominic J. O'Meara, Norfolk: ISNS, 1982, p. 4.

72. Ibid., p. 11.

that produces cosmic harmony, closely related to the musical and mathematical function of the universal Soul (Hekate, Hathor, Neith, Nut, Ishtar).

The manifested Chaldean Iynges or sounding symbols are situated within this *Anima Mundi*. They are in the life-giving womb of the goddess (a womb imitated by the chambers of initiation, burial places, tombs), thereby creating the revolving circuit, or the rhythmically weaving net, of all-embracing sympathy, the interplay of miraculous voices in the cosmic shrine of the everlasting gods.

The universal Soul may be regarded as the mother goddess who is 'pregnant' with the mummy, or the 'dead' initiate, 'nursuring his beauty' (*nefer*). Therefore the Egyptian coffin is tantamount to the alchemical body of the goddess Nut (Heaven), Neith, or Hathor, manifesting herself as a sycamore, the tree of life, who dispenses eternal noetic nourishment. In fact, this body encloses an entire divine realm (the womb of the noetic homeland) into whose 'beauty' the initiate or the deceased returns for the mysterious transmutation, in order to be delivered as Ra. The great goddess, 'the looser of bonds', whom no one knows and 'whose mummy wrappings are not loosened', says in the form of Neith.

When you enter me, I embrace your image, I am the coffin that shelters your mysterious form (Sarcophagi of King Meneptah).

For the Platonists, the visible world is a shrine (*hieron*) or a statue (*agalma*), therefore the Demiurge is a telestic priest who breaths into this statue life and intelligence. Proclus compares the theurgic consecration of *agalmata* to the act of naming: the words themselves may be likened to hieratic statues, because 'words', as divine images (*eikones*) and reason principles (*logoi*), proceed from *Nous* 'like statues of the Forms, as if the names imitated the intellective Forms' (*In Crat.* 6.13). According to S. I. Johnston:

Proclus goes on to say that the Demiurge enveloped his statue (i.e., the visible cosmos) in the *character* (or visual symbol) of the Soul and its revolutions (*periphorai*). Within the Soul's revolutions he placed names (*onomata*). He surrounded the Soul with phylacteries and in the middle of her womb inserted

noetic entities that Proclus calls the *sumbola* of the iynges. Proclus suggests that those who find the name 'iynges' a little
strange may think of them instead as divine causes.[73]

Proclus compares theurgic ascent (*anagoge*) to the process of
invocation, implying that each name recited or invoked is tantamount to the sounding statue or to the secret divine *sunthema* of
the Father. Therefore the intellectual and theurgic hymns lead the
initiate to the *huperouranios topos* (supercelestial place), described
in Plato's *Phaedrus*, and even to the ineffable One, because the
working of theurgy in Proclus is based on the theory of henads
(divine unities) by which the omnipresence of the One is established and affirmed at all levels of manifested reality.

As R. M. Van Den Berg pointed out, Proclus maintains that 'Nous in
us "moors" (*hormizon*) the soul in the Demiurge, the Maker and Father
of the universe.'[74] This Father of the universe is divine *Nous*, capable of
contemplating the Forms themselves, and is described as the Paternal
Fire and Paternal Harbour (*ho patrikos hormos*). Proclus says:

> For after the wanderings in the world of becoming and the puri-
> fication and the light of knowledge, the noetic activity (*to noeron
> energema*) finally shines out and so does *nous* in us, which
> moors the soul in the Father and establishes it in a pure way in
> the demiurgical intellections and links light with light (*phos
> photi sunapton*); this is not a thing like the light of knowledge
> but an even more beautiful, more noeric and simpler light than
> that. For this is the paternal harbour, the finding of the Father,
> the pure unification (*henosis*) with him (*In Tim.* 1.302.17–25).

The anagogic invocations are inseparable from those mystic
numbers and proportions that constitute an important part of
theurgical *paideia*. G. Shaw says:

> By coordinating his soul with the divine numbers revealed in
> nature the theurgist recovers the soul's original immortal

---

73. Sarah Iles Johnston, *Hekate Soteira*, p. 109.
74. Robert M. Van Den Berg, "Toward the Paternal Harbour. Proclean Theurgy
and the Contemplation of the Forms".—*Proclus et la Theologie Platonicienne*, ed.
A. Ph. Segonds & C. Steel, Leuven: Univ. Press; Paris: Les Belles Lettres, 2000, p. 428.

body, shaped by the Demiurge according to the proportions of the celestial gods.[75]

What the soul encounters in the hypercelestial realm are the noetic *sunthemata* which stand as the henadic symbols of the primordial Silence, of Atum's Heka that is established before the first duality (Shu and Tefnut) comes into being. The ascent to the ultimate source of all *heka* powers, of all *kheperu*-rays, is tantamount to the divine initiation which takes place not by means of intellection but by virtue of the holy silence that surpasses all gnostic (epistemic, magic, demiurgic) enterprises: only faith (understood in the Chaldean sense) 'seats us in the ineffable class of gods' (Proclus, *Plat.Theol.* IV.9.193). S. Rappe provides the following comment on Damascius' non-dual approach to metaphysics:

As a consequence, all statements about lower hypostases or about an ontology situated outside of the first principle are subject to the caveat that 'the One dissolves all things by means of its own simplicity'. All things, including Being itself, fall short of the One; their reality is merely provisional. ... Damascius recognizes that the language of metaphysics functions to signify something beyond itself. It is best thought of as a mnemonic device; its purpose is to deliver human beings from their own ignorant determinations about the nature of reality, without thereby imprisoning them in a metaphysical system that displaces reality itself.[76]

CHANTING OUT THE UNIVERSE
BY THE NAME OF EVERYTHING

One may be a 'theurgist' in the true sense of this word even without knowing the Greek term *theourgia*, presumably coined by the father and son Juliani, the legendary 'Chaldeans' of the second century. All servants of God (*hemu neter*) in the Egyptian temple are involved in what the Neoplatonists would call 'holy work', *hierourgia*. The High

---

75. Gregory Shaw, "Embodying the Stars: Iamblichus and the Transformation of Platonic Paideia".—*Alexandria*, vol. 1, Grand Rapids: Phanes Press, 1991, p. 101.

76. Sara Rappe, *Reading Neoplatonism*, p. 203 and p. 208.

Priest of Karnak, whose distinctive title is the 'Opener of the Gate of Heaven', opens not only the doors of the holy shrine (where the animated divine statue is seated) but also the invisible doors of spiritual *akhet*. It seems that those persons who may be regarded as an Egyptian equivalent of the Neoplatonic-Chaldean *theourgoi* are also called *hekau*. Ch. Zivie-Coche says:

> These were the *hekau*, those who were guardians of *heka*, and *sau*, dispensers of *sa*, magical protection. . . . Rather often, we find mention of 'lector priests', ritualists with their rolls of papyrus, who staffed the 'houses of life' attached to temples, where contemporary knowledge was elaborated in all its forms, knowledge that could be used outside as well as inside the sacred enclosure.[77]

By realizing their essential identity with Heka or with Thoth, these priests were able to ascend into the archetypal realm of Ennead (*pesedjet*). The Enneadic paradigms (like those of the Assyrian Sacred Tree, later turned into the Sephirothic Tree of Jewish mysticism) are symbolically depicted as the noetic plenitude and interplay between the different members of the divine family. They stand behind every cosmic event and every human action, thereby establishing a link between various demiurgic and theurgic *heka* powers, between the paths of descent (*katabasis*) and ascent (*anabasis*).

In the Memphite theology, centered on the god Ptah, 'he who manifested himself as heart, he who manifested himself as tongue, under the appearance of Atum', the Ennead is described as follows:

> His Ennead was before him like teeth and lips, that is, this semen and these hands of Atum, for the Ennead of Atum issued from his seed and his fingers, but the Ennead was also the teeth and the lips in his mouth that conceived the name of everything, from which Shu and Tefnut issued, and which gave birth to the Ennead.[78]

---

77. Francoise Dunand and Christiane Zivie-Coche, *Gods and Men in Egypt 3000 BCE to 395 CE*, tr. David Lorton, Ithaca and London: Cornell University Press, 2002, p. 127.
78. Ibid., p. 57.

The 'name of everything' is the Holy Word that transmits the light from the One. But Heka, like the One-Existent (*hen on*) of Iamblichus, though manifesting, revealing, and transforming all things, is essentially beyond (*epekeina*) all being. At the microcosmic level, this *Logos*-transmitting Heka is analogous to the 'one' which gathers together all the soul's faculties. The 'flower of intellect' (*anthos nou*) unites the transformed and elevated soul with the divine *Nous* and *ta noeta*, the intelligible realities (the Ennead of Atum, or the realm of *akhu*). Likewise, the *ba* of Osiris is united with the *ba* of Ra. But the 'flower of the whole soul' (analogous to the whole Eye) unites the whole human being (as a pure eidetic *imago dei*) to the ineffable One. A. Smith observes that Proclus likes to talk about the immanence of the henads as *sunthemata*:

> Thus it is likely that at the higher level of theurgy the *sunthema* concerned with ascent will be that token of the One's presence in us which is itself an *ellampsis* of a henad. . . . Of vital importance in Proclus' philosophical exposition of theurgy is its connection with unity. Theurgy depends ultimately on the One through the henads represented at different levels by *sunthemata*.[79]

In the Neoplatonic-Chaldean theurgy, the important means of conducting the initiate's ascent (whose ultimate prototype is the Horus-falcon-like pharaoh) and of effecting conjunction (*sustasis*) with the gods are the rites of invocation. They include the special 'calls' (*kleseis*) that re-sound the initial creative Word and thereby are integrated into its descending and ascending rhythms. The ascent of the soul is inseparable from the demiurgic descent of divine powers (sounds, breaths, fires, rays, *bau*). Therefore G. Shaw argues:

> Because the names were divinizing the soul ascended, yet insofar as the soul chanted the names, it descended with them into the sensible world. Since these sounds were the *agalmata* of the gods, when the soul chanted them, it imitated the activity and the will of the Demiurge in creation. . . . Since the soul itself could never grasp or initiate theurgy, the incantation, strictly

---

79. Andrew Smith, *Porphyry's Place in the Neoplatonic Tradition*, pp. 120–121.

speaking, was accomplished by the god, yet it freed the soul by allowing it to actively experience what it could never conceptually understand.[80]

Therefore by chanting these mysterious sounds which are tokens (*sunthemata*) and symbols (*sumbola*) of the gods, the caller (*kletor*) himself is turned into the perfect (*teleia*) and godlike (*theoeide*) receptacle for the god's *ba*, like the hieratic statue (*agalma, sekhem*), which is to be permeated by the divine rays. Proclus argues that

> if the Word (*Logos*) which comes-unto-light is named [by the Chaldean Oracle] as more ineffable, it is necessary that prior to the Word there should be Silence (*sigen*) which substantiates the Word, and prior to everything holy comes the cause which makes them divine. . . . As the beings posterior to the intelligibles are the words of the intelligibles, so the Word which is in them, hypostasized from another more ineffable unity, is the Word prior to the silence of the intelligibles, that is, the silence of the silent intelligibles (*De philosophia Chaldaica*, fr. 4).[81]

The illumination derived from the invoked deity, whose energies are necessary in order to accomplish all 'theurgic labours' (*theourgika energemata*), purifies the soul and its luminous vehicle (*ochema*), thereby elevating the soul on the rays of the noetic Sun. This way of ascent by invocations and hieratic rites is inseparable from contemplation (*theoria*) of the noetic lights (the Platonic Forms) that reveal themselves to the initiate's eye. 'All things are revealed in lightning' (*blepetai de [te]panta keraunois*), as the Oracle says (*Chald. Or.*, fr.147). The epiphanies that accompany the gods are manifested in such a way that the sacred fire (whirring around in a spiral, flashing more brightly than physical light or appearing without any form) seems to cover the whole horizon of one's consciousness and consume everything.

As R. Majercik observes, the theurgist is advised by the gods to 'extend an empty intellect' (*teinai keneon noon*) towards the Highest God in order to 'perceive' (*noein*) him. This intuitive perception is

---

80. Gregory Shaw, *Theurgy and the Soul: The Neoplatonism of Iamblichus*, p. 187.
81. Lucas Siorvanes, *Proclus. Neo-Platonic Philosophy and Science*, p. 198.

achieved through that part of one's intellect or thoroughly integrated soul (called the 'flower', *anthos*) which is akin to the fiery, noetic (or even supra-noetic) essence of the Father. And 'this kind of language is strikingly reminiscent of Plotinus' *via negativa* approach to the One.'[82] According to Proclus, the 'flower' of the soul unifies all that is in us and takes us to that which is beyond (*epekeina*) all being. Therefore Plato's Parmenides (the character of the *Parmenides* dialogue, himself symbolizing a henad presiding over a chain of causes) brings to completion the study of the One 'with silence' (*In Parm.* 76, Klibansky).

To say it in the terms of Heliopolitan theology, the realization of one's identity with Heka, the silent source and power of all *theourgika energemata*, means realization of nonduality at the level of Atum (or at the level of the Being-transcending Nun), before the appearance of Shu and Tefnut. The Twin Children of Atum (Shu and Tefnut, the first intelligible diad) say to the 'ontologically deconstructed' pharaoh (the sacred image of the Great One, the solar son of Atum-Ra, the paradigm of every ascending royal official, later re-named as a 'theurgist' or as a 'mystic'):

Raise yourself . . . in your name of God, and come into being, an Atum to every god (*PT* 215).

As R.O. Faulkner interprets this utterance from the *Pyramid Texts*: 'the king assumes the rank of the supreme deity and is not like Atum but *is* Atum.'[83] Therefore the pharaoh who accomplished his home-coming rites (not as an individual person, but as the re-collected and re-affirmed *pantheos*) says:

I was conceived in the night, I was born in the night, I belong to those who are in the suite of Ra, who are before the Morning Star. I was conceived in the Abyss, I was born in the Abyss; I have come and I have brought to you the bread which I found there (*PT* 211).

82. Ruth Majercik, *The Chaldean Oracles*, p. 33.
83. R.O. Faulkner, *The Ancient Egyptian Pyramid Texts*, Oxford: Oxford University Press, 1969, p. 43.

And the king's (who is restored as *pantheos*) 'bread' is the creative cultic utterance: 'Be!' (*unun; PT* 663), this imperative being like the Biblical *fiat* and the Quranic *kun*. It means that the liberated souls ('annihilated' as separate, individual entities and restored in the form of the whole solar Eye) participate in the activity (*energeia*) of the Demiurge. They 'chant out the universe', participating in the demiurgy, the eternal play of procession and return that completes the All-plenitude, namely, Atum himself. As G. Shaw explains:

> In Platonic terms this meant taking an active part in the demi-urgy of the cosmos and becoming a co-creator with the god of creation. The power and authority of Egyptian rites derived from the cooperative mimesis: according to Iamblichus they embodied the eternal ratios (*metra aidia: De myster.* 65.6) which were the guiding powers of the cosmos.[84]

WHEN ORONTES FLOWED INTO TIBER: THE REVIVED TRADITION

All these theurgic techniques of recollection, reintegration, purifi-cation, ascent, assimilation, unification, and union are based on various metaphysical and cosmological teachings of the ancients. These archaic theological doctrines appear dressed in the mythical garb of those countless cosmogonies and sacred tales that empha-size the descent of the soul from its true noetic home and its subse-quent return (in the form of royal *anthropos teleios*, the re-collected and re-affirmed hypostasis of *Purusha*) to the divine Intellect or to the ineffable Abyss, the One which is Beyond-Being. Therefore the ritual practices and invocations, allegedly revealed by the gods themselves, are intended to effect the transformation of one's body and soul (to use these quite ambivalent and rather incorrect terms) by revealing the immanent presence of the divine powers that lead, ultimately, to the highest realization of the noetic unity and tran-scendent nonduality.

The Platonic-Chaldean (that is, the Hellenized Neo-Assyrian)

---

84. Gregory Shaw, *Theurgy and the Soul. The Neoplatonism of Iamblichus,* p.22.

system of theurgy in its Graeco-Roman and Middle-Platonic philosophical form appeared, presumably, only at the reign of Marcus
Aurelius. Likewise, the first Indian Tantric texts are currently being
dated to the third-sixth centuries. However, both the Platonic
theourgia and Hindu *tantra* represent merely the revival and reinterpretation of those ancient practices which already existed (in one
form or another) and were employed from pharaonic Egypt to
Mesopotamia and India. As T. McEvilley suggests:

> But it is not necessary to posit influence. It is possible that
> there were such deep inherent linkages between Greek and
> Indian thought from an early date that the two traditions went
> on producing like forms to the end of antiquity.... The sur-
> vival of this earlier (pre-Indo-European?) substrate in Greece
> as in India, and its revival under the impact of similarly
> ancient Near Eastern practices at the time when, as Juvenal
> said, 'Orontes flowed into Tiber', seems more than likely.

> [Theurgy] involves the devotional worship of a chosen deity
> which the worshiper is in a sense to become. In tantric practice
> also an *ishtadevata*, or personal deity, is the center of each wor-
> shipper's devotional practice. In both cases the goal is to incor-
> porate the personal deity, to become it in some sense.[85]

The Platonic philosophy itself is rooted in the ancient Egyptian
metaphysical and cultic patterns, partly veiled by a new type of dialectical reasoning which, nevertheless, tacitly imitates the hieratic
rites of Osiris' dismembering and restoration, dispersion and reintegration, aimed at the initiate's (the philosopher's) ascent and his
entry into the solar barque of Ra.

In is not necessary to think that 'Iamblichus revolutionized Neoplatonic methods of exegesis through his assimilation of Plato to
the Orphic/Chaldean traditions', as S. Rappe argues,[86] because this
assimilation (or affinity) has much deeper historical and metaphysical roots.

---

85. Thomas McEvilley, *The Shape of Ancient Thought: Comparative Studies in
Greek and Indian Philosophies,* New York: Allworth Press, 2002, pp. 591–592.

86. Sara Rappe, *Reading Neoplatonism,* p. 171.

3

SACRED IMAGES AND ANIMATED STATUES IN ANTIQUITY

His face was almost square, his divine model being that of Logios Hermes (*Hermou logiou tupos hieros*). As for his eyes, how can I describe the true charm of Aphrodite herself that resided in them, how can I express the very wisdom of Athena that was contained in them? . . . To put it simply, those eyes were the true *agalmata* of his soul, and not of the soul alone, but of the divine emanation (*theias aporroes*) dwelling in it.[1]

While Plotinus says that the gods are present to the complex of temples and statues, it is really they that are in the gods, i.e., the gods are their place. The divine is the place which contains both the art and ourselves, and our experience of the art is one in which the angle of vision and distance are measured from the divine and not ourselves.[2]

MYTH AND SYMBOL:
WHAT MAKES THE IMPOSSIBLE HAPPEN?

Olympiodorus, the sixth-century Alexandrian Neoplatonist, argues that since a myth is nothing other than an image of truth (*eikon estin aletheias*)—and the human soul itself is an image of the higher noetic realities—the surface meaning is only a screen for certain metaphysical teachings concealed in the depths of the myth. Hence, the invisible is to be inferred from the visible, the incorporeal from the bodily.[3]

1. Damascius describing Isidore's appearance, *Phil. Hist.* 13 Athanassiadi.
2. Frederic M. Schroeder, *The Vigil of the One and Plotinian Iconoclasm: Neoplatonism and Western Aesthetics*, ed. A. Alexandrakis, Albany: SUNY Press, 2002, p. 68
3. Olympiodorus, *Commentary on Plato's Gorgias*, tr. Robin Jackson, Kimon Lycos, and Harold Tarrant, Leiden: Brill, 1998, p. 290.

After all, a myth is ... a false *logos* imaging truth' (*allos te kai muthos ouden heteron estin e logos pseudes eikonizon aletheian: In Gorg.* 46.3).

All myths speak riddlingly of something else, conveying 'certain other things' in symbolic terms. In this respect the question may be raised, what does it mean means to speak symbolically? In the context of the Neoplatonic-Chaldean theurgy, the symbol (*sumbolon, sunthema*) is viewed as the central link between the divine realm and human world. As P. T. Struck remarks:

> The symbol makes the impossible happen; it becomes the node on which the transcendent can meet the mundane. . . . Symbols (in daytime) along with dreams (at night) are the means by which the gods communicate with humans . . . they do the impossible: they give voice to (*ekphoneitai*) things which cannot be voiced (*aphthegta, aporrheta, arrheta*); they represent that which is above representation and put that which is beyond reason into terms accessible to humans.[4]

The unspeakable symbols (*ta aporrheta sumbola*) are in a sense analogous to 'forms of the formless': they are demiurgic traces that constitute a sacred dimension of the material world. Every such trace (*ichnos*) is endowed with the capacity to point us back to the noetic realm and the One. Thus symbols possess in themselves a transformative and elevating (anagogic) power, and thereby connect us with the divine principles through invocation, interpretation, contemplation (*sumbolike theoria*), and theurgic union (*theourgike henosis*). F. Schuon says:

> What is the role of the Symbol in the economy of spiritual life? We have shown that the object of concentration is not necessarily an Idea, but that it can also be a symbolic sign, a sound, an image or an activity: the monosyllable *Om*, mystical diagrams—*mandalas*—and images of the Divinities are in their

---

4. Peter T. Struck, *Birth of the Symbol. Ancient Readers at the Limits of their Texts*, Princeton: Princeton University Press, 2004, pp. 213, 217, 219.

way vehicles of consciousness of the Absolute, without the intervention of a doctrinal element. . . .[5]

Olympiodorus thinks it is reasonable that the soul, itself being an image (*eikon*) of the noetic realities (*ta noeta*), enjoys myths as visible images (*eikones*) of the invisible. Consequently, the soul has a natural inclination for myths.[6] But Olympiodorus argues that if 'we were entirely without reason (*alogoi*) and lived in accordance with imagination (*kata phantasian*) and this was our only protection, it would be necessary for us to live all our life as if in a myth' (*edei hemas hapanta ton bion muthode echein: In Gorg. 46.6.28–29*).

Being firmly rooted in the Hellenic rationalism, Olympiodorus argues that usually 'we should not accept the mythical accounts', these 'Phoenician falshoods', but turn instead our attention to the demonstrative arguments ('entrapped in bonds of adamant') and the best constitution (*politeia: In Gorg. 44.7*). Olympiodorus is far from suspecting that even our life in accordance with intellect is a life 'as if in a myth'. The visible world itself is a sort of miraculous 'myth', produced by the Demiurge or the divine Word.

However, this all-embracing Myth is not a human invention, but the divine dream of existence *per se*, that is, of the entire manifested reality that appears to be the magic body of *pantheos*. A human body comes 'from the Isle of Fire' (from the noetic realm), but 'the time one spends on earth is but a dream' (Neferhotep's tomb, Theban tomb 50). The cosmos itself is a myth, the play of miraculous *heka* powers irradiating from the ineffable Silence of Heka, to say it in the Egyptian terms.

THE METAPHYSICS OF CREATION
AND ITS IMAGES IN PHARAONIC EGYPT

In *The Book of Knowing the Kheperu of Ra* (*Bremner-Rhind Papyrus*), Atum appears as the primeval noetic Monad, the lord of all

---

5. Frithjof Schuon, *The Eye of the Heart. Metaphysics, Cosmology, Spiritual Life*, Bloomington: World Wisdom Books, 1997, p. 141.

6. Jean Pepin, "Le plaisir du mythe (Damascius, In Phaedonem I. 525–526, II.129–30)".—*Neoplatonisme: Melanges offerts a Jean Trouillard. Les cahiers de Fontenay*, nos. 19, 20, 21, 22, Fontenay aux Roses, 1981, p. 276.

kheperu (manifestations, irradiations, levels). He emerges from the ineffable darkness of Nun and presents himself as a creator of every noetic reality by means of Heka, his own transcendent *dunamis*:

> It was alone that I knotted my hand, before they were born, without having spat out Shu, without having expectorated Tefnut. It was my own mouth that I made us of, and my name was Heka. . . .[7]

The Egyptian verb *kheper* (come into being, manifest, develop, change, evolve) and its derivative *kheperu* (manifestations, developments) refer to any stage in the cosmogonic and demiurgic process, designating various stages, modes, and series of manifestation. The universe as the self-disclosure of Atum is the *kheperu* of the primeval transcendent Principle and of its noetic plenitude. The main constituents of human microcosm (*ka, ba, akh, sah, ren,* and so on) are regarded as *kheperu*, the immanent developments and manifestations of Atum. At the level of *kosmos noetos*, the infinite range of all *kheperu* (of all existence) is summarized in the form of the divine Ennead. According to J. P. Allen:

> The concept of *hpr* implies an ending state different from that which existed before the process began. In Egyptian, this state is expressed by means of the locative preposition *m* 'in'.[8]

The wordplay *kheper, kheperu,* and *Kheprer* conveys the metaphysical exposition of the essential unity and reciprocity between the Creator (the divine Intellect, Atum-Ra) and his names, theophanies, projections, and irradiations. The underlying conception of unity and diversity is analogous to the Anaxagorean formula adapted by Proclus and other Neoplatonists to describe the domain of *Nous* and the Platonic Forms: 'everything is in everything but in a manner appropriate to each' (*panta en pasin, all 'oikeios en hekastoi*)

---

7. Francoise Dunand and Christiane Zivie-Coche, *Gods and Men in Egypt 3000 BCE to 395 CE,* tr. David Lorton, Ithaca and London: Cornell University Press, 2002, p.58 (Zivie-Coche translates Hekau instead of Heka).

8. James P. Allen, *Genesis in Egypt. The Philosophy of Ancient Egyptian Creation Accounts,* New Haven: Yale University, 1988, p. 29.

and 'everything is everywhere existing in proportion' (*panta panta-chou ana logon esti*). As L. Siorvanes observes:

> everything that exists in some definable way is in every thing, in the epistemological and metaphysical sense. Although everything is 'in' everything, they are so in the manner distinctive to their household (*oikeios*): their level of consciousness and being.[9]

The creation itself signifies a transition from the hidden state into the intelligible visibility, and then from the intelligible invisibility (since the divine things, though being the brightest in their own activity, 'are invisible to us creatures of the night': Olympiodorus *In Gorg.* 30.3) to the sensible visibility. Therefore this revelatory cosmogony is effected through invocation, that is, through the uttering of names that constitute the single Holy Name at the level of Heka— the Word (Hu) in Atum's mouth. Atum, the intelligible plenitude concealed within the initial 'nothingness' and appearing in the form of the Scarab (Kheprer, Khopri, Khepera) says:

> When I came into being, Being came into being, Being came into being. I came into being in the form of Khopri who came into being on the First Occasion. . . . I came into being in the form of Khopri when I came into being, and that is how Being came into being. . . . (*Pap.Bremner-Rhind*).[10]

J.A. Allen provides different translation of the same passage:

> For my part, the fact is that I developed as Developer. When I developed, development developed. All development developed

---

9. Lucas Siorvanes, *Proclus. Neo-Platonic Philosophy and Science*, Edinburgh: Edinburgh University Press, 1996, p. 54.

10. R. Faulkner, "Translation of Papyrus Bremner-Rhind".—*JEA*, 24, 1938, p. 41ff. The transliteration of the Egyptian text is as follows: *nuk pu kheper em Khepera kheper-na kheper kheperu kheper kheperu neb em-khut kheper-a asht kheperu em per em re-a* (E. A. Wallis Budge *The Gods of the Egyptians or Studies in Egyptian Mythology*, vol. I, New York: Dover Publications, 1969 (first ed. 1904), pp. 308–309). Wallis Budge translates this passage as follows: 'I am he who came into being in the form of Khepera, I was (or, became) the creator of what came into being, the creator of what came into all being; after my coming into being many [were] the things which came into being coming forth from my mouth'.

after I developed, developments becoming many in emerging from my mouth.[11]

The *pleroma* which is hidden (*amun*) contains all components of the noetic heliophanies that are to appear in the form of the divine cultic body (the articulated cosmic body, *ta panta*), comparable to the hieratic statue. The universe is a display of the hieroglyphic script—the Platonic Forms made visible. And the shapes of cult statues in the Egyptian temples also imitate various hieroglyphs, that is, the divine words (*medu neter*) crystallized and revealed from the hidden (*sheta*) state.

In the Ramesside theology, God is conceived as a trinity: 'His Name is hidden as Amun, He is Ra in countenance, His body is Ptah' (*Pap. Leiden.* 1.350, IV.21–22). Ptah stands for the world as a cult statue, or as the entire cultic dimension of the divine realm through which the *ba*, the hidden power of God, can be experienced and conceived of in the plenitude of bodies, images, and symbols (like the Neoplatonic *sunthemata*). All these symbols of *deus ineffabilis* (the hidden Amun who surpasses all human and divine knowledge, but 'whose body is the millions') affirm that 'All is One' (*hen to pan*):

> The classical concept of the 'all' and the 'whole', *to pan, ta panta, omnia,* appears in Egyptian as 'millions'. It is not, however, connected with the concept of an all-embracing but closed totality, but rather with one of an endless, uncontainable plenitude. In Egyptian, 'millions' also means 'endless'... the plenitude of living beings that incessantly stream from the god's transcendent unity....[12]

The cosmic hierarchy of being is constituted by *neteru* (gods, divine names, powers): it consists of living gods whose *bau* appear as the cosmic phenomena. This cosmic dimension of divine presence, initiated by the Amunian metaphysics and its solar (noetic)

---

11. James P. Allen, ibid., p. 28.
12. Jann Assmann, *The Search for God in Ancient Egypt*, tr. David Lorton, Ithaca and London: Cornell University Press, 2001, p. 240.

discourse and maintained by the hieratic rites, is what made the manifested totality of *kheperu* intelligible and readable, or rather 'recitable'. In the Egyptian solar theology, language assumes the highly important role of symbolic mediation, though the true, secret names of the gods are never divulged. In spite of the permanent divine presence, the transcendent gods themselves and the cosmic or cultic domain, which symbolically represents and embodies them, are never entirely identical. However, R. B. Finnestad says:

> The image of the cosmos-constituting gods formulates the theogenetic implication of the cosmogony from a henotheistic point of view.... The creator and the gods arise together, constituting an entity: the cosmos. Again, it should be noted that cosmos is not conceived as a material body enlivened by a spiritual soul of god. The body consists of living gods... There is nothing in man's world that is not a form of god; there exists no 'mere' material. In the presentation of this cosmos there is an accent on the divine side of life: it all starts with god.... *Being* is subordinated to *divine being*.[13]

According to the Heliopolitan myth, humankind (*remeti*) was born from Atum's tears when he cried (*remi*). Therefore man is either Atum's image, 'issued from his body', or is made in Atum's image (*tut*) in the same way as a divine statue is made. To put it otherwise, human beings are modelled by Khnum on his wheel, using silt drawn from Nun and breathing the breath of life (*ankh*) into them, that is, animating them in the same way as statues are animated. At first, gods and men inhabited the same noetic cosmos, but under present conditions the gods are remote and manifest themselves only through the sacred images and symbols:

> The present state (in both senses of the word) is both the healing of a breach and a compensation for a loss, the loss of corporeal closeness to the gods. Real presence is replaced by

---

13. Ragnhild Bjerre Finnestad, *Image of the World and Symbol of the Creator. On the Cosmological and Iconological Values of the Temple of Edfu*, Wiesbaden: Otto Harrassowitz, 1985, p. 119 and p. 145.

representation. By virtue of their symbolic power, state and cult, temples, rites, statues, and images make present the divine and establish an irremediably indirect contact with the gods. . . . [D]ivine presence now depends upon the culturally formed possibilities of symbolic mediation and representation. The state is the institution of this closeness. The pharaoh rules as the representative of the creator god.[14]

In Egypt, a difference is made between the *rekhyet*-people, depicted as migratory birds, partly theriomorphic, partly anthropomorphic, and the *pa'et*-people, those who belong to the esoteric circle of royal initiates (or officials, whose status is thought as ontologically determined). Only the consecrated pharaoh, as *anthropos teleios* (*al-insan al-kamil* of the Sufis), both the chief mystagogue and the exemplary initiate, is an integral *imago dei* (that to some degree covers the entire state and its landscape), or the restored Eye of Horus in its true sense. Therefore the horns of the ram (*ba*) symbolizes pharaoh's sonship to Amun-Ra (the Neoplatonic *Nous*) and his union, through his royal *ka*, with the Demiurge. Only to the king (as an actualized *tut* of God) and to the righteous is granted the theurgic mimesis of the solar course, only they join the Ennead in the Place of Truth, thereby returning to the all-encompassing One. As it is related in a New Kingdom recitation which ultimately goes back to the *Pyramid Texts* (222):

May you be born like Ra
And carried in pregnancy like Thoth.
Purify yourself for yourself in the western nome,

Receive your purification in the Heliopolitan nome with Atum.
Come into being for yourself, come on high for yourself,
May it be well with you, may it be pure for you
In the embrace of your father Ra-Atum.
O Atum, take him

14. Jan Assmann, *The Mind of Egypt. History and Meaning in the Time of the Pharaohs*, New York: Metropolitan Books, 2002, p. 187.

In your embrace, together with your *ka*.
He is the son of your body, forever (*Tomb of Senenmut*).[15]

THEOGONIC APPEARANCES AND ANIMATED STONES

The Platonists faithfully followed the doctrine established in Plato's *Timaeus*, namely, that the cosmos, patterned on the eternal Living Being (or the plenitude of the noetic Forms, the Ennead of Heliopolis), itself is alive, like 'a statue (*agalma*) brought into being for the everlasting gods' (*Tim.* 37c). Hence, the Demiurge may be compared to the telestic priest who creates and consecrates the cosmos as a sacred statue. In a sense, the Creator (*Nous*), as the first Speaker, contains the archetypal realities that emanate (or are revealed and transmitted from the hidden state to the state of cultic theophany) like 'sounding statues' (*phoneenta agalmata*) of the noetic Forms.

The utterance of the Name is equivalent to a theogonic appearance, the construction of the cosmic Shrine in which the countless *agalmata* are revealed through the divine rites of demiurgy. So even if God is He-who-hides-His-Name (*amun-renf*), His face (*hra*) comes into light through the solar *sunthema* (the visible Sun disk) and through the cult statue. Therefore the revelation of the statue has a metaphysical and cosmological meaning which goes beyond the dwelling imagery of the temple: the revelation of the face of God (*un-hra hra neter*) is a cultic epiphany paralleling the cosmic theophany, according to R. B. Finnestad:

> The candle contains perfume emitted while it burns, signalizing the presence of the god. When the dark room is illuminated by the candlelight, this means that the god of Edfu has appeared—both as creator and as created: he is the revealing light, and he is the god of the statue upon which his light falls: he is himself the creator of his Horus-form. . . . Another ritual expression of the theogonic aspect of the theophany is the embracing of the statue performed by the priest who, by this act, transfer the *ka*-life to the god. The mythical image behind

15. Jan Assmann, *Death and Salvation in Ancient Egypt*, tr. David Lorton, Ithaca and London: Cornell University Press, 2005, p. 322.

this rite is that of the creator who creates the gods by embracing them and thereby transferring to them capacity to live. The priest plays the role of the theogon.[16]

In the context of Hellenic cultic practice, partly borrowed from Egypt, Mesopotamia, Phoenicia, and Anatolia, the statue (*agalma*) is regarded as a vessel and container for the divine powers that take up residence inside it. The awakening of these powers is sometimes achieved by the practice of putting *pharmaka* (remedies, drugs, herbs, magical means of power, charms, enchantments, symbols) into hollow statues and thereby animating them. This act is conducted by the telestic 'craftsman' (*demiourgos*). The physician is also designated as *demiourgos*, because

early Greek medicine and pharmacy combine theurgy (in its widest sense of supernatural or divine agencies in both diseases and their treatments) with the practical application of drugs, foreshadowing later abstractions so common in medico-philosophical thought in later Greek medicine. Theurgy remained fundamental throughout Greek history even after the accession of Christianity, and theurgy continued to exist side by side with other 'medical intervention' systems.[17]

'Animation' in its root sense implies putting *anima* (Greek *psuche*, Egyptian *ba* or *ka*) into something. Consequently, 'animation' of images and temples consists in the rite of installation and consecration, for which the terms *hidruo, anatithemi, hieroö*, and *teleo* are used, though the Hellenic sources do not reveal details of these rituals.[18] Thereby images are turned into the living *telesmata* (consecrated hieratic objects, talismans) and *agalmata* of the gods.

As the Indian *shaiva* priest would say, only when Shiva's image is fully transformed into a state of *shivata* (Shiva-ness), may the appropriate *puja* (the external ritual worship) to the image be

16. Ragnhild Bjerre Finnestad, ibid., p. 97 and pp. 100–101.
17. John Scarborough, "The Pharmacology of Sacred Plants, Herbs, and Roots".—*Magika Hiera: Ancient Greek Magic and Religion*, ed. Christopher A. Faraone, Dirk Obbink, Oxford: Oxford University Press, 1991, p. 142.
18. Deborah Tarn Steiner, *Images in Mind: Statues in Archaic and Classical Greek Literature and Thought*, Princeton and Oxford: Princeton Univ. Press, 2001, p. 115.

performed. The animated image aids one's anagogic ritual life (in spite of the fact that all human actions are considered to be forms of ritual) and helps one to attain liberation through union with a chosen deity (*ishta-devata*). 'As he is worshiped, so he becomes', according to the *Mudgala Upanishad* (3.3), because man becomes what he worships. Those who worship gods (both externally and internally, by purifications, consecrations of the different parts of their bodies to the deities with the help of seed-*mantras*, by breath control and contemplation, *dhyana*) become gods (*Bhagavadgita* 9.25).

The Greek word *telesma* derives from the verb *telein* (to initiate, to consecrate, to complete, as the Eye of Horus is made complete and alive). The practice of putting *pharmaka* and *sunthemata* (theurgic tokens) inside the statues is linked with the Chaldean talismanic lore, that is, with the Assyrian and Babylonian *hierourgia*. The animated *lamassu* and *shedu* figures, or those designated as *kuribu* (the ultimate prototype of Jewish cherubim, *al-karrubiyyun* in Arabic) and standing at the threshold of the Assyrian royal palace, are both the guardian angels of the king and external prolongations of his vital 'soul' (in the Egyptian sense of *ka*) or of his 'breaths', which are identical to the luminous and terrifying substance of the divine 'kingship'.

The Syrian and Phoenician beatyls (*baituloi*) are aniconic 'images' (not *eikones*, strictly speaking, but rather cultic instruments and vehicles of theophanies) of the same order as the Greek *xoana*—archaic cult images, carved from wood) and *daidala* (miraculous products of Daidalos, the Greek equivalent of Khotarwa-Hasis, the Ugaritic craftsman-god). Pausanias describes the curious ritual whereby trees are selected to provide wood for statues, a ritual related to the cosmological image of birds (descending souls or divine epiphanies) sitting on sacred trees:

> Wherever [the birds] may alight, cutting that tree they make the *daidalon* from it and they call by 'daidalon' the statue (*xoanon*) itself.[19]

---

19. Cited in Sarah P. Morris, *Daidalos and the Origins of Greek Art*, Princeton: Princeton University Press, 1992, p. 56.

The Near Eastern baetyls, however, are even more supernatural and miraculous habitations for divine powers. The term 'baetyl' itself derives from the Greek *baitulia*, and these baetyls are connected with Apollo, himself depicted as a bird, like the Horus-Falcon. *Beth-el* in Semitic languages means 'dwelling of the god', and this designation reminds us that the name of the golden Hathor means 'the dwelling of Horus', though the Phoenician-Aramaic god Bethel is more directly connected with the oaths and treaties of kings written on standing stones and commemorative stelae. Philo of Byblos, the second century writer, 'explains that *baitulia* were invented by the god Ouranos when he managed to create *lithoi empsuchoi*, animated stones, which fell from heaven and possessed magical power.'[20]

Damascius, the Neoplatonic philosopher from Damascus, describes the baetyl moving in air (*ton baitulon dia tou aeros kinoumenon*: *Phil. Hist.* 138). The guardian of this baetyl was certain Eusebius who met it while wandering away from the Syrian town Emesa, inspired by mysterious intuition, in the middle of the night, close to the mountain on which the ancient temple of Athena stood:

He then suddenly saw a ball of fire (*sphairan de puros*) leaping down from above and a huge lion standing beside it, which instantly vanished. He ran up to the ball as the fire was dying down and understood that this was indeed the baetyl; picking it up, he asked it which god possessed it, and the baetyl answered that it belonged to Gennaios (the Heliopolitans honour Gennaios in the temple of Zeus in the shape of a lion). . . . Eusebius was not the master of the baetyl's movement, as is the case with others, but he begged and prayed and the baetyl listened to his incantations (*Phil. Hist.* 138).[21]

The moving baetyls may be regarded as the aetherical weapons of

20. Robert Wenning, "The Betyls of Petra".—*Bulletin of the American Schools of Oriental Research*, no. 324, 2001, p. 80.
21. Damascius, *The Philosophical History*, text with translation and notes by Polymnia Athanassiadi, Athens: Apameia, 1999, p.309. The Syrian Heliopolis is Baalbek in modern Lebanon.

Zeus used in his struggle against Kronos (in the Phoenician cosmology, Hellenized by Philo of Byblos), perhaps equivalent to the fiery
thunderbolts of the Chaldean Paternal Intellect. In this respect, the
Implacable Thunders (*ameiliktoi te keraunoi: Chald.Or.* fr.35) are the
Thoughts of the Father, the multiformed Platonic Ideas that leap
forth from one Source like bees and are divided by the noeric Fire.
As we have seen, these Paternal Thoughts are called Iynges, the
demiurgic and theurgic 'wheels'. It is remarkable that the *iunx* (literally, the wryneck bird, but esoterically a sort of *yantra*) was brought
for the first time to humankind by Aphrodite, according to Pindar
(*Pyth.* 4.217–219). And Aphrodite, in this particular context, is an
exact Graeco-Phoenician equivalent of the Mesopotamian goddess
Ishtar and of the Egyptian Hathor. Therefore the Iynges (when
equated with the theurgic *sunthemata*: ineffable names and secret
mantras) function as fiery 'birds' mediating between the noetic and
sensible realms.

The divine presence may be symbolized or revealed by any thing
(or by any *kheperu*), since this presence can be perceived in all
things. For those capable of such vision, all physical, psychic, and
intellective functions themselves become a ritual that repeats the
all-embracing cosmic rites of the Demiurge and his blessed choir.
For the members of ancient Israelite cultic confederation (Yahweh's
warriors) and other *habiru*, who tacitly imitated but openly hated
Egyptian practices, the divine presence was adequately symbolized
by the cloud, the ark and certain cult-objects.[22]

But the sacred stone (like the *ben-ben* Stone in the Egyptian
Heliopolitan temple, representing the immortal *mundus intelligibilis*, the noetic 'house' of Atum-Ra) is the ultimate archaic prototype
of articulated anthropomorphic statues made of stone. In the Stone
Age metaphysics, if such expression is permissible, the stone stands
for the perfect noetic substance which is re-collected and re-actualized as *imago dei* in the stone-like 'perfect man', *anthropos teleios*.
Just as the stone may be regarded as *theos* (god in the sense of fiery

---

22. William W. Hallo, "Cult Statue and Divine Image: A Preliminary Study".—
Scripture in Context II. More Essays on the Comparative Method, ed. William W.
Hallo et alii, Winona Lake, Indiana: Eisenbrauns, 1983, p. 2.

'name' or intelligible principle), so the animated statue of a god is *theos*. Therefore Ch. A. Faraone argues that

> the Greeks did not clearly distinguish between the image and the thing represented.[23]

This distinction is required in a discursive theory, but it is less important in immediate devotional practice and in the esoteric rites of unification with a deity (like the Tantric *ishta-devata*) where an image, contemplated 'face to face', functions as a sort of theurgic *yantra* that reveals the supreme metaphysical identity (*tad ekam*) without duality (*advaita*): everything is the One who makes himself many. This realization of Brahman is regarded by A. K. Coomaraswamy as an ineffable initiation which transcends the distinction between utterance and silence:

> The secret of initiation remains inviolable by its very nature; it cannot be betrayed because it cannot be expressed—it is inexplicable (*aniruktam*), but the inexplicable is everything, at the same time all that can and all that cannot be expressed.[24]

THE THEOLOGY OF IMAGES
AND ITS ESOTERIC DIMENSION

The Hellenic worshipers of images (*eikones*), though hated and assaulted by the Christian and Jewish zealots, were perfectly aware that images of the gods are merely receptacles and symbols, not divine realities *per se*. These images are not altogether adequate representations of the gods, but the anagogic instruments that help in one's devotional, intellectual, and imaginative ascent or function as 'windows of transcendence' irradiating divine powers and graces.

Following the Egyptian cult practices, certain *xoana* were regularly carried in processions beyond the confines of the temple for

---

23. Christopher A. Faraone, *Talismans and Trojan Horses. Guardian Statues in Ancient Greek Myth and Ritual*, Oxford: Oxford University Press: 1992, p. 10.

24. Ananda K. Coomaraswamy, "The Vedic Doctrine of 'Silence'".—2: *Selected Papers. Metaphysics*, ed. Roger Lipsey, Princeton: Princeton University Press, 1987, p. 202.

the benefit of the whole environment. Likewise, Amun-Ra opens up the world: every road is filled with his light and every face lives on the sight of his beauty. The processions of his barque are regarded as real epiphanies that repeat the cosmogonic course. Normally, the statue is hidden in the dark *mesen*-chapel, and the shrine containing the statue of a deity is called *sheta* (mysterious, hidden)—for example, 'his hidden and grand *naos* of black stone.'[25] So even the opening of the temple doors is a ritual event initiating the grace-bringing divine epiphany.

The honour given to the image is transmitted to its noetic archetype, therefore the Hellenic practice of setting up images in human form is based on the premise 'that because man is godlike in his virtue and intelligence, his outward form is the best possible symbol of divinity.'[26] Olympiodorus defends the use of sacred images following the established tradition of argumentation, at first employed by Platonists themselves against the Stoic pantheists (those who rejected the cult images by saying that God is the living intelligent universe) and later borrowed by the Christian Iconodules in their apologetic defense against the Jews and the Byzantine Iconoclasts. Olympiodorus says:

> And do not think that philosophers honour representations (*ta eidola*) in stone as divine (*hos theia*). It is because we live in the sensory world, and are not able to reach up to the bodiless and immaterial power, that we devise representations as a reminder of those things, so that by seeing and respecting them we might arrive at a notion of those bodiless and immaterial powers (*In Gorg.* 47.5).

In the context of Neoplatonic-Chaldean theurgy, this theology of images acquires an esoteric dimension, because the initiate's soul (or rather its hidden *sunthema*) is awakened by means of the telestic work (*dia ton telestikon ergon*) that consists in combination of ritual activity and sacred word (*hiero logo ergon henosas: Chald.Or.* fr.110).

25. Ragnhild Bjerre Finnestad, ibid., p. 105.
26. A.H. Armstrong, "Some Comments on the Development of the Theology of Images".—*Studia Patristica*, vol. IX Berlin: Akademie-Verlag, 1966, p. 122.

The awakened soul is raised up by the seven rays (or seven vowels) of the solar Intellect to the Chaldean Paradise (*Paradeisos Chaldaikos*, as Psellus designated it: *Expositio in oracula chaldaica, P.G.* 122.1137d 5–8). This Paradise is described as the Court Open to All (*pandektike aule*), that is, the paternal order of the Father containing all the souls which have returned to the noetic realm. According to R. Majercik's remark:

> it is the 'meadow' (*leimona*) of the Father where Synesius yearns to go in order to join the 'kingly choir' (*sun anakti choro*) in 'intellectual hymns' (*noerous humnous*). . . . In light of this evidence, it is probable that the Chaldean 'paradise' was understood in Psellus' sense; i.e., as a 'choir of divine powers' which praise the Father with hymns.[27]

PRIVILEGED HABITATIONS FOR THE IMMORTAL GODS

According to Proclus, 'philosophizing about being in the manner of geometry', one has not only ideas but pictures, and these pictures might be regarded as figures (*schemata*) pertaining to all levels of manifested reality. The perfect, uniform, and ineffable figures of the gods transcend even the intelligible figures that shine everywhere with indivisible and noetic light. The ineffable divine figures impose limits upon the whole ontological hierarchy of figures. Their symbolic images are employed in the telestic operations which constitute the contemplative and sacramental path to the One. Proclus says:

> Their properties have been represented for us by the theurgic art in its statues of the gods, whom it clothes in the most varied figures. Some of them it portrays by means of mystic signs that express the unknowable divine potencies; others it represents through forms and shapes, making some standing, others sitting, some heart-shaped, some spherical, and some fashioned still otherwise; some simple, others composed of several

27. Ruth Majercik, *The Chaldean Oracles*, text, translation, and commentary by Ruth Majercik, Leiden: E. J. Brill, 1989, p. 203.

shapes; some stern, others mild and expressing the benignity of the gods; and others still fearful in shape (*In Euclid.* 138).[28]

These figures may be understood in relation to the Procline conception of the Platonic Forms: the One is analogous to the Sun, and the Forms, to its rays. The irradiating and descending Forms appear as the inferior limit of *ta noeta*, the intelligibles. Therefore each primary noetic Form is 'one', 'being', and a 'whole', and 'as such can be identically present to many different things at the same time, but transcendently; so that a Form is both everywhere and nowhere, and being present to all its instances in a non-temporal fashion is unmixed with them' (*In Parm.* 861).[29]

However, though the sensible things simultaneously partake of noeric Forms as immanently present in them, being their images in a sense—that is, resembling these archetypal Forms—one may speak of three modes of participation. Accordingly, things are likenesses of the intellective Forms, reflections of the soul-forms, and imprints or impressions of the physical forms:

> The animated statue, for example, participates by way of impression in the art which turns it on a lathe or polishes and shapes it in such and such a fashion; while from the universe it has received reflections of vitality which even cause us to say that it is alive; and as a whole it has been made like the god whose image it is. For a theurgist who sets up a statue as a likeness of a certain divine order fabricates the tokens of its identity with reference to that order, acting as does the craftsman when he makes a likeness by looking to its proper model (*In Parm.* 847).[30]

Just as the statue contains within it the divine powers that make accessible the immortal presence of the gods without directly reproducing them, so the human body functions as a vessel equipped

28. Proclus, *A Commentary on the First Book of Euclid's Elements*, tr. Glen R.Morrow, Princeton: Princeton University Press, 1992, pp. 110–111.

29. Proclus' *Commentary on Plato's Parmenides*, tr. Gleen R. Morrow and John M. Dillon, Princeton: Princeton University Press, 1992, p. 228.

30. Ibid., pp. 217–218.

with external surfaces. This 'corpse' (*soma*), being a firm enclosure (*peribolos*) that keeps the soul within its limits,[31] conceals the hidden divine spark that needs to be recollected, rekindled, and revealed. To say it in Orphico-Platonic terms, the body is a tomb (*sema*) of the soul and its immortal or divine part in us.

When the world's shape is regarded as a cosmic body, this body may be imagined as a skull deprived of the remaining bodily parts. It resembles a human head (or rather, the human skull resembles the universe which is an *agalma* created by the Demiurge), being the living creature (*zoön*) whose structure is isomorphic to the human structure. Therefore R. Brague argues:

> What is to be read in the *Laws* is still more likely to be present in the *Timaeus*: if the soul, and first of all the world soul, is constructed out of some numerical ratios, the same must be true for the body that houses the soul.... Moreover, we are justified in believing that Plato conceived of the possibility of a precise and numerical determination of this beauty. We may elicit this assertion from a passage in the *Laws* in which the proportions of the body that define the animals reproduced by painting or sculpture are called 'numbers' (*arithmoi*).[32]

Both the cult statue and the human body may be regarded as privileged habitations for the god (or the immortal *nous*). Therefore, just as the priest fills the interior of an *agalma* with *sumbola*, *sunthemata*, and *pharmaka*, while uttering verbal formulas and thereby animating the statue (making it *empnoös*), so the spiritual path of inner transformation, followed by the initiate, results in the awakening of those *sunthemata* which the Demiurge concealed within his soul and body. These secret symbols are to be re-awakened in the process of one's spiritual homecoming which opens the

31. C. J. de Vogel, "The Soma-Sema Formula: Its Function in Plato and Plotinus Compared to Christian Writers".—*Neoplatonism and Early Christian Thought: Essays in honour of A. H. Armstrong*, ed. H. J. Blumenthal and R. A. Marcus, London: Variorum, 1981, p. 80.

32. Remi Brague, *The Body of the Speech*: "A New Hypothesis on the Compositional Structure of Timaeus' Monologue".—*Platonic Investigations*, ed. Dominic J. O'Meara, Washington, D.C.: The Catholic University of America Press, 1985, p. 64.

immortal depth of the soul (*psuches bathos ambroton*). Through the perfect anagogic life (*dia tes anagogou zoes*) one is led to the union with the gods and the One. According to the *Chaldean Oracles*: 'Those who, by inhaling [the rays of the Father], drive out the soul, are free' (fr.124). Hence, the theurgist should not reject matter, but only that which is alien to the gods, because even stones, plants, and aromatic substances may be sacred, perfect, and godlike (*hiera kai telea kai theoeide*), according to Iamblichus. They are used

> as being capable of harmonizing with the construction of dwellings for the gods, the consecration of statues (*kai kathidruseis agalmaton*), and indeed for the performance of sacred rites (*tas ton thusioon hierougias*) in general. For there is no other way in which the terrestrial realm or the men who dwell here could enjoy participation in the existence that is the lot of the higher beings, if some such foundation be not laid down in advance (*De myster.* 234.2–6).[33]

In the same way, a crudely fashioned Silenus *eikon* reveals the golden *agalmata* concealed within the satyr-like shape of Socrates: his outer appearance (*schema*) is like a curtain behind which the divine essence (or the golden Osirian *eidos*) is hidden (Plato *Symp.* 216c). As D. T. Steiner relates:

> Just as the loftiest gods concealed themselves within statue-vessels that can be crude and uncouth, so, too, Socrates has taken on an external, fashioned covering that radically belies the nature of the inner person, that warns against assuming homology between visible appearance and the reality within. . . .[34]

BEHOLDING THE INEFFABLE BEAUTIES

Iamblichus, however, insists that whether we are talking of cosmic regions, cities consecrated to various gods, or of sacred statues (*hiera agalmata*), 'divinity illuminates everything from without (*exothen epilampei*), even as the sun lights everything from without

---

33. Iamblichus, *De mysteriis/On the Mysteries*, tr. Emma C. Clarke, John M. Dillon, and Jackson P. Hershbell, Atlanta: Society of Biblical Literature, 2003, p. 269.
34. Deborah Tarn Steiner, ibid., p. 89.

with its rays' (*De myster.* 30.13–14). In this context, 'from without' means 'from the transcendent dimension', therefore one equally may interpret it as meaning 'from within'—not from within the mortal domain of psychic residues (a sort of Jungian unconscious), but as if from 'nowhere'. This is so, because 'the light of the gods illuminates its subject transcendently (*choristos*)', and this single, indivisible light 'is one and the same in its entirety everywhere' (*De myster.* 31.10–11).

The practice of beholding the visible images of the gods and uttering the sacred names of the gods (or other types of *sunthemata*) has the power to raise us up to the gods and unite us with them. Thus the completely incorporeal gods are united to the visible gods who have bodies and whom the initiate contemplates, in an attempt to become assimilated to their essence by virtue of sacred liturgy (*dia tes hieras hagisteias*), consecration, and 'annihilation' of his mortal Titanic nature.

This theurgic rite implies the realization of human nothingness (*oudeneia*), because only the divine may be united with the divine. In this case, then, 'the divine is literally united with itself' (*auto to theion pros heauto sunesti: De myster.* 47.6–7). The noetic gods, by reason of their infinite unity (*dia ten apeiron auton henosin:* ibid., 60.9-10), embrace within themselves the visible gods who reside, in reality, outside their bodies, being rooted essentially in the noetic domain already. To be united with the divinity housed inside the statue is to be mounted on the divine falcon which would carry you (not as a mortal individuality or human *eidolon,* but in the form of the immortal light, as the divine falcon himself) to the land of *lux intelligibilis.*

Isidorus, the master of Damascius, however, maintained that 'the truly sacred truth . . . lies hidden in the depths.' For this reason, he did not like 'to worship the statues of the gods, but he was fast moving towards the gods themselves, not in sanctuaries but in the very mystery (*en auto to aporrheto*)—whatever this may be—of the completely unknowable' (Damascius *Phil. Hist.* 36a).

In spite of all sophisticated techniques of the Neoplatonic-Chaldean theurgic activities (*theurgika energemata*), neither the contemplation of images and epiphanies, nor invocations and liturgies, could be properly understood without the sacred dimension of beauty. For Plotinus already, the degree of participation in being directly corresponds to the degree of participation in beauty. And the *Chaldean Oracles* maintain that the theurgic *sumbola*, which the Paternal Intellect, Craftsman of the Fiery Universe (*kosmou technites puriou*), has sown throughout the cosmos, are called 'ineffable beauties' (*kalle aphrasta*: fr. 108). The Holy Name (*onoma semnon*) that leaps into the cosmoi with eternal circular motion (fr. 87) must be beautiful and carry beauty by its sounding rays.

Since the theurgist who invokes the god to appear in the form of a visionary self-manifested 'statue' (*autopton agalma*) is designated as 'caller' (*kletor*), Proclus relates the word 'beauty' (*kalon*) to the verb meaning 'to call' (*kalein*). According to W. Beierwaltes:

The beautiful itself contains an uplifting power and thereby becomes the moving force for the conversion and return through eros. Echoing Plato, Proclus derives the word *kalon* from *kalein* or *kelein*, 'to call', and from the word draws conclusions about the object. Accordingly, the effect of the beautiful is to 'call' to itself what exists and thinks', to 'captivate', and to 'enchant' (*In Alc.* 328.12ff). At the same time, what 'calls' and 'enchants' distances thought from the beautiful appearance by becoming a 'mean' that conveys or reduces the manifestation of the beautiful to its being and essence.[35]

For Proclus, Beauty itself is a life-possessing noetic Form of which each beautiful thing partakes: though intelligence is not present to everything that is beautiful, but only to ensouled things, the light of beauty is present even in stones (*In Parm.* 859). This manifested beauty is like an epiphanic beauty of the goddess Hathor (the golden house of Horus-Falcon), known as the Eye of Ra, or the whole (*uedjat*) Eye. She is the instrument of divine energy and the power (*sekhem*) of Ra, projected out into the world which is both created, animated, and illuminated by the intelligible beauty of the divine Face.

35. Werner Beierwaltes, "The Love of Beauty and the Love of God".—*Classical Mediterranean Spirituality: Egyptian, Greek, Roman*, ed. H.A. Armstrong, London: Routledge and Kegan Paul, 1986, p.307.

DIVINE BODIES AND REPRESENTATIONS
IN INDIAN TANTRISM

The Indian Tantric practices that represent the prolongation and development of the archaic spiritualities (or the so-called Bronze Age metaphysics of the post-Middle Kingdom Egypt, of Akkadian Mesopotamia and Central Asia, including Punjab) may shed more light into the purely documented areas of Neoplatonic-Chaldean theurgy. For example, the Pythagorean equation of *agalma* (statue, image) with *onoma* (name) appears to be analogous to the *rupa* (form, shape) and *nama* (name) relationship in Indian thought.

Name and form are the two fundamental aspects of divine manifestation, since the primordial unity is differentiated by name and form. Therefore 'everything has a name and a form' (*Brihadaranyaka Upanishad* 1.4.7). A. K. Coomaraswamy regards *nama* as an equivalent of the Idea, the Platonic Form, and *rupa* as an image, be it the inwardly known form (*jnana-sattva-rupa*) or the external shape, like a *pratima* (anthropomorphic icon).

Like the Greek *agalma, pratima* represents the formless (*arupa*) deity and is 'of the same kind as a *yantra*, that is, a geometrical representation of a deity, or a *mantra*, that is, an auditory representation of a deity.'[36] The Tantric universe is constituted by the basic divine powers, or theophanies, themselves regarded as deities (*devata*) that can be approached and perceived through words, images, and symbols. The representations of deities through *mantras* (thought-forms, vocal *sunthemata* of the Chaldean theology) and *yantras* (anagogic diagrams, instruments of contemplation and unification) are viewed as more accurate than those executed in the anthropomorphic fashion. As A. Danielou remarks:

> *Mantras* and *yantras* are therefore the abstract symbols, *mudra* (gesture) and *svara* (musical notes) are the subtle representations, and image and myth are the gross representations of the principles known as deities.[37]

36. Ananda K. Coomaraswamy, *The Transformation of Nature in Art*, New York: Dover Publications, 1956, p. 28.
37. Alain Danielou, *The Myths and Gods of India*, Rochester: Inner Traditions, 1991, p. 333.

However, the Indian cult statue (though inwardly conceived as a metaphysical formula) is a full-bodied representation (*murti*) of the god that is made for worship and adoration so that the worshiper may concentrate on the deity in its concrete visible or epiphanic form. At first, the worshiper contemplates the divine attributes manifested in their dispositional forms (*bhava-rupa*), in *asanas* (fixed and semiotically meaningful 'hieroglyphic' postures), in *mudras*, visible shapes, and symbols of the deity within the boundaries of the *yantra* or the cult statue. Then he mediates all these attributes as situated in the various *cakras* (wheels, formally analogous to the Chaldean *iunges*) of his own recollected and reintegrated body, like the tokens (*sunthemata*) of the Mediterranean hierurgy (*hierourgia*). These *sunthemata* need to be reawakened and reactivated (to be rotated by the erotic *shakti* like the wheels of Ishtar's or Hekate's elevating energy) in order to accomplish the theurgic *energemata*.

This is achieved partly by invocation and partly by visualization (which accompanies, to certain degree, the noetic concentration), since the power of the *yantra* resides in the *mantra*, regarded as the very body of the deity. The deity presents itself in contemplation together with the special *mantra*, the vocal-image of the particular noetic principle.

The statues and figural compositions (*pratimas*) are based on underlying but hidden *yantras* (like the *schemata* of Egyptian hieroglyphs, viewed as 'divine speech', *medu neter*). Therefore the *Vastu-Sutra-Upanishad* argues that the principles of sacred geometry (as a means of theurgy and anagogic life) are indispensable for any sculptor who tries through his symbolic construct (*pratika*) to show immaterial (*amurta*) as material (*murta*):

The first step in image-making is said to be the drawing of a compositional diagram or cage (*khilapanjara*) on the stone surface, the diagram consisting of an outer circle and a square or a rhombus within, and the whole surface then being divided into a number of straight lines—vertical, horizontal, diagonal and oblique. The limbs of the deities with their attending gods and worshippers have to be set along the lines, according to their hierarchical status, and fitted into the geometrical pattern. The resulting panel is supposed to represent the cosmos in miniature—representing in its upper, middle and lower planes, the deity, the attending gods, and the deities' vehicles and worshippers, respectively.[38]

At first, the artist visualizes an image in his contemplative vision (*dhyana*) and then constructs it in accordance with the noetic archetype. After the ritual of animation or establishment (*pratishtha*), the image is brought to life and is regarded as an efficacious *yantra* able to reveal the subtle spiritual essence (*sukshma sharira*, like the Egyptian luminous *sah*-body, the Neoplatonic ethereal vehicle of the immortal soul) through its gross material body (*sthula sharira*). Hence, the *pratishtha* ritual is thought to accomplish an actual transformation in the character of the hieratic statue.

Be that as it may, the deity can be perceived only by means of crystallization in the form of holy bodies, sacred sounds, images, and myths. The myths have the same sacramental dimension and function as consecrated images. Remember Olympiodorus, who also says that myths are produced so that we may proceed from the apparent to the invisible (*In Gorg.* 46.2).

Sharira, one of Sanskrit words for 'body', derives from the verbal root *shri* ('to rest upon', 'to support'). Hence, the body serves as a framework (like the Greek *peribolos*) by means of which the All-Worker can experience the world, though *deha*, another word for body, hints of its dark and defiled nature, similar to the Orphic conception of the body as 'prison'. However, as G. Feuerstein remarks:

If the world is in essence divine, so must be the body. If we must honor the world as a creation or an aspect of the divine Power (*shakti*), we must likewise honor the body. The body is a piece of the world and . . . the world is a piece of body. Or,

38. V. K. Chari, "Representation in India's Sacred Images: Objective vs. Metaphysical Reference".—*Bulletin of SOAS* (School of Oriental and African Studies), vol. 1, 2002, p. 66.

rather, when we truly understand the body, we discover that it is the world, which in essence is divine.[39]

SENSE PERCEPTION AND INTELLECTION
IN NEOPLATONISM

In this respect, we should indicate that the meaning of *aisthesis* (sense perception) in Neoplatonism is problematic, because even the supra-intelligent henadic perception which transcends *noesis* (intellection) and operates through the 'flower of intellect' (*anthos tou nou*) is called *aisthesis* by Proclus. Plotinus discusses a sort of *aisthesis* which belongs to *Nous*. This divine Intellect is like 'a living richly varied sphere' (*sphaira zoë poikile: Enn.* VI.7.15.25–26). Plotinus says:

> those sense-objects (*ta aistheta*), which we called so because they are bodies, are apprehended in a different way; and this sense perception here below is dimmer than the apprehension there in the intelligible, which we called sense-perception because it is of bodies and which is clearer. And for this reason this man here has sense-perception, because he has a lesser apprehension of lesser things, images (*eikonon*) of those intelligible realities; so that these sense perceptions here are dim intellections, but the intellections there are clear sense-perceptions' (*hoste einai tas aistheseis tautas amudras noeseis, tas de ekei noeseis enargeis aistheseis: Enn.* VI.7.7.24–32 Armstrong).

So, as H. J. Blumenthal explains, the noetic *aisthesis* imitates *Nous* and contains its own objects:

> It does not proceed from one set of objects to another because that is a characteristic of the divided power ... and does not 'go outside', that is operate externally. It contains in itself the

---

39. Georg Feuerstein, *Tantra, The Path of Ecstasy*, Boston and London: Shambhala, 1998, p. 53.

whole of what is perceptible and so is rather a form of reflexive consciousness.[40]

This internal noetic sense-perception is more or less identical to *noesis* (intellection), because 'true self-knowledge is a function of intellect'.[41] For Plotinus, *noesis* implies the real knowledge which is the goal of our life 'according to intellect' (human intellect being considered as a merely irradiation, *ellampsis*, of the divine *Nous*) and consists in identity of knowing subject and knowing object, analogous to the conjunction (*sustasis*) of the Chaldean 'caller' (*kletor*) and the object of his invocation.

This ontological identity is real *gnosis*, because knowledge below the level of *Nous* is only by representation. Therefore the unifying *noesis* also belongs to the theurgical activity and is considered as being superhuman and divine. *Noesis* of this type (in which subject and object are identical) is above human *noesis* and human *episteme* (rational scientific knowledge). According to A. Smith:

> The same is true for Proclus who stresses the role of *nous* at the highest levels of union. A fact which further supports this is the way in which Proclus sometimes sees theurgy as a means not merely to union with the One but as a means of achieving the unified thought of real *noesis*.[42]

However, Proclus paradoxically describes four levels of *aisthesis*, of which only the last kind is dim, passive (*pathos*) and close to natural sympathy. But the noetic *aisthesis*, which grasps the objects of its cognition as a whole and in an unchanging way (like the Sufi *dhawq*, spiritual tasting) is described by Proclus as follows:

> There is another kind of perception (*aisthesis*) prior to the one residing in the soul's vehicle (*en to ochemati tes psuches*): compared with this one it is immaterial, pure and a kind of

40. Henry J. Blumenthal, "Proclus on Perception".—*BICS* (Bulletin of Institute of Classical Studies, University of London), vol. 29, 1982, p. 2.

41. Henry J. Blumenthal, *Aristotle and Neoplatonism in Late Antiquity: Interpretations of the De Anima*, London: Duckworth, 1996, p. 166.

42. Andrew Smith, *Porphyry's Place in the Neoplatonic Tradition: A Study in Post-Plotinian Neoplatonism*, The Hague: Martinus Nijhoff, 1974, pp. 114–115.

cognition (*gnosis*) not involving affection, but it is not free from form (*morphes*) because it is itself like bodies as it acquires its existence in a body (*In Tim*. 3.286.19ff).

As H. J. Blumenthal explains, this sense-perception 'has the same nature as *phantasia*, imagination, but is called *aisthesis* when it operates externally and *phantasia* when it remains internal and contemplates forms and shapes in the *pneuma*.'[43]

By this sort of 'anagogic' *aisthesis*, the Neoplatonic philosopher or the initiate may perceive the noetic realities and through contemplation (*dhyana*, to say it in Sanskrit terms) of the hieratic image (like one's *ishta-devata*, tantamount to one's real noetic *eidos* and divine *paradeigma*) to be united with the archetypal *pleroma* of Intellect. Hence, one's chosen deity (its animated icon) is to be contemplated as one's very Self. On this level of practice, the philosophical distinction between *aisthesis* and *noesis* seems quite irrelevant. G. Feuerstein says:

> It is within the microcosm (body-mind) that, according to the *Tantras*, we find the doorway to the outer cosmos. The entire architecture of the universe is faithfully mirrored in our own body-mind. . . . We can access the cosmos by going within ourselves because objective and subjective realities coevolve from and always subsist in the same Reality. In the transcendental dimension, they are absolutely identical. In the subtle realms, they are barely distinct, and they manifest as seemingly separate lines of evolution only in the visible material dimension.[44]

DIVINE LIGHT AND LUMINOUS VEHICLE OF THE SOUL

For Proclus, the divine light irradiates from the One God (the Platonic Good, *to agathon*) and penetrates to all levels of the manifested reality, ensuring a goodness and theurgic salvation for everything. Therefore there are many different modes of light—noetic, psychical, hypercosmic, and physical:

43. Henry J. Blumenthal, *Proclus on Perception*, p. 3.
44. Georg Feuerstein, ibid., pp. 61–62.

Behind the visible sun lie the metaphysical, invisible suns, which give it power and sustenance.[45]

The Neoplatonists regarded light as an incorporeal activity: the corporeal forms of light (the visible Sun and fire) only house this incorporeal light which really does not travel but is simultaneously everywhere. Julian the Emperor says:

> Accordingly, the doctrine of the Phoenicians, who are wise and knowledgeable about divine matters, states that the sunlight that proceeds in all directions is the undefiled *energeia* of pure Intellect. Our theory is not inconsistent with theirs since light itself is incorporeal, if one should consider that its source is not a body but the undefiled *energeia* of intellect irradiating into its proper abode (*Or.* iv.134ab–b7).

All forms of divine inspiration, revelation, and true divination are possible owing to illumination by the incorporeal light of the One, the pure activity (*energeia*) of Helios (Amun-Ra), which at first 'irradiates into' (*ellampomene eis*) the noeric ('noeric' denotes the 'thinking intelligibles', *ta noeta*) realm and then shines through Apollo, the separated and transcendent monad of the visible realm. However, Iamblichus curiously maintains (in accordance to the general Platonic devaluation of images) that the image-making art (*he eidolopoietike techne*) is able to utilize only a very obscure element in these descending immaterial lights. For Iamblichus, as J. F. Finamore observes:

> This so-called art does not derive externally and separately from the gods but arises from the material and corporeal powers around matter and in bodies. . . . Far from using the revolving stars, the image-maker uses these final effluences of nature artificially (*technikos*), not theurgically (*theourgikos*).[46]

Proclus, however, insists that light, being a 'participation in the

---

45. Lucas Siorvanes, ibid., p. 242.
46. John F. Finamore, "Iamblichus on Light and the Transparent".—*The Divine Iamblichus, Philosopher and Man of Gods*, ed. H. J. Blumenthal and E. G. Clark, Bristol: Bristol Classical Press, 1993, p. 59.

divine existence' (*metousia tes theias huparxeos*), is a sort of body. The supra-celestial light is identical with the *place* of the cosmos, and this 'place', as well as the cosmos itself, is a body. Thus 'we have a case of two bodies interpenetrating', as R. Sorabji observes.[47] But Proclus, and his master Syrianus, speak about *immaterial bodies*: both 'place' and the vehicles of our souls are immaterial. According to Syrianus,

> immaterial bodies resemble the light emitted from different lamps which goes right through the whole of the same building, the light of each lamp passing through that of the other without being obliterated or divided (*In Metaph.* 85.15).

'Place' as a supra-celestial light, a sphere of light equal in volume to the cosmos (understood as an *agalma*), 'is visible not to the eyes, but only through the luminous vehicles of our rational soul. It is not affected, therefore, when visible light goes out.'[48] This vehicle (*ochema*) of the soul is ethereal and eternal. When the soul and its *augoeide ochema* revolve together, the soul enjoys perfect intellection (*noesis*), moving in a circle like the solar barque of Ra, which carries those immortal *bau* which are saved and transformed into *akhu* (intellects, noetic lights, spirits). Likewise, the chariots in the myth of Plato's *Phaedrus* (248a1–b5) are moving in a circle, thereby imitating the ouroboric nature of *Nous*. So the spherical vehicle of the human soul revolves in conjunction with the vehicles of the gods. However, as J. F. Finamore remarks, 'the relationship between a soul and its vehicle deteriorates as the soul participates less fully in the One.[49]

Although regarded by Plotinus as merely an illumination of what is below *ta noeta*, the descent (*kathodos*) into generation and involvement with material elements results in real incarnation. The subtle material covering of the soul becomes its gross corporeal

---

47. Richard Sorabji, "Proclus on Place and the Interpenetration of Bodies".— *Proclus lecteur et interprete des anciens*, ed. Jean Pepin and H.D. Saffrey, Paris: CNRS, 1987, p. 297.

48. Ibid., p. 303.

49. John F. Finamore, *Iamblichus and the Theory of the Vehicle of the Soul*, Chico, California: Scholars Press, 1985, p. 48.

body. Thereby the human soul (which is not strictly 'human' at the noetic level, but rather supernatural, *huperphues*) descends in order that theogony and all the tasks of demiurgy may be fulfilled. The soul accepts the unique task of becoming mortal, of realizing its own nothingness, as G. Shaw argues:

> Only then might it experience the supernatural death of the theurgists, a death not of the body but of the individual self. Only then may the soul's *eros* carry it to fulfillment, a journey that is necessarily anonymous.[50]

Therefore the main task of all theurgical practices is to remove the material pollution from the soul's immortal ethereal vehicle and re-unite the soul with its noetic principles and the One itself through the ascending hierarchy of intermediaries.

DIVINE PRESENCE IN IMAGES

In India, the metaphysical Principle is regarded as both transcendent and immanent, being simultaneously supreme (*paratva*) and accessible (*saulabhya*). Therefore the hieratic icons, imbued with the mysterious presence of God, are likened to the deep pools where water is always available. The god Vishnu, who manifests and incarnates himself in many different ways, instructs his devotees that he, Vishnu, can be worshiped in embodied form only. So, allegedly, this mode of worship is revealed by Vishnu himself. There is no worship without the manifest forms and icons, 'therefore humans should construct the Imperishable One in human form and worship him with utmost devotion' (*Paramasamhita* 3.6–8).[51]

In certain cases, these images are viewed as the actual incarnations of Vishnu or Shiva, being infused by the divine presence in the same manner as a soul enters and animates a human body. Therefore there is the direct analogy of a soul entering a human body

---

50. Gregory Shaw, "The Mortality and Anonymity of the Iamblichean Soul".— *Syllecta Classica*, vol. 8, The University of Iowa, 1997, p. 190.

51. Richard H. Davis, *Lives of Indian Images*, Princeton: Princeton University Press, 1997, p. 30.

(whose 'inner controller', *antaryamin*, is the transcendent All-Worker, concealed within the heart) and a deity (or its *ba*, as Egyptians would say) entering a statue—sometimes by the spontaneous self-manifestation (*svayambhu*), sometimes through the hieratic rites of animation (*pratishtha*).

In any case, the fashioned or constructed sacred image is a body (*vigraha*). Without losing its essential transcendence, the god enters this body in the form of *atman*, life breath (*prana*), noetic consciousness (*cetana*), or divine power (*shakti*), and inwardly infuses it with divine presence. This mysterious infusion is called 'animation'. Likewise, a soul or animating principle (*jiva*) enters a human body, which serves as a receptacle in the same manner as material *hupodoche* receives the Platonic Forms, poured into the womb (*kolpos*) of Hekate.

The Chaldean theology likens the Forms that enter the *kolpoi* to 'thunderbolts', 'lightnings', and 'fires' of the Father. Hekate as the noetic Life (Rhea) and the World Soul performs the role of 'nurturing' (that is, dividing and measuring) these Forms, or Ideas, also called *Iunges*. Then Hekate herself pours forth the great *alke* (strength) of the vivifying fire. On the way back to the noetic source, this *alke* assists the theurgist's soul in its ascension and liberation, guiding the works of fire (*puros erga*). This is so because 'theurgy and its goal—the unification of man's soul with the divine—were activated by the divine alone; the soul's role was strictly preparatory.'[52]

Damascius tells us that Heraiscus, the Egyptian Neoplatonist, who is credited with becoming a Bacchus (tantamount to Osiris, the vindicated 'dead', *maa-kheru*) even before his physical death, had the natural gift of distinguishing between animate and inanimate hieratic statues (*ton te zonton kai ton me zonton hieron agalmaton*) by means of certain *eumoria*, the inborn ability of noetic perception:

> He had but to look at one of them and immediately his heart was afflicted by divine frenzy while both his body and soul

---

52. Sarah Iles Johnston, *Hekate Soteira: A Study of Hekate's Roles in the Chaldean Oracles and Related Literature*, Atlanta: Scholars Press, 1990, p. 85.

leapt up as if possessed by the god. But if he was not moved in such a way, the statue (*agalma*) was inanimate (*apsuchon*) and devoid of divine inspiration (*theias epipnoias*). It was in this way that he recognized that the ineffable statue (*to arrheton agalma*) of Aion was possessed by the god who was worshipped by the Alexandrians, being at the same time Osiris and Adonis as a result of a truly mystical act of union (*Phil. Hist.* 7E).

The Neoplatonists maintained that the first name-giver revealed the attributes of the gods by means of sounds (the divine names, regarded as images) in the same way as the statue-maker embodied these sounds in stone. In this respect the model of human artists is both Apollo (the Egyptian Horus), who is in charge of cosmic harmonies, and Hephaestus (Ptah), the maker of the visible universe filled of signs (*semeion*) that the wise man can read. According to Proclus, the cosmic 'Poet' (*poietes*) works 'mythologically' (*muthologikos: In Remp.* 1.68.15 ff). Therefore the cosmos itself is both a statue (*agalma*) and a myth—a single animated body, all of whose parts are related to one another, bearing a symbolic and semiotic function: 'Texts and bodies are visible objects, meanings and souls, invisible.'[53] And 'since human beings cannot participate perfectly in the gods, they look at them through imaginary figures.[54]

Contemplating the statue of a deity and uttering the divine names, regarded as *agalmata phoneënta* (vocal images of the gods), the initiate is granted access to the invisible and ineffable reality that resides both within the statue and within the initiate's own tomb-and-temple-like body.

Since all manifested reality is established as theophany, a deity (as an aspect or *kheperu* of the Creator) is *a priori* present in the raw materials gathered to create the image, as it is already present in landscapes, animals, and human beings. Likewise, fire is regarded as being latent in the dry wood, therefore hieratic rites and spiritual practices (or contemplative life itself, which consists in a series of

53. Oiva Kuisma, *Proclus' Defense of Homer*, Helsinki: Societas Scientiarum Fennica, 1996, p. 68.
54. Ibid., p. 41.

transformative rituals) only make this fire manifest in one way or another. The *Chaldean Oracles* inform us that the world-forming Ideas of the demiurgic *Nous* (fiery principles projected like bolts of lightning) not only perceived the noetic works of the Father (*patros erga*), but concealed them by means of sense-perceptible works (*aisthetois ergois*) and bodies (fr. 40).

According to the Shaiva ritual texts, Shiva's general (*samanya*) presence is everywhere, therefore the consecration of certain places, images, or things simply marks the special re-actualization of divine presence. This 'marked' (*vishista*) divine presence in the image is achieved by the ritual of awakening which has many phases but concentrates on the opening of the statue's eyes (*netronmilana*) by a golden or a diamond needle. As R. H. Davis relates:

> By rendering God physically present in a particular fixed location, icons enable the whole liturgical system of temple transactions between God and his human worshipers[55] ... the divine image is both means (*upaya*) and end (*upeya*). It leads the devotee towards God, and it also *is* God, the devotee's object of enjoyment. Rather than simply reminding its audience of the 'mystery of the Incarnation', the Vaishnava image serves as the base within which Vishnu mysteriously does incarnate himself.[56]

This incarnation may be viewed as a central 'root manifestation' (*mulamurti*) of divinity (like the Shiva's *lingam* or the stone pedestal-throne), which becomes the animating source of *lux intelligibilis* for all other anthropomorphic images and statues in the confines of the temple. The fabricated bodies can be filled with hidden noetic light (or rather reveal it 'from within', 'from nowhere') only through the theurgic installation. All these divine works (*theia erga*) are really done by Vishvakarman, the All-Worker, who 'has painted' all the forms of all the bodies *in illo tempore*. As H. Zimmer says:

---

55. Richard H. Davis, ibid., p. 31.
56. Ibid., p. 33.

This teaching of Vishvakarman is, then, nothing less than the knowledge of the god's true manifestation, converted into norms and axioms.[57]

Since Shiva (like the All-Worker) acts in the manifested cosmos only with a 'body of *mantras*', the main task of ritual consecration is 'to impose a mantric body onto the physical body of the fabricated image.'[58] Thereby the statue becomes a 'divine body' (*divyadeha*) composed of the demiurgic *mantra*-powers. These powers are symbolically 'poured out' in the form of holy water from the ritual waterpots, like the water of celestial Nile (Osiris), whose stream carries the archetypal potencies of Nun, the ineffable One of the Heliopolitan solar theology.

LIVING IMAGES OF THE EGYPTIAN GODS

In the Ramesside theology, God as One is called *Ba sheta* (the hidden *Ba*). He is unnameable and ineffable, though a decad of his primeval noetic manifestations (*bau*) constitute the archetypal background of the visible world. These are the ten *bau* of Amun that animate and sustain the manifold universe of all *kheperu*. Being decisively transcendent, Amun is simultaneously the illustrious *Ba* of gods and humans.

From one point of view, Amun's transcendent 'body' is Nun (the ineffable Water, Inundation, which brings forth *ta noeta*). From another point of view, the visible cosmos is his immanent 'body' animated from within. Amun's breath is the 'fire of life' (*ankhet*) and the 'breath of life to all nostrils'. He is 'great of *heka* with secret form', 'his *ba* is Shu, his heart is Tefnut' (*Pap. Leiden* 1.350). J. Assmann says:

The Ramesside theologians develop the idea of light, air and water as three elements in which the life-giving power of the

---

57. Heinrich Zimmer, *Artistic Form and Yoga in the Sacred Images of India*, tr. and ed. Gerald Chapple and James B. Lawson, Princeton: Princeton University Press, 1984, p. 186.
58. Richard H. Davis, ibid., p. 36.

hidden God is manifest in the world. In the ritual of ten *Ba*'s, the first pair of *Ba*'s are the sun and the moon, which can also be explained as the right and the left eyes of god. Then come the *Ba*'s of Shu and Osiris for air and water. The fifth is that of Tefnut, the goddess of the flaming uraeus snake. . . . Sun and moon represent not light, but time, which also appears here as a cosmic life-giving energy. Light is attributed to the *Ba* of Tefnut. . . . She is the 'flaming one', the fire-spitting Cobra at the head of the sun god, the lioness. . . . Her creation at the beginning of the world, together with her twin brother Shu, refers to the primordiality of light which is also the meaning of the Biblical creation account where the creation of light comes first.[59]

Since the earth is an image of heaven (of *archetypus mundus*), the totality of deities embody the spiritual, cosmic, and political unity (*sema*) of the Two Lands, of Upper and Lower Egypt, of Seth and Horus. The Egyptian gods (*neteru*) are owners of the temple estates and houses, residing in their manors (that reproduce the entire universe in miniature) either as a cult statues located in the most sacred chambers, or as a portable processional barques and pavilion-like shrines containing animated symbols. The god's appearance in procession, his 'turning outward', is tantamount to the cosmogonic act of luminous manifestation (the *proödos* of later Neoplatonists).

The whole temple itself is invoked as the form of god and represents his living cultic 'body'. All sacred carvings, reliefs, and paintings belong to the manifest form of a deity (lord of temple) as pictorial representations of archetypal realities and theological concepts. Therefore the carved words denote the ideas and, at the same time, are images to be contemplated in an anagogic way. The painted signs (hieroglyphic images) themselves are 'bodies' for the living gods. They are awakened by the ritual invocation (not simply reading, but reciting and singing) that effects a *kheper*-creation through the re-activated *heka* power and produces divine epiphany.

---

59. Jan Assmann, "Mono-, Pan-, and Cosmotheism: Thinking the 'One' in Egyptian Theology".—*Orient*. Report of the Society for Near Eastern Studies in Japan, vol. XXXIII, 1998, p. 140.

In the Iamblichean version of Platonism, which established the direct correlation between hierurgy, musical harmony, and mathematical disciplines, the proper arrangement of images (or even of the privileged philosophical texts, the *hieroi logoi* of the Neoplatonic *paideia*) is able to re-establish the psycho-somatic energies of the soul and reveal their underlying archetypal patterns. Likewise, the sacred chants and mantric invocations make audible the noetic principles, 'sounding' through the theurgic *sunthemata* in imitation of cosmogenesis and its whirring noise (*rhoizon*). As G. Shaw pointed out:

> Chanting ineffable names or singing theurgic hymns . . . were sensible activities and therefore tied to the material gods, yet their underlying structures were arithmetic, hence immaterial.[60]

R. B. Finnestad argues that the creation texts carved in the Egyptian temples do not merely relate, but represent (we would say, re-enact) creation:

> They are their own version of the creative words of the Heavy Flood which are seen, partaking in the theophany of the creator of the cosmos; they are meant to *appear*.[61] Not only the statues in the chapels are seen during the morning ritual. When the interior of the temple is illuminated by the opening of the doors and the lighting of candles, the entire place reveals what is hidden in it: the colourful world of gods: the illumination of the building brings into light the figures of the gods carved on it, i.e., it is a coming into being of the pantheon.[62]

Truly speaking, the Egyptian gods do not dwell on earth but rather install their *bau* in images and symbols, descending from the

60. Gregory Shaw, "The Geometry of Grace: A Pythagorean Approach to Theurgy".—*The Divine Iamblichus. Philosopher and Man of Gods*, ed. H. J. Blumenthal and E. G. Clark, Bristol: Bristol Classical Press, 1993, p. 124.
61. Ragnhild Bjerre Finnestad, *Image of the World and Symbol of the Creator*, p. 122.
62. Ibid., p. 111.

noetic realm (mythically represented by the sky) on their *sekhemu* (temples, statues, reliefs, texts, ritual instruments). Thereby the divine *bau* in the form of these in-dwelled images (*sekhem* meaning both 'image' and 'power') participate in the temple liturgies.

The cult statue itself could be called the *ba, sekhem,* or *tut* (image) of the god whose divine *energeia* has entered and empowered the purified receptacle. The *naos* where the statue lives hidden (*amun, sheta*) in darkness is called *bu djeser,* 'the sacred place', where the priests invoke the primeval *bau* of Heliopolis. In the form of his solar barque the god's *ba* rests on the High Seat (*set uret*), the primeval isle (*iu*) of the Egg (or the primordial stone pillar of Heliopolis that serves as a pedestal for the *bennu* bird), with which the god's *ba* is united. Likewise, his *ba* is united with the entire temple.

The effect of this cultic union is theophany, a coming out from the hidden *sheta*-state, like a coming out from the tomb. When the divine face (*hra*) of the hieratic statue comes to light, this appearance is viewed as revelation which coincides with creation. The intelligible pantheon appears as the universe of *kheperu* and, simultaneously, the temple appears as cosmos *qua* pantheon. J. Assmann emphasizes that the cult statue, strictly speaking,

> is not the image of the deity's body, but the body itself. It does not represent his form, but rather gives him form. The deity takes form in the statue, just as in sacred animal or a natural phenomenon.[63]

Therefore the statue is not 'made' by the sculptor ('one who makes to live'), but 'born'. The verb *mesi* ('to give birth') is used for the crafting of a statue that resembles a living creature. The birthing ritual results in the statue's 'animation'. It is based on priestly knowledge that deals with the divine names (*renu*), manifestations (*bau*), and powers (*sekhemu*).

In Mesopotamia, this craft, regarded as an esoteric art, was attributed to the antediluvian sages (*apkallus*), the avatars of divine wisdom (*nemequ*). This hieratic art (*hieratike techne*) allegedly

---

63. Jan Assmann, *The Search for God in Ancient Egypt*, p. 46.

passed into the state of occultation when these *apkallus* returned to the Apsu, the mysterious realm of their lord Ea.[64]

The rite of the Opening of the Mouth (*uper-ra*), whose full title is 'Performing the Opening of the Mouth in the workshop for the *tut* of N,' constitutes only the last stage in the preparation of the hieratic statue, an image (*tut*) for the divine *bau* (whose image it is) to enter it. In fact, the god's *ba* alights on his images (*akhemu*) in the monuments which the god himself (through the pure human servant) has made as instruments of the *heka* power (analogous to the theurgic *sunthemata*).

TO BE MADE INTO A SPIRIT OF LIGHT

Any one of the Egyptian gods may have many *bau*, many names, many holy *kheperu*, and many mysterious images in the temples that constitute his text-like body. But the *bau* of the Demiurge (the Administrator, who oversees and governs the universe together with the fiery choir of his *akhu*) are concentrated in the noetic realm of *akhu*. The word *akh* may designate something radiant, intellective, made into a spirit of light, belonging to the noetic domain. Other words related with *akh* designate both the ritual ascension and the instrument of this ascent to the supercelestial region (the *huperouranios topos* of Plato's *Phaedrus*), namely, *akhet*, the place of transformation and rebirth, of ascent and re-union, represented by the stony pyramid (*akhet*). According to J. Naydler:

> The connotation of the word *akh* is that of inner illumination as well as primordial creative power. Used in its initiatory sense, an *akh* might best be translated as 'an enlightened being'—one whose consciousness has become open to the reality of the spiritual world.[65]

Being in the state of *akh* means to be like a 'lord of wisdom' (*neb*

---

64. Mehmet-Ali Ataç, "The 'Underworld Vision' of the Ninevite Intellectual Milieu".—*Iraq*, vol. LXVI, London: British School of Archeology in Iraq, 2004, p. 68.

65. Jeremy Naydler, *Shamanic Wisdom in the Pyramid Texts. The Mystical Tradition of Ancient Egypt*, Rochester: Inner Traditions, 2005, p. 254.

saibut), or like 'one who transcends wisdom' (*her sai*) and who may pronounce:

My death (*aret*) is at my own wish;
My spiritualization (*imakhu*) is at my own will (*PT* 315).[66]

This spiritualization (one's turning into the *akh iker*, 'the glorified excellent one', like into the noetic gold) is achieved by joining the Eastern *Bau* and participating in their vocal liturgies—homage to the rising Sun, the supreme *sunthema* of *Nous*. Thereby the opening of the double Sundoor at the limit of Akhet occurs. As A. K. Coomaraswamy asserts:

It is through the Sun, and only through the Sun, as Truth (*satyam*), and by the way of the Well at the World's End, that there runs the road leading from this defined Order (*rta, kosmos*) to an undefined Empyrean. It is 'through the hub of the wheel, the midst of the Sun, the cleft in heaven, that is all covered over by rays, that one is altogether liberated' (*Jaiminiya Upanishad Brahmana* 1.3.5–6).[67]

Although 'liberation' may be understood in many different senses (so that even Porphyry and Iamblichus would disagree), this inner 'solar' transfiguration from *ba* to *akh* (from soul to spirit, from *psuche* to *nous*), symbolized by the embrace of Osiris and Horus, presupposes the mystical ascent through the *djed* pillar of Osiris. Microcosmically, this royal column (or the mantric body of the deity), sometimes equated with Ptah, is analogous to the *sushumna-nadi* channel of the initiate's subtle (*sukshma*) body in Tantric practices. By opening this channel, the re-awakened Sarasvati, or *kundalini-shakti* (the serpent power, like the fiery *sekhem* of the Egyptian goddess Sekhmet-Hathor that bestows liberation on the wise and bondage on the ignorant), raises up the life force, the agency of transformation and enlightenment, to the *sahasrara-cakra*

66. Ibid., p. 302.
67. Ananda K. Coomaraswamy, "The Symbolism of the Dome".—1: *Selected Papers. Traditional Art and Symbolism*, ed. Roger Lipsey, Princeton: Princeton University Press, 1989, p. 448.

(thousand spoked wheel) where the goddess Shakti is re-united with Shiva. This esoteric process of *shakti*'s ascension through the statue-like fixed Osirian body is related with the mantric initiation, contemplation of images and *yantras*, visualization of one's chosen deity (*ishta-devata*) and other ritual actions.

The noetic sphere of *akhu* is represented by the visible Sun, from which the rays of light enter the cult statues and human bodies. The Demiurge illuminates with light the 'souls' and the statues that house these 'souls' (*bau*). The light of the Sun disk (*aten*) is filled with the noetic energy of the demiurgic Intellect (Atum-Ra) as *pan-theos*. At the Dendera temple of Hathor even Osiris is drawn into this solar theology of intelligible light:

> Osiris . . . the glorious serpent, he comes as *akher* to unite with his form in his sanctuary; he comes flying from the sky as the falcon with shining feathers, and the *bau* of the gods follow him. He flies as falcon to his chapel in Dendera.[68]

In the Neoplatonic-Chaldean theology, the reception of the Sun rays effects the final purification of the soul's vehicle and lifts it upward to union with Helios (Ra), the invisible Creator of the pharaoh (son of Ra): it is depicted over the pharaoh's head, shining forth through him. The Horus-like king, regarded as a saviour (*shed*), is really divine, however, only to the extent of being an *imago dei* and acting *in loco dei*. The archetypal *Ba* of all human beings, as one of the ten primeval *Bau* of Amun, is equated with royal *ka*, the inherited life force of the *mandala*-like state. The *ka* is viewed as generic, not individual, vital force. As L. Bell explains:

> Just as a god's *ka* took up transitory residence in a statue-body, endowing it with life, so an ancestor *ka* temporally occupied and animated the body of an ordinary person, and the royal *ka* transiently inhabited and empowered the body of an individual king. . . . The royal *ka* was the divine aspect of a mortal

---

68. Ragnhild Bjerre Finnestad, "Temples of the Ptolemaic and Roman Periods: Ancient Traditions in New Contexts".—*Temples of Ancient Egypt*, ed. Byron E. Shafer, London: I. B. Tauris, 2005, p. 308.

king, the divine principle in humankind. A ruler could legitimately be worshiped in his own cultus only as an incarnation of the royal *ka*, as a manifestation of divine kingship.[69]

Since the pharaoh is adored not in his human form, but only in his immortal divine form (the noetic archetype of *anthropos teleios*), we find some really amazing things: 'the human Ramesses II worshiping the divine Ramesses II.'[70] Ra himself acts through the king as a pilot, the one 'who guides men on all the paths.' The pharaoh is considered to have certain divine being (participating in a divine *ousia*) and holy qualities only when he performed official ceremonies[71] (though his entire life was arranged as a permanent ritual and official ceremony), or when he, like the cult statue, was illuminated by the supernatural divine light.

In a sense, the pharaoh is the main or central animated Statue of the theophanic state. He is the chief mystagogue and the cultic leader (lord of the rituals, *neb irit akhet*), involved into theogenetic and theurgic activities. His architectural and liturgical acts converge and paradoxically coincide. As a principial builder, whose programmatic works imitate and repeat theogony, the king creates the 'radiant place' (*akhet*), which represents and reveals the place of origins (*kerehet*). The same metaphysical and cosmic Heliopolis is the place where liturgical *energemata* transform the human and mortal pharaoh (or the initiate) into an immortal and divine being.

Since Maat (Truth), as a gift of Atum's own inner essence, manifest through the series of *kheperu*, is an image of offerings (the whole Eye of Horus) and of order's circular flow, the pharaoh, offering the statuette of Maat to the Creator's image 'offers part of his self, which is also part of god's self, in a reciprocal act of creation.'[72]

---

69. Lanny Bell, "The New Kingdom 'Divine' Temple: The Example of Luxor".— *Temples of Ancient Egypt*, ed. Byron E. Shafer, London: I.B. Tauris, 2005, p. 131 and p. 140.

70. Ibid., p. 188.

71. Dietrich Wildung, *Egyptian Saints. Deification in Pharaonic Egypt*, New York: New York University Press, 1977, p. 3.

72. Byron E. Shafer, "Temples, Priests, and Rituals: An Overview".—*Temples of Ancient Egypt*, ed. Byron E. Shafer, London: I. B. Tauris, 2005, p.25.

RITES OF ALCHEMICAL TRANSFORMATION

The Opening of the Mouth ritual was performed not only on statues and mummies, but also on names, Apis bulls, sarcophagi, *ushabti* figures, amulets (such as the green heart-scarabs that functioned as powerful *sunthemata*), painted images and texts, solar barques and the entire temples. Thereby hieratic rites transformed the statues of gods (or those of vindicated dead, viewed as royal initiates and knowers of the mysteries) from the potential receptacles made by human artists (servants of Ptah) into the cultic bodies within which divine powers may dwell. In this way even names and symbols were made theurgically effective.

This ritual was performed either on reassembled body-shapes in the embalming workshop (*per nefer*, the 'house of beauty) or on the vertically standing mummies (roughly equivalent to *djed* columns) set up in front of the tomb. Thereby the mummy is turned into the cultic image that reveals divine *eidos*. In other words, it is transformed into the statue-like divine *sunthema* related with the *ba*-life of the dead man—or of the initiate, if one's Osirification is achieved 'philosophically' before the mortal *khat*-body passed away.

By pointing towards the transcendent dimension, the animated mummy (*sah*) both symbolizes and reveals the noetically fixed *sah*-body of the inner alchemical gold. Its face mask, in the case of royal mummies, is also made of gold, because the noetic and supra-celestial bodies of the gods, or their *ochemata* (vehicles), are held to be of pure spiritual gold. Therefore the statues of the gods represent the golden nature of their bodies, and gold (*nebu*) is regarded as the proper material for the construction of divine images, 'as much from a symbolic perspective as from considerations of the inherent worth of the precious substance.'[73] Ra himself is called the Mountain of Gold.

Both the transformed initiate's body and the mummy prepared by the gods themselves under the guidance of Anubis (the priest performing his role) may be likened to the alchemical apparatus

73. Richard H. Wilkinson, *Symbol and Magic in Egyptian Art*, London: Thames and Hudson, 1999, p. 108.

(homologous to the universe itself which includes the alchemical passage through the mouth and womb of the goddess), employed in ritual manipulations of elements to be purified and transformed, dispersed and re-united. All sacred incantations (analogous to the Tantric *mantras*, vocal images of the gods) as well as various craft instruments, minerals, herbs, and hieroglyphic tokens are to be regarded as manifold hieratic tools (*yantras*),

> with which the alchemist may master the one divine energy that surges through both the universe and his own body. He is now prepared to embark upon the alchemical life-cycle rites (*samskaras*) that will ultimately render him a second Shiva.[74]

The *Kularnava Tantra*, a seminal text of the Kaula tradition, says: 'just as iron, penetrated by mercury, attains the state of gold, so the soul, penetrated by initiation (*diksha*), attains the state of Shiva.'[75] Shiva is the Tantric equivalent of the Egyptian god Osiris, whose dismembered and then restored and animated body (restored and re-awakened in the psychic realm of Duat, within the *Anima Mundi*) here below constitutes the very 'black soil' (*khem*) of Egypt. Therefore R.B. Finnestad rightly argues:

> The mummification is a divinization, a transmutation of the human body to a god's body. From a religious point of view the mummification is no conservation of the human body but rather the opposite: the mummification is a ritual transformation of the human and mortal to the divine and eternal. The cultic significance of the mummy thus lies in its function as a symbol of Osiris.... Hidden in the burial chamber the mummy represents the divine being who is met in the shrine in the statue. Thus the tomb is like a temple of Osiris.[76]

The ritual of the Opening makes this symbol of Osiris operative.

---

74. David Gordon White, *The Alchemical Body. Siddha Traditions in Medieval India,* Chicago and London: The University of Chicago Press, 1996, pp. 181–182.

75. Ibid., pp. 182–183.

76. Ragnhild Bjerre Finnestad, "The Meaning and Purpose of Opening the Mouth in Mortuary Contexts".—*Numen,* vol. xxv, fasc.2, p.128.

The tomb itself functions as a vehicle for regeneration where the deceased is to be 'justified with Osiris' (*maa kheru kher Usir*) in order to follow all the phases of Osirian transformation and to be reborn. In the case of the dead queen Nefertari, the great royal wife of Ramesses II, she is depicted as experiencing the mysteries of noetic rebirth and union with the solar *Nous* within the Akhet. The equation of her with Ra is made and 'the appearance of Ra' is granted to her 'through the speech of various gods and goddesses.'[77] One of the gods gives her 'the kingship of Atum'.[78]

The Apis (Hapi) bull, like other privileged sacred receptacles of divine powers, was equated with a living statue which incarnates the solar (noetic) *ba* of Ra (Ra's *ba* being called Apis-Osiris). And the ritually embalmed mummy of Apis (known as Osiris-Apis) is regarded as the transfigured and immortalized image of his noetic *sah* form.

Among the prime salvific deeds ritually performed by every pharaoh was the temple (*het neter*) construction, followed by the opening of the temple for the onto-genetic divine epiphany. This included the bringing of divine offerings in the form of the restored Eye of Horus, as well as union with the gods, resulting in a sojourn of 'a million years' in a mystic embrace of Ra. At first, the pyramid (*akhet*) functioned as a site for the theurgic activity of *heka* powers (that is, of transformation, ascent, and noetic rebirth of the ruler). Later on, the specific mansions that each pharaoh built for himself as *djeser akhet* (sacred *akhet*) were places of *unio mystica* where he and his initiates ('followers of Horus', *shemsu her*) could become *ankhu*, 'the living ones'.

Amun-United-with-Eternity (*nenmet-neheh*) and the transformed pharaoh are seen as one; therefore the king may address Amun as follows:

77. Heather Lee McCarthy, "The Osiris Nefertari: A Case Study of Decorum, Gender, and Regeneration".—*Journal of the American Research Center in Egypt*, vol. XXXIX, 2002, p. 191.

78. Ibid., p. 187.

I am your son, O Lord of Gods, Amun-Ra, the primeval one of the Two Lands. Make divine my image (*seshemu*). Protect (*khu*) my temple. Make it festive with your *ka* every day.[79]

Since the pharaohs themselves were tantamount to animated statues that incarnated the *ba* of Ra, 'they occupied the same theological category as the sacred animals.'[80] In the so-called *Demotic Chronicle* (Pap. 215 of the Biblioteque National de Paris), the Apis bull is described as the triune god in whom merge Ptah, Ra, and Horus, all these gods being related to the conception of sacred kingship.

THE OPENING OF THE STATUE'S MOUTH

There are seventy-five scenes that illustrate the *upet-ra* ritual, collected by the scholars from different sources. Our task is not to reconstruct and present its coherent version, but simply to indicate and emphasize certain theological truths related with ritual actions.

The 'opening of the mouth and eyes' is performed by the lector priest (*kher heb*, one who holds the papyrus on which the *heka* words of the hieratic rite are written), the *sem*-priest wearing the leopard-skin garment, and other officials, by touching the mouth of the statue with various instruments or by embracing it. The purifying and animating instruments include an adze called *neterty* (formed from the same root as *neter*, god), a chisel called *medjedfet* made of iron, an ostrich feather, a *pesesh-kef* (*pesesh* meaning 'dividing instrument', and *kef*, 'flint'), the *sem*-priest's finger, and other items. The *pesesh-kef* instrument is also used in cutting the umbilical cord, because death means a return to the divine womb, and rebirth is the antithesis of joining with the *ka* and implies a division or separation from the *ka*.[81]

79. Gerhard Haeny, "New Kingdom 'Mortuary Temples' and 'Mansions of Million of Years'".—*Temples of Ancient Egypt*, ed. Byron E. Shafer, London: I.B. Tauris, 2005, p. 107.

80. Jan Assmann, *The Mind of Egypt. History and Meaning in the Time of the Pharaohs,* tr. Andrew Jenkins, New York: Metropolitan Books, 2002, p. 375.

81. Ann Macy Roth, "The pss-kf and the 'Opening of the Mouth' Ceremony: A Ritual of Birth and Rebirth".—*The Journal of Egyptian Archeology,* vol. 78, 1992, p. 127.

The core of the long solemn version of the ritual is the opening of the statue's or *sah*-body's mouth with the leg of a freshly-slaughtered sacrificial bull. With the presentation of the foreleg (*khepesh*) and the heart (*haty,* meaning the same as the more common *ib*) the statue is endowed with vital strength (*khepesh*) and divine consciousness. The anointing of the statue symbolizes the uniting of its limbs. The *sem*-priest anoints the statue by touching its mouth with the index finger of his right hand:

> The entire effect of the embalming ritual is contained in this single gesture that the *sem*-priest carries out with his index finger . . . the conclusion is a censing in front of the uraeus-serpent.[82]

Only when animated is the statue enabled to breath, to see, to hear, and to speak in a subtle way (at the level of meditative consciousness and imagination of worshiper's *sukshma sharira,* to say it in Sanskrit), as a living image of a deity. By unveiling the face (*un hra*) of this image, the god comes into manifestation (in the form of visionary epiphany), and by embracing the statue the initiate worshipper is united with his archetypal lord.

The animated statue may eat sacramentally, therefore offerings made to it (repeatedly called *maat* or regarded as the whole Eye of Horus, the restored *imago dei* of one's inner being) represented the life (*ankh*) and order (*maat*) that were consubstantial with the divinity. To present the god with the *ankh* and *ib*-heart hieroglyphs meant to transfer the force of life from the food substance to the god, and vice versa, in a sacramental manner. The large *ankh*-bouquets were regarded as a means of transmitting Amun-Ra's power of life. Likewise, Osiris' *uah ny maa-kheru* (floral garland of justification) transferred a royal power from Osiris to Horus. Sometimes even the carved hieroglyphs and images were designated as gods (*neteru*), related to the metaphysical character and meaning of stone:

> The symbols are gods because they are visible, durable, eternalized forms, and at the same time refer to something invisible.

---

82. Jan Assmann, *Death and Salvation in Ancient Egypt,* p. 317.

They bridge the gap between here and not-here, now and not-now.[83]

The ability of the divine statue to act (*iri*), that is, to reveal its world-creating *heka* power and beauty, to manifest luminous graces, to speak (in a subtle manner that resembles the *rhoizon* of the Pythagoreo-Chaldean cosmic spheres and the noise of sistrum, *sesheshet*, depicted in the form of life sign, *ankh*) and respond to the cultic act (the offering of the Eye, *iret*, by the priest) depends on the properly performed rite of animation. In this context, the word for 'eye' (*iret*) is related to the noun *iru* (that which acts), thereby indicating the active manifestation of the god's *ba* through the awakened cult image.

MYSTICAL UNION
WITH THE NOETIC SUN

In all hieratic rites of animation, consecration, and divinization, the constant stress is upon the statue's contact (while standing before Ra as the mummy stands at the entrance of the tomb) with the vivifying sunlight, with the 'breaths' and 'sounds' of the demiurgic Intellect. When the Opening of the Mouth ritual is performed 'at the House of Gold', the face of a statue or a mummy is to be turned southward and bathed in the rays of the Sun.

Likewise, the initiate (equated with the statue in his Osirian posture, or *asana*, to say it in Sanskrit) stands facing the Sun (while inwardly facing *Nous*), as if standing on the primeval mound from which Atum and his archetypal City, Heliopolis, emerged. Thereby the theurgic transformation is conducted when the deceased (not only in the form of a statue, coffin, or mummy, but as a living mystic, an official of the pharaonic state) stands face to face with the Sun in order to be united through the Sun with Atum-Ra, his real metaphysical Father. Consequently he is noetically born like Ra in Atum's embrace, because

---

83. Jan Assmann, *The Mind of Egypt*, p. 57.

The sun's light not only shines in the sky, but can be contacted inwardly, and in uniting with it inwardly the soul undergoes apotheosis.[84]

This ritual of 'Unity with the Sun Disk' (*henem aten*) stands as a divine prototype and as a means of one's *unio mystica* through that solar theurgy which is enacted in the *akhet*. It is enacted both externally and inwardly. The illumination by the sunlight even may replace the Opening rite itself, which is described as performed in the sunlight as follows:

May you stand erect on the sand of Rasetau,
May you be greeted when the sun shines on you
So as to carry out your purification.

Your mouth will be opened, your limbs will be purified
Before Ra when he rises!
May he transfigure you, may he grant that you be rejuvenated,
Living among the gods![85]

The Mesopotamian *pit-pi* and *mis-pi* rituals of mouth-opening and mouth-washing, performed with incantations on the statue (*salmu*) in order that it may be reborn as a god, is conducted by setting the statue's eyes toward sunrise. Thereby the material form of the statue is inwardly animated and enabled to manifest the actual presence of the god. The Babylonians and Assyrians clearly maintained a distinction between the god as such and his receptacle produced by Ea through the human artisans. However, all enlivened images, both in Egypt and Mesopotamia, are regarded as cultic bodies not in certain illusory and metaphorical manner, but as really invested with divinity. Ch. Zivie-Coche says:

Each icon was linked to a function, or perhaps to an aspect, of the divine person. The Egyptians attempted to clarify their deities as closely as possible by means of a network of combinations that were not mutually exclusive, and a god could thus

---

84. Jeremy Naydler, *Shamanic Wisdom in the Pyramid Texts*, p. 240.
85. Jan Assmann, *Death and Salvation in Ancient Egypt*, p.320.

be presented under many aspects, each of which was considered as a facet, not as a global vision. Conversely, a single icon could serve to represent various deities, each of whom would keep his or her own name, or perhaps associate that name with another, though in a non-exclusive manner.[86]

Once or several times a year, the statue of the temple's lord and images of other deities are removed from the stone or wooden shrines which stand in the darkness of the 'interior' (*khenu*), carried out to the *uabet* ('pure place') where the divine statues are clothed and adorned with jewelry, and then put on the roof of the temple. The ritual of Unity with the Sun Disk (*aten*), aimed at statue's union with the rays of the Sun, is performed on the roof. Thereby the *ba* of Ra can alight (*khen*) upon his statue (*bes*) and unite (*sema*) with his image (*sekhem*). The golden statue (made of Sun's own substance) is united with the Sun's *energeia*, with the original and pure noetic gold of Ra. This ritual serves as a model for the initiate's spiritual ascent and union (*sema*) with the solar *Nous* as well.

After the awakening to light at dawn the cult statue is regarded as 'the living *ba*' of the god. Then it descends into the dark temple's *naos* again, as into the tomb. The *ba* (viewed as a 'spiritual body' by L. Bell)[87] is like the descending divine Form (*eidos*) which needs a certain noetic, psychic, or physical receptacle. However, the 'shadow' (*shuyt*) is also regarded as an irradiation from the noetic plenitude of Amun-Ra and as a reflection of his incarnating light-power. The god's *ka* also takes up transitory residence in a statue-body, endowing it with life, as the royal *ka* of the ancestors (of the lower World Soul) temporarily occupies and animates the mortal body of an ordinary human being. The term *ba* designates not only the divine emanations and hypostases, but the bird-like human 'soul' as well, which likewise descends on the rays of the noetic Sun (Atum-Ra, Amun-Ra).

According to the Neoplatonists, the first genesis (*genesis prote*: Plato *Tim.* 41e3) of the souls is their descend from the noetic realm

---

86. Francoise Dunand and Christiane Zivie-Coche, ibid., p.15.
87. Lanny Bell, *The New Kingdom 'Divine' Temple: The Example of Luxor*, p. 131.

(*ten apo tou noetou kathodon*: Proclus *In Tim.* III.278.31–32) and the 'sowing' of their luminous vehicles around the visible gods as patrons and saviours, that the souls might call upon them as their appropriate leaders in the cosmic rite of salvation. These saviours may be conceived as the connective rays in the particular descending and ascending chain (*seira*) of manifestations, *bau*.

The gods send souls (manifestations, emanations, and powers, in the sense of *kheperu, bau,* and *sekhemu*) for the completion (*teleiosis*) of the cosmos. Certain exceptionally pure souls (those who belong to the royal category of 'perfect man', *anthropos teleios*) descend voluntarily and turn down toward bodies in order to reveal the divine attributes, qualities, and activities (*energemata,* or *erga,* as practical manifestations of the *energeiai*). In this case

the gods come forth (*proerchontai*) into the open and show (*epideiknuntai*) themselves through the pure and immaculate lives of souls (Iamblichus *In De anima* 27).[88]

So the gods show themselves as gods through the pure Osirian souls of the royal initiates and through the cult statues and images in the temples. One may restore one's 'likeness to god' (*homoiosis pros theon*) by participating in cultic activities and their supernatural powers, that is, as if kneeling in the *henu*-posture and undergoing inner transfiguration (*sakhu*) in the presence of his Lord, shining out through the image:

The deceased is initiated into the afterlife as into a temple, and the divine presence in which he shares has the character of cultic service.[89]

Every god is without form (*amorphotos*), even if he is envisioned in images and shapes (*morphotikos*), as Proclus maintains:

For there is no form in him, but rather from him, since he who envisions is not able to see the formless (*amorphoton*) without

---

88. Iamblichus, *De Anima*, text, translation, and commentary by John F. Finamore and John M. Dillon, Leiden: Brill, 2002, p. 55 and p. 156.

89. Jan Assmann, *Death and Salvation in Ancient Egypt*, pp. 200–201.

an image (*amorphotos*) but sees according to its own nature with images (*In Remp.* 1.39.28–40.4)

Therefore the Egyptians say that the Eastern *Ba* of the transcendent, unknowable, and invisible Amun (the Only One, *ua*) descends in order to unite with his image (*sekhem*, *tut*), as his cultic body, that thereby the king then might 'lift things' (make offerings, presenting his own spiritual integrity as the restored Eye of Horus, as the mirror-like *tut* of Amun) in the presence of God's *sah*. As the theological text in the Hathor's temple in Dendera relates:

> He (the pharaoh) has built the House-of-Uniter-of-the-Two-Lands for He-who-shines-as-gold, the Serpent in the House-of-the-Serpent, to guard the image (*semen*) of his body (*djet*) in his sanctuary and to protect his 'majesty' (*hem*) in his shrine, the image (*seshem*) of his mysteriousness carved in his chapel as beautiful expressions of Isden (i.e., Thoth, Djehuti, the tongue of Ra, the god of rituals and hieroglyphs), so that when he has seen his court and embraced his images (*sekhem*), he might alight (*khen*) upon his statue (*bes*) in his chapel and praise Ra for his city in sweetness of heart, his body enveloped in joy, and give great kingship to the pharaoh.[90]

The solar divine intelligence is active in the entire dynamic hypercosmic and cosmic hierarchy of *kheperu*: all levels of being, including the sensible realm and its creatures, are dependent on the constant influx of the breath of life (*suh en ankh*), analogous to the Greek *pneuma* and Indian *prana*. Eusebius, the Christian writer, in his *Praeparatio Evangelica*, informs us that the Egyptians somewhat identified Horus, Osiris-Helios (that is, Osiris-Ra) and Zeus-Amon (the Father of all living beings) with the all-pervading *pneuma*.[91] This all-pervading breath of Shu, being immanent in all things,

---

90. Slightly altered translation from: David Lorton, "The Theology of Cult Statues in Ancient Egypt".—*Born in Heaven, Made on Earth: The Making of the Cult Image in the Ancient Near East*, ed. Michael B. Dick, Winona Lake, Indiana: Eisenbrauns, 1999, p. 198.

91. Erik Iversen, *Egyptian and Hermetic Doctrine*, Copenhagen: Museum Tusculanum Press, 1984, p. 19.

emanates from Amun-Ra, because all created worlds (even what the Greeks conceived as *phusis*, nature) consists of heliophanies, of Ra's solar *kheperu*.

The Eye of Horus symbolizes this life force in its integrity and unity, realized as *henosis* in Neoplatonism. Therefore those gnostics who know the words and actions of the Eastern *Bau*, who sing hymns to the Sun Disk and mingle with the solar apes of Thoth, become one with Amun-Ra as His own recollected, unified, and uplifted *bau*. Thereby the initiate (one who is perfect in knowledge of God's great images and able to meet every *neter* face to face) acquires a noetic quality of *akh* and becomes spiritually effective. He becomes a living *ba* endowed with divine powers (*sekhemu*). Hence, his initiatic 'mummification' is necessary for his subsequent union with the Ra's *ba* in the form of Osiris.

REVELATION OF THE DIVINE FACE

The so-called Mansions of Millions of Years, such as the *Akhmenu* (the Festival Hall of Thutmoses III) were constructed as theurgic *yantras* (instruments of power) and holy places for the union of the pharaoh (as an *imago dei*) with God (in the form of his archetypal *Ba*). In this way, Amun-Ra's powers were legitimately transferred to the ruling king.

An efficacious royal offering also functions as a model for the spiritual ascent of the initiate gnostic, one who is ready to be 're-created'. By ascending the throne and coming to embody the divine 'kingship', the pharaoh (as the symbolic *persona mystica*) becomes 'immortal'. This rite of immortalization is variously reinterpreted and repeated by his followers, those who attend the royal state mysteries in order to pass through the 'doors of heaven'.

Rebirth means 'repeating birth' (*uhem mesiut*) in the sense of restoring one's primordial 'golden' state. Gold-dust is a symbol of sunlight, since the light becomes visible by alighting on the golden image and by image's participation (*metexis*) in the pervasive 'golden luminosity' of divine light. As L. Bell pointed out:

Thus luminosity, brilliance, and radiance possessed creative power and signaled deity's presence. The king's accession to

the throne and mounting of his chariot were likened to the
sun's rising; and the king's public manifestation at the Window
of Appearance was compared to the sun's appearance on the
eastern horizon.[92]

When the *ba* of Amun-Ra (in the form of one or another iconographic member of the Egyptian Ennead) unites with the temple,
he unites simultaneously with all images and hieroglyphs in which
his *Logos* is to be seen. The statue of the temple's lord is hidden in
the dark *set-amun*, which, like the mysterious tomb, symbolizes and
represents the ineffable transcendence. The ritually enacted
sequences of going into and coming out of the temple as *imago caeli*
are analogous to the going into the body of Nut (the Netherworld,
Duat, as the intermediate *mundus imaginalis* and the Osirian temple) and emerging from her womb into the radiance of the manifest
noetic 'day'.

While discussing the two forms of theophany (cosmic and cultic), R. B. Finnestad describes the ritual of the opening of the doors
that initiates the epiphany of God as follows:

> The temple is constructed in such a way as to lead the light in a
> straight line into the *St-wrt*-sanctuary which lies axially at the
> beginning of the processional road through the temple from
> its innermost localities. When the doors of the temple and the
> sanctuary are opened the light travels along this road and hits
> the solar boat resting on the representation of the mythical
> first mound emerging from the water and uplifting the god
> who creates the world with his rays. The ingoing light has a
> double function in that it both represents the uniting of the
> god with his seat and also effects the appearance of the creator
> from the place of darkness.[93]

Thereby the divine face is revealed every morning and the world
itself re-created. When the doors of the *mesen* chapel in the Edfu

92. Lanny Bell, ibid., p. 129.
93. Ragnhild Bjerre Finnestad, *Image of the World and Symbol of the Creator*,
p. 95.

temple are opened, light travels along the temple's axial road and is 'united with' (*henem*) the image of the Falcon-of-Gold. This means that Horus himself comes to see his image (*bes*) in the sanctuary of the High Seat (*set uret*), and consequently descends to his chief image (*sekhem*) and all other images (*akhemu*). The act of seeing god (*maa neter*) or rather the appearance (*khau*) of god when he is coming out of darkness, constitutes the most significant aspect of the morning ritual.

Ra himself is the divine interpreter of his own actions, deeds, and revelations: of the solar course, granted to the righteous persons, and of the priestly books, regarded as 'manifestations of Ra'. The process of interpretation, therefore, is tantamount to transfiguration (*sakhu*), which opens one's 'embalming' noetic gaze (the royal path to immortality) and 'makes one an *akh*' by showing the beautiful and mysterious divine face shining through the image of Osiris and Ra in a single shape.

Since justification is no less than 'moral mummification', and the word for mummy, *sah*, also means 'worthy' and 'aristocrat'[94] (like the Sanskrit term *brahman*), the initiate is both equated with Osiris and regarded as the follower of Horus, one who is carried in pregnancy like Thoth and is reborn like Ra. His mouth is opened by the chisel of Ptah, so that his body may be transfigured and he himself may emerge as a living *ba* of Ra.

DIVINE STATUES AND THEIR SACRED GIFTS

Essentially, the divine statues functioned in the same way as sacred trees, stones, rough-kewn blocks, columns, pillars, and other objects. These stones were sometimes believed to be 'fallen from Zeus' (*diopetes*) and, therefore, regarded as inherently animated with the noetic breath (*empnoös*) or the psychic substance (*empsuchos*) within them.

In this respect, we should remember that not only is the consecrated statue called *seshem* or *sekhem* in Egypt, but all of creation is equally viewed as an image (*sekhemu*, used in plural) of the solar

---

94. Jan Assmann, *Death and Salvation in Ancient Egypt*, p. 75.

Nous, namely, Amun-Ra. The Two Lands (Egypt) bear God's *sekh-emu*, and His breath is in everything. Amun-Ra himself is called an image (*tut*, in the sense of a noetically visible Statue—*Ishvara*, to say it in Sanskrit terms). He appeared when neither gods, nor names (*renu*) yet existed, and produced the *kau* of all *neteru*. Therefore Amun-Ra is described in terms that also apply to every kind of body as well as to the hieratic statues in which the gods (*neteru*) reveal themselves. D. Lorton says that in a papyrus from the reign of Ramesses II,

> Amun is described as 'fashioning (*hem*) himself, none knowing his shape (*qi*), goodly nature who came into being as the sacred, secret image (*bes*) who built (*qed*) his images (*seshemu*), who himself created (*qema*) himself, goodly power (*sekhem*) who made good his desire (*ib*), who joined his seed with his body to bring his egg into being within his secret self, being (*kheper*) who came into being (*kheper*), image (or model, *tut*) of what is fashioned (*mesut*).[95]

The cult of statues is regarded as being of divine origin, initiated and revealed by Amun-Ra himself through the hierarchy of the gods who are Amun's own *kheperu* and *bau*.

The natural unworked stones (*aergoi lithoi*) and meteors called *baituloi*, or *lithoi empsuchoi*, served as images, dwellings, and altars of the gods in ancient Phoenicia and Arabia. The Greeks, partly following the example of Eastern people, used to consecrate and set up the animated stones at the gates of their cities and temples in connection with Apollo. They maintained that not only cultic and talismanic statues, but even rocks can be consecrated (*tetelesmenos*) by anointing them with oil and decorating with flowers, wreaths, and garlands.

The story related by Psellus (*Script. Min.* 1.446.28) that Julian the Theurgist created a human mask (or head) of clay that shot thunderbolts at the enemy during a battle of Marcus Aurelius against the Dacians, is not a curious and exotic example of certain 'Chaldean *telestike*', but simply an illustration of old-standing Near Eastern and Mediterranean practices. Laiios, the telestic priest and philosopher,

---

95. David Lorton, *The Theology of Cult Statues in Ancient Egypt*, pp.185–186.

during the reign of Antiochus I (280–261 BC) protected the city of Antioch-on-the-Orontes from a plaque by similar means:

this Laiios commanded the city to carve a great mask of Charon (*charonion prosopon*) into the slope of a mountain that overlooked the city, and then by inscribing some special words on it brought an end to the pest. This monument was called the *charonion* or in later Greek *charoneion* (a formation much like the *gorgoneion*), and it has actually survived intact, although its present battered condition makes it impossible to see any distinguishing features that might mark it out as a dangerous death-dealing divinity (for example, the glaring or extraordinary eyes associated with words of the stem *char-*).[96]

A legendary talismanic statue of Athena, consecrated by a telestic priest (*telestes*) at the founding of Troy and called the Palladium, was of the same sort. The animated Trojan Palladium, usually regarded as fallen from heaven (*diopetes*), protected the city like the Assyrian guardians of the temples and palaces, namely, the statues of *lamassu* and *shedu*.[97]

For the Greeks, seeing necessarily involves being seen, therefore to see or contemplate the cult stones and sacred images, *xoana* and *agalmata*, that are usually hidden, means to cause a sort of divine epiphany and experience an inward vision or revelation. The radiance of the gilded, painted, adored, and perfumed statues themselves was quite literally dazzling. D. T. Steiner argues:

The use of precious stones for the eyes and of objects inlaid with enamel, glass, silver, and gold for the attributes, the gilding of the hair, and the adornment with vestments and jewels must have turned the images into an ever-shifting play of sparkling light. . . . That a peerless beauty belonged to these statues, as it did to the immortals when they showed themselves to man, needs little demonstration.[98]

96. Christopher A. Faraone, *Talismans and Trojan Horses*, p. 57.
97. Ibid., p. 7.
98. Deborah Tarn Steiner, *Images in Mind*, pp. 101–102.

This cultic *theoria* (a contemplation full of *thauma*, awe and wonder) serves as a foundation for the esoteric techniques of theurgic dealing with *theoptike psuche* ('the soul that sees god') and its union with true being (*to on*) and the divine (*to theion*). The worshiper might be granted an inward and unifying vision of the god that he is worshiping in the shape of cult image, and thereby not only partake in his transcendent, super-celestial, and cosmic order (*taxis*), but gain release or liberation (*he apolusis*) from the generative process. This liberation is re-actualized through the hieratic modes of ascent (*dia tinon hieratikon anodon: De myster.* 271.11–12), related to the cultic *theoptike dunamis*, the contemplative power that lets us see the gods.

Divination by means of animated divine statues (sometimes removed from their original cultic settings in the temples) is based on the same theological premises and hieratic techniques. It is therefore no wonder that in the context of the Neoplatonic theurgy, 'divination' as a prediction of future in the popular and exoteric sense is not highly esteemed. Divination here functions primarily as a means of mystagogy and union with the divine through mystical and ineffable images of the gods (*ten mustiken kai aporrheton eikona ton theon*), in the soul and in the temple. Iamblichus says:

> Only divine mantic prediction (*he theia mantike*), therefore, conjoined with the gods, truly imparts to us a share in divine life (*tes theias zoes*), partaking as it does in the foreknowledge and the intellections of the gods, and renders us, in truth, divine (*hemas theious hos alethos apergazetai*). And this genuinely furnishes the good for us, because the most blessed intellection of the gods (*ton theon noesis*) is filled with all goods (*De myster.* 289.3–7).

Accordingly, along with this foreknowledge (*prognosis*), the theurgists receive Beauty itself, as well as order, since both the divine *mantike* and *telestike* are aimed at the knowledge (*gnosis*) of the Father, which leads the souls upwards. Thereby the theurgist, who was previously united to the contemplation of the gods, is conceived of as 'divinized' (*ho theotos*). The sacred and theurgic gift of well-being (*eudaimonia*), received by the means of anagogic 'divination', is called 'the gateway to the Demiurge of all things', according to Iamblichus (*De myster.* 291.10–11).

The sacred gift of *eudaimonia* (the blessed daimonic state of being, like *ananda* in Hinduism) is like the 'embrace' (*sekhen*) that culminates the animation rite in pharaonic Egypt. This 'embrace' might consist in the ritual placement of a headdress adorned with a royal uraeus snake (equivalent to the noetic Eye and truth, *maat*) on the head of the statue or on the head of the initiate. In the case of a royal initiate, this theurgic coronation awakens him to the divine light, archetypal self-consciousness, and trans-personal integrity, thus transforming him into the empowered and living *ba* of Sekhmet-Hathor and, consequently, of Ra himself.

By the means of the anagogic powers that shine through the animated divine images and those that emanate from the *sunthemata* awakened within the soul itself, the initiate is raised upwards toward the gods. The Neoplatonic-Chaldean ritual of 'evoking the light' (*photos agoge, photagogia*) may initially be related to various meditations and invocations practiced while facing the animated stones and statues considered as receptacles for the presence of a deity. This contemplation and re-unification of wholeness (the restored Eye of Horus) turns one's imagination inward, but without thereby ignoring the ideal external beauty of the divine face. To say it in J.P. Anton's words: 'Imagination, hence, is a case of spiritual sight.'[99]

The divine light, revealed both inwardly and through the sunlight, 'illuminates the aether-like and luminous vehicle surrounding the soul with the divine light (*epilampei theio photi*), from which vehicle the divine appearances (*phantasiai theiai*), set in motion by the god's will, take possession of the imaginative power (*phantastiken dunamin*) in us. For the entire life of the soul and all the powers in it move subject to the gods. . . .' (*De myster.* 132.10–14).

In the context of Hellenic philosophy and metaphysics, *dunamis* (like the Egyptian *sekhem*) is a power that causes change and transformation. When understood in the active, anagogic sense, it unifies the separated members of Osiris' body, thereby bringing multiplic-

---

99. John P. Anton, "Plotinus and Augustine on Cosmic Alienation: Proodos and Epistrophe".—*The Journal of Neoplatonic Studies*, vol. IV, no. 2, 1996, p. 21.

ity back to psycho-somatic and noetic unity. Plotinus designates the first overflow (*proödos*) from the ineffable One as 'indefinite intellect' (*nous aoristos*), which immediately desires to turn back (*epistrophein*) and return to the One, thereby becoming an Intellect contemplating the Forms, that is, the demiurgic *Nous* proper. D. Rehm says:

> From the perspective of the indefinite intellect which looks toward the One, the One becomes an intelligible object (*noeton*). Yet the One as perceived is not identical with the One as it is.[100]

Just as *nous aoristos* (referred as *opsis*, 'sight', by Plotinus) seeks the One, so the awakened *nous* of the initiate seeks to contemplate the hidden essence (*ba sheta*) of the noetic *ba*, as revealed through the image. And just as the *nous aoristos*, being unable to see or think the ineffable One, is himself actualized as the demiurgic *Nous* (referred as *horasis*, 'sight seeing', by Plotinus), so the initiate, unable to see the hidden essence of Amun, is transformed into the integral, sacrificial, noetic Eye of Horus. Thus, just as the primeval Eye of Atum at first leaves him and then returns in order to be embraced, so the soul of the initiate *theoros* returns to the noetic plenitude of Atum, carried up by the *dunamis* of his contemplative Eye.

SALVATION AS RETURN TO THE DIVINE

The Neoplatonic-Chaldean theurgists used various symbols and sacramental objects that were akin to the specific gods invoked to appear in cultic epiphanies and inward visions or dreams. In Egypt, regarded as a 'temple of the whole world' (*mundi totius templum*) by the followers of Thoth-Hermes (*Asclepius* 24), these sacred objects are hieroglyphs (*medu neter*) and images (*sekhemu, akhemu*). The images are united with the descending divine *ba* and thereby reveal the dazzling radiance and beauty of the solar *Nous*. Consequently, the worshiper's imagination is inspired and possessed by the divine

100. David Rehm, Plotinus' "Treatment of Aristotelian δυναμισ in Emanation".—*The Journal of Neoplatonic Studies*, vol. ɪɪ, no.1, 1993, pp. 13–14.

light. The royal initiate (one who has already passed through the spiritual stations of death, dismemberment and inward mummification, having being transformed into the *ba* of 'living Osiris') hopes to see a certain unifying vision in his inner *akhet*, and for himself to be transformed into a flash of lightning, 'a flame moving before the wind to the end of the sky and of the earth' (*PT* 261).

Apart from the telestic statues, the theurgists alternatively used incantations (*epodai*) in order to evoke the uniform *phasmata ta ton theon*, the appearances of the gods in self-revelatory images (*ton autophanon agalmaton*) that shine forth distinctly and whose 'visions (*ta theamata*) are seen more clearly than the truth itself' (*De myster.* 77.1). Iamblichus says:

> Sometimes, moreover, they also conduct the light through water, since this, being transparent, is naturally well suited for the light's reception. At other times they cause it to shine on a wall, having expertly prepared in advance a place on the wall for the light, with sacred inscriptions of magical symbols (*tais hierais ton charakteron*). . . . There might be many other ways for conducting the light (*tes tou photos agoges*), but all are reduced to one, i.e. the shining of the bright light in whatever way and through whatever instruments it may shine forth (*De myster.* 134.2–10).

All these prescribed rituals and exercises are intended to effect the transformation that enables the theurgic soul (*theourgike psuche*) to understand the God (who himself is beyond being and transcends intellection) as the ultimate principle of all manifested life and well-being, because 'in all things an image of the Good carries God in it' (*eikon tagathou ton theon empheretai: De myster.* 164.11). By connecting all things to all, one may be perfectly established in the activities (*energeiai*) and intellections (*noeseis*) of the demiurgic powers. This kind of salvation means 'bringing Egypt (in the sense of the entire creation as an *imago*) to its Father Amun.' The initiate is to be saved through union with the 'eternal *Logos*', not as a particular individual, but as a priest of the solar *Nous* (Amun-Ra), now become the *akh*-intellect.

To say it in the Plotinian terms, by adoring and contemplating the divine image, made 'true and beautiful' by the animating force of the noetic Form, the soul discovers its own divine nature and essential inner beauty:

And in its own self-recognition it is lightened, because it now can aspire to its own inner harmony and seek to re-ascend to that principle inside itself which regulates, unifies and appeases.[101]

The enlightened bodies and images manifest the radiance and splendor of the divine beauty (*nefer*) which belongs to the Solar realms of *Nous* (Atum-Kheprer-Ra, Amun-Ra, or Ptah-Sekhmet-Nefertum) and shows itself as the life-bearing light. Hence, every true life (*ankh*) belongs to the realm of *akhu* (lights, intellects, spirits). As Plotinus would say, 'every life is an intellection' (*noesis: Enn.* iii.8.8.16–17) and 'living contemplation' (*theoria zosa*: ibid., iii.8.8.11), because being, truth, noetic perception (*noesis*), and beauty at the level of *Nous* coincide.

The metaphysical conception of *sekhem* or *tut* (*eikon*), to which the rays of deity descend in order that this image itself may ascend to the divine as a vehicle of the soul intended to reach the domain of archetypes, is inherited by the Christian mysticism of Dionysius the Areopagite, a tacit follower of Proclus:

The visible icon in Dionysius is the presence of the divine light. The light ray which originates in the divine is present in the icon. The divine itself is within the icon and the icon is the manifestation (*ekphansis*) of the divine. The icon is possessed by the divine light. The divine is entirely present in the icon, its stamp is on each impression.... The icon is a representation of divine light, of divine beauty. It appears through its light. Without light there can be no appearance.... As a figure which reveals the divine the icon refers to it in the same way as oral speech refers to internal thoughts.... In reality the icon with its beauty constitutes the principle of ascending return to

---

101. Jean-Marc Narbonne, "Action, Contemplation and Interiority in the Thinking of Beauty in Plotinus".—*Neoplatonism and Western Aesthetics*, ed. Aphrodite Alexandrakis, Albany: SUNY Press, 2002, p. 5.

the divine. The ascending function of the icon is due to God's illumination through the process of emanation. Again, the emanation of light from God constitutes for the icon a real ascent (*anagoge*) which is analogous to the actualized reception of light by it.[102]

As in the later Indian Tantric practices of divine worship and spiritual alchemy, the animated images in ancient Near Eastern and Mediterranean cultures served multiform theurgic purposes. They were related to the royal path of divinization and noetic rebirth. This path employed various esoteric rites of the soul's descent and ascent, aimed at one's spiritual recollection, reintegration, illumination, and union with the gods. However, for the modern mentality, shaped by the Biblical iconoclastic tradition and post-Enlightenment positivism, it is difficult if not impossible to comprehend all these divine self-disclosures, theophanies, and theurgic activities related to sacramental images and animated statues.

---

102. Dimitrios N. Koutras, "The Beautiful According to Dionysius".—*Neoplatonism and Western Aesthetics*, ed. Aphrodite Alexandrakis, Albany: SUNY Press, 2002, p. 36.

4

METAPHYSICAL SYMBOLS
& THEIR FUNCTION
IN THEURGY

Thus the universe and its contents were created in order to make known
the Creator, and to make known the good is to praise it; the means of making it known is to reflect it or shadow it; and a symbol is the reflection or
shadow of a higher reality. . . . Therefore, in respect of our having said that
a symbol worthy of the name is that in which the Archetype's radiation pre-
dominates over its projection, it is necessary to add that the sacramental
symbol proceeds from its Source, relatively speaking, by pure radiation.[1]

SYMBOLS AS ONTOLOGICAL TRACES OF THE DIVINE

The contemporary metaphysical understanding of symbol, as
opposed to the neoclassical conception of *mimesis*, is inherited from
the Neoplatonic theory of symbolic language which represents that
which by definition is beyond every representation but, nevertheless, shows the bodiless by means of bodies and serves as a ladder
for ascent to the divine.

F. W. Schelling and other Romantic writers, those who invented
the modern distinction between the mysterious symbol and allegory, followed Proclus in this respect, borrowing his theory of the
theurgic symbol, partly transmitted in the Christianized form
through Dionysius the Areopagite. But the term *allegoria* meant
rather different things for Proclus and for those Romantic thinkers
who rejected the 'classical' genre of writing related to Aristotelian

1. Martin Lings, *Symbol and Archetype. A Study of the Meaning of Existence,*
Cambridge: Quinta Essentia, 1991, p. 1 and p. 11.

poetics, labelling it as 'allegorical' and futile. However, our present task is not to investigate certain modern developments and mis-placements of ancient terms, concepts, or theories, but rather to reveal the Neoplatonic notion of the symbolic in the context of theu-rgy and in relation to the ancient Egyptian theological doctrines—to certain extent, at least, inherited by the later Pythagorean and Pla-tonic tradition.

In Neoplatonism, the divine symbols have a transformative and elevating power, like the noetic rays, because they are regarded as the things demiurgically woven into the very fabric of being and therefore directly attached to, and united with, the gods themselves, the principles of being. One should not be deceived by the Greek term *sumbolon*, which has so many different meanings, sometimes far removed from the realm of metaphysics. What is important is the underlying theological and cosmological conception of the divine principles and powers that appear and become visible through certain images, objects, numbers, sounds, omens, or other traces of presence.

Even in the iconoclastic Amarna theology (established in the reign of Akhenaten, 1352–1338 BC), that is theology which abolishes the mythical imagery, Aten is the One in whom million lives: the light creates everything and by seeing this light, the eye is created. J. Assmann says:

> God creates the eyes in order that they might look on him as he looks on them, and that his look might be returned and that light might assume a communicative meaning, uniting every-thing existing in a common space of intervision. God and men commune in light.[2]

In a sense, symbols are tantamount to the divine names that con-stitute the whole 'cultic' universe and ensure its cyclic dynamics: procession and return, descent and ascent. The Neoplatonic theory of the symbolic is only the late conceptualization (within the Hel-lenic philosophical tradition of onto-semiotics) of those ancient

---

2. Jan Assmann, *Moses the Egyptian. The Memory of Egypt in Western Monothe-ism*, Cambridge: Harvard University Press, 2002, p. 185.

metaphysical doctrines (such as the Ramesside theology of *bau* powers) which constitute the theurgic foundation of ancient civilizations and mythically express the dialectic of the One and the Many. Therefore those hieratic realities, entities, and things that are described as the ineffable (or esoteric) symbols and tokens (*ta aporrheta sumbola kai sunthemata*) of the gods might equally well be designated by many other terms, unrelated to the specific Hellenic conception of the symbolic and equated, for example, with the Egyptian 'divine words' (*medu neter*, hieroglyphs) which constitute the entire visible world. If the universe is a manifestation (as the Egyptian term *kheperu* indicates), then all manifested noetic and material entities are nothing but the multiform images, symbols, and traces of the ineffable One shining through the intellective rays of *deus revelatus*, the demiurgic Intellect.

The gods create everything by means of representations (images which reflect their noetic archetypes) and establish the hidden 'thoughts' of the Father through the symbolic traces or tokens (*dia sunthematon*) that are intelligible only to the gods themselves and possess the uplifting *heka* power, to say it in the Egyptian terms. As P. Struck pointed out:

> Here the material world is fabricated by representations, but it is meaningful (that is, has a semantic dimension) through its being a *sunthema/sumbolon*. The image (*eikon*) marks the material world in its status as a fainter reproduction of a higher principle, but the world seen as symbol indicates its status as a manifestation—that is, something that works according to the logic of the trace, with the capacity to point us back up to the higher orders that produced it.[3]

Sumbola and *sunthemata*, understood in this particular metaphysical sense, are not arbitrary signs, but ontological traces of the divine, inseparable from the entire body of manifestation (*ellampsis*): the cosmos, as the revealed divine *agalma* (statue, shrine), itself is the Symbol *par excellence* of the noetic realm and the Creator. It

---

3. Peter T. Struck, *Birth of the Symbol. Ancient Readers at the Limits of their Texts*, Princeton: Princeton University Press, 2004, p. 221.

represents that which is above representation and is an immanent receptacle of the transcendent principles.

Therefore the demiurgic *Logos* is both the sower and distributor of all ontological symbols (or rather, symbols constituting its own manifested totality), and these symbols (when gathered, awakened, re-kindled) lead up to the noetic and supra-noetic unity. As J. F. Finamore observes, 'the *sumbola* become passwords or tokens in the soul's ritual ascent.'[4] This is so, not because of our thinking (if thoughts, *ennoiai*, themselves are not regarded as a special sort of *sunthemata*), but by virtue of the ritual accomplishment (*telesiourgia*) of ineffable acts and the mysterious power of the unspeakable symbols that allow us to re-establish theurgic union with the gods (Iamblichus *De mysteriis* 96.13 ff).

Hence, through the proper actualization (and recollection) of these divine symbols, the hypercosmic life of the soul is re-actualized. The ascent (*anodos*) through invocations (*kleseis*), symbolic contemplations, and rites (*erga*), results in revelation of the blessed sights (*makaria theamata*) and the activity (*energeia*) which is no longer human.

THE ANAGOGIC POWER
OF SECRET NAMES AND TOKENS

The Greek term *sumbolon* (derived from the verb *sumballein*, meaning 'to join') initially denoted a half of a whole object, such as *tessera hospitalis*, which could be joined with the other half in order that two contracting parties (or members of certain secret, esoteric brotherhoods) might have proof of their identity. Therefore the symbol appears and becomes significant only when two parties make an intentional rupture of the whole, or when the One manifests itself as plurality, that is, when Osiris or Dionysus is rent asunder. In this original sense, the symbol 'reveals its meaning by the fact that one of its halves fits in with or corresponds to the other.'[5]

---

4. John F. Finamore, "Plotinus and Iamblichus on Magic and Theurgy".— *Dionysius*, vol. XVII, 1999, p. 83.

5. James A. Coulter, *The Literary Microcosm: Theories of Interpretation of the Later Neoplatonists*, Leiden: E. J. Brill, 1976, p. 61.

When viewed in accordance with the 'vertical' metaphysical asymmetry, one half of the imagined *tessera hospitalis* represents the visible thing (the symbol proper) and another half stands for the invisible noetic or supra-noetic reality symbolized by the lower visible part. The initiation and spiritual ascent consists in joining these two separate parts. That means re-uniting the manifested *sumbolon* (as a trace) and the hidden principle which is 'symbolized' by it. In this way Osiris (or Dionysus) is re-assembled, and the symbol itself is dissolved in the symbol-transcending unity (*henosis*). According to Damascius:

> The object of the initiatory rites (*ton teleton*) is to take souls back to a final destination (*eis telos anagagein*), which was also the starting point from which they first set out on their downward journey, and where Dionysus gave them being, seated on his Father's throne, that is to say, firmly established in the integral Zeusian life (*In Phaed.* 1.168.1–4).

When symbols are reassembled into a completed whole, this means both that the microcosmic Eye of Horus (or *imago dei*) is restored and that the macrocosmic theophany of *pantheos* (the Lord of All, *neb tem*, the All-Worker) is reaffirmed as the transcendent unity. Within this kind of ancient cosmology, the descending and ascending rays of manifestation are considered as a multi-leveled hierarchy of *sumbola* and *sunthemata* that constitute the universal 'language' of Being and its existential body. R. Lamberton says:

> Just as there are various modes of perception that correspond to the successive modes of being, extending from the total, unified perception exercised by a god down to the passivity of our sense-impressions in this world, so there are different levels of language that correspond to these modes of perception — a hierarchy of systems of meaning, of kinds of utterances — that extend from a creative, divine 'language' (not, presumably, recognizable as such by us) down to the 'language' that exists on the final fragmented level of the senses.... Each lower language is actually the 'interpreter' (*hermeneus*) of the

higher one, in that it renders it comprehensible at a lower level, at the expense of its (opaque, inaccessible) coherence.[6]

The secret names of the gods are the anagogic symbols: they function both as *epodai* (recitations, elevating spells) and as the gnostic passwords for entry into the other-worldly realm, the subsequent transformation, and noetic rebirth. Therefore the 'symbolic life' is the life of knowledge which enables one's recollection, reintegration, and return to the *archetypus mundus*. The Egyptian *Book of the Dead* says:

As for him who knows this spell (or symbolic utterance), he will be a worthy spirit in the realm of the dead, and he will not die again in the realm of the dead, and he will eat in the presence of Osiris. As for him who knows it on earth, he will be like Thoth. . . . (*BD* 135).[7]

By knowing the proper words of power (*hekau, sunthemata*), the Osiris-like initiate or the 'deceased' might proceed to the throne of the integral archetypal Osiris and be united (as the *ba* of Osiris) with the *ba* of Ra. The process of transformation, *sakhu*, literally means 'making an *akh*' (the shining noetic spirit, divine *nous*). This ritualized transformation is designated as 'going forth by (or into) day' (*pert em hru*), that is, ascending to the noetic realm and 'going out' from the Duat (the alchemical body of Osiris or Nut) into the intelligible 'day' of Ra and appearing as Ra. So in the *Pyramid Texts* the paradigmatic royal initiate ascends on the wing of Thoth, flying up as a falcon and alighting on the divine throne like a scarab, saying:

My seat is with you, O Ra. . . . I will ascend to the sky to you, Ra, for my face is that of falcons, my wings are those of ducks. . . . O men, I fly away from you (*PT* 302).[8]

6. Robert Lamberton, *Homer the Theologian: Neoplatonist Allegorical Reading and the Growth of the Epic Tradition,* Berkeley: University of California Press, 1986, p. 167 and p. 169.

7. *The Ancient Egyptian Book of the Dead,* tr. Raymond O. Faulkner, ed. Carol Andrews, Austin: University of Texas Press, 2001, p. 123.

8. *The Ancient Egyptian Pyramid Texts,* tr. R. O. Faulkner, Warminster: Aris and Phillips, 1969, p. 92.

Thereby one's *ba* (as a symbol) is made *akh*-effective in the Isle of Fire (the solar realm of Platonic Forms). The theurgic texts to be ritually recited as a means of ascent themselves are regarded as *akhu* that are 'pleasing to the heart of Ra.' The Egyptian initiatory rite is based on the mutual *akh*-effectiveness of father and son, as of the Greek *sumbolon*: 'akh is a son for his father, *akh* is a father for his son', both appearing in the presence of Thoth, the lord of hieroglyphs (*medu neter*) and wisdom.

The ultimate goal (*telos*) of this 'symbolic wisdom' is to make the Eye of Horus sound and whole, that is, to restore one's primordial 'golden' nature, like the pure mirror (*ankh*) which reflects the intelligible light of Ra and is 'sacrificially' reintegrated into the realm of the *akhu*. This involves one's spiritual and alchemical transmutation in the 'tomb' built (in the ideal archetypal sense) by the gods themselves, including Seshat, the goddess of writing.

Everything has two designations, one in the realm of terrestrial *sumbola*, another in the realm of the gods whose names are viewed as anagogic passwords known only to the initiate. At the same time, every element in the domain of the temple liturgy, be it a priest, a thing, or a place, becomes the 'name' (*ren*) of a deity whom it reveals or interprets. Likewise, every offering (designated as the Eye of Horus) represents a substance that restores truth (*maat*) and unity (*sema*) or reassembles something that had fallen apart. As J. Assmann says, it is the symbol of a reversibility that might heal everything, even death:

> There is a close connection between cultic commentaries, with their principle of sacramental explanation, and initiatory examinations, with their principle of secret passwords that relate to the divine realm.... In the initiatory examinations, there is a secret language, and the initiate demonstrates his mastery of it. He who knows the secret language belongs to the secret world to which it refers, and he may enter it. In the cultic commentaries, there is a sacramental explanation of the ritual by means of which the cultic acts are transposed into the context of the divine realm.[9]

9. Jan Assmann, *Death and Salvation in Ancient Egypt*, p. 353.

In the context of the Hellenic Mysteries and Orphico-Pythagorean tradition, the symbol may be a deity's secret name, an omen or a cultic formula (that may include the divine cultic epithets, themselves regarded as *sunthemata*). These symbols allow the initiate to pass into the realm of the gods, the Netherworld, doing this like the Egyptian pharaoh who takes the night-journey 'as the representative of all human beings'[10] and sails with the *Ba* of Ra in the solar barque. The acquired Apollonian wisdom enables one to perceive the hidden divine 'thoughts', the immaterial archetypes, or Ideas.

The Pythagorean *sumbola* are also *ainigmata* (riddles, obscure hieratic sayings). The prophetic utterances and sneezes, related to Demeter of Eleusis, are called 'symbols' as well. Since an understanding of the symbols as a sort of secret code of both demiurgy and theurgy stems from the Orphico-Pythagorean tradition, inherited and conceptualized by the Neoplatonists, P. Struck rightly emphasizes that 'the power of the symbol is born out of the power of the secret.'[11] He says:

> In both the mysteries and esoteric philosophy, symbols are passwords of authentication that just happen to be enigmatic, interpretable speech.[12]

ANIMATED THEURGIC HIEROGLYPHS
OF THE HIDDEN AMUN

The Greeks themselves, contrary to the modern scholarly tastes and prejudices, related the Pythagorean symbolism to the Egyptian theory of 'divine speech'. The symbol as hieroglyph (the visible shape of the invisible Platonic Form), as gnostic password and word of power (*heka*), is inseparable from the Egyptian ways of thought. Therefore the ancient Hellenic writers correctly maintained that

---

10. Theodor Abt and Erik Hornung, *Knowledge for the Afterlife. The Egyptian Amduat—A Quest for Immortality*, Zurich: Living Human Heritage Publications, 2003, p. 24.

11. Peter T. Struck, *Birth of the Symbol*, p. 103.

12. Ibid., p. 88.

symbols (or secret names of the gods that work 'symbolically', *sumbolikos*, and ensure union, *henosis*) are a particularly Egyptian mode of imitating the demiurgic activity of the gods. According to Plutarch's trustworthy remark:

> Pythagoras, as it seems, was greatly admired, and he also greatly admired the Egyptian priests, and, copying their symbolism (*to sumbolikon auton*) and esoteric teachings (*musteriodes*), incorporated his doctrines in riddles (*ainigmasi*). As a matter of fact most of the Pythagorean precepts do not at all fall short of the writings that are called hieroglyphs (*De Iside et Osiride*, 354ef).

The majority of contemporary classicists (following the erroneous suggestions of positivistic Egyptology) misunderstood Porphyry's claim regarding the symbolic (*sumbolike*) aspect of the Egyptian hieroglyphs. Porphyry the Phoenician says:

> In Egypt he (Pythagoras) lived among the priests and learned the wisdom and language of the Egyptians, and three kinds of writing, epistolographic, hieroglyphic, and symbolic, of which some is ordinary speech according to *mimesis*, and some allegorizes according to certain riddles' (*kata tinas ainigmous: Vita Pyth.* 11–12).

J. Assmann ensures us that Porphyry was right in describing a variant of the Egyptian script as symbolic, because, in fact, there are four distinct forms of writing in Egypt: demotic, hieratic, hieroglyphic, and cryptographic (or symbolic). The latter was a secret code accessible only to the initiate and based on the priestly notion that this symbolic script (whose signs are laden with the symbolic knowledge) is an imitation of divine demiurgy: here the hieroglyphs are regarded as tokens of creation conceived by Ptah, the Memphite Demiurge, and recorded by Thoth. Consequently, they are imbued with the theurgic function as well. In addition, both script and sacred images in their unity are designated as 'gods' (*neteru*). The symbols are gods made visible in stone, the manifest substance of immortality. J. Assmann says:

Iamblichus perfectly expresses the principle of 'direct significa-
tion' that underlies the cryptography of the late temple
inscriptions. . . . This specifically Egyptian view is the foundation of the Greek's mythical vision of hieroglyphs. The mistake
of the Greeks was not that they interpreted hieroglyphic script
as a secret code rather than a normal writing system. The Egyptians had in fact transformed it into a secret code and so
described it to the Greeks. The real misunderstanding of the
Greeks was to have failed to identify the aesthetic significance of
cryptography as calligraphy. The question then arises whether
their misunderstanding might not also have been encouraged
by the Egyptian priests. It surely cannot be pure chance that the
systematic complication of hieroglyphic script coincided with
the Greek invasion and Ptolemaic foreign rule.[13]

The members (*hau*) of the animated body may be regarded as
symbols that are to be spiritually reassembled into the image (*tut*) of
Osiris, itself constituted by the *sunthemata*, which modern scholars
conventionally designate by the word 'amulet', not forgetting to add
(almost mechanically) the label 'magical'. These alleged 'amulets'
might be viewed as the fundamental theurgic tokens or metaphysical symbols that appear in the form of certain basic hieroglyphs,
such as *ib* (heart), *pet* (sky), *kheper* (scarab beetle), *sema* (union),
ta-uer (the symbol of Abydos and its lord Osiris), *bik* (falcon of
Horus), *tiet* (Isis knot), *seshen* (lotus), *ankh* (life, mirror), the *djed*
column of Osiris, *shen* (ring, symbol of eternity, also mirrored in
the shape of *ouroboros*), *djeneh* (wing), *shut* (feather), *mehyt* (the
papyrus scepter), *uedjat* (the restored Eye of Horus), *sekhem* scepter,
uas scepter, *menit* necklace and so on.

By putting these hieroglyphs on the eidetic *sah*-body (now habitually called 'mummy'), a sort of the alchemical Osirian statue is
constructed and the symbolic composition of *heka* powers is
arranged. The divinized royal initiate, who is theurgically united
with the gods (symbolically identified as hieroglyphs and members

13. Jan Assmann, *The Mind of Egypt. History and Meaning in the Time of the Pharaohs,* tr. Andrew Jenkins, New York: Metropolitan Books, 2002, p. 419.

of his metaphysical body) and turned into the reestablished *tut neter*, the overwhelming image of the ineffable God, revealed as a Statue of the reassembled pantheon, speaks as follows:

> I am Ra, continually praised; I am the knot of the god within the tamarisk. . . . My hair is Nun; my face is Ra; my eyes are Hathor; my ears are Upuat; my nose is She who presides over her lotus-leaf; my lips are Anubis; my molars are Selket; my incisors are Isis the goddess; my arms are the Ram (*Ba*), the Lord of Mendes; my breast is Neith, Lady of Sais; my phallus is Osiris; my muscles are the Lords of Kheraha; my chest is He who is greatly majestic; my belly and my spine are Sekhmet; my buttocks are the Eye of Horus; my thighs and my calves are Nut; my feet are Ptah, my toes are living falcons; there is no member of mine devoid of a god, and Thoth is the protection of all my flesh. . . . I am the Lord of Eternity; may I be recognized as Kheprer, for I am the Lord of the Uereret-crown. I am he in whom is the Sacred Eye, and who is in the Egg, and it is granted to me to live by them. I am he in whom is the Sacred Eye, namely the Closed Eye, I am under its protection. I have gone out, I have risen up, I have gone in, I am alive. I am he in whom is the Sacred Eye, my seat is on my throne, I dwell in my abode with it, for I am Horus who treads down millions, my throne is ordered for me, and I will rule from it (*BD* 42).

Regarding the claim that there is no member of the divinized initiate devoid of god (when he is transformed into *pantheos*), Iamblichus says almost the same thing. Raising the problem as to how the gods may receive the allotment of certain places—for example, how Athena (Neith) may be allotted both Athens and Sais in Egypt—Iamblichus inquires:

> How would any part of the All be completely devoid of God? And how would any place survive entirely unprotected by the superior ones? (Proclus *In Tim.* 1.145.5).[14]

14. *Iamblichi Chalcidensis in Platonis dialogos commentariorum fragmenta*, ed.and tr. John M. Dillon, Leiden: E.J. Brill, 1973, p. 119.

Consequently, everything is theophany, and all manifested reality is 'full of gods' (*panta plere theon*). The *Logos* which is in the Soul of All (*ho logos ho en te psuche pantos*: Proclus *In Tim.* II.309.11) knows everything and rules everything. The liberated *ba* of the theurgist is the *Ba* of the All.

Words and tokens give life to the realities by drawing into manifest existence the powers that are named or revealed in images. The human figure (as a living statue) itself is a hieroglyph: its different positions (like Tantric *asanas* and *mudras*) represent the dynamic ritual of 'writing', which is tantamount to the manifestation of life (*ankh*). The written word might be imbued with the life of the thing represented, like the animated hieratic statue or the human body, itself being viewed as a sort of 'written word'.

As the demiurgic and theurgic tokens, able to embody the powers (*sekhemu*) and 'textual' epiphanies of the gods, the hieroglyphs were regarded virtually as living things. They are receptacles of the divine rays, like the statues (whose shapes imitate the forms of hieroglyphs), or even these very powers themselves, possessing 'a magical life of their own'.[15] They can function theurgically: not only within the written text, but within the text-like universe as a whole.

Though symbols by definition stand for something other than what they depict, or something other than they are as the manifested *kheperu*, the Egyptian hieroglyphic script hardly emphasizes any division between 'inner' and 'outer'. However, the Egyptian symbols clearly presuppose the hidden (*sheta*) dimension, or the hidden meaning (*huponoia*, to say it in the terms of Hellenic hermeneutical tradition).

Therefore symbolism is aptly described as 'a primary form of ancient Egyptian thought', which is symbolically oriented to 'a degree rarely equaled by other cultures.'[16] The Egyptian universe of symbols simultaneously exhibits different meanings and shows different hermeneutical perspectives, even consciously encouraging the ambiguity and theological polysemy of their symbolism.

---

15. Richard H. Wilkinson, *Symbol and Magic in Egyptian Art*, London: Thames and Hudson, 1999, p. 150.

16. Ibid., p. 7.

When we translate this metaphysical language of *medu neter* (the language that constitutes millions of *kheperu*: images, signs, symbols, breaths of life, heliophanies) into the language of Neoplatonic philosophical discourse, we can say, along with Plotinus, that 'all things are filled full of signs' (*semeion*: *Enn.* II.3.7.12), or rather that all things *are* signs and images of the vast ontological Text. The multiplicity of gods (*neteru*) is the multiplicity of symbols, images, and names of the hidden God (Amun), the One who is One-in-the-many, the *Ba* that assumes form in the many gods and, simultaneously, remains concealed from them. As O. Kuisma remarks:

> Since all things are ultimately dependent on the One, each and every thing can be thought of as hinting at it either directly or via mediating stages. Every particular thing in the hierarchy of being is in this sense a sign, which points towards its causes, either because of similarity or because of analogy.[17]

Like the Neoplatonic term *to hen*, the Egyptian name Amun (meaning 'hidden', 'invisible', 'transcendent') is merely an epithet which, nevertheless, might be regarded as the supreme *sunthema* of the ineffable Principle, simply because every divine name is a name of this hidden God. He is called *Ba*, the paradigm of all life-bearing *bau* that constitute millions of forms (*kheperu*), millions of symbols, but really there is no name for him:

> His hidden all-embracing abundance of essence cannot be apprehended.[18]

To say it in late Neoplatonic terms, the ineffable One, regarded as pure unity, is above *dunamis*, power, be it creative or revealing, because it is above division and above the first noetic duality (like Atum's Heka, *hen on*, is above Shu and Tefnut in the Egyptian theology). But the One is also the source of manifestation (*ellampsis*) and the source of the duality of *dunamis*, which results in Being, regarded as 'mixture' (*mikton*) that is posterior to the principles of

17. Oiva Kuisma, *Proclus' Defense of Homer*, Helsinki: Societas Scientiarum Fennica, 1996, p. 54.
18. Jan Assmann, *Moses the Egyptian*, p. 197.

Limit and the Unlimited. This triad is approximately analogous to the Memphite theological triad of Ptah-Sekhmet-Nefertum. Being as procession and return is the totality of *kheperu*, which affirm both the divine transcendence and immanence. As J. M. P. Lowry relates:

On the side of division *qua* division, being would turn out to be simply nothing, or matter: the pure *dunamis* as possibility. On the side of unity *qua* unity being would turn out to be everything, simply, or the One: the pure *dunamis* as *energeia*. Accordingly, Being can be neither the one nor the other but is the procession and return of the One.[19]

NEOPLATONIC RITES OF METAPHYSICAL REVERSION

For Proclus, the terms theurgy (*theourgia*), hieratic art (*hieratike techne*), and theosophy (*theosophia*, literally: 'divine wisdom', 'wisdom of the gods') are synonymous. They designate the spiritual path and method of ascent, revealed and established by the gods themselves.

By means of this *theourgike techne*, the soul is purified, transformed, and conducted to the divine realm, as if carried 'on the wing of Thoth'. Thereby the vindicated soul is separated from the mortal receptacle and re-united with the noetic principles. Symbolically ('in the most mystic of all initiations': *en te mustikotate ton teleton*: Proclus *Plat. Theol.* IV.9, p.193, 38) this separation from the gross body is represented by burying the initiate's body with the exception of the head:

The head is not buried, because the soul which abides in it does not undergo 'death'. This sacramental act has an additional peculiar feature: it is the initiate who at the binding of the theurgists buries his own body.[20]

---

19. J. M. P. Lowry, *The Logical Principles of Proclus' ΣΤΟΙΧΕΙΩΣΙΣ ΘΕΟΛΟΓΙΚΗ as Systematic Ground of the Cosmos,* Amsterdam: Rodopi, 1980, pp. 66–67.

20. Hans Lewy, *Chaldean Oracles and Theurgy. Mysticism, Magic and Platonism in the Later Roman Empire,* Nouvelle edition par Michael Tardieu, Paris: Etudes Augustiniennes, 1978, p. 205.

This separation, purification, and elevation to the realm of eternal, noetic 'day' (as well as subsequent return to the ineffable One) is regarded as the existential and metaphysical rite of 'homecoming'. The Neoplatonists maintained that the lowest things are in the highest and the highest things in the lowest (*en te tois protois ta eschata kai en tois eschatois ta protista*: Proclus *Hier. Art.* 148). In the depths of its own nature, each manifested thing keeps the mysterious and hidden 'symbol of the universal Father' (*to sumbolon tou panton patros*), the secret hieroglyph of Atum, like the unspeakable (*aporrhetos*) token of one's essential apophatic identity with the One.

The initiatory priests and the practitioners of the telestic science (*he telestike episteme*), those who deal with the divine *sunthemata*, are called *telestai*. They purify both the body as material receptacle of the divine rays and the soul as the immortal divine seed or the wingéd bird, detached from the inanimate body and the related psychosomatic self-consciousness. As the *Pyramid Texts* say:

[*Ba*] to heaven, *shat* (body in the sense of corpse, *khat*) to earth (*PT* 474).

Similarly, the priests consecrate (*telein*) cult statues of the gods. Thereby the statues are animated, illuminated, and imbued with the divine powers (*sekhemu*). In both cases, the *telestai* call forth the gods, or rather their *bau* (to say it in the Egyptian parlance), that 'fill' the purified and properly prepared receptacles, either statues, or the divinized bodies, themselves transformed into hieroglyphs.

Eventually, by his own eidetic and henadic nature, the *telestes* worships the Lord of All (*neb tem*), being unified with Him by the soul's mystic *sunthema* (or hieroglyph), *in illo tempore* inserted by the Father Himself. This unification is possible, because the Father himself has sown the secret symbols (*sumbolois arrhetois ton theon*) in the soul, according to Proclus (*In Tim.* 1.211.1). And these symbols are explicitly designated as *ta arrheta onomata ton theon*, the unspeakable divine names (*In Alcib.* 441.27). In this respect Proclus follows the Chaldean theurgists, namely, the famous fragment of the *Chaldean Oracles* (fr. 108 = Proclus *In Crat.* 21.1–2).

In a sense, the paternal symbols, or the unspeakable divine

names, are identical with the thoughts of the Paternal Intellect. These demiurgic thoughts are the noetic Forms, manifested as the Chaldean Iynges, as *voces mysticae*, or the hieroglyphic 'building-blocks' that constitute the very textual fabric of our existence. Because of its noetic origins, the soul has an inborn (albeit temporarily forgotten) knowledge of these world-creating, world-ruling, and, simultaneously, elevating names.

As Proclus argues, everything is unified by means of its own mystic *sunthema*. By becoming one with this re-activated divine *sunthema*, the telestic priest is theurgically united with the unknowable Source of all good.[21] When the essential hidden *sunthema* is remembered, re-awakened, and re-sounded, the soul, mythically speaking, returns through the fiery ray to its noetic and supra-noetic Principle. But, esoterically speaking, we might say that God returns to God, even if, ultimately, this 'return' is only a sort of the divine dream, or illusion, when viewed from the point of the all-embracing, ineffable God himself.

H. Lewy argues that a *sunthema* which is uttered in prayers, supplications, and invocations (*entuchiai kai kleseis*) disposes the Paternal Intellect in favour of the soul's wish to be elevated, and this *sunthema* is identical with the one of the symbols which the demiurgic *Nous* has sown throughout the universe and which are laden with the ineffable beauty of the Ideas.[22] These *sunthemata*, like the divine sparks of the soul, or the internal fiery seeds, enable the rite of *anagoge* (ascent) and *apathanatismos* (immortalization). Thereby the soul is lifted upwards by means of the solar (noetic) rays of Apollo or the Egyptian Amun-Ra. This ascent is regarded by H. Lewy as 'the chief mystery of the Chaldean sacramental community.'[23]

According to Proclus, every soul is composed of *noeroi logoi* (intellective reason principles) and *theia sumbola* (divine symbols). The former are related to the intelligible Forms, reflected or manifested at the level of the soul, and, consequently, with *Nous*; the

---

21. Laurence Jay Rosan, *The Philosophy of Proclus. The Final Phase of Ancient Thought*, New York: Cosmos, 1949, pp. 213–214.

22. Hans Lewy, ibid., p. 191.

23. Ibid., p. 177.

latter is related to the divine henads (the fundamental supra-noetic unities) and the One itself.

For Proclus, the One (*to hen*) is God, and the multiplicity of gods is the multiplicity of self-complete henads (*henades eisin outoteleis hoi theoi: ET* 114). He argues that there are two orders of henads, one consisting of self-complete principles, the other of irradiations (*ellampseis*) from them. These irradiations are like the Egyptian *bau* that constitute the descending divine series whose members (*bau*) appear at different levels of reality. They may be designated as symbols that function as a means of transformative ascent and re-union of the soul (itself regarded as the *ba* in the multiple sequence of divine *bau*).

In this sense, the word *ba* means any noetic and psychic 'manifestation' (as an image or a symbol of some higher principle), imbued with being, life, and intelligence, albeit in different degrees and proportions. In the descending chain (analogous to the Neoplatonic *seira*) of theogony, cosmogony, and demiurgic irradiation, Ra, for instance, is the manifested *ba* of the ineffable Principle; Sekhmet, the *ba* of Ra; Bastet, the *ba* of Sekhmet, and every living cat (or rather its hidden *sunthema*, which may dwell within the statuette or mummy of the sacred cat), the *ba* of Bastet.

There are 'millions' of such descending and ascending chains, the rays or 'sounding breaths' of the intelligible Sun. The 'horizontal' levels of these 'vertical' rays constitute both the theophanic being itself (its eidetic orders, *taxeis*) and the hierarchy of divine *sunthemata*. However, the range of possible theological perspectives and possible meanings for any given symbol is very wide. So one may equally say that God's *ba* is Ra 'in the sky' (in the noetic realm), his body is Osiris 'in the West' (in the psychic Netherworld, *Anima Mundi*), and his cult image is in southern Heliopolis (Thebes, the City of Amun, here standing for the entire terrestrial world).

The rite of metaphysical reversion (*epistrophe*) consists in the soul's ability to identify itself with its hidden *sunthema*, and through it with the higher cause.[24] However, the telestic priest uses

---

24. E.R. Dodds, in Proclus *The Elements of Theology*, tr. E.R. Dodds, Oxford: Clarendon Press, 1992, p. 223.

many different visible, audible, and tangible symbols in his rites, including various metals, minerals, stones, plants, and animals, since all of them belong to one or another particular chain of manifestation and, therefore, may lead back to the initial monad.

Accordingly, the theurgic *sumbola* and *sunthemata* do not merely stand for invisible and divine things, but are inherently connected with them: in a sense, they *are* 'gods', as the being-constructing hieroglyphs are 'gods', and for this reason manifest reality is sacred both in principle and *de facto*. The *sumbola* of the noetic realm are immanently woven into the very fabric of the material world and constitute its unifying divine foundation.

Proclus compares the animated statues which contain both visible and invisible *sunthemata* (also regarded as *pharmaka*—drugs, charms, secret means) of the gods to the entire sensible universe which is constructed like a statue by the Demiurge and contains all kinds of visible and invisible *sumbola* of the noetic and supra-noetic realms.

For Proclus, not only are words *sumbola*, but even myths are *sumbola*, and consequently serve as a means of esoteric mystagogy (*arrhetos mustagogia*). All these symbols are the constituent parts of the manifested cosmos, itself regarded as a divine statue (*agalma*), the well-ordered *sphaira* of light, having many different eidetic faces, levels of being, and chains of irradiation. As A. Sheppard pointed out:

> Thinking of it diagrammatically, we may say that the world was conceived as organized into both horizontal and vertical lines. The heliotrope, on the low level of plant life, is a *sumbolon* of the sun which is in the same *seira*, the same 'vertical line', but on a higher level of being, a higher 'horizontal' line. The sun in turn is a *sumbolon* of higher realities in the same *seira* such as the god Apollo, and ultimately, as in Plato *Rep.* VI, of the transcendent Good which is the Neoplatonic One. The belief that such 'vertical line' relationships hold between the natural world and the intelligible world, is equally essential both to theurgy and to Proclus' metaphysics.[25]

25. Anne D. R. Sheppard, *Studies on the 5th and 6th Essays of Proclus' Commentary on the Republic*, Göttingen: Vandenhoeck and Ruprecht, 1980, p. 152.

The symbol of the transcendent One, hidden in the soul, is regarded as the essential henadic aspect of the soul (called the 'one of the soul') by which the mystical union with the One is realized. In this sense, the soul-complex must be deconstructed and reduced to this essential *sunthema*, the hidden and ineffable 'flower' (*anthos*), which is tantamount to the self-subsisting unity beyond being and substance.

Hence, to be unified and to be divinized are the same, insofar as all gods, according to Iamblichus, Syrianus, and Proclus, are 'self-subsistent hypostases' or *huparxeis* (pure supra-noetic entities) beyond being and substance.[26] At the lower levels of reality, the *sunthemata* function as receptacles for the gods (for their *bau*, to say it in Egyptian terms), because 'the gods illuminate matter and are present immaterially in material things.'[27]

Even spices, aromatics, sounds, and numbers may serve as the proper receptacles for the anagogic divine powers. The Demiurge and his assistant *neteru* themselves determine and conduct the theurgic rites that put the soul into correspondence and *sustasis* (conjunction) with the gods. H. Lewy argues that the term *sustasis* is often applied to the prayer (*logos*) which effects conjunction. He says:

> Proclus reports that the Chaldeans communicated in their Oracles the 'divine names' of the night, of the day, of the month and of the year which effected the 'conjunction'. Thus we learn that 'conjunction' was brought about by a recital of the 'divine names' (that is, the *voces mysticae*) of the gods who were called upon to participate in it.[28]

---

26. Carlos G. Steel, "Iamblichus and the Theological Interpretation of the Parmenides".—*Syllecta Classica*, vol. 8: Iamblichus: The Philosopher, The University of Iowa, 1997, p. 18.

27. Gregory Shaw, "Theurgy as Demiurgy: Iamblichus' Solution to the Problem of Embodiment".—*Dionysius*, vol. xii, Dalhousie University Press, 1988, p.53 (cf. Iamblichus De mysteriis 232.14–16).

28. Hans Lewy, ibid., p. 229.

THE INEFFABLE STATUES OF TRANSCENDENT LIGHT

Though the Greek terms *eikon* (image) and *sumbolon* may be used interchangeably in Neoplatonism, their more technically articulated distinction is based on the assumption that *eikon* is to be regarded as a mirror-image (a direct reflection or representation of its archetype), whereas a *sumbolon* has no such direct resemblance, even if it mystically 'fits together' with the corresponding divine reality or serves as its proper vehicle.

According to Proclus, 'symbols are not imitations of that which they symbolize' (*In Remp.* 1.198.15–16). However, neither are images plain imitations, because any image (related to its archetype as an effect is related to its cause) 'by its very nature embodies simultaneously the characteristics of similarity and dissimilarity.'[29]

Proclus (or perhaps Iamblichus, paraphrased in Proclus' *Commentary on Plato's Timaeus*) argues that the Pythagoreans, before their *epistemonike didaskalia* (strictly scientific instruction) usually reveal the subjects under consideration through similitudes and images (*dia ton homoion kai ton eikonon*). Then they introduced the same subjects through the esoteric symbols (*dia ton sumbolon aporrheton*). Thereby the soul's ability to comprehend the noetic realm is reactivated (*In Tim.* 1.30.2 ff). In addition, certain causal principles of creation are represented 'in images through symbols' (*en eikosi dia tinon sumbolon*).

J.M. Dillon confesses as being unable to draw any clear distinction between *eikon* and *sumbolon* in Proclus' metaphysics or 'system of allegory'. He says:

If one takes the most obvious Platonic example, the comparison of the Sun as *eikon* with the Good as *paradeigma*, we have arrived at the point of difficulty. Why is the Sun an *eikon* (*Rep.* 509a9), and not a *sumbolon*?[30]

---

29. S.E. Gersh, *ΚΙΝΗΣΙΣ ΑΚΙΝΗΤΟΣ, A Study of Spiritual Motion in the Philosophy of Proclus,* Leiden: E.J. Brill, 1973, p. 85.

30. John Dillon, "Image, Symbol and Analogy: Three Basic Concepts of Neoplatonic Allegorical Exegesis".—*The Significance of Neoplatonism,* ed. R. Baine Harris, Norfolk: ISNS, Old Dominion University, 1976, p.250.

In fact, the Sun indeed is the supreme visible *sunthema* of both the One and the Demiurge. In these matters of metaphysical designation, we should avoid of any one-sided rigidity in our classifications. As Proclus says, certain things may be understood 'in some such symbolic sense . . . without reading too much into them' (*In Tim.* I.200.2–3).

Since the language of metaphysics is at its best allusive (in both its symbolic and iconic mode), we can speak of the divine things only provisionally (*kata endeixin*). Neither the ineffable One, nor the henads (or *ta aporrheta sumbola*) can be the subject of a discursive philosophical argument. The theurgic symbolism of 'divine names' is initially bound to a radical reversion (*peritrope*) of human language. S. Rappe asserts:

Thus Proclus and Simplicius both allow that any teaching about realities such as intellect and soul must take place by means of *endeixis*, by means of coded language. . . . In Neoplatonic texts, the word *endeixis* is linked to Pythagorean symbolism and conveys the sense of allusive or enigmatic language. . . . As used by Damascius, the word *endeixis* suggests that the language of metaphysics must be acknowledged to be at most a prompting toward inquiry into something that exceeds its own domain as descriptive. The result of this inquiry tells us more about our own states of ignorance than about the goal of our search.[31]

However, as a symbol of the unspeakable noetic fire, the *sunthema* of the Sun is 'the central mystery of Neoplatonic theurgy.'[32] In a threefold classification of reality, established by Proclus, the notion of an image is employed in connection with relationship within the noetic realm, though 'the spiritual world contains images in a strictly relative sense, whereas images proper are confined to

---

31. Sara Rappe, *Reading Neoplatonism. Non-discursive Thinking in the Texts of Plotinus, Proclus, and Damascius,* Cambridge: Cambridge University Press, 2000, pp. 210–211.

32. Gregory Shaw, *Theurgy and the Soul. The Neoplatonism of Iamblichus,* University Park: The Pennsylvania State University Press, 1995, p. 227.

the sensible and mathematical realm.'[33] In short, the lower reality is present in the higher which relates to it 'archetypally as a cause' (*kat' aitian archoeidos*), and is manifested at its own level 'accordingly to its *huparxis*' (existential essence). But the higher reality is present in the lower 'by participation in a manner of an image' (*kata methexin eikonikos: ET* 62).

The realities of any higher level of being constitute the metalanguage (regarded as an esoteric *theoria*) by means of which the realities of the immediately lower level are to be interpreted or contemplated. Likewise, in the hierarchy of poetic art, the highest poetry proceeds either by pure *sumbola*, which are antithetical and dissimilar to their metaphysical referents, or it proceeds 'by employing *eikones* to refer to transcendent *paradeigmata*.'[34]

When viewed in accordance with the schematic duality between 'here' (*entautha*) and 'there' (*eikei*), the contents of the lower reality are to be viewed 'according to the esoteric (or unspeakable) doctrine (or contemplative vision)'—*kata ten aporrheton theorian*. This point of view implies a mode of understanding related to the 'first-working causes' (*en tois protourgois aitiais*), in contrast to the category of understanding known as *kata to phainomenon*, 'according to the apparent sense'.

Consequently, the apparent sense of the cosmic text, and the written philosophical, mythological, and liturgical text, is to be regarded as a symbolic 'screen' (*parapetasma*) which simultaneously reveals and conceals the underlying hidden meaning (*huponoia*). This is because the image of ultimate reality, constructed using tools of language (whose polysemous structure is analogous to the polysemous world it mirrors), inevitably distorts and fragments that reality. These limitations are partly resolved and transcended by ascent to a higher level of unity, that is, by restoring the fragmented Eye of Horus, the unified *imago dei*. As R. Lamberton says:

> The highest and most perfect 'life' of the soul is on the level of the gods: the soul utterly abandons its own identity, transcends

33. S.E. Gersh, ibid., p. 85.
34. Robert Lamberton, *Homer the Theologian*, p. 215.

its individual *nous* and attaches 'its light to the transcendent light, and the most unified element of its own being and life to the One beyond all being and all life' (Proclus *In Remp.* 1.177.20–23). Poetry that corresponds to this condition is characterized by the absolute fusion of subject and object. It is divine madness (*mania*), which is a greater thing even than reasonableness (*sophrosune*) and fills the soul with symmetry.[35]

In Neoplatonism, the gods themselves are beyond all representation. However, the divine names are both images and symbols of the invisible gods. H.D. Saffrey assumes that the equation of the divine names with the statues (*agalmata*), which became an important feature of late Neoplatonic metaphysics, is due to specific historical circumstances. The Platonists of Athens (the school of Syrianus and Proclus) presumably developed this theory of divine names as spiritual substitutes for the cult statues of the gods that began at that time to disappear from their temples.[36] Since the Neoplatonic philosophers started to celebrate divinity through the systematic metaphysical interpretation of Plato's *Parmenides* and the creation of scientific theology, worship was allegedly reduced to the *religio mentis*, an entirely intellectual process.[37]

However, it seems that H.D. Saffrey is subtly incorrect in this respect, because even in pharaonic Egypt hieroglyphs functioned as the 'divine names' in the form of *agalmata*, be it visualized mental figures, written pictures or the divine statues made of stone and precious metals. The divine names are objects of adoration like the statues of the gods, because, according to Proclus, the demiurgic Intellect produces each name as a statue of the gods:

35. Ibid., p. 189.
36. H.D. Saffrey, "Nouveaux liens objectifs entre le Pseudo-Denys et Proclus".— *Recherches sur le Neoplatonisme apres Plotin*, Paris: Librairie philosophique J. Vrin, 1990, p. 241.
37. H.D. Saffrey, "From Iamblichus to Proclus and Damascius".—*Classical Mediterranean Spirituality. Egyptian, Greek, Roman*, ed. A.H. Armstrong, London: Routledge and Kegan Paul, 1986, p.253.

And just as theurgy by certain symbols (*dia de tinon sumbolon*) invokes the generous goodness of the gods with a view to the illumination of statues artificially constructed (*ten ton techne-ton agalmaton ellampsin*), so also intellective knowledge related to divine beings, by composition and divisions of articulated sounds, reveals the hidden being (*ten apokekrummenen ousian*) of the gods (*Plat. Theol.* 1.29.124.12–125.2 Saffrey-Westerink).

In his *Commentary to Plato's Cratylus*, Proclus speaks about the *eikastike dunamis*, a certain power by which the soul has the capac-ity to make images and assimilate itself to the gods, angels, and dai-mons. For this reason the soul makes statues (*agalmata...* *demiourgei*) of the gods and superior beings. Likewise, it produces out of itself (with the help of *lektike phantasia*, linguistic imagina-tion) the substance (*ousia*) of the names. Proclus says:

And just as the telestic art by means of certain symbols and inef-fable tokens (*dia de tinon sumbolon kai aporrheton sunthematon*) makes the statues (*agalmata*) here below like the gods and ready to receive the divine illuminations (*ellampseon*), in the same way the art of the regular formation of words, by that same power of assim-ilation, brings into existence names like statues of the [metaphysi-cal] realities (*agalmata ton pragmaton: In Crat.* 19.12–16).

Accordingly, the names are images and symbols of the gods as well as intellective statues (*agalmata*) of divine realities: primarily they are the names of the noetic Forms and secondarily the names of sensible forms. As the 'vocal statues' (*agalmata phoneënta*), these names are identical with the theurgic *sumbola* and *sunthemata*. As G. Shaw pointed out:

Neither Iamblichus nor any of his Platonic successors provide concrete examples of how names, sounds, or musical incanta-tions were used in theurgic rites. There is a great wealth of evi-dence from non-theurgical circles, however, to suggest that theurgists used the *asema onomata* according to Pythagorean cosmological theories and a spiritualization of the rules of grammar.[38]

38. Gregory Shaw, *Theurgy and the Soul*, p. 183.

By these incantations and contemplations constituting the complex set of the hieratic 'work' (*ergon*), the theurgist tried to join the gods through his inner ascension and assimilation to the Demiurge, thereby (by means of the ineffable symbols) entering the solar barque of Ra.

5

DIVINE RITES
AND PHILOSOPHY
IN NEOPLATONISM

Human existence is nothing but the divine life unlived.[1]

We should always have philosophy as our patron, since it is she who performs the task of Homer's Athena scattering mist.[2]

RITUAL AND COSMIC ORDER

The contemporary spokesman of archetypal psychology, J. Hillman, argues that 'we can imagine nothing or perform nothing that is not already formally given by the archetypal imagination of the gods'.[3] Thus he turns (though maintaining, paradoxically, that one of the most available paths of the *imitatio dei* is through 'infirmity') to the main Neoplatonic theme of philosophy as an imitation of the gods and a striving for the 'golden' life. But life, as the Hellenic myths and dramas tell us, is trouble, and it is never going to be any better. In contrast to the lofty dreams of grandeur, 'humankind is weak and small, it sees but little and has nothingness in its nature', according to Iamblichus. Therefore the only cure for this congenital nothingness (*oudeneia*), confusion and unceasing change is 'its sharing to the extent possible in divine light' (*metousian theiou photos kata to dunaton metalaboi: De myster.* 144.13).

---

1. Peter Kingsley, *Reality*, p. 340.
2. Olympiodorus, *In Gorg.* 26.13.
3. *The Essential James Hillman: A Blue Fire*, ed. by Thomas Moore, Routledge, London, 1994, p. 150.

For Neoplatonists, everything—despite different levels, ranks, and orders—is an irradiation of the One. The task of every being is not only to follow his own noetic archetypes, but to come back, as far as possible, to the supreme and ineffable source of light. This is accomplished by rejecting the ontological multiplicity through a sacrificial death. Therefore we can ask whether philosophy itself is not a sort of 'modernized' theurgy. Would it be possible to propose that *theoria* and *theourgia*, or *telesiourgia*, are somewhat convertible terms, if regarded as means of ascent in the grand cosmic theatre— in the world which reveals the power of unspeakable symbols known only to the gods, the world that is itself a Myth? Indeed, for Sallustius, 'the cosmos itself can be called a myth, since bodies and material objects are apparent in it, while souls and intellects are concealed' (*De diis*, III.8–10).

It is almost impossible to reveal the exact meaning of such crucial but rather Proteian terms as 'philosophy', 'myth', 'ritual', 'theurgy'. Any attempt to produce a firmly established solution raises more questions than answers. However, our humble task is not to solve the fundamental riddles of human civilization, but simply to show that, in the context of Neoplatonism and Hellenic culture, theurgy cannot be regarded as a strange misunderstanding incompatible with rational philosophizing. This is because theurgy follows certain universal patterns—universal in a historically determined sense of spiritual 'genre'—and philosophy itself is partly based on ritual transformed into discursive and rational 'ceremonies' of thought. Similarly, one can see the analogy between ritual and grammar. The grammarian undertakes the same operations with respect to the text as the priest undertakes with respect to the sacrifice: both of them decompose the primal unity, then identify the separated parts according to a new set of relationships, and finally produce or confirm the unity on a higher level of synthesis. The Neoplatonic science of dialectic follows a similar course which clearly resembles the divine manifestation and the gradual integration of the manifested parts into their single archetypal source. Ritual is both work, deed, enterprise (*to ergon*, Sanskrit *kriya*) and order, rule, law (*telete* as an accomplishment of perfect revolution while moving in a circle, Sanskrit *rta*).

As Proclus says in his *Commentary on Plato's Parmenides* VII.1161:

the Intellect, through its unchanging reversion towards the intelligible, anticipates causally circular motion; and not only the Intellect, but every divine soul, by reason of its 'dance' round Intellect, takes on incorporeal circular motion.... The theologians also know of incorporeal circular motion, seeing that the theologian of the Hellenes (sc. Orpheus) declares about the primary and hidden god, who is prior to Phanes, 'And he was borne unceasingly about/ In an endless circle' (fr.71). And the Oracles lay down that 'all the founts and the beginnings whirl, and yet always remain fixed in an unwearying eddy' (fr. 49).

Therefore ritual and cosmic order, including order of seasons and order of *logos*, are inseparable. The cosmos itself is *ton aidion theon gegonos agalma*—'a shrine brought into being for the everlasting gods' (*Tim.* 37c). In its outward aspect, ritual is a program of demonstrative acts and patterns which try to establish the identity and solidarity of the closed group and determine its *skopos* and *telos*.

THE AIM OF PHILOSOPHY

Ancient Hellenic philosophy intended to transform souls through various 'spiritual exercises', because the task of the philosopher was not primarily to communicate 'an encyclopedic knowledge in the form of a system,'[4] but to live the philosophical life. In Neoplatonism, psychagogy is tantamount to mystagogy, and the Delphic maxim 'know thyself' means 'return to the source, the first principle of all'. This 'reversion' (*epistrophe*) is both *epistrophe pros heauton* (a return to one's immortal self through self-reflexivity) and elevation through the ontological symbols accomplished by the divine energies.

Although humans are not able to attain knowledge of the gods by their discursive reason, according to Iamblichus, philosophy in the

---

4. Pierre Hadot, *Philosophy as a Way of Life. Spiritual Exercises from Socrates to Foucault*, ed. A.I. Davidson, Blackwell, Oxford, 1995, p. 21.

Pythagorean manner is a road to wisdom in which one will pro-pound, not contradictions, but firm and unchanging truths strengthened by scientific demonstration through sciences (*mathematon*) and contemplations (*theorias*). He is wise who contemplates the One, the goal of all contemplation and is able to see from here, as if from a watch-tower, god (who presides over all truth, happiness, all being, causes, principles) and all in the train of god.

The goal of the Platonic philosophy is wisdom and immortality achieved through the ascent (*anagoge*) of the soul. It is coming to be like a god (*homoiosis theo*) and union with the divine at the level of noetic theophanies or the ineffable source itself. Therefore philosophy as a rational discourse is the hermeneutically developed substitute for the ancient rituals which were viewed as an integral part of the cosmic events. Philosophical games and contests for truth themselves could be regarded as special and partly individualized cases of ritualized cosmogony which is an imitation of the gods and a sort of divine service.

DIFFERENT ASPECTS OF DIVINE ACTS

We know little about the Neoplatonic hieratic art as such, and different scholars present different pictures of it. According to H. Lewy, theurgy and philosophy were two parallel methods aimed at the same goal, union with the gods.[5] L. J. Rosan was able to distinguish between a lower and a higher theurgy.[6] A. Sheppard divided the Procline theurgy (as attested by Hermeias) into three types, claiming that 'Proclus still thinks of the final union as a Plotinian mystical experience, not as some magically induced trance',[7] as if the so-called lower theurgy was nothing but a silly striving for hallucinations. Arguing that Proclus re-interpreted the Plotinian mys-

5. Hans Lewy, *Chaldean Oracles and Theurgy. Mysticism, Magic and Platonism in the Later Roman Empire*, ed. Michel Tardieu, Etudes Augustiniennes, Paris, 1978, pp. 462–463.

6. Laurence Jay Rosan, *The Philosophy of Proclus. The Final Phase of Ancient Thought*, Cosmos, New York, 1949, p. 213.

7. Anne Sheppard, "Proclus' Attitude to Theurgy".—*Classical Quarterly* 32, 1982, p. 224.

tical experience in terms of the theory behind theurgy, A. Sheppard describes mystical union as 'a lofty kind of theurgy because turning the 'one in the soul' towards the supreme One was thought of as activating a *sumbolon* in the direction of what is symbolized'.[8] Therefore the supreme theurgy is also a *theia philosophia* (divine philosophy).

G. Shaw discerns material, intermediate and noetic theurgies, because *theia erga*, divine acts, in the last analysis constitute the whole path of *proödos* and *epistrophe*. They are the manifested reality as such, or rather a set of *sumbola* and *sunthemata* which reveal both the demiurgic and the anagogic power of the Forms and their henadic background. Therefore, as G.Shaw pointed out:

> The law of theurgy was the law of cosmogony in ritual expression; hence one could never ascend to the gods by favouring one 'part' of the soul over another, however transcendently the soul was imagined. . . . In this sense, Neoplatonic theurgy was profoundly anti-gnostic, for it never allowed the disoriented condition of the embodied soul to be projected on the cosmos as an 'ontological' conflict.[9]

Despite the different classifications derived from the painstaking analysis of the extent texts[10] and the widely disseminated myth of Plotinus' exceptional and purely intellectual mysticism—which stands behind various approaches tending to ridicule *le mirage de la theurgie* (as H.D. Saffrey did in fact)[11], or to defend it as no more than a material basis for one's philosophical development—it should be clear that it is one thing to dispute endlessly about details, and quite another to explore the metaphysical principles that

---

8. Ibid., p. 221.

9. Gregory Shaw, "Theurgy: Rituals of Unification in the Neoplatonism of Iamblichus".—*Traditio*, vol. XLI, 1985, p. 27.

10. See, for example, Andrew Smith, *Porphyry's Place in the Neoplatonic Tradition: A Study in Post-Plotinian Neoplatonism*, Martinus Nijhoff, The Hague, 1974; John F. Finamore, "Plotinus and Iamblichus on Magic and Theurgy".—*Dionysius*, vol. XVII, Dec. 1999.

11. H.D. Saffrey, *Recherches sur le neoplatonisme apres Plotin*, Librairie philosophique J. Vrin, Paris, 1990, p. 48.

provide the foundation for the whole super-structure of ancient hieratic life and thought.

As A. H. Armstrong has emphasized, the later Neoplatonists simply 'give strong and carefully worked out arguments for the importance of sacred rites and ceremonies and the use of material symbols in our approach to the Divine and the Divine's approach to us. And the principles upon which they base these arguments are by no means always non-Hellenic or altogether incompatible with the thought of Plotinus, or even of Plato'.[12]

THEURGY AND SPIRITUAL HERMENEUTICS

The Neoplatonic *telestike* (which includes purifications, *katharmoi*, and rites, *teletai*) can be hermeneutically deduced from the several texts of Plato, especially from the *Laws, Timaeus, Phaedrus* and *Symposium*. However, it seems that in a certain sense the philosophy of Plato himself is the disguised reinterpretation of Orphic and Homeric myths and motifs, or those of Parmenides, the initiated healer and priest of Apollo, as P. Kingsley tries to persuade us.[13] But there is actually much more to it. According to Ch. Evangeliou, the Platonic tradition is closer to the Eastern ways of thinking (especially the Indian), than to a narrowly defined 'Western rationality'.[14] And the genesis of the entire Hellenic philosophy corresponds precisely to the time when *Hellas* met *Aiguptos*.[15]

It means that Hellenic philosophy, albeit in a radically emancipated manner, still appears as the direct prolongation of an ancient wisdom. Neoplatonism simply tries to restore the supposed primordial and sacred unity of the cosmos, regarded as a cultic body of the divinity. Therefore it is no wonder that theurgy, viewed in Platonic terms, fulfilled the goal of philosophy understood as a *homoiosis*

12. A. Hilary Armstrong, "Iamblichus and Egypt".—*Les Etudes philosophiques*, no.2–3, 1987, p. 181.

13. Peter Kingsley, *In the Dark Places of Wisdom*, The Golden Sufi Center, Inverness, California, 1999, p. 44; p. 140.

14. Christos C. Evangeliou, *The Hellenic Philosophy: Between Europe, Asia, and Africa*, Institute of Global Cultural Studies, Binhamton University, 1997, p. 51.

15. Ibid., p. 104.

theo. As G. Shaw pointed out, 'both cultic acts and philosophic *paideia* were rooted in one source: the ineffable power of the gods'.[16] For Iamblichus and Proclus, the idea of the sacred tradition, received from the gods themselves and transmitted through the *Hermaike seira* (a sort of *silsilah*, to say it in the Sufi parlance, though regarded more in vertical than in horizontal sense), becomes the central issue.

Although Iamblichus insists that theurgy must be exalted above discursive philosophy and exempt from philosophical criticism considered as merely human reasoning, he also emphasizes the necessity of proceeding in short steps, i.e. starting with material gods as a step toward elevation (*anabasis*) to the immaterial gods (*De myster.* 217.8–11). Instead of saying that Iamblichus fully harmonized (1) the Chaldean rites of soteriological elevation in terms of a divinely guided spiritual journey and (2) the late Neoplatonic doctrine of procession and return, we prefer to assert that instead he made explicit the initial harmony of divine rites and divinely inspired sacred knowledge which only gradually, and due to the physiological, cosmological, ethical, and metaphysical interpretations, was turned into a sort of philosophical discourse. The structure of the syllogistic procedures and the ancient logic itself is still bound to the ritualistic patterns of order as represented by the traditional cosmogonies, and this scientific logic still functions in the cosmos which is the 'most sacred temple of the Demiurge' (Procl. *In Tim.* 1.124.16–22).

Iamblichus harmonized Platonic epistemology with the notion of the anagogical force residing within rituals as such (be they corporeal rites and sacrifices or rituals of thought and noetic liturgies), claiming that the *sunthemata* accomplish the work by their own power. An ascent to the truth which is accomplished by contemplations, noetic sacrifices and inspired interpretations of symbols assists in establishing the hermeneutical meta-structure of philosophy as a discourse based on systematic reasoning and logic. Such philosophy is coextensive with the sacred rites. Iamblichus says:

16. Gregory Shaw, *Theurgy and the Soul. The Neoplatonism of Iamblichus,* Pennsylvania State University Press, 1995, p. 5.

Listen therefore to the intellectual interpretation of symbols according to the mind of the Egyptians (*kata ton Aiguption noun ten ton sumbolon noeran diermeneusin*), at the same time removing from your imagination (*tes phantasias*) and your ears the image (*eidolon*) of things symbolical (*ton sumbolikon*), but elevating yourself to the intellectual truth (*ten noeran aletheian: De myster.* 250.13–18).

Phantasia, like a mirror, can reproduce images of higher princi-ples, and by its image-making power (*eikastike dunamis*) the soul can make itself like beings superior to it. Therefore Proclus argues that 'by the same power it also makes its inferior products like itself and even like things greater than itself because it fashions statues of gods and daemons' (*theon te agalmata kai daimonon demiourgei: In Crat.* 19.6f).

The hermeneutical elevation, aimed at intellectual truth, follows the same anagogic call to participation in the perfection of the One, directed by the 'calling power' (*he anakletike dunamis*). With the help of this all-pervading power, some of the divinely inspired phi-losophers and theurgists (*hoi hieratikoi*) can achieve union with the divine. According to Pythagoras, as recounted by Aristides Quintil-ianus, 'Souls cannot ascend without music'. But neither can they ascend without the exegesis, or *sumbolike theoria*, of sacred rites (*teletai*), myths, and fundamental metaphysical texts, such as the *Parmenides* of Plato. In the Islamic Sufi tradition, which is partly based on the Neoplatonic intellectual heritage, *ta'wil*, or the exegesis of soul, leads the soul back to its truth (*haqiqat*)—and, according to H. Corbin, 'transmutes all cosmic realities and relations and restores them to symbols; each becomes an Event of the soul, which, in its ascent, its *Mi'raj*, passes beyond them and makes them inte-rior to itself.'[17]

By asserting that every soul and every intellect has a twofold activity—(1) the unitary activities (*tas men henoeideis*) which are better than the intellectual, and (2) the intelligible activities (*tas de*

17. Henry Corbin, *Avicenna and the Visionary Recital*, tr. W.R. Trask, Princeton University Press, 1988, p. 34.

noetikas)—Proclus makes a sort of division between rational philosophy and the ultimate knowledge which is higher than science *(In Parm.* VII.63k). According to Proclus, the 'dialectical operations are the preparation for the struggle towards the One, but are not themselves the struggle' *(In Parm.* VII.75k). Therefore 'after going through all the negations, one ought to set aside this dialectical method also' (ibid.).

HIERATIC RITES OF ASCENT

In the extant fragments of his *Commentary on the Chaldean Oracles*, Proclus discusses the 'theurgic race' *(to theourgon phulon)* which is beneficent and devoted to a zealous imitation of the goodness of God *(tes tou theou agathotetos: De phil. Chald.* 27–28, p.208 des Places) and elevation by means of the anagogic life *(dia tes anagogou zoes*: ibid., A 14, p. 206).

The end of all spiritual elevation is participation in divine fruits and filling the soul with divine fire, which allows the contemplation of God. The soul is placed in the presence of the Father (ibid., A 17–19, p.206). The sacred rites of ascent are equated

with the intellectual and invisible hymns of the ascending soul *(kai noeroi kai aphaneis humnoi tes anagomenes psuches)*, awakening the memory of the 'harmonic reasons' *(ton harmonikon logon)*, which bear the inexpressible images of the divine powers *(aporrhetous eikonas ton theion en ante dunameon*: ibid., A 25–26, p.206–207).

Despite the splendid images of the Chaldean rhetoric, this fiery elevation is at the same time understood as a Platonic *anamnesis* of the ultimate truth and a way to the pure noetic contemplation, and thus as an escape from the transient nature of *genesis*. But the true end of the Father-loving soul, argues Proclus—that soul which obeys the call to 'run to the hot (since the spirit is elevated by heat) and fly from the cold'—is the all-receptive temple of the Father who receives and unites the ascending souls (ibid., A 3–6, p.206). 'Let us become fire, let us travel through fire' *(pur genometha, dia puros hodeusomen*: ibid., B 2, p.208) he says, and explains the two integral sides of this 'hymn', consecrated to God as an act of assimilation to him, as a laying aside of all multiplicity and union with the hypernoetic *huparxis*:

Philosophy says that to forget the eternal reasons (*ton aidion logon*) is the cause of the departure of the soul from the Gods, and to recall the knowledge of the eternal reasons or Ideas is the cause of the return to them, but the Oracles assert that the forgetfulness and remembering of the paternal synthems (*ton patrikon sunthematon*) are respectively the causes of the departure and return. Both statements are in harmony. For the soul is constituted from sacred reasons and divine symbols (*apo ton hieron logon kai ton theion sumbolon*), of which the former proceed from the intellectual forms (*apo ton noeron eidon*), but the latter from the divine henads (*apo ton theoin henadon*); and we are images of the intellectual essences, but statues of the unknown synthems (*kai esmen eikones men ton noeron ousion, agalmata [ta] de ton agnoston sunthematon*). And just as every soul is a fullness (*pleroma*) of forms, but subsists wholly or simply according to one cause, thus also it indeed participates in all synthems, through which it is united to divine things (*De phil. Chald.* E 18–26, p. 211, 1–4, p. 212).

Here we have the famous distinction made between an *eikon* and a *sumbolon*. In the later Neoplatonism, higher realities may be revealed either through *eikones* (related to their respective *paradeigmata*), or through *sumbola* which cannot resemble the objects symbolized. However, 'similarity' (*homoiotetes*) is a key term in both cases, because everywhere the similar is naturally united to the similar, according to Proclus. Therefore just as noetic objects are known by *noesis*, so that which is prior to intellect is related to the so-called 'flower' of the intellect.

It would be rather incorrect to restrict philosophy to that limited faculty of the soul which knows true and divine beings *kata to dianoetikon* or investigates cosmos through *eikones* (in a Procline sense, for instance, regarding the recapitulation of the *Republic* at the beginning of Plato's *Timaeus* as an *eikon*, in contrast to the Atlantis myth understood as a *sumbolon*). Likewise, to think that there is such a thing as an 'empty ritual', somewhat detached from the fundamental noetic structure of being and intellect, is too naïve. The Neoplatonic philosophy itself is a homecoming rite, *nostos,* paradigmatically accomplished by the Homeric hero Odysseus. The path of return is the path of an archetypal hero in conjunction with a corresponding god. There are thematic connections between the conception of the 'ancestor' (or sage, *sophos*) and that of the 'hero', related to the 'seasonal eschatology'.

THE COMMON METAPHYSICAL BACKGROUND

It would be incorrect to relate the Neoplatonic telestic art exclusively to the *Chaldean Oracles* and regard this cosmological and soteriological poem as the single mysterious source of all theurgy. Rather we should accept as a fruitful hypothesis that the Neoplatonic theurgy is only a hellenized branch of various ancient beliefs that prevailed in the Middle East and Egypt in the form of 'theurgic' kingship and the ideologies of the all-embracing cosmic state. These sacred ontologies and their entirely pragmatic technologies of the temple magic, related to the supernatural cosmic bureaucracy for the purpose of ensuring a harmonious flow of energy between the different levels of being, were transformed into, and survived as, the efficacious means of personal gnostic 'salvation'—the task which constitutes *raison d'être* of Platonism as well.

Regarding Near Eastern parallelisms, we ought to remember that even the most striking convergences in detail may turn out to be nothing more than a typological analogue. However, the common metaphysical background of the various paths of rebirth and solar immortality, including those of the Pythagoreans, Orphics, Chaldeans, Egyptians and the Neo-Vedic initiates of the 'five fires' and the 'two ways', is quite evident, notwithstanding considerable differences in detail. According to the assertion made by H. Zimmer:

The late Vedic-Gnostic reincarnation doctrine of the 'knower' who through his gnosis escapes from the sublunar world and its cycle of death and rebirth, must have had its ultimate roots in Mesopotamia ... a Sumerian-Babylonian spiritual heritage, diffused to the Orient and there creatively transformed, also travelled westward to become the Greek Orphism, and finally, nourished anew by the old energies of its Near Eastern mother soil, celebrated its resurrection in Gnosticism.[18]

Perhaps a picture of the ideal theurgic cosmos is always the result of reconstruction, even if we understand the term *theourgia* not in a strictly Neoplatonic sense (as a Chaldean neologism, coined in the third century AD), but simply as a working of the gods (*theon erga*) and their theophanies, including:

(1) the creative or magical divine power that underpins and pervades all that exists in the spiritual, psychic and material world (since spirit and matter are woven out of the same substance);

(2) the whole eidetic meta-structure of the cosmic state and the hieratic (ontogenetic and eschatological) institute of kingship, supported by certain myths and daily rituals, and thus following the macrocosmic and microcosmic 'rhythms'.

PHILOSOPHERS AS SACRED STATUES

In the world of real hierophanies, the gods are not to be distinguished from their statues or images, since the image, by invoking the name (or the essence) of the substance imaged, is itself animated, i.e. magically transformed from a mere image to an image infused with the spiritual (or noetic) substance it portrays. This world is a manifestation of the life-giving and sounding noetic Light, of sound made substantial. The sacred images (seasons, landscapes, temples, statues, animals, trees, human beings as *dramatis personae*, or their body-members as identified part by part with a number of different deities) are vehicles of an indwelling divine presence.

In the Egyptian theology (revered by theurgical Platonism for its ability to imitate the nature of the universe and the creative energy of the gods), the sacred action is the action performed ritually, and

18. Heinrich Zimmer, "Death and Rebirth in the Light of India".—*Man and Transformation: Papers from the Eranos Yearbooks*, ed. By J. Campbell, Princeton University Press, 1980, p. 341.

such action is no longer personal. And self-identification with a god is common also in the magical papyri. Similarly, the Hermetic philosopher or the Chaldean sage (representative of the sacred philosophy, *maghdim*) are not self-determined individual 'authors', but rather divine masks and symbols, ranks and archetypal functions. This attitude partly survived into the late Neoplatonism and Neopythagoreanism.

Regarding the animating of statues, we should draw certain parallels from both the Hindu and the Egyptian worlds. According to the Tantric view, purification of the elements and *nyasa* is the ritual infusion of life force into an object, including one's own body, by which it is divinized, transformed into a divine body, externally symbolized by the *asanas*—the 'postures' which make the practitioner immune against the onslaught of the pairs of opposites. An action or a state of consciousness that is not ritualized is merely human, but through the ritualized action or the ritualized mental (eidetic) pattern, the initiate becomes a mediator of the divine light. Therefore, as J. Naydler observes, for the Egyptians:

Ritual action is invocatory; by means of it the magician invokes spiritual powers. The ritual act thus takes place as much in the spiritual dimension as in the physical. Rituals occur in the realm of the gods; the gods are necessarily witnesses of and participants in the sacred rites—for this is precisely what makes them sacred.[19]

Whatever external rituals may be performed, the noetic component is never absent, and the intense visualization (as in the case of visualizing oneself as one's chosen deity, *ishta-devata*, in the Tantric ascent) is always the crucial step. Here the material body is also regarded as a temple of the divinity, an *agalma*, or a living statue, raised up in accordance with the sacred iconography. And certain Hellenic philosophers (Syrianus, for instance) indeed were regarded as divine statues. In a sense, the philosopher is analogous to the *agathos aner* who is build up like a solid and stable statue, or *kouros*-like

19. Jeremy Naydler, *Temple of the Cosmos. The Ancient Egyptian Experience of the Sacred*, Inner Traditions, Rochester, Vermont, 1996, p.144.

hero, fixed forever in the brilliance of an unchanging youth where *panta kala*, 'everything is beautiful'.

TO BE REBORN INTO THE SOLAR WORLD

Syrianus, the famous master of Proclus and Hermeias, conceived the rites of the sacrifice, offered by the Homeric Achilles at the funeral pyre of Patroklos (*Iliad*, XXIII.192f), as an imitation of the soul's immortalization, performed by the theurgists (Procl. *In Remp.* 1.152.7). This analogy cannot be regarded as entirely fabulous, because the funeral of Patroklos in *Iliad* are strikingly close to the royal funerary rituals that are recorded in official Hittite documents.[20] The Vedic god Agni as the supreme model and guide of rebirth himself is a psychopomp, by virtue of cremation of the dead. In his aspect of terrestrial fire, he provides the dead hero with a direct link to Agni as celestial fire: the divine Sun.

In various parts of the ancient world, the initiatory or real death was conceived as the ritualized contest for immortality in bliss, as a prize to be won by those who had wished to live in accordance with virtue and to be reborn into the solar world of Agni, Ra, or Apollo-Helias. The statue-like body of Osiris is awakened by the solar rays issuing from the falcon head of Horus. And Horus himself is reborn through Osiris, thus becoming a shining spirit, or *akh*.

Such texts as the Egyptian *Book of Coming Forth into the Day* (*pert em hru*), known as the *Book of the Dead*, should not be regarded simply as funerary texts. There is a firm correspondence between the temple rituals, performed by and for living, and the night journey of the Sun. The temple rituals served the purpose of achieving rebirth and bringing the soul back to its solar origins. However, they were performed for the benefit of the world as a whole (for the Beloved Land, *ta-meri*, which is *mundi totius templum* and *imago caeli*) and regarded as the actual return (or ascent) to the First Time (*tep sepi*), the realm of metaphysical realities conceived in terms of certain symbolic images that are comparable to

---

20. Gregory Nagy, *Greek Mythology and Poetics*, Cornell University Press, Ithaca and London, 1992, p.128.

the realm of the Platonic Ideas, understood as the beautiful, intelligent and everlasting gods, and their hieroglyphs (*medu neter*).

The same task, albeit on the level of individualized and rationalized discursive thought, is performed by philosophy and, especially, by various branches of Platonism. According to D. Frame, in ancient times the worship of the Sun normally ends by rationalizing itself and becoming the secret possession of the initiates and philosophers.[21] Therefore there is a close relationship between solar theologies and the elite—be they kings, magicians, initiates, heroes, or philosophers. The philosophers represent the last link in the chain of those elect, who completed the secularization of the solar hierophanies by turning them into ideas. The *Chaldean Oracles* simply re-mythologized these philosophical ideas (as the Persian theosopher al-Suhrawardi, the Shaykh of Ishraq, who moved in the same direction) by turning them back into the living mythical beings of the pious hieratic imagination: the Iynges, Connectors (*sunocheis*), Teletarchs, angels, and daemons.

THE COSMIC THEATRE OF SACRIFICIAL FIRES

The Chaldean cosmology as a whole is also informed by a heliocentrism in which the Sun represents the hearth or centre of the cosmos. The three worlds (Empyrean, Ethereal, and Material: cf. Procl., *In Tim.* II. 57. 10–14) can be regarded as fiery circles dominated by the visible Sun and Moon. The architecture of the cosmic spheres constituted the theatre for the soul's journey, both down and up. Descent and ascent are each conducted by the use of different vehicles (*ochemata*) in the course of embodiment and disembodiment. Thus there are two cosmological vectors: (1) the descent and appearance on the stage of the world (Sanskrit *avatarana*), comparable to that of the actor who emerges from the green room, and, (2) the heroic ascent through the cosmic spheres, which in Platonism is partly accomplished by dialectical reasoning.

The cosmic theatre with its puppets (*thaumata*), suspended by

---

21. Douglas Frame, *The Myth of Return in Early Greek Epic*, Yale University Press, New Haven and London, 1978, p. 32.

golden threads or solar rays from above and exciting a sort of wonder (*to thaumazein*) that, according to Plato, is the source of philosophy, has a well-ordered structure. The Year is the great symbol of
the whole. As the Sun belongs to the Year, so the Moon belongs to
the months. Therefore the idealized cosmology (today regarded
merely as a symbol of the noetic and psychic functions) reveals the
energies of the gods in action and embodies the path (*hodos*) along
which not only mythical heroes are led to Olympus, but even that
by which Parmenides is driven by the goddess—perhaps the same
'right road to truth' that was mentioned by Pindar (*III Pythian* 103).

In the all-embracing cosmic structure, *aion* is visualized as the
synthesis of the finite and the infinite in the form of a circle. The
seasons (*rtu*) are the doorkeepers of the spheres in the late Vedic
tradition of sacrifice. The sacrifice itself is tantamount to a theurgic
elevation. Among the five sacrificial fires that constitute the Vedic
cosmos, the first is that through which the gods make their offerings
in the upper noetic world. Its fuel is the Sun, whose rays are the
smoke; the day is its flame; the four cardinal points are its coals, and
the intermediate directions its sparks. In this fire the gods offer up
faith (Sanskrit *sraddha*, Greek *pistis*) as unconditional certainty.
According to the Upanishads:

> Those who know all this, and those, too, who in forest solitude
> revere Faith (*sraddha*) in their mind and concentration as the
> truly real, pass into the flame of the [cremation] fire; and from
> the flame, into the day, from the day, into the half-month of
> the waxing moon; from the half-month of the waxing Moon
> into the six months (the half-year) during which the Sun
> moves northward [i.e., into the rising year between winter sol-
> stice and summer solstice]. From those months they pass to
> the realm of the gods (*deva-loka*), and from the realm of the
> gods to the Sun; from the Sun to the sphere of lighting.(...)
> That is the Way of the Gods (*Brihadaranyaka Upanishad*
> 6.2.15).[22]

22. Heinrich Zimmer, ibid., p. 346.

THE GOLDEN CORDS OF APOLLO

According to the *Chaldean Oracles*, the soul hastens towards the streams of light. Thus the soul is drawn upward and mingles with the solar rays (fr. 66). Proclus explains that 'in the callings and self-manifestations (*en tais klesesi kai autophaneiais*) it seems as if the gods would approach men, whereas in fact the latter are drawn upwards by the former. For in reality the mystes is moved, while the godhead does not leave its place' (*In Alcib.* 398.14).

Moving away from concrete, sensible images through the fiery flower or flame of intellect, the soul extends an empty mind (*teinai kenon noon*) towards the highest God. As R. Majercik observes, the emphasis here lies on sameness, not difference.[23] But it is paradoxical that the one-sided Platonic anthropology, with its 'immortal soul' which outlasts the 'philosophically' rejected body, is built upon much older and more 'materialistic' (or rather magic) cosmology and the member-based psychology where qualities of the soul are regarded as parts of the body. Understood both symbolically and literally, fire is here of the utmost importance. It is related to the ancient conceptions of a transcendent and universal Fire of which our fires are only pale reflections.

The *Jaiminiya Brahmana* speaks of man's twofold possibility of rebirth:

(1) in the sublunar world of mortal beings, through the womb of a woman;
(2) in the imperishable transcendent world (the *kosmos noetos* of the Hellenic tradition), through the womb of the sacred votive fire, whose flame is a messenger and intermediary between men and the gods.[24]

The initiate is aware of his solar self and is certain of his imperishable solar nature. As H. Zimmer pointed out:

---

23. Ruth Majercik, *The Chaldean Oracles*. Text, translation, and commentary, E.J. Brill, Leiden, 1988, p. 24.
24. Heinrich Zimmer, ibid., p. 335.

In the closing period of Vedic thought the dominant features of the ritual—the sacrificial fire and the burnt offering—still give symbolic form and structure to this secret doctrine: a man comes into being on earth through a transformation and rebirth, brought about by a fivefold burnt offering of the gods.[25]

According to the *Jaiminiya Upanishad Brahmana* (I.28.29), whoever speaks, hears, or thinks, does so by the ray of the solar Indra to whom all names belong, but who in fact has no name. The functional powers of Brahma (compared to a sparkling fiery wheel in *Maitri Upanishad* VI.24) are the solar rays or reins by which the one and only Seer and Thinker sees, hears, thinks and eats within us (ibid., II.6; VI.31). The active powers of speech, vision and thought are only the names of His acts.

Similarly, Apollo binds all things to himself, and orders them. A. K. Coomaraswamy argues that this bond, activated and controlled by *sutra-dhara* as a stage manager of Hindu tradition, is precisely Plato's 'golden cord' by which the puppet should be guided if it is to play its proper part.[26] Since we are God's toys, we ought 'to dance' accordingly, and this cosmic dance includes, (1) irradiation, the demiurgical descent, and, (2) elevation (measured by the eternal ratios, *metra aidia: De myster.* 65.6), the theurgical ascent. And these are merely the two sides of the same divine rite, the same cosmic game.

This doctrine of the supernal Sun implies the equivalence of life-creating light and sound, since to shine (*bha*) means to speak (*bhan*), and 'utterance' is 'raying'. The divine Sun speaks and what he has to say is the great and hidden name (*nama guhyam*). A similar doctrine is attributed to the Egyptian prophet Bitys by Iamblichus (*De myster.* 268.2–3).

Therefore the theurgist himself—as an animated divine statue (*agalma*)—is tantamount to a solar ray or the microcosmic *axis*

25. Ibid., p. 344.
26. Ananda K. Coomaraswamy, *The Bugbear of Literacy*, Denis Dorson, London, 1947, p. 106.

mundi: the channel of the fiery light in the chain (*seira*) of descent and ascent, *proödos* and *epistrophe*. According to the *Chaldean Oracles*, the theurgist stands as a warrior whose battle cry echoes the primordial sound of creation. He stands as a hero 'arrayed from head to toe with a clamorous light (the all-armored vigor of sounding light, according to H. Lewy),[27] armed in intellect and soul with a triple-barbed strength'. He must cast into his imagination *pan triados sunthema* and approach the empyrean channels in a state of recollection (fr. 2).

The initiate must rush to centre of the sounding light: to the Sun (which is the supreme Death as well) and the central hearth of fiery transformation and rebirth. Like the supreme *sunthema* itself, he stands in the centre of the primordial *mandala* of the cosmos, equivalent to the shining sphere of light.

SHINING FORTH LIKE A GOD

This position is similar to that of the god Horus-Ra, the Egyptian king as an ogre who eats men and lives on gods. He eats their *heka* (magic power of being, life, and intelligence) and devours their glory (*Pyramid Texts*, 393–404). Placing himself at the hub of theophanies and assimilating their powers, he is the ritual model and prototype not only of the magician, but the philosopher as well, the only difference being that for the Hellenic philosopher the distinction between the 'subjective' inner world and the 'objective' outer world is more or less firmly established.

In Egypt, the *ka* of the solar and lunar king permeated the whole country and was the focus of the collective consciousness. 'He was the *ka* of Egypt, and he was the personification of *ka* as experienced in each individual', according to J. Naydler.[28] *Ka*, sometimes translated as 'double', is the principle symbolizing physical, social, moral and spiritual appetites and tendencies, such as subsistence, creative power of food, nutrition, force, splendor, magic, illumination and so on.

27. Hans Lewy, ibid., p. 192.
28. Jeremy Naydler, ibid., p. 197.

The rudiments of the Plotinian metaphysics in mythological form can be seen already in the Egyptian conception of

(1) *ka* energy of the god Horus, whom the king embodied;
(2) *ba* as the vehicle of ascent, depicted as human-headed falcon, which exists in relation to both the physical and the spiritual worlds; literally it means 'manifestation', but is rendered 'soul' (and therefore can be related to the *Phaedrus* myth);
(3) *akh* as a state of radiance and inner illumination, connected with the solar Ra and representing the king's (who is the paradigmatic initiate and the supreme philosopher) transcendent identity with Ra, who himself emerged from the ineffable transcendence of Nun.

The appearance of the king, his shining forth, is equivalent to the theophany of Ra on the primordial hill *in illo tempore*. The Neoplatonic philosopher is dramatically striving to reach this ineffable glory as well, but, at the same time, he likes to leave this world only after it is fully 'catalogized' according to the rules of the post-Aristotelian logic, and hymned in terms of the scientific enthusiasm—not in the same manner as it was done by his predecessors from the Middle East and Egypt, but nonetheless with the same practical and theoretical zeal.

Philosophy as a sort of rational and critical discourse, a set of *problemata*, or as an interrogation and *torture* of reality, was born out of the ritualized combat (*agon*) for wisdom, initially related to the art of solving riddles and to cosmological contests for the purpose of winning knowledge of the principles. Only after the sharp separation of inner and outer reality was made did philosophy became a mistress of the newly-discovered and personalized inner world. Owing to this transformation, spiritual and psychic events were no longer experienced by the collective imagination as outer events.

The introduction of the ancient hieratic theurgy into the onesided and therefore excessively ambitious Greek philosophy was an attempt to re-create the sacred ways of thinking in accordance with the new scientific thought of the Hellenistic period. Perhaps it is theoretically possible—through sophisticated metaphysical exegesis—

to deduce theurgy directly from the dialogues of Plato, such as the *Timaeus,* the *Phaedrus,* or the *Laws.* However, the writings of Plato himself cannot be explained without references to the transmutation of archaic symbols into his own patterns of thought.

Contemplation of the wondrous works (*thaumata erga*) of the gods and interpretation of the mysterious cosmic order marked the start of philosophy both as physiology and as metaphysics. However, despite early attempts to reject the traditional myths as such, philosophy (still determined by the old patterns of thought, hidden beneath the screens, *parapetasmata,* of scepticism and rationalism) inevitably turned towards the 'divine light', claiming that we cannot become happy unless, by the aid of philosophy we acquire and contemplate the wisdom of truly existing beings.

Philosophy is the science of living perfectly, according to Iamblichus. But if the summit of perfection is achieved only through the union with the divine principles themselves and, if they are called 'gods', the traditional means of ascent should be rehabilitated and reused. Therefore, both historically and metaphysically, the marriage of philosophy and the Platonized branch of theurgy was determined and destined *a priori* by the soteriological attitude, prevailing among contemporary philosophers, towards *telos,* man's last end.

APPENDIX

THE LIMITS OF
SPECULATION IN NEOPLATONISM

But even denial is a form of discourse, and that makes what is denied an object of discourse, but the transcendent is nothing, not even something to be denied, in no way expressible, not knowable at all, so that one can not even negate its negation. Rather the only way of revealing that of which we speak is simply the deferral of language and of conceptions about it.[1]

THE HERMENEUTICAL PROGRAM
OF READING NEOPLATONISM

While trying to understand the Neoplatonic notion about the limits of thinking and human understanding (realized at the threshold of the Ineffable whose 'nothingness', *oudeneia*, constitutes and penetrates being itself), one should remember that discursive (especially academic) interpretation of ancient philosophies and religions does not transcend questions of ultimate truth, as it boldly claims. Such presumably innocent interpretation still maintains its own standards of reason and its own hidden premises of truth, raised in accordance to its ideologically determined and culturally constructed sense of the real.

Following this hermeneutical program of modern positivistic study, the universe that the Neoplatonic philosophers and theurgists believed themselves to inhabit, contemplate, and describe, is regarded as being fictitious, illusory, and unfit for inclusion in the 'objective' model of reality. This model (itself not 'natural', but learned and imposed by training and socio-political magic) *a priori* rejects metaphysical categories, entities, or things, such as gods,

---

1. Damascius *De Principiis* 1.21.14–18.

henads, divine principles, noetic lights, angels, and daimons. However, certain contemporary scholars surmise that this so-called 'objective reality' (idolized in its unholy materialistic hypostasis by modern science) is not reality *per se*, but merely that which presently possesses mythical, onto-theological, ideological, social or simply pragmatic consensus. As J. D. BeDuhn remarks:

> When consensus changes, the old objective reality is displaced to the realm of the subjective.[2]

Leaving aside the deceptive task of defining what is 'objective' and what is 'subjective', or how history is shaped 'objectively' by the myths, theological doctrines, and ideological dreams assented to, we simply wish to remind of the fact that each historically attested tradition and metaphysical perspective may be viewed as real in itself. It is not necessary in every case to search behind these traditions, theories, and rituals for that kind of 'real' meaning which makes sense only to the profane contemporary student, and only according to modern standards of coherence and social benefit. As J. D. BeDuhn says about the cultures of the past:

> Whether or not they prove to be true according to our standards—in isolation, divorced from their operative context or displaced to another—is entirely trivial to the role they played in past human behavior. We understand nothing of religious behavior by grappling over whether gods, mystical experiences, possessions, visions, even healings, are true by some supposed objective or empirically verifiable standard.[3]

Therefore we cannot produce any 'better' reading of Neoplatonism than the ancient Neoplatonists themselves. However, by trying to make sense of their philosophical practice according to our own philosophical *askesis* (which involves hermeneutical construction, reconstruction, and deconstruction of metaphysical *mandalas*

---

2. Jason David BeDuhn, *The Manichean Body in Discipline and Ritual*, Baltimore and London: The Johns Hopkins University Press, 2002, p. 269
3. Ibid., p. 270.

as traditionally established gates towards the Ineffable), we can share the same field of philosophical knowledge (*episteme*) and participate in the salvific divine activity (*theourgia*) related to it.

NON-DISCURSIVE DIVINE PRESENCE
AND RELATIONAL TRANSCENDENCE

According to Proclus, both ancient Hellenic theology and Pythagorean philosophy stem from the Orphic mystagogy. Consequently, the doctrines of Plato may be regarded as the revelations of Apollo translated into the discursive language of rational dialectic.

Since the One is exempt from all things (*exeremenon panton*), it is ineffable. But if everything (*ta panta*) is a manifestation or revelation of the Ineffable, this means that, in a certain fundamental respect, being itself is ineffable, in spite of its noetic articulation, sensible crystallization, and visibility.

The inevitable conclusion is that the entire hierarchy of being (which includes the graded hierarchy of transcendence and immanence), when regarded as a display of the One, is equivalent to a kind of miraculous divine 'myth'. This 'myth', revealed in the form of the all-embracing and dynamic cosmic *agalma* (hieratic statue, image, shrine) is analogous to the obscuring power of *maya* which (in the Trika philosophy of Kashmir), though being an aspect of *Parama Shiva*, acts as a veil thrown over the supreme ineffable Principle.[4]

Thereby the Parama Shiva presumably does not 'experience' (to use this rather misleading term) the whole of the manifested universe (*vishva*) as the transcendent oneness, but as the noetic multiplicity. This multiplicity shows itself as the Dionysian fragmentation reflected in the countless mirrors of divine Imagination. The entire hierarchy of paradigms and images shines within the unspeakable unity of the One, this hierarchy itself being nothing but a single unity, unified by Apollo whose full multitude of powers is 'incom-

---

4. Deba Brata SenSharma, *The Philosophy of Sadhana with Special Reference to the Trika Philosophy of Kashmir*, Albany: SUNY Press, 1990, p. 37

prehensible to us and indescribable' (*aperilepton hemin kai aperiege-ton*: Proclus *In Crat.* 97.2–3).[5] As Proclus says:

Indeed, how could human reason ever become able to grasp all the properties together, not only of Apollo, but of any God at all? (ibid., 97.4–6)

Aristotle has defined wisdom as the knowledge of *ousia* (being, essence), but the Neoplatonic conception of knowledge includes both privation (*steresis*) and negation (*apophasis*), thereby contemplating not only that which can be spoken, but the speakable and the unspeakable simultaneously. For the late Neoplatonists, both kathaphatic and apophatic assertions apply to being, but the *huperousios* (beyond-being) is beyond both affirmation and negation. Only silence is appropriate to the realm of that which lies beyond *ousia*, and which consequently transcends affirmations and negations, which may be comprehended only in their reciprocal relationship.

Now the Neoplatonists maintained that knowledge is both an archetypal ideal and actual presence, in varying forms, at all levels of divine irradiation (*ellampsis*) or theophany. The real knowledge consists, however, in 'the identity of a *nous* with the content of its thought.'[6]

Since the One is the unspeakable ground of everything, it is not beyond (*ouk epekeina*) those things of which it is a measure (Proclus *In Parm.* 1209.24). Rather the manifested reality itself constitutes the gradable scale of transcendence (*to exeremenon*), because the *exeremenon* is relational and always implies being transcendent with respect to something else. Accordingly, transcendence as exemption is relational, not absolute. In Neoplatonism, as L. Siorvanes argues:

5. Proclus, *On Plato's Cratylus*, tr. Brian Duvick, ed. Harold Tarrant, London: Duckworth, 2007, p.96; *Proclo Lezioni sul 'Cratilo' di Platone*, tr. Francesco Romano, Catania/Roma, 1989, p. 97

6. A.C. Lloyd, *The Anatomy of Neoplatonism*, Oxford: Clarendon Press, 1991, p.141

Transcendence may mean a going beyond or above what is given (normally in experience and sense-perception), but the transcendent is relative to the base which it transcends.[7]

The divine *Nous*, which (in its unparticipated and transcendent dimension) cannot be attributed to the individual proper, is the source of intellectual intuition (*noesis*). This Neoplatonic intellection is understood in a sense of noetic immediacy and self-presence. In this respect, it transcends all kinds of discursive reasoning.

Therefore the Neoplatonic wisdom does not consist of propositions. Being non-representational, it reveals the limitations of discursive thinking and establishes the philosophical *askesis* related to *apophasis* (that which involves the indefinite and indicates the absence of something without any kathaphatic implications), described as 'practice of non-discursive mode of awareness' by S. Rappe.[8] She argues that non-discursive truth is the foundation of entire Neoplatonic philosophical enterprise:

> The discursive strategies that inform Neoplatonic texts are a configuration of non-discursive truth, just as the tradition as a whole is a record of its own appeal to what can only be called an unwritten tradition.[9]

MASKS AND TONGUES OF THE INEFFABLE

Proclus himself speaks of the human weakness that restricts us to probabilities and unreliable descriptions based on sensible phenomena. Thereby he makes a clear distinction between different ontological levels of being and thinking:

---

7. Lucas Siorvanes, "Proclus on Transcendence".—*Documenti e studi sulla tradizione filosofica Medievale*. An International Journal on the Philosophical Tradition from Late Antiquity to the Late Middle Ages of the Societa Internazionale per lo Studio del Medioevo Latino, vol.IX, Sismel: Edizione del Galluzzo, 1998, p. 6.

8. Sara Rappe, *Reading Neoplatonism. Non-discursive Thinking in the Texts of Plotinus, Proclus, and Damascius*, Cambridge: Cambridge University Press, 2000, p. xvi.

9. Ibid, p. xv.

Speaking generally, just as what we say about intelligible objects does not fit the objects of discursive thinking, so what we say about the objects of scientific knowledge does not fit perceptible objects. For the intelligible objects are the models of those of discursive thinking and these in turn of the perceptible (*In Tim.* 1.349.25–28).

But since Intellect makes its own contents known to itself alone, what kind of language is to be used to convey noetic (or even hyper-noetic) truths?[10] The answer may be paradoxical indeed, if we put aside for a while our suspicion regarding metaphors and literary tropes, and simply confirm reality as an henadic theophany of theurgic symbols and tokens (*sumbola kai sunthemata*). Since any manifested 'mask' of the Ineffable itself may be described as a sort of ineffable symbol displayed within the Ineffable (which is nowhere and everywhere), it makes little difference what kind of language we choose to use, in spite of the ontological and hermeneutical hierarchy of *ta aporrheta sumbola* and *ta pragmata*.

These divine symbols (and every created thing plays this paradoxical role), sowed by the demiurgic *Nous* through the cosmos, do in fact (throughout the invisible *huparxis* of the One, themselves equivalent to its miraculous 'faces' and 'mouths') accomplish the impossible: 'They give voice to things which cannot be voiced . . . they represent that which is above representation and put that which is beyond reason into terms accessible to humans.'[11] Or rather, they constitute human beings themselves; they *are* human beings, and all manifested things, images, and veils, revealed as the unspeakable symbols of the One.

Consequently, the Orphic myths and the elaborated abstract metaphysical constructions of the Neoplatonists are equally based on the Ineffable—and equally aimed at *epopteia* and *henosis*, mystical vision and mystical union—which alone provides the non-discursive anagogic foundation for discursive reasoning itself, thereby

10. Ibid., p. xiv.
11. Peter T. Struck, *Birth of the Symbol. Ancient Readers at the Limits of their Texts*, Princeton and Oxford: Princeton University Press, 2004, p. 219.

turning it into a sort of theurgic *yantra*, to say it in Sanskrit. Therefore both Neoplatonic scholasticism (the Platonic theology of Proclus, for instance) and the ritualized visionary flights reveal the same divine Presence: the Ineffable, not capable of receiving a name and, at the same time, possessing all names.

The multiplicity of names (irradiations, manifestations, things) derives from the single noetic Name that reveals the divine *Nous* in the act of reverting to the One in its perennial contemplation of itself and its ineffable Source. Therefore '*Nous* as it exists in the divine can be apprehended when we have purified the intellect in ourselves' (Plotinus *Enn.* v.8.3), and the soul, being the 'image of *Nous*', attains to identification with *Nous* (which is universal) through the practice of concentration, hermeneutical reading, and ascent.

The cosmos (constituted by the circle of the Same and the circle of the Other that enclose the soul within the *agalma* of manifested being) is a symbol for God, the One which shows itself through the *Nous*, the 'divine name' as the principle of metaphysical translation, creative articulation, and revelation. According to Proclus:

> Yet this name is ineffable and unutterable and is made known to the gods alone. For there are names appropriate to each level of reality: divine names for the gods, discursive names for the discursive intellect, and names rooted in appearances for the sensible faculty (*Plat. Theol.* II.6.92).

THE DISTINCTION BETWEEN LOOKING UP AT
THE SUN AND LOOKING DOWN AT REFLECTIONS

Plato already distinguished reason from intellection, though for him both (albeit at different levels) are aimed at and depends on the Forms. For Plato, geometry music theory are related to reflections and images (*eikones*) of the eternal Forms (*eide*), thereby exercising *dianoia* (rational discursive thought) and leading towards dialectic.

The process of dialectic is analogous to looking up at the stars and at the Sun itself, as described in Plato's *Republic* 516 bc, and thus recognizing the first cause of all Being, the Form of the Good, which is *epekeina tes ousias*, beyond Being. In this respect, *episteme* (direct metaphysical knowledge, science) is contrasted with *dianoia* as looking up at the Sun is contrasted with looking down at reflections of the Sun.[12]

According to the famous myth of the Cave (*Rep.* 514 ff), noetic realities may be comprehended only outside the Cave (outside the tomb-like corporeal cosmos), thereby drawing a contrast between *doxa* (opinion) and *noesis* (intellection), between intelligible light and psycho-somatic darkness.

J. Ferguson maintains that the figure of the Cave is Orphic in origin. Likewise, Plato's notion that the Good is *epekeina tes ousias*, beyond Being, may be traced back to the Parmenidean metaphysics.[13] In this context, as J. Ferguson aptly remarks, truth (*aletheia*) is coupled with intellect (*nous*). Both these terms are key-words for Parmenides, to whom 'the way of truth is continually associated with the verb *noein*.'[14]

All followers of Platonic and Aristotelian traditions (*haireseis*) usually made a distinction between discursive reason and intellect. This distinction is emphasized by Aristotle himself in *De anima*, 3.5, and elaborated by the commentators (including Alexander of Aphrodisias and Plotinus) in different ways.

The Neoplatonists always maintained this crucial classificatory distinction (forgotten, neglected, or rejected as artificial and unreal by the majority of modern thinkers) between *dianoia* and *nous*. Discursive reason (*dianoia*) operates with material either derived from the *nous* above, or from the sensible world below, and presented to it by imagination (*phantasia*).

Intellect (the second divine hypostasis of Plotinus) perceives its objects (its own noetic contents) instantly, directly, and permanently, thereby recognizing and confirming its own noetic identity with them. In contrast, *dianoia* may be described as reasoning moving from one object, premise, or argument to another, thus involv-

12. R.G. Tanner, "Διανοια and Plato's Cave".—*The Classical Quarterly* 20, Oxford: Clarendon Press, 1970, p. 86.

13. John Ferguson, "Sun, Line, and Cave Again".—*The Classical Quarterly* 13, Oxford: Clarendon Press, 1963, p. 193.

14. Ibid., p. 191.

ing transition, division, and fragmentation. Therefore reason stands as an intermediate between the indivisible *nous* (either macrocosmic, or microcosmic) and the divided irrational soul which is involved with the body and its passions.[15] Proclus says:

> The intellect in us is Dionysian and truly an image (or hieratic statue: *agalma*) of Dionysus. Therefore, anyone that transgress against it and, like the Titans, scatters its undivided nature (*ten amere autou phusin*) by fragmented falsehood, this person clearly sins against Dionysus himself, even more than those who transgress against external statues of God (*ta ektos tou theou agalmata*), to the extent that the intellect more than other things is akin (*sungenes*) to the God' (*In Crat.* 77.25–78.4).

MODES OF INTELLECTION AND UNION

According to Porphyry, the soul is consubstantial with *nous* insofar as it is pre-existent in *nous* which acts as its metaphysical principle (*arche*) and demiurgic source, though the soul itself cannot become *nous*.[16] However, the 'inner man' is somewhat identical with *nous* (ultimately with the divine hypostasis, *Nous* as the universal Demiurge), and individual minds are inevitably related to *Nous* which encompasses all of them. Therefore Porphyry

> clearly puts *nous* as the fourth goal of the ascent of the soul. The third stage is that of the soul acting intelligently.... At this stage soul is directed towards and filled by *nous*. It receives, then, only images of the *noeta*....[17]

As regards the supreme union with *nous* (which implies certain degree of identity of one's real self and *nous*), A. Smith argues as follows:

---

15. Henry J. Blumenthal, *Aristotle and Neoplatonism in Late Antiquity: Interpretations of the De Anima*, London: Duckworth, 1996, p.165.

16. Andrew Smith, *Porphyry's Place in the Neoplatonic Tradition. A Study in Post-Platonian Neoplatonism*, The Hague: Martinus Nijhoff, 1974, pp. 48–49.

17. Ibid., p. 50.

This is something permanent and the floating self must now make contact and become identified in some way with this higher self. But Porphyry does not seem to make any definite identification of an ego with the higher self.[18]

This is so because when the soul is united to the gods in contemplation or in theurgic prayer, it is not united as an individual or an ego. The later Neoplatonists are much more radical in this respect: they speak about supernatural (*huperhues*) death of those theurgists whose souls are transformed from individuality to universality, even though the soul's self-alienation and descent into the realm of mortality are activities of the gods themselves.[19]

A.Smith argues that the supreme union with *Nous*, as well as a stage higher than the contemplation of the noetic realities (*ta noeta*), are both attested in Porphyry. While asking what sort of union might be meant by the identification of one's real self with *nous*, he says:

> Plotinus, too, seems to consider the normal constitutive *epistrophe* of a hypostasis towards its prior as different from its spiritual *epistrophe* or union. This is particularly clear in his treatment of the relationship of *Nous* and the One. *Nous* is formed by a constitutive *epistrophe*, and its turning in mystical contemplation towards the One, by which it indulges in an activity whose scope lies outside its mere existence as *Nous*, is a further type of *epistrophe*. Porphyry would appear to be making a similar distinction here and it is an important distinction, for by it the metaphysical structure in virtue of which soul exists and is related to *nous* (and thus to *Nous*) in the realm of existence is distinguished from the spiritual ascent or mystical relationship. . . . Salvation is achieved not through the unity of soul and *nous* but by the reflection in the logical soul of *noeseis* in the form of *ennoiai*.[20]

18. Ibid., pp. 50–51.
19. Gregory Shaw, "The Mortality and Anonymity of the Iamblichean Soul".— *Syllecta Classica*, vol. 8, The University of Iowa, 1997, p. 189.
20. Andrew Smith, ibid., pp. 52–53.

A. Smith further argues that the late Neoplatonists tend to separate unity with the *noeton* (intelligible realities, paradigms, archetypal Forms), or with the highest member of the noetic realm (which is 'beyond' *nous*, when *nous* is depicted as the noeric, that is 'thinking', agent of cosmic demiurgy), from unity with the contemplating *nous* proper. Thereby different modes of intellection at different levels of being are established.[21]

Therefore even theurgy may be viewed in conjunction with *noesis*, though Iamblichus, contrary to Porphyry and Plotinus, relates *noesis* to the elevating and transforming powers of the gods which are, strictly speaking, *huper pasan noesin*, transcending all intellection. The ascending philosopher must return (in co-operation with the divine *dunameis*) to the realm of pure *noesis* and pure *theoria* (mystical contemplation which results in *epopteia*).

Such *noesis* 'is attainable only through the workings of theurgy',[22] that is, by the grace of God and the mysterious activity of the ineffable divine *sunthemata*. Therefore *noesis* of this higher divine order is 'an aspect of the actual union with the gods which Iamblichus calls theurgic union (*ten theourgiken henosin*).'[23]

For Proclus, the essential unity of the soul lies in its inward depths, because in its depths the soul coincides to a degree with the henadic *huparxis* and the ineffable One itself. It follows, accordingly, that the union (*henosis*) of soul with the One underpins the entire Procline thesis 'that everything can be known, and that Platonism can offer a comprehensive Theology.'[24]

All the gods, according to Proclus, are henads above being (*huperousioi*), or rather they transcend the multiplicity of beings and are the summits of beings (*kai tou plethous ton onton huperanechousai kai akrotetes ton ousion*: Proclus *In Parm.* 1066.27–28). However, the series of self-subsistent henads (or 'ones'), posited after the One, are specified 'through the diverse classes of beings depending

21. Ibid., p. 87.
22. Ibid.
23. Ibid., p. 86.
24. Lucas Siorvanes, "The Problem of Truth in the Platonic Theology".—*Proclus et la théologie platonicienne*, ed. A. Ph. Segonds and C. Steel, Leuven: University Press; Paris: Les Belles Lettres, 2000, p. 55.

upon them,'[25] and, in a certain sense, are identical with the *sumbola* and *sunthemata* that constitute the entire manifested reality.

In one respect, henads are beyond being, perhaps even beyond *peras* and *apeiria*, the Limit and the Unlimited, that is, the two metaphysical principles which determine all subsequent manifestation of multiplicity. In another respect, henads proceed on all levels of being-life-intelligence, from the *noeton* proper to the angelic and daimonic orders (*taxeis*) to all divinized souls and bodies, reaching as far as the realm of plants and minerals.

Although Being (*to on*) extends wider than Life (*zoë*) and Intelligence (*nous*), for the philosopher aimed at the dialectical ascent, *nous* as *theoria* (contemplation) proves to be the most important. This is so because he tries to achieve the union of all activities in one *energeia* (or the union of subject, predicate, and object), thereby accomplishing the union of the divine and human. 'The human soul, as particular, is never saved, however', as G. Shaw aptly remarks, because the soul's unity with the *Nous*, the gods, and the One, is not an individual or personal experience:[26] 'It is impossible to participate as an individual in the universal orders of existence', as Iamblichus declares, paraphrased by Damascius (*In Phileb.* 227.4–5).[27]

The same is true regarding real metaphysical knowledge and 'divine speculation'.

Nous may be described as the union of *ousia* (being, essence) and *energeia* (activity, act), which contemplates itself, but 'for *nous* to be *nous* it must look beyond itself'.[28] Likewise, the soul elevated to the level of *nous*, or rather re-established as *nous*, contemplates the Ineffable (the One which is beyond Intellect and, at the same time, is the ultimate *dunamis* of everything) through the contemplative gaze of the divine Intellect itself. As M. Sells explains:

25. Carlos G. Steel, "Iamblichus and the Theological Interpretation of the *Parmenides*".—*Syllecta Classica*, vol. 8, The University of Iowa, 1997, p. 18.

26. Gregory Shaw, ibid., p. 189.

27. *Damascius' Lectures on the Philebus, wrongly attributed to Olympiodorus*, text and tr. L. G. Westerink, Amsterdam: Adolf M. Hakkert, Publisher, 1982, pp. 106–107; also cited by G. Shaw, ibid., p. 190.

28. Michael A. Sells, *Mystical Languages of Unsaying*, Chicago and London: The University of Chicago Press, 1994, p. 23.

Nous is contemplation, but the 'object' of its contemplation is constantly being pulled away through apophatic abstraction (*aphairesis*). . . . Plotinus called this *apophasis* a symbolic use of language... It 'proceeds' out into delimited language reference, only to 'return' back towards a referential openness.[29]

TO LIVE MEANS TO READ

For the Neoplatonists, *Nous* is in the One, not the One in *Nous*, and likewise *Psuche* is in *Nous*, not vice versa. And the first Hypothesis of Plato's *Parmenides* indicates that the One under consideration is not really one at all (*to hen oute hen estin oute estin*: *Parm.* 141e12).

According to the Neopythagorean tradition, this ineffable Principle was named Apollo not just to indicate its unity (the name Apollo is interpreted as constituted of *a-*, the privative, and *polla*, 'multiplicity', 'many'), but rather to show the First Principle's 'transcendence of all qualities, even that of unity, as J. Whittaker pointed out.[30]

Consequently, awareness (*sunesis*) of the One is provided not by intellection (*noesis*), but by a presence that surpasses knowledge itself, given that the very possibility of knowledge is based on the noetic articulation of *peras* and *apeiria* at the level of the Platonic Forms and below—down to the level of discursive principles (*dianoetikoi logoi*). The discursive thinking, *dianoia*, related to the mathematical method (*logismos*), operates by means of the reasoning process, whereas a non-discursive *noesis* grasps its objects (the intelligible Forms) as if 'by touch' (*kat' epaphen*).[31]

But this awareness of the One is itself hyper-noetic, though related to the One's *parousia*—Its mysterious presence in the *Nous*. Therefore J. Rist argues:

---

29. Ibid., p. 31.
30. John Whittaker, "Neopythagoreanism and the Transcendent Absolute".— *Studies in Platonism and Patristic Thought,* London: Variorum Reprints, 1984, ch. XI, p. 79 (reprinted from *Symbolae Osloenses* XLVIII, 1973, pp. 77–86).
31. Dominic J. O'Meara, *Pythagoras Revived: Mathematics and Philosophy in Late Antiquity,* Oxford: Clarendon Press, 1997, p. 47.

We may conclude that there is within *nous* a kind of unity derived from the One's presence, but not damaging to the One's transcendence, which is actualized at the moment of the return to the One in the mystical union. . . . We should not regard it as an indication that *nous* has in its own nature the means of transcending itself. *Nous* can transcend itself only in virtue of what is not itself, but is in itself. . . . [32]

The limits of speculation and, ultimately, the limits of noetic contemplation, reflection, and vision, are established as the limits of the fundamental power of *Nous*, derived from the Ineffable and aimed at a return to the same Ineffable. M. J. Edwards says:

And, since the mind acquires its formal being by a process which necessitates reversion, the life which is implied in that reversion is as much the cause of mind as its effect.[33]

Thereby the ouroboric archetypal circle of being-life-intelligence is established, within which all manifested reality is revealed through the *dunamis* of Hekate, to say it in terms of the *Chaldean Oracles*.

Philosophical discourse imitates the contemplative gaze of *Nous* at the discursive level of images and syllogistic reasoning. Therefore it reflects, paradoxically, the ambiquity of the relationship between the Ineffable (though the term 'ineffable', in this metaphysical context, does not possess an ordinary meaning: since it has absolutely no reality, according to Damascius, it is not even a term)[34] and the intelligible splendor of *Nous* as *deus revelatus*.

Consequently, the limit of philosophical speculation (which may be labeled as 'inspired' or not) is silence that frees the dialectician (as any other 'inspired' speaker) both from his own production and from the revealed divine mythology translated into the human fables. At the same time, any image and any symbol, when under-

---

32. John M. Rist, "Mysticism and Transcendence in Later Neoplatonism".—*Platonism and its Christian Heritage*, London: Variorum Reprints, 1985, ch. xv, p. 214.

33. Mark J. Edwards, "Being, Life and Mind: a Brief Inquiry".—*Syllecta Classica*, vol. 8, The University of Iowa, 1997, p.197.

34. Sara Rappe, ibid., p.209.

stood as a veil (*parapetasma*) thrown over the unspeakable Transcendence, may serve as a limit of philosophical speculation, inviting one to accept the miraculous presence revealed by silence. In this second sense, a sophisticated philosophical system, as well as a particular doctrine, may be regarded as an *upaya* (an effective soteriological ‚mirage‘) and *yantra* (the theurgic vehicle of concentration, re-integration, and union), to say it in Sanskrit.

Likewise, the term *endeixis*, used by Damascius, suggests

> that the language of metaphysics must be acknowledged to be at most a prompting towards inquiry into something that exceeds its own domain as descriptive. The result of this inquiry tells us more about our own states of ignorance than about the goal of the search... To describe philosophical discourse as *endeixis* is to limit its ambitions. *Endeixis* in this sense is not a descriptive use of language, but encompasses a number of different linguistic devices.[35]

However, in spite of the fact that all speech is only provisional, *kata endeixin*, discursive reasoning is not to be despised or rejected. It is perfectly valid in the same sense as any *sunthema* (anagogic token, sign, symbol) and any archetypally based *muthos* (myth, narrative, hermeneutical story) are valid, because all of them are direct or indirect self-disclosures, testimonies, traces, faces, playthings, or even tricks, of the One. And the One embraces everything: even deviation from the noetic standard and manifestation of the absurd cannot fall outside the Ineffable, because no such 'outsideness' can exist. Nonetheless the noetic gaze establishes its own 'inner' hierarchy of paradigms and images that constitute the 'mirage' of transcendence revealed as the immanent text of being.

To live means to read and interpret the countless chapters of this divine text, though every chapter has its own limits and its own existential logic. They are revealed in time and concealed again in the chain (*seira*) of births and deaths that constitute the ouroboric crown of the One (or *Aion*), miraculously displayed through the contemplative gaze (or rather, through the creative Imagination) of

35. Ibid., p. 211.

Nous. Ultimately, silence is the harbour of 'salvation' (*soteria*) where every thought and every discourse find their ineffable repose, their metaphysical limit. As S. Rappe says:

> Language turns back upon itself because its purpose is to negate its own function. Damascius' chosen name for this style of metaphysics is *peritrope*, and this word too has a history in the annals of Scepticism... If the Sceptics embrace *epoche*, suspension of beliefs, as their solution to the impending dangers of *peritrope*, one could argue that, in a parallel way, Damascius embraces silence or ineffability... The 'limit of philosophical discourse' (*peras tou logou*) refers to the complete removal of any proposition or any statement about reality. This limit is 'silence without recourse'.... (C-W 1.22)[36]

---

36. Ibid., pp.212–213; C-W, *Damascius' Doubts and Solutions Concerning First Principles*, 3 volumes, ed. J. Combes and L.G. Westerink, Paris: Les Belles Lettres, 1986–1991 (Greek text and French translation).

BIBLIOGRAPHY OF WORKS
ON PHILOSOPHY AND THEURGY

Abt, Theodor, and Hornung, Erik, *Knowledge for the Afterlife. The Egyptian Amduat—A Quest for Immortality,* Zurich: Living Human Heritage Publications, 2003.

Abusch, Tzvi, *Ascent to the Stars in a Mesopotamian Ritual: Social Metaphor and Religious Experience,* in *Death, Ecstasy, and Other Worldly Journeys,* ed. J.J. Collins and M. Fishbane, Albany: SUNY Press, 1995

Allen, James P., *Genesis in Egypt. The Philosophy of Ancient Egyptian Creation Accounts,* New Haven: Yale University, 1988.

Annus, Amar, "Ninurta and the Son of Man".— *Melammu Symposia II: Mythology and Mythologies, Methodological Approaches to Intercultural Influences,* ed. R.M. Whiting, Helsinki: The Neo-Assyrian Text Corpus Project, 2001.

Anton, John P., "Plotinus and the Neoplatonic Conception of Dialectic".—*The Journal of Neoplatonic Studies,* vol. 1, no. 1, Fall 1982.

⸻. *Plotinus and Augustine on Cosmic Alienation: Proodos and Epistrophe,* in *The Journal of Neoplatonic Studies,* vol. 4, no. 2, 1996.

Armstrong, A. Hilary, *Expectations of Immortality in Late Antiquity,* Milwaukee: Marquette University Press, 1987.

⸻. "Aristotle in Plotinus: The Continuity and Discontinuity of Psyche and Nous".— *Aristotle and the Later Tradition,* ed. Henry Blumenthal and Howard Robinson, Oxford: Clarendon Press, 1991.

⸻. "Iamblichus and Egypt".—*Les Etudes philosoph-iques,* nos. 2–3, 1987.

⸻. "Some Comments on the Development of the Theology of Images".—*Studia Patristica,* vol. IX, Berlin: Akademie-Verlag, 1966.

Assmann, Jan, *The Search for God in Ancient Egypt,* tr. David Lorton, Ithaca and London: Cornell University Press, 2001.

⸻. *Moses the Egyptian: The Memory of Egypt in Western Monotheism,* Cambridge: Harvard University Press, 2002.

Assmann, Jan, *The Mind of Egypt. History and Meaning in the Time of the Pharaohs,* tr. Andrew Jenkins, New York: Metropolitan Books, 2002.

_____. *Death and Salvation in Ancient Egypt*, tr. David Lorton, Ithaca and London: Cornell University Press, 2005

_____. "Death and Initiation in the Funerary Religion of Ancient Egypt".— *Religion and Philosophy in Ancient Egypt*, ed. J.P. Alen et alii, New Haven: Yale University Press, 1989.

_____. "Mono-, Pan-, and Cosmotheism: Thinking the 'One' in Egyptian Theology".— *Orient: Report of the Society for Near Eastern Studies in Japan*, vol. XXXIII, 1998.

Atac, Mehmet-Ali "The 'Underworld Vision' of the Ninevite Intellectual Milieu", in *Iraq*, vol. LXVI, London: British School of Archeology in Iraq, 2004.

Athanassiadi, Polymnia, *Introduction* to *Damascius: The Philosophical History*, ed. and tr. Polymnia Athanassiadi, Athens: Apameia, 1999.

Atwill, Janet M., *Rhetoric Reclaimed. Aristotle and the Liberal Arts Tradition*, Ithaca and London: Cornell University Press, 1999.

Aune, David E., "Heracles and Christ: Heracles Imagery in the Christology of Early Christianity".— *Greeks, Romans, and Christian: Essays in Honor of Abraham J.Malherbe*, ed. David L. Balch et alii, Minneapolis: Fortress Press, 1990.

BeDuhn, Jason David, *The Manichean Body in Discipline and Ritual*, Baltimore and London: The Johns Hopkins University Press, 2002.

Bell, Lanny, "The New Kingdom 'Divine' Temple: The Example of Luxor".—*Temples of Ancient Egypt*, ed. Byron E. Shafer, London: I.B. Tauris, 2005.

Beierwaltes, Werner, "The Love of Beauty and the Love of God".— *Classical Mediterranean Spirituality. Egyptian, Greek, Roman*, ed. A.H. Armstrong, London: Routledge and Kegan Paul, 1986.

Betz, Hans Pieter (ed. and tr.), *The Greek Magical Papyri in Translation Including the Demotic Spells*, Chicago and London: University of Chicago Press, 1996.

Blumenthal, Henry J., *Aristotle and Neoplatonism in Late Antiquity. Interpretations of the De anima*, London: Duckworth, 1996.

_____. *Proclus on Perception*, in *Bulletin of Institute of Classical Studies*, London: University of London, vol. 29, 1982.

Brague, Remi, "The Body of the Speech: A New Hypothesis on the Compositional Structure of Timaeus' Monologue".— *Platonic Investigations*, ed. Dominic J. O'Meara, Washington, DC: The Catholic University of America Press, 1985

Burkert, Walter, *Greek Religion*, tr. John Raffan, Cambridge, MA: Harvard University Press, 2000.

————. *Babylon, Memphis, Persepolis: Eastern Contexts of Greek Culture*, Cambridge, MA: Harvard University Press, 2004.

Bussanich, John, "Mystical Theology and Spiritual Experience in Proclus' Platonic Theology", in *Proclus et la Theologie Platonicienne*, ed. A. Ph. Segonds and C. Steel, Leuven: University Press, Paris: Les Belles Lettres, 2000.

Bychkov, Oleg, "Alexej Losev: A Neoplatonic View of the Dialectic of Absence and Presence in the Nature of Artistic Form".—*Neoplatonism and Contemporary Thought*, Part II, ed. R. Baine Harris, Albany: SUNY Press, 2002.

Chari, V. K. "Representation in India's Sacred Images: Objective vs. Metaphysical Reference".— Bulletin of SOAS (School of Oriental and African Studies), vol. 1, 2002.

Cleary, John J. "Working Through Puzzles with Aristotle".—*The Journal of Neoplatonic Studies*, vol. 1, no. 2, Spring 1983.

Cole, Susan Guettel, *Voices from Beyond the Grave: Dionysus and the Dead*, in *Masks of Dionysus*, ed. Thomas H. Carpenter and Christopher A. Faraone, Ithaca and London: Cornell University Press, 1993.

Coomaraswamy, Ananda K., "The Vedic Doctrine of 'Silence'".—2. *Selected Papers: Metaphysics*, ed. Roger Lipsey, Princeton: Princeton University Press, 1987.

————. "Vedic 'Monotheism'".—2. *Selected Papers: Metaphysics*, ed. Roger Lipsey, Princeton: Princeton University Press, 1987.

————. "On the Indian and Traditional Psychology or Rather Pneumatology".—2. *Selected Papers: Metaphysics*, ed. Roger Lipsey, Princeton: Princeton University Press, 1987.

————. "The Symbolism of the Dome".— *Selected Papers: Traditional Art and Symbolism*, ed. Roger Lipsey, Princeton: Princeton University Press, 1989.

————. *The Transformation of Nature in Art*, New York: Dover Publications, 1956.

————. *The Bugbear of Literacy*, London: Denis Dorson, 1947.

Corbin, Henry, *Avicenna and the Visionary Recital*, tr. W. R. Trask, Princeton: Princeton University Press, 1988.

Cornford, Francis MacDonald, *Plato's Cosmology: The Timaeus of Plato*, Indianapolis: Hackett Publishing Company, 1997.

Coulter, James A., *The Literary Microcosm: Theories of Interpretation of the Later Neoplatonists*, Leiden: E. J. Brill, 1976.

Damascius, *The Greek Commentaries on Plato's Phaedo, vol. II: Damascius*, ed. and tr. L. G. Westerink, Amsterdam: North-Holland Publishing Company, 1977.

Damascius, *Lectures on the Philebus, wrongly attributed to Olympiodorus*, text and tr. L.G. Westerink, Amsterdam: Adolf M. Hakkert Publisher, 1982.

Damascius, *The Philosophical History*, text with translation and notes, ed. and tr. Polymnia Athanassiadi, Athens: Apameia, 1999.

Danielou, Alain, *The Myths and Gods of India*, Rochester: Inner Traditions, 1991.

Davidson, Arnold I., "Introduction: Pierre Hadot and the Spiritual Phenomenon of Ancient Philosophy.—Pierre Hadot", *Philosophy as a Way of Life: Spiritual Exercises from Socrates to Foucault*, ed. A.I. Davidson, tr. M. Chase, Oxford: Blackwell, 1995.

Davidson, Ronald M., *Indian Esoteric Buddhism: Social History of the Tantric Movement*, Delhi: Motilal Banarsidas Publishers, 2004.

Davis, Richard H., *Lives of Indian Images*, Princeton: Princeton University Press, 1997.

Desjardins, Rosemary, *The Rational Enterprise: Logos in Plato's Theaetetus*, Albany: SUNY Press, 1990.

Dillon, John, "Philosophy and Theology in Proclus: Some Remarks on the 'Philosophical' and 'Theological' Modes of Exegesis in Proclus' Platonic Commentaries".— *From Augustine to Eriugena: Essays on Neoplatonism and Christianity in Honor of John O'Meara*, ed. F.X. Martin et alii, Washington, DC: The Catholic University of America Press, 1991.

_____. "Plato and the Golden Age".— *Hermathen: A Trinity College Dublin Review*, no. CLIII, Winter 1992.

_____. (ed. and tr.) *Iamblichi Chalcidensis in Platonis dialogos commentariorum fragmenta*, Leiden: E.J. Brill, 1973.

_____. "Image, Symbol and Analogy: Three Basic Concepts of Neoplatonic Allegorical Exegesis".— *The Significance of Neoplatonism*, ed. R. Baine Harris, Norfolk: ISNS (International Society for Neoplatonic Studies), Old Dominion University, 1976.

Dodds, E. R., *The Greeks and the Irrational*, Berkeley: University of California Press, 1984.

Dunand, Francoise and Zivie-Coche, Christiane, *Gods and Men in Egypt, 3000 BCE to 395 CE*, tr. David Lorton, Ithaca and London: Cornell University Press, 2002

Edwards, Mark J., "Being, Life and Mind: a Brief Inquiry".—*Syllecta Classica*, vol. 8, The University of Iowa, 1997.

Evangeliou, Christos C., *The Hellenic Philosophy: Between Europe, Asia and Africa*, Binghamton: Institute of Global Cultural Studies, Binghamton University, 1997.

Faraone, Christopher A., *Talismans and Trojan Horses: Guardian Statues in Ancient Greek Myth and Ritual*, Oxford: Oxford University Press, 1992.

Faulkner, Raymond O., (tr.) *The Ancient Egyptian Pyramid Texts*, Warminster: Aris and Phillips, 1969.

————. (tr.), *The Ancient Egyptian Book of the Dead*, ed. Carol Andrews, Austin: University of Texas Press, 2001.

Federn, Walter, "The 'Transformations' in the Coffin Texts: A New Approach".—*Journal of Near Eastern Studies*, vol. xix, no. 4, October 1960.

Ferguson, John, "Sun, Line, and Cave Again".- *The Classical Quarterly* 13, Oxford: Clarendon Press, 1963.

Feuerstein, Georg, *Tantra: The Path of Ecstasy*, Boston and London: Shambala, 1998.

Finamore, John F., *Iamblichus and the Theory of the Vehicle of the Soul*, Chico, CA: Scholars Press, 1985.

————. "Plotinus and Iamblichus on Magic and Theurgy", in *Dionysius*, vol. xvii, December 1999.

————. *Iamblichus on Light and the Transparent*, in *The Divine Iamblichus: Philosopher and Man of Gods*, ed. H. J. Blumenthal and E. G. Clark, Bristol: Bristol Classical Press, 1993.

————. "Julian and the Descent of Asclepius", in *The Journal of Neoplatonic Studies*, vol. 7, no. 2

Finamore, John F. and Dillon, John M., *Commentary to the De anima*, in *Iamblichus' De anima*, text, translation and commentary by John F. Finamore and John M. Dillon, Leiden: J. E. Brill, 2002.

Finnestad, R. Bjerre "The Meaning and Purpose of Opening the Mouth in Mortuary Contexts".— *Numen*, vol. xxv, 2.

————. *Image of the World and Symbol of the Creator: On the Cosmological and Iconological Values of the Temple of Edfu*, Wiesbaden: Otto Harrassowitz, 1985.

————. *Temples of the Ptolemaic and Roman Periods: Ancient Traditions in New Contexts*, in *Temples of Ancient Egypt*, ed. Byron E. Shafer, London: I. B. Tauris, 2005.

Frame, Douglas, *The Myth of Return in Early Greek Epic*, New Haven and London: Yale University Press, 1978.

Fowden, Garth, *The Egyptian Hermes: A Historical Approach to the Late Pagan Mind*, Princeton: Princeton University Press, 1993.

Gersh, Stephen E., ΚΙΝΗΣΙΣ ΑΚΙΝΗΤΟΣ: *A Study of Spiritual Motion in the Philosophy of Proclus*, Leiden: E. J. Brill, 1973.

Gerson, Lloyd P. "Επιστροφη προς εαυτον: History and Meaning".— *Documenti e studi sulla tradizione filosofica Medievale*. An International Journal on the Philosophical Tradition from Antiquity to the Late Middle Ages, vol. VIII, 1997.

Graf, Fritz, "Dionysian and Orphic Eschatology: New Texts and Old Questions", in *Masks of Dionysius*, ed. Thomas H. Carpenter and Christopher A. Faraone, Ithaca and London: Cornell University Press, 1993.

————. "Prayer in Magic and Religious Ritual".—*Magica Hiera: Ancient Greek Magic and Religion*, ed. Christopher A. Faraone and Dirk Obbink, Oxford: Oxford University Press, 1997.

Griffith, R. Drew "Sailing to Elysium: Menelaus' Afterlife: *Odyssey* 4.561–569 and Egyptian Religion".— *Phoenix*, vol. 55, 2001.

Griswold, Charles, "Plato's Metaphilosophy".—*Investigations*, ed. Dominic J. O'Meara, Washington, DC: The Catholic University of America Press, 1985.

Guénon, René, *Symbols of Sacred Science*, Hillside, NY: Sophia Perennis, 2004.

Hadot, Ilsetraut, "The Spiritual Guide".— *Classical Mediterranean Spirituality: Egyptian, Greek, Roman*, ed. A. H. Armstrong, London: Routledge and Kegan Paul, 1986.

Hadot, Pierre, *Philosophy as a Way of Life: Spiritual Exercises from Socrates to Foucault*, ed. Arnold I. Davidson, tr. Michael Chase, Oxford: Blackwell, 1992.

Haeny, Gerhard, "New Kingdom 'Mortuary Temples' and 'Mansions of Million Years'".—*Temples of Ancient Egypt*, ed. Byron E. Shafer, London: I. B. Tauris, 2005.

Hallo, William W., "Cult Statue and Divine Image: A Preliminary Study". —*Scripture in Context II: More Essays on the Comparative Method*, ed. William W. Hallo et alii, Winona Lake, IN: Eisenbrauns, 1983.

Helleman, Wendy E., "Philo of Alexandria on Deification and Assimilation to God".—*The Studia Philonica in Hellenistic Judaism*, vol. 2, ed. David T. Runia, Atlanta: Scholars Press, 1990.

Hillman, James, *The Essential James Hillman: A Blue Fire*, ed. Thomas Moore, London: Routledge, 1984.

Hornung, Erik, *The Egyptian Books of the Afterlife*, tr. David Lorton, Ithaca and London: Cornell University Press, 1999.

Iamblichus, *De mysteriis/On the Mysteries*, tr. Emma C. Clarke, John M. Dillon, and Jackson P. Hershbell, Atlanta: Society of Biblical Literature, 2003.

————.*De Anima*, text, translation, and commentary by John F. Finamore and John M. Dillon, Leiden: Brill, 2002

Igal, J. "The Gnostics and 'the Ancient Philosophy': Porphyry and Plotinus".—*Neoplatonism and Early Christian Thought: Essays in honour of A. H. Armstrong*, ed. H. J. Blumenthal and R. A. Marcus, London: Variorum Publications, 1981.

Iversen, Erik. *Egyptian and Hermetic Doctrine*, Copenhagen: Museum Tusculanum Press, 1984.

Johnston, Sarah Iles, *Hekate Soteir: A Study of Hekate's Role in the Chaldean Oracles and Related Literature*, Atlanta: Scholars Press, 1990.

Kay, Peter A. "Dialectic as the Science of Wisdom in Plotinus".—*The Journal of Neoplatonic Studies*, vol. 4, no.1, fall 1995.

Kilmer, Anne Draffkorn, "The Symbolism of the Flies in the Mesopotamian Flood Myth and Some Future Implications".—*Language, Literature, and History: Philosophical and Historical Studies presented to Erica Reiner*, ed. Francesca Rocherberg-Halton, New Haven: American Oriental Society, 1987.

Kingsley, Peter, *In the Dark Places of Wisdom*, Inverness, CA: The Golden Sufi Center, 1999.

———. *Reality*, Inverness, CA: The Golden Sufi Center, 2003.

Kotansky, Roy, *Incantations and Prayers for Salvation on Inscribed Greek Amulets*, in *Magica Hiera: Ancient Greek Magic and Religion*, ed. Christopher A. Faraone and Dirk Obbink, Oxford: Oxford University Press, 1997.

Koutras, Dimitrios N. "The Beautiful According to Dionysius".— *Neoplatonism and Western Aesthetics*, ed. Aphrodite Alexandrakis, Albany: SUNY Press, 2002.

Kuisma, Oiva, *Proclus' Defense of Homer*, Helsinki: Societas Scientiarum Fennica, 1996.

Lamberton, Robert, *Homer the Theologian: Neoplatonist Allegorical Reading and the Growth of the Epic Tradition*, Berkeley: University of California Press, 1986.

Lesko, Leonard H. (tr.), *The Ancient Egyptian Book of Two Ways*, Berkeley: University of California Press, 1977.

Lewy, Hans, *Chaldean Oracles and Theurgy: Mysticism, Magic and Platonism in the Later Roman Empire*, Nouvelle edition par Michael Tardieu, Paris: Etudes Augustiniennes, 1978.

Lings, Martin, *Symbol and Archetype: A Study of the Meaning of Existence*, Cambridge: Quinta Essentia, 1991.

Lloyd, A. C., *The Anatomy of Neoplatonism*, Oxford: Clarendon Press, 1991.

Lorton, David, "The Theology of Cult Statues in Ancient Egypt".—*Born in Heaven, Made on Earth: The Making of the Cult Image in the Ancient Near East*, ed. Michael B. Dick, Winona Lake, IN: Eisenbrauns, 1999.

Lowry, J.M.P. *The Logical Principles of Proclus'* ΣΤΟΙΧΕΙΩΣΙΣ ΘΕΟΛΟΓΙΚΗ *as Systematic Ground of the Cosmos*, Amsterdam: Rodopi, 1980.

Louth, Andrew, "Pagan Theurgy and Christian Sacramentalism in Denys the Areopagite".—*The Journal of Theological Studies*, vol. 37, Oxford: Clarendon Press, 1986.

McCarthy, Heather Lee, "The Osiris Nefertari: A Case Study of Decorum, Gender, and Regeneration".—*Journal of the American Research Center in Egypt*, vol. xxxix, 2002.

McEvilley, Thomas, *The Shape of Ancient Thought: Comparative Studies in Greek and Indian Philosophies*, New York: Allworth Press, 2002.

Majercik, Ruth (tr.), *The Chaldean Oracles: Text, Translation, and Commentary*, Leiden: E.J. Brill, 1989.

Mamo, Plato, "Is Plotinian Mysticism Monistic"?—*The Significance of Neoplatonism*, ed. R.Baine Harris, Norfolk: ISNS, Old Dominion University, 1976.

Marinatos, Nanno. "The Cosmic Journey of Odysseus", in *Numen*, vol. 48, Leiden: Koninklijke Brill NV, 2001.

Marlen, J.C., "Proclus on Causal Reasoning, I: Alcibiades and the Doctrine of Anamnesis".— *The Journal of Neoplatonic Studies*, vol. 1 no. 2, spring 1993.

Miller, Patricia Cox, *In Praise of Nonsense*, in *Classical Mediterranean Spirituality: Egyptian, Greek, Roman*, ed. H.A. Armstrong, London: Routledge and Kegan Paul, 1986.

Morris, Sarah P., *Daidalos and the Origins of Greek Art*, Princeton: Princeton University Press, 1992.

Musser, Robert, "Notes on Plotinian Purification".— *The Journal of Neoplatonic Studies*, vol. 5, no. 1, fall 1996.

Nagy, Gregory *Greek Mythology and Poetics*, Ithaca and London: Cornell University Press, 1992.

Naydler, Jeremy, *Temple of the Cosmos: The Ancient Egyptian Experience of the Sacred*, Rochester: Inner Traditions, 1996.

————. "Plato, Shamanism and Ancient Egypt".— *Temenos Academy Review*, vol. 9, London, 2006.

————. *Shamanic Wisdom in the Pyramid Texts: The Mystical Tradition of Ancient Egypt*, Rochester: Inner Traditions, 2005.

Narbonne, Jean-Marc, "Action, Contemplation and Interiority in the Thinking of Beauty in Plotinus".— *Neoplatonism and Western Aesthetics*, ed. Aphrodite Alexandrakis, Albany: SUNY Press, 2002.

Nock, Arthur Darby, "Notes on Ruler-Cult I–IV".— A.D. Nock, *Essays on Religion and the Ancient World*, vol. 1, ed. Zeph Stewart, Oxford: Clarendon Press, 1986.

Oosthout, Henri, *Modes of Knowledge and the Transcendental: An Intro-duction to Plotinus's Ennead* 5.3 (49) *with a Commentary and Transla-tion*, Amsterdam: B.R.Gruner, 1991.

Olympiodorus, *The Greek Commentaries on Plato's Phaedo, vol.I: Olympi-odorus*, ed. and tr. L.G. Westerink, Amsterdam: North-Holland Pub-lishing Company, 1977.

———. *Commentary on Plato's Gorgias*, tr. Robin Jackson, Kimon Lycos, and Harold Tarrant, Leiden: Brill, 1995.

O'Meara, Dominic J., *Pythagoras Revived: Mathematics and Philosophy in Late Antiquity*, Oxford: Clarendon Press, 1997.

Parpola, Simo, "The Assyrian Tree of Life: Tracing the Origins of Jewish Monotheism and Greek Philosophy".— *Journal of Near Eastern Stud-ies*, vol. 52, no. 3, 1993.

———. *Mesopotamian Precursors of the Hymn of the Pearl*, in *Melammu Symposia II: Mythology and Mythologies. Methodological Approaches to Intercultural Influences*, ed. R.M. Whiting, Helsinki: The Neo-Assyrian Text Corpus Project, 2001.

———. "The Mesopotamian Soul of Western Culture", in *Bulletin of Canadian Society for Mesopotamian Studies* 35, 2000.

Pepin, Jean, "The Platonic and Christian Ulysses".— *Neoplatonism and Christian Thought*, ed. Dominic J. O'Meara, Norfolk: ISNS (Interna-tional Society for Neoplatonic Studies), 1982.

———. "Le plaisir du mythe (Damascius, In Phaedonem 1.525–526, II.129-130)".—*Neoplatonisme: Melanges offerts a Jean Trouillard.*—Les cahiers de Fontenay, nos. 19, 20, 21, 22, Fontenay aux Roses, 1981.

Phillips III, C.R., "Nullum Crimen sine Lege: Socioreligious Sanctions on Magic".—*Magica Hiera: Ancient Greek Magic and Religion*, New York and Oxford: Oxford University Press, 1991.

Press, Gerald A., "Knowledge as Vision in Plato's Dialogues".—*The Jour-nal of Neoplatonic Studies*, vol. 3, no. 2, spring 1995.

Proclus, *The Elements of Theology*, tr. E.R. Dodds, Oxford: Clarendon Press, 1992.

———. *A Commentary on the First Book of Euclid's Elements*, tr. Glen R. Morrow, Princeton: Princeton University Press, 1992.

———. *Proclus' Commentary on Plato's Parmenides*, tr. Glen Morrow and John M. Dillon, Princeton: Princeton University Press, 1992.

———. *On Plato's Cratylus*, tr. Brian Duvick, ed. Harold Tarrant, Lon-don: Duckworth, 2007.

Rappe, Sara, *Reading Neoplatonism: Non-discursive Thinking in the Texts of Plotinus, Proclus, and Damascius*, Cambridge: Cambridge Univer-sity Press, 2000.

Rehm, David Plotinus' "Treatment of Aristotelian δυναμις in Emanation".—*The Journal of Neoplatonic Studies*, vol. 2, no. 1, 1993.

Rist, John M., "Mysticism and Transcendence in Later Neoplatonism".- *Platonism and its Christian Heritage*, London: Variorum Reprints, 1985.

———. "Plato Says That We Have Tripartite Souls. If He Is Right, What Can We Do About It?".— *ΣΟΦΙΗΣ ΜΑΙΗΤΟΡΕΣ "Chercheurs de sagesse."* *Hommage a Jean Pepin*, ed. Marie-Odile Goulet-Caze et alii, Paris: Institut d'Etudes Augustiniennes, 1992.

Roberts, Alison, *Hathor Rising: The Serpent Power of Ancient Egypt*, Rottingdean: Northgate Publishers, 1995.

Ronan, Stephen, "Hekate's Iynx: An Ancient Theurgical Tool", in *Alexandria*, vol. 1, Grand Rapids: Phanes Press, 1991.

Rosan, Laurence Jay, *The Philosophy of Proclus. The Final Phase of Ancient Thought*, New York: Cosmos, 1949.

Roth, Ann Mary, "The pss-kf and the 'Opening of the Mouth' Ceremony: A Ritual of Birth and Rebirth".—*The Journal of Egyptian Archeology*, vol. 78, 1992.

Saffrey, H.D., "From Iamblichus to Proclus and Damascius".—*Classical Mediterranean Spirituality: Egyptian, Greek, Roman*, ed. A.H. Armstrong, London: Routledge and Kegan Paul, 1986.

———. "Nouveaux liens objectifs entre le Pseudo-Denys et Proclus".— H.D. Saffrey, *Recherches sur le Neoplatonisme apres Plotin*, Paris: Librairie philosophique, J. Vrin, 1990.

Scarborough, John, "The Pharmacology of Sacred Plants, Herbs, and Roots",—*Magica Hiera: Ancient Greek Magic and Religion*, ed. Christopher A. Faraone and Dirk Obbink, Oxford: Oxford University Press, 1991.

Schuon, Frithjof, *Logic and Transcendence*, tr. Peter N. Townsend, London: Perennial Books, 1984.

———. *The Eye of the Heart: Metaphysics, Cosmology, Spiritual Life*, Bloomington: World Wisdom Books, 1997.

Sells, Michael A., *Mystical Languages of Unsaying*, Chicago and London: The University of Chicago Press, 1994.

SenSharma, Deba Brata, *The Philosophy of Sadhana, With Special Reference to the Trika Philosophy of Kashmir*, Albany: SUNY Press, 1990.

Shafer, Byron E., *Temples, Priests, and Rituals: An Overview*, in *Temples of Ancient Egypt*, ed. Byron E. Shafer, London: I.B. Tauris, 2005.

Shaw, Gregory, *Theurgy as Demiurgy: Iamblichus' Solution to the Problem of Embodiment.*—*Dionysus*, vol. XII, Dalhousie University Press, 1988.

Shaw, Gregory, "Theurgy: Rituals of Unification in the Neoplatonism of Iamblichus".—*Traditio: Studies in Ancient and Medieval History, Thought, and Religion*, vol. XLI, NY: Fordham University Press, 1985.

————. *Theurgy and the Soul: The Neoplatonism of Iamblichus*, The Pennsylvania State University Press, 1995.

————. "Embodying the Stars: Iamblichus and the Transformation of Platonic Paideia", in *Alexandria*, vol. 1, Grand Rapids: Phanes Press, 1991.

————. "The Mortality and Anonymity of the Iamblichean Soul", in *Syllecta Classica*, vol. 8, The University of Iowa, 1997.

————. "The Geometry of Grace: A Pythagorean Approach to Theurgy", in *The Divine Iamblichus, Philosopher and Man of Gods*, ed. H.J. Blumenthal and E.G. Clark, Bristol: Bristol Classical Press, 1993.

Sheppard, Anne D.R., *Studies on the 5th and 6th Essays of Proclus' Commentary on the Republic*, Göttingen: Vandenhoeck and Ruprecht, 1980

————. "Proclus' Attitude to Theurgy".— *Classical Quarterly* 32, 1, 1982.

————. "Proclus' Philosophical Method of Exegesis: The Use of Aristotle and the Stoics in the Commentary on the *Cratylus*".—*Proclus lecteur et interprete des anciens*, ed. Jean Pepin and H.D. Saffrey, Paris: CNRS, 1987.

Siorvanes, Lucas, *Proclus, Neo-Platonic Philosophy and Science*, Edinburgh: Edinburgh University Press, 1996.

————. "Proclus on Transcendence".—*Documenti e studi sulla tradizione filosofica Medievale*, vol. IX, Sismel: Edizione de Galluzzo, 1998.

————. "The Problem of Truth in the Platonic Theology".- *Proclus et la theologie platonicienne*, ed. A. Ph. Segonds and C. Steel, Leuven: University Press; Paris: Les Belles Lettres, 2000.

Smith, Andrew, *Porphyry's Place in the Neoplatonic Tradition: A Study in Post-Plotinian Neoplatonism*, The Hague: Martinus Nijhoff, 1974.

Sorabji, Richard, "Proclus on Place and the Interpenetration of Bodies".—*Proclus lecteur et interprete des anciens*, ed. Jean Pepin and H.D. Saffrey, Paris: CNRS, 1987.

Steel, Carlos G., "Iamblichus and the Theological Interpretation of the Parmenides", in *Syllecta Classica*, vol. 8: *Iamblichus: The Philosopher*, The University of Iowa, 1997.

Steiner, Deborah Tarn, *Images in Mind: Statues in Archaic and Classical Greek Literature and Thought*, Princeton and Oxford: Princeton University Press, 2001.

Sterling, Gregory E., "Platonizing Moses: Philo and Middle Platonism", in *The Studia Philonica Annual: Studies in Hellenistic Judaism*, vol. 5, ed. David T. Runia, Atlanta: Scholars Press, 1993.

Struck, Peter T., *Birth of the Symbol: Ancient Readers at the Limits of their Texts*, Princeton: Princeton University Press, 2004.

Suhrawardi, *The Philosophy of Illumination: A New Critical Edition of the Text of Hikmat al-Ishraq*, tr. John Walbridge and Hossein Ziai, Provo, Utah: Brigham Young University Press, 1999.

Tanner, R.G., "Διανοια and Plato's Cave".—*The Classical Quarterly* 20, Oxford: Clarendon Press, 1970.

Uzdavinys, Algis, "Putting on the Form of the Gods: Sacramental Theurgy in Neoplatonism".—*Sacred Web: A Journal of Tradition and Modernity*, vol. 5, 2000, pp. 107–180.

_____."Divine Light in Plotinus and al-Suhrawardi".— *Sacred Web: A Journal of Tradition and Modernity*, vol. 10, 2003, pp. 73–89.

_____."Being in Ancient Egyptian and Neoplatonic Thought".— *Being or Good? Metamorphoses of Neoplatonism*, ed. Agnieszka Kijewska, Lublin: Wydawictwo KUL, 2004, pp. 33–64.

_____.(ed.), *The Golden Chain: An Anthology of Pythagorean and Platonic Philosophy*, selected and edited by A.Uzdavinys, foreword by John F. Finamore, Bloomington: World Wisdom Books, 2004.

_____."The Egyptian Book of the Dead and Neoplatonic Philosophy".—*History of Platonism: Plato Redivivus*, ed. Robert Berchman and John Finamore, New Orleans: University Press of the South, 2005, pp. 163–180.

_____."Chaldean Divination and the Ascent to Heaven".—*Seeing with Different Eyes: Essays in Astrology and Divination*, ed. Patrick Curry and Angela Voss, Cambridge: Cambridge Scholars Publishing, 2007, pp. 21–34.

_____.*Philosophy as a Rite of Rebirth. From Ancient Egypt to Neoplatonism*, Westbury: The Prometheus Trust, 2008.

_____."Animation of Statues in Ancient Civilizations and Neoplatonism".—*Late Antique Epistemology. Other Ways to Truth*, ed. Panayiota Vassilopoulu and Stephen R.L. Clark, New York: Palgrave Macmillan, 2009, pp. 118–140.

_____.(ed.), *The Heart of Plotinus. The Essential Enneads including Porphyry's On the Cave of Nymphs*, ed. Algis Uzdavinys, foreword by Jay Bregman, Bloomington: World Wisdom Books, 2009.

Van Den Berg, Robert M., "Towards the Paternal Harbour: Proclean Theurgy and the Contemplation of the Forms".— *Proclus et la Theologie Platonicienne*, ed. A. Ph. Segonds and C. Steel, Leuven: University Press, Paris: Les Belles Lettres, 2000.

Van Winden, J.C.M. *True Philosophy—Ancient Philosophy.—*ΣΟΦΙΗΣ

ΜΑΙΗΤΟΡΕΣ "Chercheurs de sagesse". Hommage a Jean Pepin, ed. Marie-Odile Goulet-Caze et alii, Paris: Institut d'Etudes Augustiniennes, 1992.

Vernant, Jean-Pierre, *Mortals and Immortals: Collected Essays*, ed. Froma I. Zeitlin, Princeton: Princeton University Press, 1991.

Vogel, C.J. de, "The Soma-Sema Formula: Its Function in Plato and Plotinus Compared to Christian Writers".—*Neoplatonism and Early Christian Thought: Essays in honour of A.H. Armstrong*, ed. H.J. Blumenthal and R. A. Marcus, London: Variorum, 1981.

Wallis, R.T., *Neoplatonism*, second ed. with a Foreword and Bibliography by Lloyd P. Gerson, London: Gerald Duckworth, 1995.

Wallis Budge, E.A., *The Gods of the Egyptians, or Studies in Egyptian Mythology*, vol. 1, New York: Dover Publications, 1969 (1st ed. 1904)

Weiss, Herold, "A Schema of 'the Road' in Philo and Lucan".— *The Studia Philonica Annual: Studies in Hellenistic Judaism*, vol. 1, ed. David T. Runia, Atlanta: Scholars Press, 1993.

Wenning, Robert, "The Betyls of Petra".—*Bulletin of the American Schools of Oriental Research*, no. 324, 2001.

Wente, Edward F., "Mysticism in Pharaonic Egypt?".—*Journal of Near Eastern Studies*, vol. 41, no. 3, 1982.

White, David Gordon, *The Alchemical Body: Siddha Traditions in Medieval India*, Chicago: The University of Chicago Press, 1996.

Whittaker, John, "Neopythagoreanism and the Transcendent Absolute".-*Studies in Platonism and Patristic Thought*, London: Variorum Reprints, 1984.

Wildung, Dietrich, *Egyptian Saint: Deification in Pharaonic Egypt*, New York: New York University Press, 1977.

Wilkinson, Richard H. *Symbol and Magic in Egyptian Art*, London: Thames and Hudson, 1999.

Wilkinson, Richard H., *Reading Egyptian Art: A Hieroglyphic Guide to Ancient Egyptian Painting and Sculpture*, London: Thames and Hudson, 1994.

Zimmer, Heinrich, Death and Rebirth in the Light of India.—*Man and Transformation: Papers from the Eranos Yearbooks*, ed. J. Campbell, Princeton: Princeton University Press, 1980.

Zimmer, Heinrich, *Artistic Form and Yoga in the Sacred Images of India*, tr. and ed. Gerald Chapple and James B. Lawson, Princeton: Princeton University Press, 1984.

GLOSSARY OF TERMS

Agalma: image, cult-statue, ornament, shrine, object of worship, something in which one takes delight; *theon agalmata* is the common phrase for 'images of the gods' and 'cult-statues' which may be 'animated' by the theurgists; the word *agalma* contains no implication of likeness and is not a synonym of *eikon*; for Plato, the created cosmos is 'a shrine brought into being for the ever-lasting gods' (*ton aidion theon gegonos agalma: Tim.* 37c); for the Emperor Julian, the visible Sun is 'the living *agalma*, endowed with soul and intelligence and beneficent, of the noetic Father' (*Ep.* 51.434).

Aisthesis: sensation, perception, as an opposite of intellection (*noesis*), understanding and pure thought; more loosely—any awareness; for Plato, some *aistheseis* have names, such as sights, sounds, smells, cold and heat, distress, pleasures, fears, but nameless *aistheseis* are countless (*Theaet.* 156b); for Plotinus, perceptions in this world are dim intellections (*noeseis*), and intellections in the noetic world are vivid perceptions; Philo of Alexandria postulates an Idea of *aisthesis*, along with an Idea of *nous*, in the Intellect of God (*Leg. Alleg.* 1.21–27).

Akh: the ancient Egyptian term for intelligence, spiritual light, illumination, irradiation; it may designate both a spiritual being (the winged soul, *ba*, divinized and raised above the Osiris state) and the entire spiritual dimension that corresponds to the Neoplatonic *kosmos noetos*; through the celestial ascent a pharaoh (the prototype of the philosopher-mystic of later times) becomes a 'shining one' (*akh*), a star irradiating light throughout the cosmos, and is united with Ra (the divine Intellect) as his 'son'.

Akhet: the Egyptian term meaning 'horizon', a kind of the sun-door for entering or coming from the Duat (the Osirian Netherworld); the hieroglyphic sign for 'horizon' shows two peaks with the solar disk between them, protected by the *aker*, a double lion; *akhet* is a threshold realm (comparable to the Islamic notion of *barzakh*) between the Heaven, the Earth, and the Duat; etymologically it is connected with other words meaning radiance, intelligence, noetic light, spirit, 'making into a spirit of light'; *akhet* is symbolized by the pyramid, therefore the pharaoh ascends to Heaven (in order to be integrated into the circuit of Ra) by way of this *akhet*, i.e., the threshold of light; the *akhet* hieroglyph was applied in Egyptian art, especially, in architectural forms: the two pylons which flanked temples entrance represented the two peaks of akhet, and the statue of Atum-Ra, or Amun-Ra, was displayed for the god's epiphany (*khaai*) between these mountain-like towers.

Al-insan al-kamil: the Arabic term for the Sufi concept of a Perfect Man which, ultimately, derives from the ancient cosmogonies centered on the macrocosmic Man (Vedic *Purusha*, Gnostic *Anthropos*); in the Egyptian solar theology, it is represented by the pharaoh, the son of Ra, who unites in himself both Horus and Seth, or is identified with Thoth in all respects; in Sufism, the Perfect Man is God's deputy on earth, because he manifests perfection of all divine attributes; the Prophet Muhammad, Khidr, Solomon, Jesus and other Islamic prophets belong to this category; the Perfect Man is a manifestation of the Muhammadan Reality (like a manifestation of the Neoplatonic *Nous*); the term *haqiqa muhammadiyya* (Muhammadan Reality) is a term of the first thing that God created (i.e., *Nous*, Atum-Ra), and this Reality is manifested within the world (in terms of finality and *telos*) as the Perfect Man; although each individual thing of the world is God's mirror, the Perfect Man, as an apex of all creation (i.e., the Horus-like royal entity), is the perfect mirror and therefore he is both the goal of creation and the link between God and His creation by which God sees Himself; Ibn al-'Arabi contrasts the Perfect Man with the animal man (*al-insan al-hayawan*).

Anagoge: ascent, elevation, bringing up; the approach to the divine realm by means of purifications (*katharmoi*), initiations (*teletai*), the Platonic dialectic and allegorical exegesis, contemplation (*theoria*), and the ineffable sacred rites employed in theurgy; it is prefigured by the sacred way which the initiates of mysteries (*mustai*) walk, the path to the mountain (*oreibasia*); typological analogies of the Neoplatonic ascent to the divine may be seen in the *Pyramid Texts* and the accounts of *mi'raj* of the Prophet Muhammad in the later Islamic tradition.

Anamnesis: recollection, remembrance; in the Orphico-Pythagorean context, it is understood as a remembrance of one's true divine nature, revealed through the sacred initiation; the idea of memory and restoration of the soul's true identity is crucial for the Egyptian tradition as reflected in the *Book of the Dead* and later employed by Pythagoreans and Plato who explains *anamnesis* as recollection of things known before birth and since forgotten *(Meno, 85d)*; thus Platonic learning is equated with remembering (*Phaed. 72e*).

Ankh: the Egyptian term meaning 'life'; the hieroglyph *ankh*, originally perhaps representing a knot or a bow, is a symbol for divine life, for the 'breath of life', provided by Shu and other gods, and for regenerating power of water. *Ankh* also designates a floral bouquet (offered to the gods) and a mirror, itself an important metaphysical symbol; various items used in hieratic rites (e.g., the hooped sistrum) were fashioned in the shape of this hieroglyph. The *ankh* survived into the Coptic period and was inherited by the Christians as the *crux ansata*.

Anthropos: man; in Gnosticism, the macrocosmic *anthropos* is regarded as the Platonic 'ideal animal', *autozoön*, or a divine *pleroma*, which contains all the archetypes of creation and manifestation.

Apatheia: impassivity or freedom from emotions, understood as a philosophical virtue; *apatheia* means not being affected in any way and is applied both to the sages and to transcendent entities by the Neoplatonists.

Apeiron (*apeiros, apeiria*): lacking in limit, unlimited, as opposed to *peras*, a bound; the even as opposed to the odd. This is a fundamental Pythagorean term, designating one of the main principles of manifested being. The Pythagorean Unlimited is indefinite and in need of Limit, it is infinite in the negative sense of infinitely divisible. In Neoplatonism, *peras* and *apeiron* constitute the primal archetypal duality located somewhere between the ineffable One and the noetic cosmos.

Aporrhetos: secret, prohibited, unspeakable; the common designation of mysteries and sacred rites of initiation; in Neoplatonism, the term is used in metaphysics and negative theology, frequently understood as a characteristic of the First Principle.

Apotheosis: divinization; in the esoteric sense it is accomplished by the philosophical purification and theurgical *anagoge* which reveals one's primal and true identity with the divine principles. This is not a Homeric conception, because Homer clearly separates the gods and men; however, following the ancient Egyptian spiritual patterns, the Orphic texts already promised *apotheosis* and immortality for the initiated soul who (like the Egyptian *ba* and the *psuche* in Plato's *Phaedrus*) restores her wings and ascends in flight back to the divine homeland.

Arche: beginning, starting point, authority, government, heart, principle; *archai* are understood as the first principles by Neoplatonists; the term *archetupos*, an archetype, is used already by Plotinus in a sense of the divine paradigm or the noetic model of the manifested entity.

Arete: excellence, goodness, virtue. Plotinus makes a distinction between the civic virtues (*politikai aretai*) and the purificatory virtues (*kathartikai aretai*); Porphyry adds two other grades—the theoretic virtues (*theoretikai aretai*) and the paradigmatic virtues (*paradeigmatikai aretai*): the former being those of the soul that beholds *nous* within itself, the latter being the virtues proper to the divine Intellect, *Nous*, itself. Iamblichus discerns seven grades of virtue which in an ascending order illustrate the anagogic path to the divine: natural, ethical, civic, purificatory, theoretic and paradigmatic virtues are crowned by the hieratic virtues (*hieratikai aretai*) that are proper to the One—those that make the soul godlike (*theoeides*) and unite it through theurgy with the First Principle.

Arrhetos: ineffable, unspeakable; this term is close to *aporrhetos* and is used to designate the rites and visions of the mysteries and the transcendent nature of the One in Neoplatonism.

Arithmos: number; for the Pythagoreans, number is the first principle (Arist. *Metaph.* 986a15); Iamblichus sometimes identifies the gods with *arithmoi*, regarding the first numbers from the monad to the decad as deities and archetypal models of manifestation. The numerical organization of the cosmos requires the organizing principles of bodies to be considered as physical numbers and distinguishes them from mathematical numbers, which are the paradigms of physical numbers; but the ideal, noetic, or eidetic (*eidetikos*), numbers transcend even mathematical numbers.

Askesis: in ancient philosophy, this term designates not an 'asceticism', but spiritual exercises, therefore *philosophia* is understood not as a theory of knowledge but as a lived wisdom, a way of living according to intellect (*nous*); an *askesis* includes remembrance of God, the 'watch of the heart', or vigilance (*nepsis*), *prosoche*, or attention to the beauty of the soul, the examination of our conscience, and knowledge of ourselves.

Aten: the Egyptian term for the 'sun globe' or 'sun disk', regarded as a visible icon of Ra; represented as the simple sun disk, the disk with uraeus, the disk with rays emanating from it, or as the sun disk containing the scarab beetle (*kheper*) and the ram (*ba*); under the reign of Akhenaten (Amenhotep IV) the sun disk is worshiped as the solar deity Aten whose rays are depicted as arms proffering *ankh* hieroglyphs.

Atman: the Sanskrit term designating the innermost nature of all divinities, of all living beings, of all manifested forms; according to *Manu Smrti*: 'All the gods are this one *atman*, and all dwell in *atman*' (12.119); this is the universal continuum of consciousness, the Self; as an unqualified consciousness one with *Brahman*, *atman* is self-luminous; it is not 'this' nor 'that', unseizable, indestructible, unbound, it is not born, nor does it die when the body is slain; it is hidden in all things, but can be perceived only by the sages with the Eye of Intellect (the Egyptian Eye of Ra) when *atman* reveals itself; as *Paramatma* it is the complete and integral supreme Self (the Egyptian Atum-Ra); the ego-personality, or individual self, called *jiva*, is regarded as primal ignorance and, therefore, contrasted to one's true identity—the transcendent Self, or *atman*.

Autozoön: the essential living Being, or noetic Animal, that contains within it the Ideas of all the living creatures and Archetypes of the four elements (*Tim.* 30b); it is a completely coherent *archetypus mundus*, a timeless, ungenerated, immaterial and perfect matrix of the psychic and physical cosmos; for Plotinus, it is a well-rounded-whole, composed of individual intellects, or noetic lights; 'a globe of faces radiant with faces all living' (*Enn.* VI.7.15).

Ba: the ancient Egyptian term which indicates the 'manifestation' of certain divine qualities, arranged in the descending and ascending hierarchy; in the eschatological and soteriological context, it may be understood as 'soul' moving up and down, as an individual in an out-of-body state which is attained through either initiation or death, when the physical body (*khat, soma*) is experienced as a corpse. *Ba* is the vehicle of ascent, pictured as a human-headed bird which flies into the spheres of light and finally becomes aware of oneself as an *akh*; the concept of *ba* influenced the Pythagorean and Platonic concept of soul (*psuche*) who tries to restore her wings through *anamnesis*—initiation into philosophy—and then ascends to the divine realm.

Barzakh: the Arabic term for 'isthmus'. An imaginal reality, regarded as a mirror image, is a *barzakh* between the reflected object and the mirror: an imaginal (not imaginary) thing is both the same as and different from each of the sides that define it; in Islamic Sufi theology, *barzakh* is taken to mean a certain intermediate state or realm, like the Egyptian Duat, which constitutes a barrier between the two seas of the Quranic cosmology or between any two different ontological levels of being; it may be compared 1) to a mediating prism which breaks down the noetic light into the varied colors of a sensible realm, and 2) to a lens which concentrates the rays from above; the period in the *barzakh* (comparable to the Osirian Fields of Rushes) prepares the deceased for the resurrection, just as the time spent in the womb prepares him for birth into this world; according to Ibn al-'Arabi: 'The resurrection is a *barzakh*. There is nothing in existence but *barzakhs*, since a *barzakh* is the arrangement of one thing between two other things, like the present moment between the past and future' (*Futuhat,* III.156.27, W. Chittick); as a mediating instance, *barzakh* is equated 1) with the heart (*qalb*) which mediates between the realm of Spirit (*Ruh*) and that of the individual soul (*nafs*), or 2) with the pole (*qutb*) which, in the Sufi hierarchy, functions as the world sustaining and saving *Logos*, i.e., as the Horus-like pharaoh, albeit hidden (hidden because Egyptian Sufism, since it was opposed to the official 'state metaphysics', often stood against the corrupt official powers, and was consequently forced to elaborate a parallel esoteric hierarchy constituted by externally unrecognized 'spies of God').

Ben-ben: an Egyptian word carrying the connotation of 'outflow'. The pyramid-like sacred stone or pillar that came to be the cult object of Ra in the Heliopolitan temple represents the primordial *ben-ben*, i.e., the noetic 'stone', or the primeval hill, which emerges from the apophatic abyss of Nun as the first self-projection of Atum ('All' and 'Nothing'), as the seed of the Neoplatonic *kosmos noetos*: 'Atum-Khepera, you culminate as hill, you raise yourself up as the *bennu*-bird from the ben-ben stone in the abode of the Phoenix at Heliopolis' (*PT* 1652). The wondrous *bennu*-bird, sitting on the top of the *ben-ben*, is said to come from the Isle of Fire having filled its body with the demiurgic *heka*-power and may be compared to the self-created original solar Word (*Logos*) which brings light into darkness; this bird of light is the primeval hypostasis of Ra, that is, the light-like intelligible Being; Heliopolis represents the symbolic centre of the manifested world, of all theophanies.

Bios: life, or a way of life, analogous to the Hindu *darshana*; therefore one can speak of the Pythagorean way of life, the Orphic way of life; to be a philosopher implies a rupture with the daily life (*bios*) and purification of one's passions in order to experience the transcendence of the divine Intellect and the soul with respect to the mortal body.

Bomiskos: bomos is the Greek sacrificial altar; being the most important element for the sacred work (more important than the cult stone, tree, and spring) the altar is ritually set up in the *temenos*, the sacred enclosure, when the first sacrifice is performed *in illo tempore* by Heracles or some other hero. The Greek altar is constructed of bricks and white-washed with lime, sometimes decorated with volutes in between of which lies the metal tablet on which the fire burns; in Pythagorean philosophy, *bomiskos* designates the irregular volume from which body is produced; the theurgist's physical body is also regarded as the sacrificial altar on the way to the divine realm.

Brahman: the Sanskrit term for the ultimate non-dual and un-manifest Principle, in certain respect tantamount to Nun of Egyptians or the ineffable One of Neoplatonists; it is the supreme reality without quality or distinction. As *Brahma nirguna* it is the unqualified Beyond-Being; as *Brahma saguna* it is Being, or Ishwara, tantamount to Atum-Khepera-Ra who emerges from the abyss of Nun; when designated as *saccidananda*, *Brahman* is the fullness of being (*sat*), consciousness (*cit*), and bliss (*ananda*); however, it is can only be described by the negation of everything (*neti-neti*, not this, not that). *Brahman* transcends Intellect and everything that is thinkable; it is invisible, inconceivable, 'that which speech cannot express, but through which speech is expressed . . . that which thought cannot conceive but through which thought is thought . . . that which breath cannot breath but through which breathing is breathed' (*Kena Upanishad,* 1.4ff); it is 'the light of lights beyond darkness' which dwells in the hearts of all; the human person, who genealogically belongs to the priestly *varna,* is called a *brahman* and conventionally regarded as a legal representative of the *sattva* quality or even as a direct embodiment of this Principle, though, in fact, he may be an ordinary man, actually devoid of any real 'divine wisdom'.

Daimon: in the ancient Greek religion, *daimon* designates not a specific class of divine beings, but a peculiar mode of activity: it is an occult power that drives man forward or acts against him: since *daimon* is the veiled countenance of divine activity, every god can act as *daimon*; a special knowledge of *daimones* is claimed by Pythagoreans. For Plato, *daimon*, is a spiritual being who watches over each individual, and is tantamount to his higher self, or an angel; whereas Plato is called 'divine' by Neoplatonists, Aristotle is regarded as *daimonios*, meaning 'an intermediary to god"—therefore Aristotle stands to Plato as an angel to a god. For Proclus, *daimones* are the intermediary beings located between the celestial objects and the terrestrial inhabitants.

Demiourgike seira: The vertical series of gods, irradiating in time from the Creator (*demiourgos*) in his timeless act of creation and crossing different levels of being, is called *demiourgike seira*, a demiurgic chain; therefore a series of philosophers emanating in time from Orpheus, Pythagoras and Plato is called *chruse seira*, the golden chain; the appellation 'golden' refers to the vertical rays of the divine light and godlike nature of wisdom preserved by a 'chosen race' (or 'golden race') of philosophers.

Demiourgos: Creator in Plato's *Timaeus*, literally 'craftsman', who as the Father and King contains all things in one perfection. When things are distributed to the particularized or manifested world, they become diversified and come under the power of different ruling principles. The Platonic Creator creates by appealing to a higher Paradigm, *autozoön*, which, for the Neoplatonists, lies at the highest noetic level; for Proclus, *demiourgos* is the intellective Living-Being (*noeron zoön*), and the Forms in the Creator's Intellect are compared to the notions of public offices in the mind of a statesman. He is the efficient (*poieti-kos*), the formal (*eidetikos*), and the final (*telikos*) cause of the temporal, physical world. Initially, the Greek concept of the divine craftsman was related to the Egyptian god Ptah and the Ugaritian Kothar-wa-Hasis.

Dhawq: the Arabic term meaning 'tasting'; understood by the Sufis as a direct experience of theophanies, of certain spiritual states and stations (for instance those belonging to the *mundus imaginalis*, the cosmological and psychic realm where invisible realities become visible and corporeal things are spiritualized), or of 'that which truly is', i.e., the Divine Being; in a sense, *dhawq* is analogous to unveiling, or finding (*kashf*), which means to perceive and to be that which is perceived at one and the same time; this direct 'tasting' (along with its semi-sensual implications) is aimed at the 'true knowledge' which makes it possible to combine similarity and incomparability, or imagination and reason; the concept of *dhawq*, regarded as heart-vision, heart-savour, or '*aisthesis* of the heart', is originally Peripatetic; it may also be understood as the creative intuition, or as the first state of mystical intoxication, or as 'the first degree of contemplative vision (*shuhud*) of God within God' (Tahanawi, d.1745).

Dhikr: the Arabic (Quranic) term for 'remembrance', 'recollection', 'invocation', regarded by certain metaphysicians as an equivalent of the Platonic term *anamnesis*; in Sufism, *dhikr Allah* means the constant mentioning of the supreme name of God (*al-ism al-a'zam*), that is, *Allah*, or of certain other divine names, formulas, and verses of the *Qur'an*; this practice (analogous to the repetition of Hindu mantras and Egyptian 'words of power', *hekau*) consists of invocation of the tongue (*dhikr al-lisan*), invocation of the heart (*dhikr al-qalb*), and invocation of one's secret innermost self (*dhikr al-sirr*); it is aimed at the sacramental purification, at the overcoming and transcending of one's lower soul (*nafs*), at the alchemical restoration of *al-fitrah*, one's primordial nature equivalent to the cleansed mirror able to reflect a radiant image of God; it is thought that *dhikr* (transmitted by the spiritual master through initiation) brings perfection and enables the initiate to approach God as closely as possible; the supreme *dhikr* is regarded as a means of subsistence (after experiencing of annihilation, *fana'*) and of mystical union, although the concept of 'union' frequently is treated with suspicion in the Islamic theological milieu.

Diadochos: successor, the head of the Platonic Academy in the chain of transmission; however, the *diadoche* is hardly a matter of institutional continuity, and may be understood in the sense of the golden chain of philosophers which serves to transmit the sacred knowledge and principles of pure (*diakekat-harmene*) philosophy.

Dialektike: dialectic; for Plato, only those who philosophize purely and righteously bear the title of dialectician (*Soph.* 253e); sometimes the method of *sunagoge* (collection) and *diairesis* (division) is identified as dialectic; for Proclus, the Forms at the intelligible (*noetic*) and intellectual level cannot be defined, but they are definable at the level of soul and below; therefore dialectic defines, by *diairesis*, these images of the Forms, though it can only contemplate the Forms themselves. There are three processes of dialectic: 1) cathartic, used to purge ignorance, 2) recollective, which raises to the *anamnesis* of true reality, 3) a mixture of the two; usually Proclus makes a sharp distinction between the so-called Parmenidean dialectic, which provides a path to the divine realities, and the dialectical method (*epicheirematike*) of the Peripatetics.

Dianoia: discursive reason, mind; discursive knowledge, located between immediate apprehension and fallible opinion (*Rep.* 511d). According to Proclus, the One, when we apprehend its presence in each of the Forms, 'ought not to be viewed by the faculty of opinion, nor by discursive reason (*dianoia*), for these kinds of knowledge are not cognate with intellectual monads, which are neither objects of opinion nor of discursive reason, as we learn from the *Republic* (VI.511a). Rather it is proper to see by intuitive apprehension that simple and unitary existence of Forms' (*In Parm.* 880).

Dikaiosune: justice; its opposite is *adikia*, injustice; giving to each man his due is just, according to Plato (*Rep.* 331e). *Dikaiosune* may be understood in a cosmic and divine sense, since to perform the task for which one is naturally equipped is to follow one's divine archetype, one's own *dharma*, to put it in Hindu terms, which is *lex aeterna*, the eternal law of creation.

Djed: the Egyptian hieroglyph meaning 'stability' and representing both the macrocosmic and microcosmic *axis mundi*, the backbone of Osiris. The sign is depicted as a stylized representation of a pillar or a column around which sheaves of grain were tied; during the Old Kingdom, it was associated with Ptah, the chief Memphite Demiurge, called the Noble *Djed*; during the New Kingdom, it was used as a symbol of Osiris and represents his regenerative power. This symbol was sometimes pictured with a pair of eyes and regarded as a receptacle of a living god, as a sacred icon animated through the Opening of the Mouth ritual; the royal ritual of Rising the *Djed* Pillar was aimed at the re-establishment of stability, of the cosmic order, and symbolized the rebirth both of the deceased pharaoh and of the initiate; accordingly, the pillar represents the path of alchemical transformation (passing through death and resurrection) and theurgic ascent, that is, the philosophical way leading to the union of Osiris and Ra; the *djed* pillar, supported by Isis and Nephtys, is analogous to the Tantric *sushumna*, the spinal column, which shows the royal way to immortality, leading to the crown of the head (the golden lotus-flower of Ra-Nefertum); the baboons of Thoth, i.e., the eastern *bau*, who praise the noetic sun rising from the top of vertical *djed* pillar, indicate that the Osirian transformation is accomplished through the wisdom of Thoth, through his supernatural knowledge (*rekh*) and theurgic power (*heka*).

Djet: the Egyptian term related to Tefnut, the daughter of Atum, identified as the principle of the intelligible Order, *Maat* (analogous to the Pythagorean Limit, *Peras*); sometimes rendered as Eternal Sameness, *djet* stands as a complementary opposite term to *neheh*, or Eternal Recurrence, identified as the noetic Life of Shu, the son of Atum. On the lower levels of manifestation, *djet* carries Osirian attributes and signifies a certain eidetic completeness; *djet*-time, or *djet*-eternity, is tantamount to 'the enduring continuation of that which, acting and changing, has been completed in time' (J. Assmann), to the cosmic wholeness and plenitude, often represented by spacial categories, or understood as the accomplished ideal totality of Forms; if *neheh* carries attributes of Ra and represents a cyclical infinitude of creation, manifested through the breath of Shu (the Pythagorean series of *apeiria*), *djet*, instead, represents an unchanging permanence (the structure imposed by peras and oriented towards an *epistrophe*, therefore related to the mortuary cult and the continuation of the completed image).

Doxa: opinion; in Platonism, a sharp distinction is made between the eternal noetic world of Forms (Ideas, Archetypes) of which knowledge (*gnosis*) is possible and the perceptible world of becoming which is only opinable (*doxastos*); for Proclus, the perceptible entities are opinable, but true being is an object of intellect (*Elements of Theology*, 123); opinions may be true or false, whereas knowledge can only be true.

Dunamis: power, capacity; for Aristotle, *dunamis* is one of the fundamental principles (*archai*); Plotinus describes the One as the seminal power of all things (*dunamis panton*: *Enn.* III.8.10.1). A net of divine powers in their descending and ascending order is a net of theophanies; in this respect *dunamis* is analogous to the ancient Egyptian *sekhem*. The powers of the divine Intellect and Soul are present at every part of the cosmos, but the physical world (and the human body) are unable to receive the full power of their incorporeal Reality; *dunameis* may sometimes be equated with the daimonic forces.

Eidolon: image, idol, double, apparition, phantom, ghost; in Homer, there are three kinds of supernatural apparitions that are called by the term *eidolon*: 1) the phantom (*phasma*), created by a god in the semblance of a living person, 2) the dream-image, regarded as a ghostly double that is sent by the gods in the image of a real being, 3) the *psuche* of the dead; the Homeric *psuche* is not a soul, but a phantom, a thin vapor that proves to be ungraspable; for Pythagoreans and Plato, *psuche* is no longer the *eidolon* of the body, but the immortal soul that constitutes one's real being; for Plotinus, the soul is the *eidolon nou*, a *simulacrum* of *nous*, an image that is already obscured. The conception of *eidolon* is partly related to the ancient Egyptian concept of *ka*.

Eidos: visible shape, form, a kind of thing; the intelligible Form or noetic Idea of Platonism. The word is etymologically connected with *video*, and the term *idea* also comes from the same root as Greek verb *idein* and the Latin verb *videre*, both meaning 'to see'; therefore *eidos* is closely connected with contemplation (*theoria*), transcendental or divine imagination, and mystical vision.

Eikon: image, icon; a mirror-image as a direct representation of its *paradeigma*; for Plotinus and other Neoplatonists, the sensible world is an image of the noetic world and time is an image of eternity *(Enn. III.7.11)*, therefore the lower realities may be contemplated in ascending hierarchy as images, or traces, of the higher paradigms. Proclus distinguishes between an *eikon* and a *sumbolon*: the Pythagoreans, before revealing directly the truths of their doctrine, present *eikones* of reality (*In Tim.* 1.29.31ff).

Ellampsis: irradiation, shining forth, manifestation, illumination, flowing from the principle as a cause; for Proclus, 'only an illumination *(ellampsis)* from the intellective gods renders us capable of being connected to those intelligible-and-intellective Forms.... For this reason, indeed, Socrates in *Phaedrus* (249d) compares the contemplation to mystery-rites *(teletais)*, initiations *(muesesi)* and visions *(epopteias)*, elevating our souls under the arch of Heaven, and to Heaven itself, and to the place above Heaven' (*In Parm.* 949).

Episteme: knowledge, scientific knowledge of that which is unchanging and necessary, e.g. the Platonic Forms; since *episteme* is regarded as a certain knowledge of reality, the objects of *doxa* (opinion) cannot be assigned to *episteme*. For Proclus, the task of science is the recognition *(gnosis)* of causes, and only when we recognize the causes of things do we say that we know them (*Elements of Theology* 11); science or scientific knowledge *(epistemonike gnosis)* depends on the synthesizing power of mind, but 'intellect *(nous)* is the proper spectator of the Forms, because it is the same nature as them' (*In Parm.* 924.32–37).

Epistrophe: reversion, return; in the Neoplatonic threefold scheme of manifestation, a thing, or rather intelligible entity, proceeds from itself to multiplicity, and returns to itself, while its essential characteristic identity remains unchanged at the initial level; the three moments—remaining *(mone)*, procession *(proödos)* and reversion *(epistrophe)*—are phases of a simple continuous and dynamic process (sometimes regarded as simultaneous) that infuses unity-diversity, causation and predication; it is essentially a metaphysical and logical relationship.

Epopteia: the most important mystical vision that culminates the Eleusinian mysteries, the beholding of the secret symbols or epiphanies of the gods. *Epopteia* is the highest stage of initiation; the *epoptai* (beholders) are those who came back to watch the rituals again; in a similar way, the philosophical purification and instruction culminates in *epoptika*—the direct revelation of truth and contemplation of the Forms, or divine realities.

Eros: love, sometimes personified as a deity, a *daimon*, or a cosmogonical, pedagogical and soteriological force, manifested in the process of demiurgy and within the domain of providence; for Plato, philosophy is a sort of erotic madness *(mania)*, because Eros, though implying need, can inspire us with the love of wisdom; Diotima in Plato's *Symposium* describes education in erotics as an upward journey or ascent towards the perfect noetic Beauty; Plotinus uses the union of lovers as a symbol of the soul's union with the One (*Enn.* VI.7.34.14–16). Proclus distinguishes two forms of love: 1) ascending love which urges lower principles to aspire towards their superiors, 2) descending or providential love (*eros pronoetikos*) which obligates the superiors to care for their products and transmit divine grace (*In Alcib.* 54–56); for Dionysius the Areopagite, who follows Proclus, the *eros ekstatikos* becomes the unifying factor of the cosmos.

Eusebeia: piety, meritorious piety; 'to change nothing of what our forefathers have left behind'—this is *eusebeia* (Isocr. 7.30). For Platonists, piety means not simply bringing the sacrificial offerings and fulfilling of cultic duties, but also humility, supported by philosophy and combined with the love (*eros*), faith (*pistis*) and knowledge (*gnosis*) that finally lead to assimilation to God.

Gnosis: knowledge; *gnosis* is contrasted with *doxa* (opinion) by Plato; the object of *gnosis* is *to on*, reality or being, and the fully real is the fully knowable (*Rep.* 477a). The Egyptian Hermetists made distinction between two types of knowledge: 1) science (*episteme*), produced by reason (*logos*), and 2) *gnosis*, produced by understanding and faith (*Corpus Hermeticum* IX); therefore *gnosis* is regarded as the goal of *episteme* (ibid., fl.9). The idea that one may 'know God' (*gnosis theou*) is very rare in the classical Hellenic literature, which rather praises *episteme* and hieratic vision, *epopteia*, but it is common in Hermetism, Gnosticism and early Christianity; following the Platonic tradition (especially Plotinus and Porphyry). Augustine introduced a distinction between knowledge and wisdom, *scientia* and *sapientia*, claiming that the fallen soul knows only *scientia*, but before the Fall she knew *sapientia* (*De Trinitate* XII).

Goeteia: magic; the sharp distinction is made between 1) the sinister *goeteia* and 2) *theourgia*, the sacramental divine work, by Iamblichus in *De mysteriis*; however, magic is sometimes interpreted as *gnosis*, and *gnosis* pertains to the secret divine names as facilitating the power of magic; the Hellenistic magic (frequently equated with the mysteries and labeled *musteria, musterion, musterion tou theou*) is related to the ancient mystery-cult initiation and the Egyptian doctrine of *heka*—the miraculous power of creation, governed by the god Heka, who distributes *hekau*, the cultic words of power (like the Hindu mantras) that perform divine liturgies and transformations of the soul; Hermes-Thoth, *Isidos pater*, is regarded as the founder of the holy tradition (*paradosis*) of the magic arts and the author of the secret names 'wrote in Heliopolis with hieroglyphic letters'; therefore the magician is sometimes called the mystagogue (*mustagogos*).

Hairesis: taking, choice, course of action, election, decision; this term (plural, *haireseis*) refers to any group of people perceived to have a clear doctrinal identity; *hairesis* is a group with fairly coherent and distinctive theories, with an acknowledged founder (*hairesi-arches*) and leaders who articulate their rejection of rival theories through theoretically founded polemics; Diodorus of Sicily complains that the Hellenes, unlike the Orientals, always introduce doctrinal innovations in important matters, thus 'founding new *haireseis*' (2.29.6). By the II century AD, *hairesis* had become a standard term for philosophical school; the early Christians use of *hairesis* to refer to a body of false beliefs.

Heka: although this Egyptian term designates both demiurgic and theurgic power, it is usually rendered as 'magic'; in its role as the creative power, the personified god Heka (analogous to Hindu *Maha-Maya*) stems from the primeval creative utterance of Atum and is contained in the divine *Logos:* being regarded as the father of the gods and of all that becomes manifested, Heka constitutes and permeats every level of manifested reality, be it noetic, psychic, or physical; by the permanent work of Heka the different levels of being are woven into an integral magic carpet, therefore the *heka*-power fulfills the transforming and elevating function on the path of an inner alchemy and ascent of the soul The conception of *heka* is intimately connected with that of *maat*, correct cosmic order and justice; therefore the *heka*-magic is inseparable from the cultic, political, social, economic, scientific, artistic, and philosophical aspects of the Egyptian state-life; in the rite of the pharaoh's ascent and his assimilation to the supreme divine Principle (that is, his equation to the transcendent and immanent *pantheos*, the Reality of all that exist), the *heka* of the gods is to be sacramentally 'eaten' and contained in his 'belly'. The possession of magical words of power (*hekau*) is essential for the initiate in the Osirian realm of Duat where the soul (*ba*) is tested, transformed, and (if proved to be *maakheru*) turned into *akh* through the *heka*-based theurgic power and knowledge.

Hen (to hen): the one, which can mean: 1) Unity or Oneness in general; 2) the unity of anything that has unity or is one thing; 3) that which has unity, anything that is one; 4) the one thing we are speaking of, as opposed to 'other ones' (see: F.M. Cornford, *Plato and Parmenides*, London, 1969, p.111). For Neoplatonists, the One is the ineffable source of Being, the Supreme Principle, explicitly regarded as God by Proclus; *to hen* transcends the demiurgic Intellect and constitutes the first divine *hupostasis* of Plotinus; it corresponds to Nun, the Father of the gods (*neteru*) in the ancient Egyptian theology.

Henas: henad, unit; the term is taken by Iamblichus, Syrianus and Proclus from Plato's *Philebus*, where it is used interchangeably with the term 'monad'; since for every real being there is a unit, and for every unit a real being (Procl. *Elements of Theology,* 136), the henads are pure unities, the sources of being's identity, located between the pure One and the noetic One (or Being); more precisely, the henad is the first principle (*arche*) and the measure (*metron*) of being; the One is unparticipable, but the henads are participable, therefore they correlate with real beings; Proclus divides henads into transcendent or independent units and those that are immanent and belong to their participants and are irradiations of the first; in theurgy, henads constitute a set of theophanies, i.e. divinity in its many different forms at all the different levels of reality; therefore divine henad stands for the god-entity as a whole. The dif-

ference between the One and the participable henads (which may be compared with the Egyptian *neteru*), opens the theurgic way of adoration, worship
and ascent; according to Proclus, 'the most divine thing in us is the 'one' in us,
which Socrates called the illumination of the soul (*Rep.* 540a7), just as he
called truth itself light' (*In Parm.* VII.48); since like is apprehensible by like, the
'one of the soul' makes union with the ineffable One possible.

Henosis: unity; unity as the characteristic that everything has in common; anything depends on unity and unity alone is the goal of all things. In Neoplatonism, the soul's purification, accomplished primarily through philosophy,
culminates in noetic vision and finally in mystical union (Plot. *Enn.* VI.7.36);
the divine truth is an indivisible *henosis* of real beings.

Hermaike seira: Hermaic chain (of transmission, or heavenly initiation). The
Neoplatonists commonly associated themselves with the Hermaic chain,
i.e., the vertical 'golden' chain of the noetic light and wisdom that emanate
through Hermes Logios and other angelic powers from the divine Intellect
(*nous*).

Hermeneus: interpreter; the *hermeneus* owes his name to Hermes, the messenger
of the gods; *hermeneus* is an interpreter of the hieratic rites and liturgies (in
Egypt, such hermeneutical procedures, called 'illuminations', were practiced at
least from the times of the Middle Kingdom), divine omens, tokens, symbols,
oracular utterances, and, in the case of Neoplatonists, the Homeric poems,
Plato, Aristotle and the *Chaldean Oracles*. The goal of *hermeneutike* is to reveal
the inner meaning (*huponoia*) of the texts and indicate the highest truth that
points beyond the discourses, thus elevating the soul to the first principles
themselves; there is an ontological hierarchy of interpreters and interpretations, therefore each lower language of theophany functions as the *hermeneus*
of the higher one and renders it comprehensible at a lower level at the expense
of its coherence.

Hieratike techne: sacred art, hieratic art, namely the priestly art, theurgy, accomplished by the gods themselves through different degrees of initiation, transformation, elevation (*anagoge*) and ineffable mystagogy; it represents the
ascending path to unification with the One through scientific training (*agoge
epistemonike*) regarding certain henadic qualities, ontological symbols, sacred
rites, divine names and theurgic powers; according to Proclus: 'the theurgists
established their sacred knowledge after observing that all things were in all
things from the sympathy that exists between all phenomena and between
them and their invisible causes, and being amazed that they saw the lowest
things in the highest and the highest in the lowest' (*Hier. Art,* 148).

Hierophantes: hierophant, priest of Eleusis, he who shows sacred things; since the
language of mysteries was employed by Plato and the later Platonists, philosophy is often regarded in terms of a mystery initiation, and a true philosopher
or a spiritual leader of *hairesis* is equated to the hierophant of the mysteries.

Hieros logos: sacred tale, sacred word or book (e.g. that possessed by the initiation priests of Dionysus and Pythagoreans); there were *logoi* (accounts, explanations) embraced by the practical mysteries and additional *logoi* adduced from the outside; they were both exoteric and esoteric, both about the mysteries and within the mysteries, and were developed on three different hermeneutical levels: those of myth, allegory, and metaphysics.

Homoiosis theo: likeness to God; the phrase is derived from the famous passage of Plato's *Theaetetus* 176bc; it is understood as the end (*telos*) of life which is to be attained by knowledge (*gnosis*); for Iamblichus, 'knowledge of the gods is virtue and wisdom and perfect happiness, and makes us like to the gods' (*Protrep.* ch. 3).

Huparxis: pure existence of a thing, an essential foundation; the term covers the level of pure unity (which is the foundation of all manifested realities) and the divine; for Proclus, being's pure essence is no actual being, but a unity (*henas*) with existence (*huparxis*), and this unity is the spark of divinity; the *huparxis* of henads is not the existence of certain concrete subjects, but unqualified existence, unconditioned even by being.

Hupodoche: reception; the receptacle underlying all the world of becoming; for Plato—the material principle, the mother and receptacle of the whole visible cosmos (*Tim.*51a); *hupodoche* is equivalent to space (*chora*) and nurse (*tithene*); according to Iamblichus, the pure and divine matter receives and reveals the gods in cosmogony (*De myster.* 232.17); each level on the Neoplatonic chain (*seira*) of theophany is regarded as the receptacle of its superior (which functions as a 'form' in respect to 'matter'); the embodied soul is a *hupodoche* of the god due to the soul's capacity or theurgic suitability (*epitedeiotes*); in theurgy, minerals, plants, animals, divine statues and icons, temples and sacred landscapes can be regarded as the receptacles of the descending divine light or power; initially, this is the Egyptian doctrine of *descensio* and *translatio*: the gods and divine powers descend into their images (*akhemu*) and animate the material world, understood as an *imago caeli*.

Hupostasis: standing under, sediment, foundation; in Neoplatonism, *hupostasis* is a synonym of *ousia*, that means being, substance, existence; the three *hupostaseis* of Plotinus are three fundamental levels, or dimensions, of divine reality: the One, Intellect, and Soul.

Hupothesis: proposal, intention, argument, hypothesis, the premise of a syllogism; the nine hypotheses of dialectic in Plato's *Parmenides* are regarded by the Neoplatonists as the nine *hupostaseis*, or levels of reality, extending from the ineffable One to pure matter, or non-being.

Idea: in non-technical use the term refers to the visual aspect of anything; for Plato and Platonists, it is the highest noetic entity, the eternal unchanging Form, the archetype of the manifested material thing; in Plato, *idea* is a synonym of *eidos*, but in Neoplatonism these two terms have a slightly different meaning.

Imago dei: 'the image of God' in Latin, the Egyptian *tut neter*; the numerous con-

ceptions of likeness (*homoiosis*) to God were elaborated in Platonic philosophical tradition and the Scripture-based Christian theology, namely, that man
(though shaped from the earth and therefore a mortal, passable, short-lived
being) is honoured with God's own image which (sometimes equated with the
microcosmic *nous*) reflects the immortal, pure, and everlasting divine nature;
accordingly, as the image of God, the immortal human soul (or heart-intellect) is viewed as a mirror of God, both to others and to itself; in the case of
Christ (analogous to the Horus-like pharaoh, *Ra sa*, Osiris resurrected, the
Perfect Man of Sufi metaphysics), the overwhelming cosmological 'image'
(*eikon*) stands for living and active essence, which thereby establishes dominion over all creatures; being made in the image of God, man (who has recov-
ered his pure, primordial nature and realized his final spiritual perfection) is
the vicegerent of the Lord; though ultimately of the Egyptian origin, 'this very
concept of the *Imago Dei* which formed a synthesis between the Platonic-Aris-
totelian-Stoic view and the Christian view of man . . . dominated the whole of
the Patristic period and the Christian Middle Ages' (E. Brunner).

Isefet: the Egyptian term which designates 'lack', or 'deviation' from the meaningful divine order (*maat*), that is, all negative Sethian qualities, such as false-
hood, violence, sickness, enmity, and so on; the meaning of creation
(constituted by the different levels and modes of manifestation, the *kheperu*)
lies in its noetic plenitude, that which yields being, order, life, and justice,
therefore all suffering, rebellion, crime, and injustice (the symptoms of lack,
delusion, and non-being) are indications of the world's loss of its original
intelligible plenitude for the reason of its moving away from the primeval
noetic source and, as a consequence, of its deviation from the correct archetypal patterns; the sacred institution of kingship is revealed and established as
a means to overcome *isefet* and reconstitute the disfigured *imago dei*, that is, to
recover one's true spiritual identity, according to the Egyptian theology: 'Ra
has placed the pharaoh in the land of the living, forever and ever, judging
humankind and satisfying the gods, realizing *maat* and destroying *isefet*'.

Ka: the Egyptian term for one's vital power, or for one's 'double', which also may
be understood as an abstract principle symbolizing an individual psychic tendencies, moral qualities, and appetites; *ka* may indicate male potency and the
sustaining power of life; the ka hieroglyph represents two extended arms, perhaps suggesting the gesture of praise, prayer, or one of embrace (since the
hieratic power of *ka* is ritually transmitted through the priestly embrace—that
is, through embracing statues and spiritual disciples—which imitates the
archetypal 'event' when Atum embraced Shu and Tefnut *in illo tempore*); the
ka-double is fashioned along with the material human body by the ram-
headed god Khnum on his potter's wheel; to 'go to one's *ka*' meant to die;
however, the *ka* (when located in the vital realm of the dead ancestors) needs
the continuing nourishment provided in the funerary sanctuaries/residences
to the animated statues: the food-offerings themselves are designated as *kau*
and are thought of as being imbued with the life-power of *ka*; the fundamental

qualities attached to the notion of *ka* included subsistence, nutrition, penetration, force, splendor, magic, worth, radiance, greenness, vassalage (that of serving an official, or a spiritual master, who often occupied the rank of official or administrator of the pharaonic state); all ancestors are regarded as *kau*, therefore to beget a child is to re-establish a vital link with them; Osiris is viewed as the *ka* of Horus (in the role of his father and the source of his fortune), and Horus is viewed as the *ka* of Osiris when he embraces and revives his father Osiris; the pharaoh's *ka* is the source of prosperity to the whole world and to all inhabitants of the theocratic state.

Katharsis: purification, purgation of passions; the term occurs in Aristotle's definition of tragedy (*Poetics*, 1449b 24) and seems to be borrowed from medicine, religious initiations and magic.

Kheper: the Egyptian hieroglyph depicting the sacred scarab (*Scarabaeus sacer*), representing both this insect itself as well as the metamorphoses or transformations involved in all possible 'becomings'; *kheper* means coming into being, manifestation, development, changing, and so on; different ontological manifestations (such as one's corpse, shadow, *ka, ba, akh, sah*) are regarded as *kheperu*. Atum, as the source of all existence, is the 'lord of *kheperu*'; he is described as developing 'in this your identity of the Scarab', meaning in his hypostasis as the noetic sun at the dawn of creation. Ra emerged from the abyss of Nun in his identity of Khepera, therefore Atum (*neb tem*, the lord of totality) is the transcendent completeness and the supreme noetic source of being, Khepera (Kheprer) the proximate cause of all manifestations (*kheperu*), and Horus the final cause. While Khepera is the entity embodied in the sun as it rises in the morning, it is the symbol of the initiate's rebirth.

Kosmos noetos: the intelligible cosmos of divine Forms and intellects, located between the One and the Soul; it embraces the hierarchy of the different levels and orders (*taxeis*) of divine reality (such as Being, Life, and Intellect), filled with the various triads of the intelligible (noetic), intelligible-intellective (noetic-noeric) and intellective (noeric) gods; among the metaphysical categories and triads of *kosmos noetos* are: existence (*huparxis*); power (*dunamis*); activity (*energeia*); remaining (*mone*); procession (*proödos*); reversion (*epistrophe*); symmetry (*summetria*); truth (*aletheia*); and beauty (*kallos*).

Logismos: numerical calculation, the power of reasoning, reason.

Logos: the basic meaning is 'something said', 'account'; the term is used for the explanation and definition of a certain kind of thing, but it also means reason, measure, proportion, analogy, word, speech, discourse, discursive reasoning, noetic apprehension of the first principles; the demiurgic *Logos* (like the Egyptian *Hu*, equated with Thoth, the tongue of Ra, who transforms the Thoughts of the Heart into spoken and written Language, thus creating and articulating the world as a script and icon of the gods) is the intermediary divine power: as an image of the noetic cosmos, the physical cosmos is regarded as a multiple *Logos* containing a plurality of individual *logoi* (*Enn.* IV.3.8.17–22). In Plotinus,

Logos is not a separate *hupostasis*, but rather that which determines the relation of any *hupostasis* to its source on the one hand and its products on the
other, serving as the formative principle from which the lower realities evolve;
external speech (*logos prophorikos*) constitutes the external expression of internal thought (*logos endiathetos*).

Maat: the ancient Egyptian term for measure, harmony, canon, justice and truth,
shared by the gods and humans alike; *maat* is the essence of sacred law that
keeps a human community and the entire cosmic order; it establishes the link
between above and below; 'letting *maat* ascend' is a language-offering during
the hieratic rites and an interpretation of the cosmic processes in terms of
their mystic and salvational meaning; for Plato, who admired the Egyptian
patterns, the well-ordered cosmos, truth, and justice are among the main
objects of philosophical discourse.

Mania: madness, frenzy; the state of frenzy is connected with the psychic state
called *entheos*, 'a god within'; being possessed by a god entails a loss of one's
understanding (*nous*); the god Dionysus is the Frenzied One, therefore a certain kind of enthusiasm, madness and inspiration is related to the prophecy
and mystical experience; Plato distinguishes the prophetic *mania* of Apollo
from the telestic *mania* of Dionysus, adding two other types of *mania*—the
poetic and erotic enthusiasm and the philosophical one (*Phaedr.* 244a–245a);
the philosopher is the erotic madman, but in him the divine erotic madness
and divine *sophrosune* (temperance, virtue, prudence) are to be united in the
successful experience of love which elevates one, through *anamnesis*, towards
the divine realm.

Mathema: any study or discipline which a person may learn (*manthanein*); later
the term is confined to the mathematical sciences, harmonics and astronomy.

Maya: the Sanskrit term related to the root *ma* (measure, fashion, making); it is a
divine property or power involved in creation of the world and, therefore,
regarded both as the demiurgic wisdom and (when compared to the supreme
Principle *per se*) as the universal delusion; thus, creation is viewed as a product
of *maya*'s art and, ultimately, is an illusion, if regarded as self-sufficient, i.e., as
separated from its source; the power of *maya* is analogous to the power of *heka*
which is either combined with *maat* (order, justice, proper measure, truth), or
misused in the context of *isefet* (which includes an irrational passion) and
thereby turned into a dream-like illusion and magic; the cosmic play (*lila*) is
based on the inexhaustible power of divine *Maya* which is transcended only by
the ineffable union with the supreme Principle, the archetypal Thaumaturgus
himself; in Platonic epistemology, the realm of *maya* should be equated to the
realm of human opinion, *doxa*, contrasted to the true knowledge, *episteme*.

Me: the Sumerian term (rendered as *parsu* in Akkadian) designates the properties
and powers of the gods close to those both transcendent and immanent archetypes which are called Forms, or Ideas, in Platonism. the concept of *me*, however, is expressed in the language of myth; it covers the ideas, models, things,

and activities that are central to the theocentric universe and to civilized human life. The related term *gish-hur* (demiurgic plan, design) denotes how these noetic prototypes are manifested in an orderly manner in the realm of the state-based economic, social, cultic, and spiritual life; when the *me* are forgotten (or the *dharma* neglected, to say in Sanskrit terms), the well-attuned political, social, and religious cosmos falls into disorder.

Medu neter: 'divine words', 'divine speech', i.e., the Egyptian hieroglyphs; in certain respect, they may be regarded as the visible symbolic images, if not 'incarnations', of the Platonic Forms, that is, of the intelligible Hieroglyphs which are the archetypes of manifestation; all *medu neter* (in their noetic *akhu* aspect) originated from that which was thought by the heart of Ptah and commanded by his tongue, i.e., by Thoth; the manifested universe is an articulation of the noetic hieroglyphs; the Memphite theology argues that Ptah created all things and all hieroglyphs, after he formed the gods. The concept of *medu neter* is based on the theory of creation by the Word (*Hu, Logos*), therefore the sacred script (which is also the chief form of the Egyptian sacred art) on its own level reflects the structure of reality, the configuration of the noetic archetypes.

Methexis: participation; for the Pythagoreans, things are imitations of numbers, but for Plato, the particulars participate in their Forms; Iamblichus extended 'participation' into a general term for the informing of lower principles by higher ones, and thus established the triad of transcendent Form, immanent universal, and material particular; this general scheme of unparticipated (*amethekton*), participated (*metechomenon*) and participant (*metechon*) terms may be applied to different levels of manifestation; the unparticipated terms operate on lower realities only indirectly, through the intermediary of the participated terms which they produce; thus the ontological levels are multiplied and divine transcendence is preserved.

Mimesis: imitation, representation; in *Poetics*, 1447ab, Aristotle includes all the fine arts under *mimesis*, among them epic, tragedy, comedy, painting and sculpture; the images produced by *mimesis* are not at all like photographic images; according to H. Armstrong, the images of the classical Hellenic artists are mimetically closer to those of the traditional arts of the East than to those of nineteenth-century Europe: 'if we establish in our imagination the figure of the masked singing actor as our image of *mimesis* we shall not do too bad' (*Platonic Mirrors*, p.151); however, in a vocabulary used by Proclus the terms *mimesis* and *mimema* are usually reserved for art of an inferior type, though Proclus says that 'the congenital vehicles (*ochemata*) imitate (*mimeitai*) the lives of the souls' (*Elements of theology* 209), and 'each of the souls perpetually attendant upon gods, imitating its Q. divine soul, is sovereign over a number of particular souls' (ibid., 204).

Morphe: shape; e.g. *kata somatos morphen*—'in a bodily shape' (*Phaedr.* 271a); sometimes *morphe* is used as a synonym of *idea* and *eidos*.

Mundus imaginalis: 'imaginal world', the world of the Imaginable; the conception of *mundus imaginalis* was popularized by the French scholar Henry Corbin as a possible rendering of the Arabic *al-alam al-mithal*; this *alam* is the world of symbolic visions and of typifications, viewed as an intermediate isthmus (*barzakh*) between the intelligible and the sensible, i.e., the world in which spirits are corporealized and bodies spiritualized; this realm is prominent in the later Sufi cosmologies, though some contemporary scholars argue that the faculty of imagination (compared to the mirror which reflects both noetic and sensible sides of reality) was turned into a separate ontological world (the whole dream-like universe of symbols and animated mythological figures, established within, that was initially the hypostasis of Soul in Plotinus) due to the creative misinterpretations of al-Ghazali's texts and the Peripatetic mis-readings of the Neoplatonic meta-cosmic hierarchy; however, one of its proto-types may be found in Plato's description of the 'real earth' which is full of 'sanctuaries and temples truly inhabited by gods, and oracles and prophecies and visions and all other kinds of communion with the gods which occur there face to face' (*Phaed.* 111c ff). According to the philosophy of Ishraq, developed by al-Suhrawardi and his Persian followers, it is called the 'interme-diate Orient' (*al-mashriq al-awsat*) of Angels-Souls (those who move the heavens and are endowed with pure active Imagination), situated below the pure Orient of the higher pleroma; Ibn al-'Arabi describes it as the plane of images (*amthal*) and imagination (*khayal*) which is located between the plane of the sensible experience and the plane of the Presence of Lordship (*rubu-biyah*); to regard it as a world *sui generis* of eternal archetypes would be (according to the Greek Neoplatonists) tantamount to locating these arche-types at the level of mathematical *phantasia* which, in the case of Ishraqis, assumes the mythological status of a living wonderland in which the noetic Ideas present themselves in imaginal forms and in which the material things appear as subtle bodies; however, far from being the realm of intelligible archetypes, this is the dream-world of magicians, the twilight realm of Osirian Duat, or of Anima Mundi, integrated into the Islamic Sufi theory of prophetic and visionary experiences; the imaginal faculty (*khayal*) works by an inner perception that perceives ideas in sensory form. In the school of Ibn al-'Arabi, imagination is considered 1) as the universe itself, 2) as an intermediate mac-rocosmic world, and 3) as an intermediate microcosmic world.

Mustagogia: an initiation into a mystery; leading and guidance of the initiate (*mustes*, plural, *mustai*) to the *telesterion* where initiations take place; a mysta-gogue is the introducer into the mysteries, the leading priest, instructor or spiritual guide. Proclus viewed the philosophy of Plato as a 'mystagogy', an 'initiation into the holy mysteries themselves' (*Plat. Theol.* I.1); for the Byzan-tine Christians, a mystagogy means a liturgical contemplation of the mystery of the Church.

Musteria: the proceedings of initiation and sacred rites are called mysteries; the Eleusinian festival is known simply as *ta musteria* or *arrhetos teletai*; the initiates—*mustai* and *bacchoi*—walk a sacred way, the goal of which is inner transformation and eternal bliss: 'happy and blessed one, god will you be instead of a mortal'; the Orphic mysteries have striking parallels in the Egyptian *Book of the Dead* and the *Coffin Texts*; the mysteries are characterized as esoteric, secret, forbidden (*aporrheton*) and unspeakable (*arrheton*); the special states, attained through initiation (*telete*), are claimed to be valid even beyond death; the mystery-language is adopted by Plato and used by his followers; even the Stoic Seneca speaks of the initiatory rites of philosophy, 'which open not some local shrine, but wast temple of all the gods, the universe itself, whose true images and true likeness philosophy has brought before the mind's eye' *(Ep.* 90.28).

Muthos: myth, tale; *legomena*; the 'things recited', in the Eleusinian mysteries, i.e. the recitations of the *hieros logos*, belong to the sphere of myth. The one-sided opposition between an irrational *muthos* and rational *logos* in Hellenic philosophy and culture, established by modern scholarship, is wrong, because even in Plato myths constitute the essential part of philosophy. All true myths require a proper cosmological and metaphysical *exegesis*; according to Proclus, the hieratic myths have a certain inner meaning (*huponoia*) and conceal secret or unspoken (*apporrheton*) doctrines, sometimes inspired or revealed by the gods themselves; Sallustius associates the highest level of myth with the transcendent divine reality and the lowest with the deceptive perceptions within the realm of the senses; thus a Myth (like Hindu *Maya*) is tantamount to the manifested cosmos itself, understood as the visible veil of the hidden invisible truth.

Neheh: the Egyptian term related to the ontological series of Shu and sometimes rendered as Eternal Recurrence; *neheh*-eternity, or *neheh*-time, perhaps should be conceived as the cyclic time of Ra which is reflected as our everyday time of a constant rhythmic change, therefore it is not completed in the sense of the Osirian *djet*-time; this is time of eternal return which is emphasized by the regular repetition of temple rituals.

Neter, neteret (pl. *neteru, neterut*): the Egyptian term for 'god' and 'goddess' respectively; the *neter* hieroglyph depicts a figure sitting in profile while knees bent and feet drawn back toward the body; another related hieroglyph looks like a staff wrapped with cloth, or like a cultic flag; in both cases an association with wrapping and binding (*ut*) is evident, and the mummy-like nature of the tightly wrapped body of the sitting figure indicates an idea of deification (or that of an immanent participation in the divine) through the soul-transforming death and rebirth; in the Ptolemaic period, the hieroglyph of a star also signified 'god'; the series of all gods are viewed as manifestations or hypostases of the supreme Principle ('Lord of All', 'Sole Lord who bore all by means of Heka') which Itself may be called by different names; *neteru* may be also rendered as 'divine principles', 'archetypal names', 'hieroglyphs', 'paradigms and energies of the manifested being'; the totality of divine forces that constitute the Egyptian universe is summarized by the term 'Ennead' (*psdt*), that is, 'group of nine'

which means both the chief noetic meta-structure of archetypes and the inde-
terminate number of divine forces, the plurality of gods. In the *Instruction for
Merikare* the Creator is referred simply as *neter* and human beings regarded as
images (*snn*) of this God; the gnostic identification with the *neteru* was indispensable if the initiate wished to attune oneself to the power of a particular
divine principle and to re-establish his true identity through sacred hermeneutics, purification, integration, assimilation, illumination, and theurgic union.

Noesis: intellection, thought, intellectual intuition, pure intuitive apprehension
which transcends the discursive reason and is related to *nous*; unified noetic
intuition at different levels of reality. For Proclus, intelligible and at the same
time intellective (*noeton hama kai noeron*) Life, which is characteristic of the
self-substantiated henads, exemplifies *noesis* as a process; at the highest ontological level, *noesis* provides union with the intelligible (*noeton*) world
through the so-called 'flower of intellect' (*anthos nou*); for Iamblichus, the
unifying power of the gods transcends all human *noesis* (which appears to
resemble the Plotinian *dianoia*), but this human *noesis* is a necessary part of
ascent and co-operation with the divine; the supreme *noesis* is attainable only
through the working of theurgy by the grace of god.

Nous: intelligence, immediate awareness, intuition, intuitive intellect; Plato distinguished *nous* from *dianoia*—discursive reason; *Nous* is the second hupostasis of Plotinus; every intelligence is its own object, therefore the act of
intellection always involves self-consciousness: the substance of intelligence is
its noetic content (*noeton*), its power of intellection (*nous*), and its activity—
the act of *noesis*. In a macrocosmic sense, *Nous* is the divine Intellect, the Second God, who embraces and personifies the entire noetic cosmos (Being-Life-
Intelligence), the Demiurge of the manifested universe; this *Nous* may be compared to the Hindu *Ishvara* and be represented by such solar gods as the Egyptian Ra; *Nous* is independent of body and thus immune from destruction—it
is the unitary and divine element, or the spark of divine light, which is present
in men and through which the ascent to the divine Sun is made possible.

Ochema: vehicle; a boat which conveys the souls of the dead, the soul's chariot in
Plato's *Phaedrus*; *ochema* is understood by Aristotle as *pneuma*—the seat of
imagination (*phantasia*), analogous to that element of which the stars are
made; the *ochema-pneuma* as an astral body functions as a quasi-immaterial
carrier of the irrational soul; daimons have a misty *pneuma* which alters its
form in response to their imaginings and thus causes them to appear in ever
changing shapes; for Iamblichus, an aethereal and luminous vehicle (*aitherodes
kai augoeides ochema*) which is the recipient of divine *phantasia*. *Ochema* carries soul down to the state of embodiment and is darkened until it becomes
fully material and visible: the material or fleshly body is also a sort of *ochem.;*
Proclus distinguished 1) the higher immaterial and luminous *ochema* into
which Plato's Demiurge puts the soul (*Tim.* 41e), and 2) the lower, *pneumatikon ochema*, which is composite of the four elements and serves as a vehicle of
the irrational soul; it survives bodily death, but finally is purged away.

Onoma: word, name; a noun as distinct from a verb; for Proclus, a name is an *eikon* of a *paradeigma*, a copy of a model. The words (*onomata*) are *agalmata*, the audible 'icons' or 'statues' of the higher divine realities; therefore true names are naturally appropriate, like images that reflect the form of the object, or like artistic icons that reflect the Platonic Forms rather than objects of the sensible world.

Ousia: being, substance, nature, essence; as P. Hadot pointed out: 'If we consider the series formed by *ousia* in Plato, *ousia* in Aristotle, *ousia* in the Stoics, *ousia* in the Neoplatonists, and the *substantia* and *essentia* in the church Fathers and the Scholastics, we shall find that the idea of *ousia* or essence is amongst the most confused and confusing notions' (*Philosophy as a Way of Life*, p.76). Since the true being is permanent and intelligible, the substance (*ousia*) of beings is their *logos* and their essence, according to Plato (*Phaed.* 65d–66a); Proclus identifies pure Being (*on*) with the Essence and Substance itself (*autoousia*); for Neoplatonists, being, real existence and essence are insepara- ble: beings exist insofar as they are accessible to intellect and have a fixed defi- nition: in the intelligibles the essence is never distinguished from real being.

Paideia: education, culture; the programme of traditional Hellenic education based on imitation of the Homeric exemplars. Plato initiated a philosophically oriented *paideia* that challenged the traditional pattern of poetically sanc- tioned culture and shifted the emphasis from body to soul (see: W. Jaeger *Pai- deia: The Ideals of Greek Culture*, Oxford University Press, 1943, 3 vols.).

Paradeigma: exemplar, paradigm, archetype, pattern, model; according to Plato, a paradigm of his perfect state is laid up in Heaven (*Rep.* 592b). The noetic Para- digm is regarded as the model for the creation: the visible world is a living creature made after the likeness of an eternal original, i.e. the ideal Living Ani- mal in the world of Forms; thus the world is an image of the eternal paradigms (*paradeigmata*). Therefore the Demiurge makes the cosmos as an *agalma* (hieratic statue, cultic image, ornament) and sets up within it the *agalmata* of the individual gods.

Paradosis: transmission, tradition; e.g., *Orpheos paradosis*, the Orphic tradition.

Per ankh: the Egyptian term meaning the House of Life, i.e., the temple scripto- rium and a high school for esoteric training whose priests maintained an oral tradition of initiation and also produced writings in different branches of knowledge, including theology, mathematics, ritual expertise, hieratic liturgy, hermeneutics, genealogy, astrology, sacred geography, mineralogy, medicine, mythography, architecture, the science of theurgic talismans and image-mak- ing; the staff of every *per ankh* was constituted by the lector-priests (*heri heb*) whose role was associated with the sacred books and the *heka*-power, as well as with preservation of *maat*, the cosmic order, and maintaining the theurgic tra- dition of mystical ascent and assimilation to the gods; only through the eso- teric knowledge and initiation into the invisible realm, that is, through the symbolic death and rebirth, accomplished in the House of Life, one was able to reveal his *akh*-identity and be united with the immortal divine principles. The diagram of the *per ankh* (*Pap. Salt* 825) appears as a symbolic mandala with Osiris at the center; Isis and Nepthys occupy the corners by the side of his feet; Horus and Thoth, the corners by the side of the head; Geb represents the ground; Nut, the sky. The priests of the House of Life follow 'the secret way of Thoth'; one of the chief lector-priests (*heri tep*) said, regarding a formula imbued with the *heka*-power: 'Do not reveal it to the common man—it is a mystery of the House of Life' (*Pap. Leiden* 344r).

Peras: limit, boundary; the fundamental cosmological principle of the Pythagore-ans. The Unlimited (*apeiron*) is indefinite and in need of Limit, which in the table of opposites is related to Odd, One, Right, Male, Rest, Straight, Light, Good, Square. The principles of Limit and the Unlimited (discussed in Plato's *Philebus*) are the Pythagorean monad and dyad that constitute the order of henads in Proclus and play a central role in the constitution of reality; Limit and the Unlimited serve as two principles (*archai*) of mathematical reality (*ousia*).

Phantasia: imagination; for Plato, *phantasia* belongs to the realm of appearance and illusion; for Aristotle, *phantasia* is neither perception nor judgment but a distinct capacity of the soul, the capacity which responds to appearances derived from memory, dreams and sense-perception. The II century AD soph-ist Philostratus was the first to call the faculty of producing visual images *phantasia* which is contrasted with *mimesis*: 'For *mimesis* will produce only what she has seen, but *phantasia* even what she has not seen as well; and she will produce it by referring to the standard of the perfect reality' (*Life of Apol-lonius*, 6.19). The Neoplatonists lack the concept of creative imagination, though the Neoplatonic *phantasia* can reproduce images of the higher princi-ples of mathematics and language; therefore *phantasia*, as a mirror, is placed at the junction of two different levels of being: the mirror of imagination not only reflects images of phenomena but also images of the noetic Forms, Ideas, thus translating revelations and divine epiphanies into the visible icons and symbols of the higher realities; at the junction of *phantasia* (which is identified with *nous pathetikos* by Proclus) rational and irrational meet; the objects of *phantasia* are *tupos* (imprint), *schema* (figure) and *morphe* (shape).

Philosophia: love of wisdom; the intellectual and 'erotic' path which leads to vir-tue and knowledge; the term itself was perhaps coined by Pythagoras; the Hel-lenic *philosophia* is a prolongation, modification and 'modernization' of the Egyptian and Near Eastern sapiential ways of life; *philosophia* cannot be reduced to philosophical discourse; for Aristotle, metaphysics is *prote philosophia*, or *theologike*, but philosophy as *theoria* means dedication to the *bios theoretikos*, the life of contemplation; thus the philosophical life means the participation in the divine and the actualization of the divine in the human through the personal *askesis* and inner transformation. Plato defines philosophy as a training for death (*Phaed.* 67cd); the Platonic *philosophia* helps the soul to become aware of its own immateriality, liberating it from passions and stripping away everything that is not truly itself; for Plotinus, philosophy does not wish only 'to be a discourse about objects, be they even the highest, but it wishes actually to lead the soul to a living, concrete union with the Intellect and the Good'; in late Neoplatonism, the ineffable theurgy is regarded as the culmination of philosophy.

Phronesis: thought, understanding, practical wisdom, sagacity, prudence; according to some modern scholars, *phronesis* is closer to the English 'wisdom' than *sophia*, because 'wisdom' is, in standard English, applied to practical matters; but this is still a disputed issue, since, for Aristotle, *sophia* covers bodily, aesthetic, political, theoretical, and religious or metaphysical areas of human activity (*On Philosophy*, fr. 8).

Phusis: (*physis* in the more conventional English transcription): nature (of something), nature as opposed to the artificial; for Proclus, it is the last immaterial reality or power that exists immediately prior to the material world and is responsible for all the motion and change within it.

Pragmata: things; in Proclus *ta pragmata* also denotes transcendent realities, noetic entities, real beings.

Pronoia: providence; the well ordered arrangement of things in the cosmos is based on a guiding and planning providence; the concept developed before Socrates; according to Proclus, since all proceeding things in their essential aspect 'remain' in their higher causes, or archetypes, the higher causes not only contain their lower effects but they know, or fore-know, (*pro-noein*) these effects; foreknowledge is also a kind of love—the providential love (*eros pronoetikos*) by which the higher causes care for their effects.

Proödos: procession; the metaphysical term in the Neoplatonic scheme of *mone-proödos-epistrophe* (primarily a non-phenomenal process) that indicates manifestation. The noetic Life embraces multiplication, the unlimited, and potency or power (*dunamis*) as factors that lead to *proödos*; for Proclus, the trinity *remaining-procession-reversion* applies to every form, property, or entity, except the One and matter.

Psuche (usually transcribed as *psyche*): soul; breath of life, life-stuff; Homer distinguishes between a free soul such as a soul of the dead, corresponding to *psuche* (and still regarded as an *eidolon*), and the embodied soul, corresponding to *thumos*, *noös*, and *menos*: following the Egyptian theological patterns, the Pythagoreans defined *psuche* as the reflection of the unchanging and immortal principles; from Plato onwards, *psuchai* are no longer regarded as *eidola*, phantoms or doubles of the body; rather, the human body is viewed as the perishable *simulacrum* of an immaterial and immortal soul. There are different degrees of soul (or different souls), therefore anything that is alive has a soul (Aristotle *De anima*, 414b32); in *Phaedrus* 248b the soul is regarded as a separate, self-moving and immortal entity (cf. Proclus *Elements of Theology*, 186); *Psuche* is the third *hupostasis* of Plotinus.

Rekh: the Egyptian term for 'knowledge' which, first and foremost, is the knowledge of spiritual realities, divine names and hieroglyphs, of the sacred cosmic topography, the mythical iconography, and all the beings of the Netherworld; this elaborate store of knowledge, including scientific observations and theological interpretations, had a cultic function and culminated in *gnosis*, that is, in the realization of one's different archetypal identities and in restoration of one's divine nature; knowledge of the Duat conferred a nether-worldly identity on the initiate as 'a holy *neter* in the following of Thoth'; Thoth (Djehuty), regarded as Hermes Trismegistus by the Hellenes, and his consort Sesheta, or Maat, are the chief guardians and providers of all knowledge and wisdom; knowledge of Ra, or of his images and noetic rituals expressed in the sun's daily course, conferred upon the sage or the initiate a noetic identity: 'He who knows it is a *ba* of the *bau* with Ra'; 'He who knows these mysterious representations (or symbols) is a well-provided *akh*'; the pharaoh, standing at the apex of all creation, is the Gnostic *par excellence*: he knows the theurgic way of ascent and his own metaphysical identity, knows the mysterious words that the eastern *bau* (the 'angels' of Thoth) speak, knows the cosmogonical birthings of Ra and his self-generations in the waters of Nun; in the *Amduat*, the pharaoh, or the priest who represents him in the cult (and, consequently, every initiate, sage, or philosopher), knows the mysterious *bau* of the Netherworld, the gates and the roads that Ra (the solar *Nous*) travels, knows 'what is in the hours and their gods', the transfigurations of Ra and his images; the spiritual knowledge of the Netherworld determines one's 'Osirification', alchemical transformation, and immortalization, thereby allowing one to face Ra or to be united with Atum-Ra.

Ren: the Egyptian term for 'name'; the divine light, or the sacred, may be present in the divine names as it is present in the hieratic statues and all divine manifestations (*kheperu*), therefore it is maintained that an essential relationship exists between the name and the named; accordingly, the sacred language is regarded as a dimension of divine presence. The Egyptian hymns with name formulas (analogous to the *dhikr*-formulas in Sufism and the Hindu mantras) themselves are called 'transfigurations' (*sakhu*) and are related to the root *akh*, meaning to radiate, to illuminate, to be a divine spirit or an intelligible light; therefore *akhu* (the radiant noetic quality) refers to the theurgic power of the sacred word which is able to illuminate, elevate, or reveal the divine realities as well as their hidden meaning. In the cultic dimension, the sacred language is viewed as the language of the deities themselves, since only deities can make use of the theurgic power of names, along with the pharaoh (the son of Ra) and the initiated priests to whom the pharaoh delegates his priestly and 'philosophical' function.

Sah: the Egyptian term for one's 'golden' spiritual body which serves as a vehicle of the *akh*-intellect; the idealized shape of the mummy (viewed as an icon and receptacle of the animating divine forces) is a visible symbol of the immortal *sah* body and itself is called *sah*; the 'germination' of the spiritual body constitutes a long path of initiations and alchemical transformations based on metaphysical knowledge and the correct performance of hieratic rites; the initiate is to be identified with the sacred Scarab, the god of self-renewal, who represents the cosmogonical emergence of Being from the ineffable Beyond-Being: 'I am the god Khepera, and my members shall have an everlasting existence. . . .' The germination of the spiritual body, that is, of the noetic body of light, follows the patterns of the body-structure and the archaic psychology based on the significance of the bodily members: all the members of one's body must be transformed into their spiritual equivalents; the re-membering of the Osirian body (i.e., the restoration of the members of the dismembered body) as well as the passage beyond the realm of Osiris to that of Ra, are the essential components of the germination of the immortal *sah*-body. The initiate himself (as the radiant *akh* saturated with the rays that shine out from the intelligible Demiurge) claims to be both the primordial lotus (a symbol of self-transformation and rebirth) which shines in the Land of Purity, and the golden child, Ra-Nefertum, who emerges from the divine lotus-flower or from the Lake of Flames in his glorious solar form. *Khat* (or *shat*) is one's mortal body, one's corpse; *sah* (or *sahu*) is one's immortal spiritual body.

Sekhem: the Egyptian term designating 'power', an active emanation of deity or the divine power which (as a sort of *shakti*) can be attached to any god; in certain respect, *sekhem* is made visible in the *sekhem* scepter held by the Egyptian officials as a symbol of royal authority; the initiate or the deceased, who is united with the noetic principles, also acquires the quality of *sekhem* which, however, may differ in its measure and intensity; the receptacle of a god (its sculptured or painted image) is called *sekhem* as well, therefore the numerous texts describe the *ba* of the god which alights on his *sekhem*: thereby the image is animated and is able to reveal divine presence, provide oracles, or irradiate divine grace (like the Sufi *barakah*) and glory. The *sekhem*-power is often associated with Hathor, known as 'Eye of Ra', the whole (restored) *Iret*-eye, the vehicle of divine energy projected into the world; this power has both demiurgic and theurgic, as well as destructive and salvific, aspects.

Seira: chain, series; the term, derived from Orphism and Homer, refers here to the vertical series, consisting of a single principle, monad or henad, and repeated at different levels of reality; *seira* and *taxis* may denote both transverse and vertical series'; each level of *seira* (which may be compared to a ray of light) reproduces those above it, therefore the god's names refer not only to the henad as the source of each procession, but also to all the members of that procession: 'For each chain bears the name of its monad and the partial spirits enjoy having the same names as their wholes. Thus there are many Apollos and Poseidons and Hephaestuses of all sorts' (Proclus *In Remp.* 1.92.2ff). Manifested reality is thus arranged as the hierarchy of chains that embrace divine, angelic, daimonic, heroic, human and irrational levels (including animals, plants and minerals), all dependent on their proper divine henad, in the sense of being in its *seira*; in some respect *seira* is tantamount to the Arabic Sufi term *silsilah*.

Sema: the Egyptian term for 'union'; the *sema* hieroglyph represents two lungs attached to the trachea and symbolizes the unification of equal parts (e.g., the union of Two Lands—Upper and Lower Egypt—or of two gods such as Horus and Seth, Horus and Thoth); the *sema* hieroglyph reflects the royal prerogatives of union, however, in funerary and esoteric initiatory contexts it may signify the initiate's becoming a royal *ba*, or a *neter*, that is, to indicate a kind of mystical union, or union between different divine principles themselves.

Shakti: the Sanskrit term for 'power' and the name of the goddess; while the Advaita Vedanta considers *shakti* as material and different from the spiritual *Brahman*, certain Tantric schools regard Shakti as being identical to the supreme Principle (*Parama Shiva*, whose possession of *Svatantrya Shakti* indicates his absolute integral nature which acts through his power of action, *kriya shakti*); accordingly, the manifestation of the universe is a mode of the supreme Lord's self-revelation through his own Shakti which functions on the different levels of being and acquires different qualities; as a feminine aspect of the divine, *shakti* both creates the universe of theophanies (functioning as *spanda-shakti* or the ultimate vibratory energy) and reveals the divine glory (*aishvarya*); *shakti* is both 'closing' (*nimesha*) and 'opening' (*unmesha*), that is, involved in the process of progressive manifestation, characterized by obscuring or concealing of spiritual realities, and in the process of spiritual realization and dissolution of cosmos either macrocosmically (at the end of a world cycle), or microcosmically (by the annihilation of one's lower nature); the *shri-yantra*, which depicts the complementary relationship between Shiva and Shakti, consists of five upward-pointing triangles which represent Shiva, and four downward-pointing triangles which represent Shakti: their interweaving stands for cosmic existence as a whole. As the primordial life force (*mukhya-prana*) *shakti* is universally present in the cosmos; as the serpent power (*kundalini-shakti*) it is depicted as being coiled around a *shiva-lingam* or as ascending through the spinal column, *sushumna*, and leading the initiate (*sadhaka*) to immortality and enlightenment; thus, it is analogous to the power of the Egyptian goddess Hathor.

Skopos: aim, purpose, target; Iamblichus developed the doctrine that each philosophical source-work, especially Plato's dialogues (since the dialogue is regarded as a microcosmic reflection of the divine macrocosm) must have one basic subject matter, or *skopos*, to which all parts of the text are related; consequently, the introductory portion of the dialogues now assume an allegorical and metaphysical significance.

Sunthema: token, passport, parole, symbol (in the most cases meaning the same as *sumbolon*); a plaited basket (*cista mystica*) of the Eleusinian mysteries is called the 'watchword' (*to sunthema Eleusinion musterion*: Clement of Alex., *Protrep.* 2.21.2); the *sunthemata* of the *Chaldean Oracles* are considered as the 'thoughts of the Father' and have a cosmogonic role similar to that of the Forms in Middle Platonism; they have an anagogic function: when the soul remembers the paternal *sunthema*, it returns to the paternal Intellect. According to Iamblichus, the gods create all things by means of images and signify all things through *sunhemata* (*De myster.* 136.6 ff); there are material *sunthemata* and immaterial *sunthemata* (among them—stones, shells, parts of animals, plants, flowers, sacred statues and icons, sounds, rhythms, melodies, incantations, lights, numbers, ineffable names of the gods); the material objects that preserve the power of the gods are regarded as *sunthemata* by the theurgists and function as receptacles for the gods; the *sunthema*, understood as the impression and power of the god (similar to Hindu *yantra*), awakens the soul to the divinity which it presents or symbolizes.

Sumbolon: symbol (*sumballein* means 'to join'); a fragment of a whole object, such as a *tessera hospitalis*, which can be joined with the other half. *Sumbolon* suggests both incompleteness and the hinting power of secret meaning; the so-called Pythagorean symbols are maxims (*akousmata*, 'things heard') representing in an enigmatic and archaic form the basic teachings on the proper conduct of life. Only in the allegorical tradition of Neoplatonic hermeneutics was the theory of metaphysical, cosmogonic, and theurgic symbolism elaborated, whereby *sumbolon* achieved the status of a major critical concept; in the *Chaldean Oracles*, the *sumbola* are sown throughout the cosmos by the Paternal Demiurge and serve as the essential means of ascent and return to the gods. Every soul was created by the Demiurge with harmonic ratios (*logoi*) and divine symbols (*sumbola theia*: Proclus, *In Tim.* 1.4.32–33); the *logoi* that constitute the soul's essence are *sumbola* and may be awakened through the theurgic rites; for Proclus, the inspired myths of Homer communicate their truth not by making images (*eikones*) and imitations (*mimemata*), but by making symbols (*sumbola* or *sunthemata*), because 'symbols are not imitations of that which they symbolize' (*In Remp.* 1.198.15–16).

Sophia: wisdom; the term covers all spheres of human activity—all ingenious invention aimed at satisfying one's material, political and religious needs; Hephaistos (like his prototypes, the Ugaritian Kothar-wa-Hasis and the Egyptian Ptah) is *poluphronos*, very wise, and *klutometis*, renowned in wisdom; here 'wisdom' means not simply some divine quality, but wondrous skill, cleverness, technical ability, magic power; in Egypt all sacred wisdom (especially, knowledge of the secret divine names and words of power, *hekau*, or demiurgic and theurgic mantras, which are able to restore one's true divine identity) was under the patronage of Thoth. In classical Greece the inspired poet, the lawgiver, the politician, the magician, the natural philosopher and the sophist—all claimed to possess wisdom; indeed 'philosophy' is the 'love of wisdom', *philo-sophia*, a life lived so as to attain wisdom as its goal; the ideal of the *sophos* (sage) in the newly established Platonic *paideia* is exemplified by Socrates; in Neoplatonism, the theoretical wisdom (though the term *sophia* is rarely used) entails contemplation of the eternal Forms so as to become like the *nous*, or a god. The characteristic properties which constitute the divine nature and which spread to all the divine classes are the good (*agathotes*), wisdom (*sophia*), and beauty (*kallos*).

Taxis: order, series; any level of reality, constituted by *seira* in which the distinctive property of a particular god or henad is successively mirrored; the chain of being proceeds from simplicity to complexity and subsequently from complexity to simplicity; the hierarchy of *taxeis* establish the planes of being or world-orders (*diakosmoi*).

Telestike: one of the Neoplatonic names for theurgy and the hieratic rituals; the animation of statues. *Telestike mania* of *Phaedrus*, 244e employs purifications and rites; according to Hermeias (*In Phaedr.* 92.16–24), the telestic madness is ranked above all the others inasmuch as it gathers all the others together (that is, theology, the whole of philosophy and the erotic mania) and possesses them. There are various different kinds of *telestike*.

Telete: initiation, the rite of initiation; to initiate is *telein* or else *muein;* the initiate is called *mustes*, the ritual of initiation, *telete*, and the building where initiation takes place, *telesterion*. *Telete* is also used for religious celebrations generally; the mysteries are called *teletai;* in Neoplatonism, souls follow the mystery-rites (*teletai*) and prepare for the beholding of the realities of Being; according to Proclus, faith (*pistis*) is the cause of the ineffable initiation: 'for on the whole the initiation does not happen through intellection and judgment, but through the silence which is unifying and is superior to every cognitive activity' (*Plat. Theol.* IV.31.8–16).

Theios aner: divine man, a god-like sage; the Neoplatonic ideal of 'sainthood'.

Theologia: divine science, theology, *logos* about the gods, considered to be the essence of *teletai;* for Aristotle, a synonym of metaphysics or first philosophy (*prote philosophia*) in contrast to physics (*Metaph.* 1026a18); however, physics (*phusiologia*) is sometimes considered a kind of theology (Proclus *In Tim.* 1.217.25). Among the ancient theologians (*theologoi*), according to the Neoplatonists, are Orpheus, Homer, Hesiod and other divinely inspired poets, the creators of theogonies and the keepers of sacred rites.

Theoria: contemplation, theory; the contemplative virtue is called *theoretike*. Philosophy introduces the notion of the beholding of the well-ordered cosmos, considered analogous to the witnessing of the festivals of the gods and their epiphanies, and still called by the same word, *theoria;* in Neoplatonism, the creative power of the cosmos is contemplation (*theoria*) and intellection (*noesis*), therefore divine *praxis* is *theoria;* for Plotinus, on every level of reality creation is the result of the energy produced by contemplation (*Enn.* 8.3–4); every intellect contemplates itself directly; contemplation may be compared to the mystery-rites (*teletai*).

Theos: god; the term sometimes is used in a wide and loose sense; 'everything is full of gods' (*panta plere theon*), according to Thales; the cosmos may be regarded as a theophany—the manifestation of the One (likened to the supreme transcendent Sun) and the divine *Nous* that constitute the different levels of divine presence concealed by screens or veils (*parapetasmata*). In ancient Greece, when speaking of *theos* or *theoi*, one posits an absolute point of reference for everything that has impact, validity, and permanence, while indistinct influences which affect man directly can be called *daimones;* for Plato and Plotinus, the *nous*, the universal soul, the stars, and also the human soul are divine, thus there are both invisible and visible gods, arranged in a hierarchy of henads that follows the arrangement of the nine hypotheses in Plato's *Parmenides*. *Theoi* are the first principles, henads (as *protos theoi*), intellects and divine souls, whereas the supreme God is the ineffable One, or the Good; in some respects, *theos* is an equivalent of the Egyptian *neter;* the *neteru* are the gods, the first principles, divine powers, manifestations—both transcendent and immanent.

Theourgia: theurgy; the rites understood as divine acts (*theia erga*) or the working of the gods (*theon erga*). Theurgy is not intellectual theorizing about God (*theologia*), but elevation to God; the term was coined by the editors of the *Chaldean Oracles,* but the ancient practice of contacting the gods and ascent to the divine goes back to the Mesopotamian and Egyptian hieratic traditions; the Neoplatonic theurgy is based both on the Chaldean patterns and the *exegesis* of Plato's *Phaedrus, Timaeus, Symposium,* and other dialogues, and is thus to be regarded as an outgrowth of the Platonic philosophy and the Pythagorean negative theology; therefore the theurgical *praxis* does not contradict the dialectic of Plato; theurgy deifies the soul through the series of the ontological symbols and *sunthemata* that cover the entire hierarchy of being and lead to unification and the ineffable unity with the gods; theurgy is based on the laws of cosmogony in their ritual expression and imitates the orders of the gods; for Iamblichus, it transcends all rational philosophy (or intellectual understanding) and transforms man into a divine being.

Upaya: the Sanskrit term meaning 'way', 'path', 'method', 'means of approach'; F. Schuon regards the exoteric forms of all religions as a sort of *upaya*, that is, both as an indispensable means for one's spiritual life and as a 'soteriological mirage'—a providential formal veil of the 'formless truth'.

Yantra: the Sanskrit term for the symbolic geometric design which functions as a means for the accomplishment of various ritual practices, contemplation, visualization, concentration, theurgic ascent and assimilation to the divine principles; *yantra* is a hieratic instrument, device for immortalization which saves (*trayate*) all beings from the Lord of Death; if *mantra* is regarded as the soul of the initiate's chosen deity (*ishta-devata*), *yantra* is the deity's receptacle, its sacred body; in certain respect, *yantra* is a graphic image of the entire universe, viewed as a well-structured play of theophanies; usually *yantra* is a simplified geometric representation of a *mandala*-like palace that has four gates plus the central dot (*bindu*); the so-called *puja-yantras* are the cultic instruments of worship, while the *raksha-yantras* are the protective amulets; the *shri-yantra* is a geometric representation of the Macroanthropos (*purusha*); *yantras* belong to the same class of hieratic items as the theurgic *sumbola* and *sunthemata* employed by the Hellenic Neoplatonists and the Egyptian priests skilled in sacred geometry, contemplative mathematics, and talismanic lore.

BIOGRAPHICAL NOTE

ALGIS UZDAVINYS is Head of the Department of Humanities and a Senior Research Fellow at Vilnius Academy of Fine Arts, Kaunas Faculty in his native Lithuania. He is a published scholar in English and Lithuanian. His most recent books include (in English): *Philosophy as a Rite of Rebirth, From Ancient Egypt to Neoplatonism* (The Prometheus Trust, 2008), *Sufism and Ancient Wisdom* (forthcoming), and (in Lithuanian): *Sufism in Islamic Civilization* (2007), *Understanding of Symbols and Images in Ancient Civilizations* (2006), *Hermes Trismegistus: The Way of Wisdom* (2005), *Hellenic Philosophy from Numenius to Syrianus* (2003), and *Egyptian Book of the Dead* (2003). He has also edited *The Golden Chain: An Anthology of Pythagorean and Platonic Philosophy* (World Wisdom Books, 2004) and *The Heart of Plotinus, The Essential Enneads* (World Wisdom Books, 2009). His research includes work on Hellenic philosophy, especially Platonism and Neoplatonism, as well as traditional mythology and metaphysics, Sufism, and traditional art. In 2005 he was awarded the Andrew Mellon fellowship to the American Center of Oriental Research in Amman, Jordan. From September 2007 to March 2009 Prof. Uzdavinys was a Research Officer at the La Trobe University, Bendigo, Australia.

JOHN F. FINAMORE is Associate Professor of Classics at the University of Iowa and the President of the ISNS (International Society for Neoplatonic Studies). He has published extensively on the Neoplatonic philosophers, including *Iamblichus and the Vehicle of the Soul* (1985).

Made in the USA
Columbia, SC
08 September 2020